FIELDWORKING

FieldWorking
Reading and Writing Research

Elizabeth Chiseri-Strater

University of North Carolina—Greensboro

Bonnie Stone Sunstein

University of Iowa

A BLAIR PRESS BOOK

Prentice Hall, Upper Saddle River, New Jersey 07458

Library of Congress Cataloging-in-Publication Data

Chiseri-Strater, Elizabeth

      FieldWorking: reading and writing research / Elizabeth Chiseri-Strater and Bonnie Stone Sunstein

          p.   cm.

      Includes bibliographical references and index.

      ISBN 0-13-300211-X (pbk.)

         1. Ethnology—Field work.   2. Ethnology—Authorship.

         3. Communication in ethnology.   4. Ethnology—Research.

I. Sunstein, Bonnie Stone. II. Title.

GN346.S86   1997   96–36211

305.8'00723—dc20   CIP

Editorial Director: *Charlyce Jones Owen*

Publisher: *Nancy Perry*

Acquisitions Editor: *Mary Jo Southern*

Director of Production and Manufacturing: *Barbara Kittle*

Managing Editor: *Bonnie Biller*

Project Manager: *Karen Trost*

Project Liaison: *Shelly Kupperman*

Manufacturing Manager: *Nick Sklitsis*

Prepress and Manufacturing Buyer: *Bob Anderson*

Marketing Manager: *Rob Mejia*

Interior and Cover Designer: *Amy Rosen*

Cover Art: Hundertwasser (8080A), End of the Waters on the Roof, *Japanese Color Woodcut,*
1985, Kyoto, Japan, 57 X 42 cm, © 1997 Harel, Vienna, Austria

This book was set in 10/12 Galliard by Innodata Publishing Services Inc.
and printed and bound by R.R. Donnelley & Sons Company.
The cover was printed by Phoenix Color Corp.

Acknowledgments appear on pages 321–323, which constitute
a continuation of this copyright page.

A BLAIR PRESS BOOK

Printed in the United States of America
10 9 8 7 6 5 4 3 2 1

ISBN 0-13-300211-X

Prentice-Hall International (UK) Limited, *London*
Prentice-Hall of Australia Pty. Limited, *Sydney*
Prentice-Hall Canada Inc., *Toronto*
Prentice-Hall Hispanoamericana, S.A., *Mexico*
Prentice-Hall of India Private Limited, *New Delhi*
Prentice-Hall of Japan, Inc., *Tokyo*
Simon & Schuster Asian Pte. Ltd., *Singapore*
Editora Prentice-Hall do Brasil, Ltda., *Rio de Janeiro*

Implicit in this book is our philosophy of teaching: that teaching is a way of learning. We dedicate this book to all the students who have been our teachers.

To the Instructor

Adopting a new book takes a certain kind of courage. It's risky to depart from what you already know and try out new approaches and new ideas. So it's inevitable that as you think about using *FieldWorking*, you might wonder, "Can fieldwork really be part of a research writing course?"

Our answer: "Yes, of course, we think so. Try it for a semester or two."

As you leaf through *FieldWorking*, attracted by the idea, perhaps, but not quite sure about just how it would fit in your course, you might ask, "Why teach students to do fieldwork? How?" We've asked those questions over our years of teaching, and we'd like to offer you some reasons to try it.

Why Do Fieldwork?

Fieldwork allows students to be more engaged and involved in the research process. Instead of working only in a library, students who work in field sites and archives learn to observe, listen, interpret, and analyze the behaviors and language of the "others" around them—through more than written text. *FieldWorking* exposes students to cultures different from their own through actual contact in their research projects in addition to reading about those cultures. Doing fieldwork encourages understanding of self as each student reads, writes, researches, and reflects on relationships with the "other." But the most compelling reason for anyone to use this book is that, through the process of fieldworking, students will become better researchers and writers.

How Might Fieldwork Happen for Students in a College Class?

FieldWorking integrates skills for research, reading, and writing in each of its first five chapters with a final chapter devoted entirely to the writing process. Each chapter introduces specific research skills and then offers short writing options ("Boxes") for trying them out. Within the boxes, under the heading "Response," we've included samples from our own students' work to provide models. As students learn about new fieldworking skills and try them, they begin to build (and interpret) a cumulative record of the process of their work—a research portfolio. We've designed the book to accommodate either a single large fieldwork project or a collection of shorter fieldwork projects on different topics, from various research sites. But in both cases, the writing students do can become part of a research portfolio. In fact, a special feature of this book is the section called "The Research Portfolio," which appears at the end of each of the first five chapters. We've designed these sections to show students how to develop, reflect, interpret, and share both the processes and the products of their research.

What About Reading? How Can Students Become Better Readers While Doing Fieldwork?

Students also learn to write research by reading examples from both professional and student writers. As we chose readings for *FieldWorking*, we drew from a wide range of voices across the related disciplines of anthropology, folklore, sociology, journalism, natural science, and education in the genres of fiction and nonfiction, both historical and contemporary. We present three complete and accessible student research essays (in Chapters 1, 3, and 5) to help students set realistic goals for their own projects. We treat student essays with the same level of analysis and explication as the professional writing samples. We hope this range will challenge and encourage students to develop the complex skills and strategies to make them better readers, writers, and, of course, researchers.

What About Time? How Can a Whole Course Be Devoted to Doing Fieldwork?

We've designed this book to provide enough material for a semester-long course; however, you can easily organize or assign its content in different or abbreviated ways. It's not necessary, for example, to read the book from beginning to end, although we intended the order to offer the most complete introduction to reading, writing, and research on cultures. Students could start with the introductory two chapters, "Stepping in and Stepping Out: Understanding Cultures" and "Reading Self, Reading Cultures: Understanding Texts," which expose them to key concepts, and then move around in the book, depending on their interests and on the assignments that they choose to complete. Chapter 3, "Researching Place: The Spatial Gaze," focuses mainly on fieldnote and research skills within a specific field site. Chapter 5, "Researching People: The Collaborative Listener," emphasizes the interviewing skills that often grow out of interest in field investigation but also would be useful for a course that examines family stories and oral history in conjunction with interviews. Chapter 4, "Researching Language: The Cultural Translator," includes many short readings and exercises about language and culture; these readings could serve as a unit of language study within any course. The final chapter, Chapter 6, "FieldWriting: From Talk to Text," pulls together the elements of the writing process we've described throughout the book: freewriting, double-entry notetaking, drafting in stages or layers, and various approaches to revising and editing.

How you use this book will depend on your overall course purpose or theme and the other readings you intend to use. It might serve alone in an undergraduate composition/research course. But it also might complement an intensive ethnographic reading/writing course in which students read several full-length ethnographies such as *Mules and Men, Translated Woman, Coming of Age in New Jersey, Ways with Words*, or a collection of ethnographic essays such as *Women Writing Culture*. We've compiled our current favorite options for further reading, including the above books, in our "FieldReading" bibliographies at the end of each chapter.

What About the Specialized Words and Terms Used in Fieldwork?

Terms like "reflexivity" and "positionality" and even "culture" can seem problematic, vague, and annoying to instructors and students who are unfamiliar with them in the context of research and writing. We've included a special section called "FieldWords," a short glossary of specific terms we've introduced, in each of the first five chapters. Both students and instructors can consult these glossaries when an unfamiliar word or concept comes up during the work of any given chapter.

Will This Book Require Supplemental Texts?

We've tried to anticipate many of the writing and documenting skills students will need for effective fieldwork in our special sections called "FieldWriting" at the end of each of the first five chapters. These sections address strategies relevant to good writing such as discovering voice, using active verbs, and revising for specific detail. We also include issues specific to good research: documentation of published and unpublished sources, and taping and transcribing interviews. But if you want to present skills beyond those we've described in conjunction with the projects in this book, a handbook would serve as a good supplemental text.

As we mentioned earlier, appropriate readings are important models for students' writing. The readings we've included in our book may very well provide enough material for a semester-long course. But some instructors and students might want to add a cultural reader, a collection of ethnographic essays, a full-length ethnography, or group choices from a list of relevant readings in related disciplines.

And So?

We believe strong teaching requires the courage to learn alongside your students. It also requires love and patience and the hope that students will reflect on their lives through the processes of reading and writing. This book, we hope, will invite you and your students to engage in that reflective process together.

Effective writing, as we have tried to teach in this book, requires more than just writers. It requires a subculture of selected readers—writers' trusted "insiders"—before it moves on to an outside audience. For this book, each re-framed idea, each revision came out of our subculture of colleagues. Julie Cheville has been as devoted to this book as we have, acting as our primary reader of drafts and our coach throughout three years of writing, reading, and research. Quite often Julie knew what we wanted to say when we didn't.

We would also like to thank our long-lived writing group of academic sisters, the "Daughters of Discourse," Donna Qualley, Danling Fu, Pat Sullivan, Cindy Gannett, and Sherrie Gradin, whose voices mix with our own and always blur the boundary between "self" and "other." We've checked drafts and thoughts with colleagues in our three academic homes: Rich Horwitz, Sandie Hughes, Jim Marshall, and Mary Trachsel at the University of Iowa (UI); Janet Bean, Hepsie Roskelly, and Jim Stafford at the University of North Carolina at Greensboro (UNCG); Bob Connors, Burt Feintuch, Don Graves, Jane Hansen, Don Murray, Tom Newkirk, and Becky Rule at the University of New Hampshire (UNH) as well as the entire faculty of the UNH Summer Writing Program. Other colleagues have offered important "fresh reads" when we've needed them: Hanna Griff at Sanyo Gaiken University in Okayama-Shi, Japan, Jonathan Lovell at San Jose State University, Jack Kugelmass at the University of Wisconsin, Paul Lizotte and Sharon Dean at Rivier College, and Janet Wikler of Wikler & Co., Inc. in New York City.

Our confidence about *FieldWorking's* value in different kinds of classes is the result of so many students having used our drafts. We thank them all for their responses, their revisions, and their fieldwork. Ethnographic essays by Karen Downing, Cindie Marshall, and Rick Zollo appear in this book after extra work to prepare them for publication. Our teaching assistants tried out pieces of this book in draft: Janet Bean and Jim Stafford at the UNCG in Freshman 101 and102, and Julie Cheville at the UI in Rhetoric 10:003 and 10:004. We would also like to thank our undergraduate and graduate students, Bonnie's at UI in the Ph.D. Seminar 8P:425/7S:415 "Ethnographic Methods, Theories and Texts," in English 8W: 255 "The Ethnographic Essay," and American Studies 45:290 "Seminar in Writing about Cultures," Elizabeth's at UNCG in the Freshman 101 Seminar "Reading and Writing Culture," and Paul Russ's MFA thesis in Film Studies; our students together at UNH in English 914 "Writing Culture: Family Stories, Oral Histories, and Interviews." Our universities were generous with course reductions and research fellowships to help us complete our project. Because of our colleagues' and students' enthusiasm, careful work, and faith in us, we can share our confidence with our readers.

As *FieldWorking* stepped out of these personal subcultures and into the more public subculture of text reviewers, we were lucky to have other colleagues who offered crucial responses which re-shaped it (and us) between drafts. Our special thanks to Wendy Bishop of Florida State University and Jim Zebroski of Syracuse University (to whom we dedicate Chapter 6), Kathleen Shine Cain of Merrimack College (for street accolades and marketplace wisdom), Mark Shadle of Eastern Oregon State University (to whom we dedicate Chapter 4, as well as the word "because" each time it appears), and Sandra Clark of Anderson University, Patricia Connors of the University of Memphis, Nancy Downs of the University of Illinois at Chicago, and Lucille McCarthy of the University of Maryland Baltimore County.

And, between one important taxicab ride in 1991 and one published book, Nancy Perry's vision, judgment, expertise, business acumen, and personal support has helped us to both envision this project and carry it through the way we wanted to do it. No meeting, meal, or phone call was too much. We thank, too, Nancy's editorial assistant Michael Kramer, and Prentice Hall's professional liaison Shelly Kupperman. And this book would simply not exist without Karen Trost's meticulous production work, Bruce Emmer's detailed copyediting, and Elsa Peterson and her staff's permissions sleuthing.

Elizabeth would like to acknowledge the support of Happy Strater, who helped out with family matters for three summers while the book was being written and published. Bonnie drew special family support from Jane Anderson, Helen Honorow, Heather Molkentine, and as always, Janet Stone.

Finally, we thank our children: Tosca Chiseri, Alisha Strater, Amy Sunstein, and Stephen Sunstein. In four very different ways, each of them grew and shared with each—and with both—of us over three school years and three New Hampshire summers. As we wrote this book, they taught us, as our students do, more than we ever thought we could learn.

ELIZABETH CHISERI-STRATER

BONNIE STONE SUNSTEIN

To the Student

There's both joy and satisfaction in understanding people and situations different from our own. *FieldWorking* will give you special license and formal ways to hang out, observe carefully, and speculate about talk and behavior. This book will show you how to interpret the lives and surroundings of others through their eyes—not just your own. And this book will also help you see yourself and your own cultural attitudes more clearly since any study of an "other" is also a study of a "self."

FieldWorking assumes that you will *do* fieldwork, not just read about it. In the doing of fieldwork, we want you to consider your process as both art and craft: art in the writing and craft in the research. Fieldwork as an artistic craft implies cultural methods and expectations in the same way that woodcarving, quilting, and music making showcase the cultures they represent. Understanding and presenting other cultures requires the engaged reading, writing, listening, speaking, and researching activities we will share with you in this book.

There is no single way to read our book. We imagine that you'll work through the first two introductory chapters, complete our fieldworking exercises (called "boxes"), and then design research projects of your own. We'd like to assume that you'll want to read the entire book, but the way you proceed within it will depend entirely on your own research plans. If, for example, your project focuses mainly on a cultural setting, you'll naturally turn to Chapter 3, "Researching Place." But if you're more interested in looking closely at the language behaviors of a person or group, you may want to read Chapter 4, "Researching Language," after the two introductory chapters. And if your research centers on interviews or oral histories, you may wish to go directly to Chapter 5, "Researching People." The last chapter, "FieldWriting: From Talk to Text," draws together the many threads about writing that we've woven thoughout the book. This last chapter is deeply important to the actual writing of your study. We hope that you'll consult it whenever you begin your drafting process.

With the help of our students and colleagues, we've designed some special features in our book. First, we include many fieldwork exercises that provide opportunities to try out research skills before working them into a major research project. You may want to try them with a range of people and places, or you may already know your research site and want to explore it with each exercise. Whichever way you choose to use the exercises, we (and our students) have found them good ways to confirm or change the direction or focus of a project. We hope they'll help you avoid obstacles or problems you may not have thought about. Second, we offer you a wide range of writing samples. We hope that you'll enjoy reading our students' and colleagues' actual writing from their fieldwork—as well as the previously published professional pieces—and that their writing will give you confidence to do your own research. Finally, five of our chapters include information about and practice in keeping a research portfolio. The portfolio, we believe, offers a place for a fieldworker to gather work, review it, and decide what needs to be accomplished next. We suggest that you work with a portfolio partner to exchange your ideas and writing throughout your fieldwork project.

About us: the voice that addresses you in this book is really a double voice. We wrote this book together—every single word of it—many drafts' worth, on a laptop Macintosh Powerbook. We hope you'll find your own voice in your fieldwriting. Because we've used drafts of our book in our own courses, from freshman classes to graduate classes, we acknowledge the huge role that our students' voices and contributions played in helping us shape and reshape this text. As you read through *FieldWorking*, take what is useful to you. Ignore what you can't use. Skip around—or read it from beginning to end. But please remember this: the field research you do should be meaningful and valuable to yourself and to the "others" you study. Work on a project you care about, and you'll make others care about it too.

One final note. Throughout this book, we've chosen to use the personal pronoun "you" rather than he/she, s/he, he/she, they, or the more traditionally used "he." We do this not to be radical or off-putting, but to encompass and embrace everyone, male and female, who reads this book.

ELIZABETH CHISERI-STRATER

BONNIE STONE SUNSTEIN

Contents

CHAPTER 3

Researching Place: The Spatial Gaze   97

CHAPTER 6

FieldWriting: From Talk to Text   277

groping for a footing with oneself
   assessing the images of others
attempting to find oneself
   by explaining the other,

deflating them
   with our pins of inquiry
we collect them like butterflies
   pinned to a page,

often we ignore the breathing
   behind the images,
the sentence behind
   our seen patterns,

can we explain their shimmering
   by pinning them to a page,
can we forestall our loneliness
   with our explanations,

we can only reach out,
   allowing another's vibrations to
affect our own shimmering,
   glimpsing for a moment the same
you from another perspective,

not a synchrony,
   or a harmony,
but rather a momentary
   change in oneself,

to experience the same life
   in a new way,
to compare that experience
   with the unchanged you,

thereby glimpsing for a moment
   another world,
another possible you.

Sal Biondello
Commonwealth of the Northern Marianas

FieldWorking

Stepping In and Stepping Out: Understanding Cultures

Long before I ever heard of anthropology, I was being conditioned for the role of stepping in and out of society. It was part of my growing up process to question the traditional values and norms of the family and to experiment with behavior patterns and ideologies. This is not an uncommon process of finding oneself. . . . Why should a contented and satisfied person think of standing outside his or any other society and studying it?

Hortense Powdermaker

Ordinary living involves all the skills of fieldworking—looking, listening, collecting, questioning, and interpreting—even though we are not always conscious of these skills. Many of us enjoy people-watching from the corners of our eyes, checking out how others talk, dress, behave, and interact. We question the significance of someone wearing pig earrings or displaying a dragon tattoo on the left shoulder. We wonder how a certain couple sitting in a restaurant booth can communicate when they don't look each other in the eye or wonder who made the rules for children we see playing stickball in the middle of a busy street. Fieldworkers question such behaviors in a systematic way.

What is a "field"? And how does a person "work" in it? The word *field* carries a wide range of connotations. It can mean open cleared land, such as a field of corn, and it can also mean the ground devoted to playing sports, such as a soccer field. In military operations, the word suggests a battleground, whereas at the university, a field relates to an area of professional study, such as the field of rhetoric and composition or the field of Latin American studies. In science, it relates to a region of space under the influence of some agent, as an electrical field or a magnetic field. In photography and in art, a field can mean a visible surface on which an image is displayed, like a field of color or a field of view. Business people, naturalists, and anthropologists all talk about "being in the field" as part of their jobs. Working "in the field" for an anthropologist means talking, listening, recording, observing, participating, and sometimes even living in a particular place. The field is the site for doing research, and fieldworking is the process of doing it.

Close looking and listening skills mark trained fieldworkers who study groups of people in contexts—others' and their own. The job of this book is to help you become more conscious as you observe, participate in, read, and write about your own world and the worlds of others. Although we don't claim to turn you into a professional ethnographer, we borrow ethnographic strategies to help you become a fieldworker, and we show you ways to write about your process. We'll guide you as you conduct and write up your own fieldwork and as you read about the fieldwork of others. *FieldWorking* will make you consider your everyday experiences in new ways and help you interpret other people's behaviors, language, and thoughts. But most of all, the fieldwork itself will help you understand why you react and respond in the ways you do—based on your assumptions. Sometimes, without much consciousness, we watch others. This book will encourage you not only to watch others but also to watch yourself as you watch them—consciously.

You've probably spent many hours noticing behavior patterns and questioning inexplicable routines among the people you've lived with and learned from. In the quotation that introduces this chapter, anthropologist Hortense Powdermaker suggests that as we grow up, we "step out" a bit; we "adopt the outsider stance" as we watch the people inside our own group. We also "step in" to unfamiliar groups and examine them closely, which is the fieldworker's "insider stance." As insiders, we wonder if there might be a better technique for mincing garlic or cooling pies that is less laborious than our family's method. Or we wonder if it is always necessary to dry dishes with a towel since, after all, they *do* dry by themselves. As outsiders moving to a new school, we might question the ritual cheers aimed against the rival or different rules for submitting papers. When we visit another country, we need to learn new rules for introductions and farewells in order to behave appropriately. Fieldworkers study the customs of groups of people in the spaces they inhabit.

Inquiry into the behavior patterns of others prepares us for doing fieldwork. Powdermaker also asks why any "satisfied and contented person" would want to research everyday ways of behaving, talking, and interacting. One answer is that fieldworking sharpens our abilities to look closely at surroundings. People, places, languages, and behaviors can be familiar because we've lived with them, but when we move or travel and find ourselves strangers, the very same things can be unfamiliar or uncomfortable. Another answer is that knowing our assumptions and recognizing our stereotypes helps develop tolerance and respect for customs and groups different from ours. For example, head coverings—turbans, veils, yarmulkas, ceremonial headdresses, and even baseball caps worn backward—may seem strange to us until we understand their history and significance. Studying diverse people and cultures does not necessarily make us accept difference, but it can make us aware of our assumptions and sometimes even of our prejudices.

Defining Culture: Fieldwork and Ethnography

Culture is a slippery term. To some, it implies "high culture"—concert music, etiquette, museum art, books called "classics," or extensive knowledge of Western history. For those people, culture is gained through exposure and socioeconomic status. But fieldworkers who have studied cultures around the world and in their own backyards know that individuals acquire culture from others in their group. Every group has a culture, so there is no useful distinction between "high" and "low" cultures. Anthropologists have tried to define what culture is for as long as they've been thinking about it, and they have developed contrasting definitions.

We define culture as an invisible web of behaviors, patterns, rules, and rituals of a group of people who have contact with one another and share common languages. Our definition draws from the work of many anthropologists:

- "Culture is local and manmade and hugely variable. It tends also to be integrated. A culture, like an individual, is a more or less consistent pattern of thought and action" (Benedict 46).
- "A society's culture consists of whatever it is one has to know or believe in order to operate in a manner acceptable to its members. . . . [I]t does not consist of things, people, behavior, or emotions. It is rather an organization of those things" (Goodenough 167).
- "Cultures are, after all, collective, untidy assemblages, authenticated by belief and agreement" (Myerhoff 10).
- "Man is an animal suspended in webs of significance which he himself has created. I take culture to be those webs" (Geertz).

Cultural theorist Raymond Williams writes that *culture* is one of the most difficult words to define, and these anthropologists' definitions illustrate it. While Benedict and Goodenough emphasize patterns in their definitions, Barbara Myerhoff highlights messiness. Geertz uses the metaphor of a web to describe how a culture hangs together invisibly. And still another anthropologist, James Peacock, draws a metaphor from photography. Using the lens of a camera, he describes its "harsh light" and "soft focus" to show how ethnographers try to capture the background and the foreground of a group. As you can see, definitions of culture can be both metaphorical ("webs" and "lenses") and structured (patterns of belief and behavior as well as untidy deviations from those patterns).

In your fieldworking experiences, you will be constantly asking yourself, "Where is the culture?" of the group you are investigating. The goal of fieldworking is to find it. You will find evidence in the language of the group you study, in its cultural artifacts, or in its rituals and behaviors. Fieldworkers investigate the cultural landscape, the larger picture of how a culture functions: its rituals, its rules, its traditions, and its behaviors. And they poke around the edges at the stories people tell, the items people collect and value, and the materials people use to go about their daily living. By learning from people in a culture what it is like to be part of their world, fieldworkers discover a culture's ways of being, knowing, and understanding.

Fieldworkers who live, observe, and describe the daily life, behaviors, and language of a group of people for long periods of time are called *ethnographers*. This book draws on the work of classic and contemporary anthropologists and folklorists: Hortense Powdermaker, Henry Glassie, Barbara Myerhoff, Zora Neale Hurston, Paul Stoller, and Renato Rosaldo, among others. Ethnography, the written product of their work, is a researched study that synthesizes information about the life of a people or group. Researchers in many disciplines rely on ethnographic methods: anthropologists, folklorists, linguists, sociologists, oral historians, and those who study popular culture. Ethnographic researchers conduct fieldwork in an attempt to understand the cultures they study. And as they study the culture of others, they learn patterns that connect their own lives and traditions.

Hortense Powdermaker, who did her fieldwork during the 1930s and 1940s, wrote about the Melanesians she studied as both "strangers" and "friends." Her book, in fact, is called *Stranger and Friend*. Powdermaker, a product of her time, also refers to the Melanesians as "stone-aged" and "natives," revealing an unconscious Westernized attitude toward people different from herself. Without realizing it, Powdermaker judged the Melanesian culture to be less sophisticated or developed than her own. This attitude—domination of one culture by the values of another—is called *colonization*, and fieldworkers must guard against it.

Like Powdermaker, fieldworkers historically studied foreign or exotic cultures, but no longer do they restrict their research to non-Western cultures. Contemporary fieldworkers also investigate local cultures and subcultures. Jennifer Toth, for example, wrote a book called *The Mole People: Life in the Tunnels beneath New York City*, describing her time with homeless people who shelter themselves in subways, sewer systems, and work stations under city streets. Rather than depicting these people as somehow less than herself, Toth's attitude likens them to people who have more conventional homes. Because all fieldworkers risk projecting their own assumptions onto the groups they study, they must be ready and willing to unpack their own cultural baggage and embark on a collaborative journey with those they study.

Stepping In: Revealing Our Subcultures

As coauthors of this book, we have ourselves come to our interest in ethnography from membership in a dizzying array of subcultures. As collaborators, we share the culture of academia. We are graduates of the same PhD program in which we learned to conduct ethnographic fieldwork. As middle-aged professors, we've both taught in public urban, suburban, and rural schools, directed college writing centers and programs, and taught many college English and education courses. And as mothers of young adults, both of us have spent years navigating the child-centered cultures of nursery school carpools, pediatric waiting rooms, and soccer and Special Olympics teams.

Yet our subcultures vary. Although she doesn't think about it much, Bonnie grew up with one Yiddish-speaking Jewish grandmother and another grandmother who denied her Jewish heritage. Elizabeth is a midwestern WASP whose grandfather was a farmer and whose father became a businessman who spoke Spanish and traveled to Cuba before Castro came to power. We both grew up as American baby boomers, with conformity and optimism in the post–World War II '50s, which by the '60s turned to protest of the Vietnam War. Bonnie played the guitar, wrote folk songs for a friend's coffeehouse, and joined the civil rights march on Selma. Elizabeth belonged to the Anti-Complicity War Movement, hung out in Greenwich Village wearing black clothes, and grew organic vegetables on a cooperative farm. But we were not only followers of these "countersubcultures"; we also belonged to more mainstream American ones. Bonnie, who was vice-president of her high school student council, skipped school occasionally to take the train downtown to sneak into a broadcast of *American Bandstand* but also wrote features for her college newspaper and joined a sorority. Elizabeth was a member of the National Honor Society, drag-raced a souped-up red and cream-colored Chevy, and was sent off to finishing school, where she wore white gloves and little hats.

In each of these subcultures, we communicated through special languages with insiders. We knew the ways of behaving and interacting, and we shared belief systems with the others in each group. Yet we held membership in many subcultures at the same time, and we could move among them. As members over the years, we were unaware of those groups as actual cultures, but looking back as fieldworkers, we now understand that we, like you, have always been in a position to research the people around us. And we probably did do some informal inquiry, but not the disciplined fieldwork of the ethnographer that this book will describe.

As researchers, we've both studied the literacies of American subcultures. Because we are interested in language, both written and oral, we research everyday places where people read, write, speak, and listen. Elizabeth has studied college students' conversation patterns, collaborative journal writing, middle school writing workshops, and kindergarteners' book talk. Bonnie has studied talk in a high school teachers' lounge, interactions in a college writing center, a recording session for a Hollywood movie, the writing and reading of handicapped teenagers, and a school superintendent's writing portfolio.

Neither of us has "stepped out" of our North American culture to find our research sites, but the more research we do, the more interest we have in researching familiar places. We are a bit like tourists who need only to travel a little way from home to find something very different and very fascinating to research. Less than an hour away from Elizabeth's home, for example, is a small town called Seagrove that has over 50 working potters. They form a community that shares similar technical language, crafting skills, and aesthetic values. Each spring, the potters of Seagrove stage a ritual opening of the kilns to the public. Pots are thrown and glazes are applied as potters share their insider knowledge with outsiders. This group of artisans, whose craft goes back eight or nine generations, represents a subculture unknown to Elizabeth and many others who live just outside Seagrove. We don't always need to go very far from home to find groups of people whose ways of behaving and communicating are different and interesting, yet unfamiliar to us.

B O X 1
LOOKING AT SUBCULTURES

We would consider any self-identified group of people—who share language, stories, rituals, behaviors, and values—as a subculture. Some subcultures define themselves by geography (southerners, Texans, New Yorkers). Others define themselves by ethnicity or language (Mexicano, Irish, Flemish, Filipino, Ghanaian). And others define their interests by shared rituals and behaviors (fraternity brothers, Girl Scouts, Masons, Daughters of the American Revolution, computer hackers). Whether it's your bowling league, your neighborhood pickup basketball team, or bicycle freestylers, your church, your community government, or your school's ecology club, you simultaneously belong to many different subcultures.

List some of the subcultures to which you belong. With each subculture you mention, jot down a few key details that distinguish the group: behaviors, insider phrases, rules, rituals, and the specific locations where these behaviors usually occur. You might want to divide your list into categories or columns. Then write a short paragraph describing one of these subcultures either seriously or satirically.

Response

Some of our students listed these subcultures to which they belong: computer interest groups, home pages or online discussion groups, deer hunters, gospel singers, specialty book clubs, volleyball team members, science fiction conventioneers, auctiongoers, fly fishermen, billiard players, day-care center families, bluegrass musicians, and stock car racers. Karen Downing wrote this description of her fellow lap swimmers:

> Ritual freaks! We swim at the same time in the same lane on the same day of the week in the same swim suit. We don't speak much to one another in between "sets" because we know just how long our workout will take and have to be sure to beat the clock so our "splits pan out." We lick our goggles to keep the fog out and log our miles on a wall chart for all to see. If we have to share a lane, we are territorial, claiming one side of the gray line that will not be crossed by the other swimmer. No "circle swimming" for this bunch. Most of us do crawl stroke or "freestyle." A few do breast stroke to rest and stretch out. Pullbuoys and kick boards and fins, plus an underwater watch, are signs of a serious swimmer.

Notice that Karen uses the special language ("sets," "splits pan out," "freestyle," "circle swimming") and puts the words in quotation marks to suggest that this group of lap swimmers shares these insider terms.

Investigating Perspectives: Insider and Outsider

Fieldworkers realize that ordinary events in one culture might seem extraordinary in another. When people say "that's really weird" or "aren't they strange," a fieldworker hears these comments as signals for investigation. When you first ate dinner at someone's home other than yours, you may have felt like an outsider. You "stepped out" of your own home and "stepped in" to a set of routines and rituals different from your own. You may have noticed who set the table, passed the food, served, ate first, talked, signaled that the meal was over, cleared off the table, and washed the dishes. Or as an insider among your own relatives, you always observed their own quirky behaviors: you learned not to disturb the bronze baby shoes in Aunt Sonia's TV room or never to descend into Uncle Fred's cellar. To avoid a head cold, your mother may use crystals and a spiritual chant, but your best friend's mother may depend on warm milk and honey, minted tea, or vitamin C.

Although we would not classify modern families as subcultures, they do have some of the features of a subculture and prepare us to observe outside our own home territory. When you visit another place, you may notice that people move and talk more slowly or quickly, more quietly or noisily, or that they use space differently than you're used to. A fieldworker "steps out" to adopt an outsider's perspective when investigating unfamiliar (or even familiar) patterns, attempting to penetrate or unveil the many layers of behaviors and beliefs that make people think as they think and act as they act.

Anthropologist Renato Rosaldo offers a good example of "stepping out," using the outsider's detached perspective to look at a familiar routine, the family ritual of making breakfast:

> Every morning, the reigning patriarch, as if in from the hunt, shouts from the kitchen, "How many people would like a poached egg?" Women and children take turns saying yes or no.
>
> In the meantime, the women talk among themselves and designate one among them the toastmaker. As the eggs near readiness, the reigning patriarch calls out to the designated toastmaker, "The eggs are about ready. Is there enough toast?"
>
> "Yes" comes the deferential reply. "The last two pieces are about to pop up." The reigning patriarch then proudly enters, bearing a plate of poached eggs before him. Throughout the course of the meal, the women and children, including the designated toastmaker, perform the obligatory ritual praise song, saying, "These sure are great eggs, Dad" (47).

In this passage, Rosaldo has made a familiar routine seem unfamiliar: father makes poached eggs, women make toast; all eat. By analyzing his family's well-known breakfast-making process, Rosaldo exposes the power and gender relationships involved in this ordinary event. He describes the father as the "reigning patriarch" and the women as subsidiary toast makers and praise singers. With his detached language and his careful detailing of their routine, he depicts this North American middle-class family as if it were part of a different tribe or culture. He uses his interpretive skills as an ethnographer to create a parody—in jest and fun—to allow his family to see them as an outsider might describe them.

But fieldworkers do not depend on detachment or on the objectivity that comes from stepping out of a culture. They rely on basic human involvement—their gut reactions or subjective responses to cultural practices. In another example from Rosaldo's fieldwork, he shows how his own personal life experience shaped his ability to understand headhunters. As a ritual of revenge and grief over a deceased relative, the Ilongots of the Philippines sever human heads. When Rosaldo and his anthropologist wife, Michelle, lived and studied among the Ilongot people for several years, they were unable to understand the complex emotions surrounding headhunting. But after Michelle died in an accident during fieldwork, Rosaldo began to understand the headhunters' practice of killing for retribution. It was his own experience—rage and grief over his wife's death—that allowed him insight into the cultural practice of the people he was studying. Rosaldo writes:

> [N]othing in my own experience equipped me even to imagine the anger possible in bereavement until after Michelle Rosaldo's death in 1981. Only then was I in a position to grasp the force of what the Ilongots had repeatedly told me about grief, rage, and headhunting (19).

Rosaldo's reaction to Michelle's dying, his subjective feelings, connected him with the Ilongots' practice of killing as an act of revenge. Even though their value systems were different, Rosaldo and the Ilongots shared the basic human response to a loved one's death.

So it is not always objectivity or detachment that allows us to study culture, our own or that of others. Subjectivity—our inner feelings and belief systems—allows us to uncover some features of culture that are not always apparent. As a fieldworker, you will conduct an internal dialogue between your subjective and objective selves, listening to both, questioning both. You combine the viewpoints of an outsider "stepping in" and an insider "stepping out" of the culture you study. And studying culture is as much about the everyday practices of cooking and eating, like poaching eggs, as it is about the exotic tribal practices of killing and grieving, of achieving revenge by severing a human head. Detachment and involvement, subjectivity and objectivity, insider and outsider stances are equally coupled in fieldworking.

Stepping Out: Making the Familiar Strange and the Strange Familiar

Rosaldo's parody of the family breakfast and his understanding of the Ilongots' headhunting practices display the coupled skills of detachment and involvement a fieldworker needs. In order to understand the Ilongots' perspective on headhunting, or what anthropologists call their *worldview*, Rosaldo had to suffer the intensity of rage and grief that they did. Though not intentionally, he achieved this empathy by making what seemed to him a strange event (cutting off people's heads for revenge) totally familiar as a researcher. What is often more difficult to achieve than making the unknown become familiar is making the familiar seem strange. Rosaldo was able to accomplish the outsider view of his family's breakfast-making practices mainly through satire, a technique that distances the reader from the event or practice under consideration.

In the following reading written in 1956, "Body Ritual among the Nacirema," anthropologist Horace Miner also depends on satire to depict an ordinary set of daily practices as strange and unfamiliar.

Body Ritual among the Nacirema

Horace Miner

The anthropologist has become so familiar with the diversity of ways in which different peoples behave in similar situations that he is not apt to be surprised by even the most exotic customs. In fact, if all of the logically possible combinations of behavior have not been found somewhere in the world, he is apt to suspect that they must be present in some yet undescribed tribe. This point has, in fact, been expressed with respect to clan organization by Murdock (1949:71). In this light, the magical beliefs and practices of the Nacirema present such unusual aspects that it seems desirable to describe them as an example of the extremes to which human behavior can go.

Professor Linton first brought the ritual of the Nacirema to the attention of anthropologists twenty years ago (1936:326), but the culture of this people is still very poorly understood. They are a North American group living in the territory between the Canadian Cree, the Yaqui and Tarahumare of Mexico, and the Carib and Arawak of the Antilles. Little is known of their origin, although tradition states that they came from the east. According to Nacirema mythology, their nation was originated by a culture hero, Notgnihsaw, who is otherwise known for two great feats of strength—the throwing of a piece of wampum across the river Pa-To-Mac and the chopping down of a cherry tree in which the Spirit of Truth resided.

Nacirema culture is characterized by a highly developed market economy which has evolved in a rich natural habitat. While much of the people's time is devoted to economic pursuits, a large part of the fruits of these labors and a considerable portion of the day are spent in ritual activity. The focus of this activity is the human body, the appearance and health of which loom as a dominant concern in the ethos of the people. While such a concern is certainly not unusual, its ceremonial aspect and associated philosophy are unique.

The fundamental belief underlying the whole system appears to be that the human body is ugly and that its natural tendency is to debility and disease. Incarcerated in such a body, man's only hope is to avert these characteristics through the use of the powerful influences of ritual and ceremony. Every household has one or more shrines devoted to this purpose. The more powerful individuals in the society have several shrines in their houses and, in fact, the opulence of a house is often referred to in terms of the number of such ritual centers it possesses. Most houses are of wattle and daub construction, but the shrine rooms of the more wealthy are walled with stone. Poorer families imitate the rich by applying pottery plaques to their shrine walls.

While each family has at least one such shrine, the rituals associated with it are not family ceremonies but are private and secret. The rites are normally only discussed with children, and then only during the period when they are being initiated into these mysteries. I was able, however, to establish sufficient rapport with the natives to examine these shrines and to have the rituals described to me.

The focal point of the shrine is a box or chest which is built into the wall. In this chest are kept the many charms and magical potions without which no native believes he could live. These preparations are secured from a variety of specialized practitioners. The most powerful of these are the medicine men, whose assistance must be rewarded with substantial gifts. However, the medicine men do not provide the curative potions for their clients, but decide what the ingredients should be and then write them down in an ancient and secret language. This writing is understood only by the medicine men and by the herbalists who, for another gift, provide the required charm.

The charm is not disposed of after it has served its purpose, but is placed in the charm-box of the household shrine. As these magical materials are specific for certain ills, and the real or imagined maladies of the people are many, the charm-box is usually full to overflowing. The magical packets are so numerous that people forget what their purposes were and fear to use them again. While the natives are very vague on this point, we can only assume that the idea in retaining all the old magical materials is that their presence in the charm-box, before which the body rituals are conducted, will in some way protect the worshipper.

Beneath the charm-box is a small font. Each day every member of the family, in succession, enters the shrine room, bows his head before the charm-box, mingles different sorts of holy water in the font, and proceeds with a brief rite of ablution. The holy waters are secured from the Water Temple of the community, where the priests conduct elaborate ceremonies to make the liquid ritually pure.

In the hierarchy of magical practitioners, and below the medicine men in prestige, are specialists whose designation is best translated "holy-mouth-men." The Nacirema have an almost pathological horror of and fascination with the mouth, the condition of which is believed to have a supernatural influence on all social relationships. Were it not for the rituals of the mouth, they believe that their teeth would fall out, their gums bleed, their jaws shrink, their friends desert them, and their lovers reject them. They also believe that a strong relationship exists between oral and moral characteristics. For example, there is a ritual ablution of the mouth for children which is supposed to improve their moral fiber.

The daily body ritual performed by everyone includes a mouth-rite. Despite the fact that these people are so punctilious about care of the mouth, this rite involves a practice which strikes the uninitiated stranger as revolting. It was reported to me that the ritual consists of inserting a small bundle of hog hairs into the mouth, along with certain magical powders, and then moving the bundle in a highly formalized series of gestures.

In addition to the private mouth-rite, the people seek out a holy-mouth-man once or twice a year. These practitioners have an impressive set of paraphernalia, consisting of a variety of augers, awls, probes, and prods. The use of these objects in the exorcism of the evils of the mouth involves almost unbelievable ritual torture of the client. The holy-mouth-man opens the client's mouth and, using the above mentioned tools, enlarges any holes which decay may have created in the teeth. Magical materials are put into these holes. If there are no naturally occurring holes in the teeth, large sections of one or more teeth are gouged out so that the supernatural substance can be applied. In the client's view, the purpose of these ministrations is to arrest decay and to draw friends. The extremely sacred and traditional character of the rite is evident in the fact that the natives return to the holy-mouth-men year after year, despite the fact that their teeth continue to decay.

It is to be hoped that, when a thorough study of the Nacirema is made, there will be careful inquiry into the personality structure of these people. One has but to watch the gleam in the eye of a holy-mouth-man, as he jabs an awl into an exposed nerve, to suspect that a certain amount of sadism is involved. If this can be established, a very interesting pattern emerges, for most of the population shows definite masochistic tendencies. It was to these that Professor Linton referred in discussing a distinctive part of the daily body ritual which is performed only by men. This part of the rite involves scraping and lacerating the surface of the face with a sharp instrument. Special women's rites are performed only four times during each lunar month, but what they lack in frequency is made up in barbarity. As part of this ceremony, women bake their heads in small ovens for about an hour. The theoretically interesting point is that what seems to be a preponderantly masochistic people have developed sadistic specialists.

The medicine men have an imposing temple, or *latipso*, in every community of any size. The more elaborate ceremonies required to treat very sick patients can only be performed at this temple. These ceremonies involve not only the thaumaturge but a permanent group of vestal maidens who move sedately about the temple chambers in distinctive costume and headdress.

The *latipso* ceremonies are so harsh that it is phenomenal that a fair proportion of the really sick natives who enter the temple ever recover. Small children whose indoctrination is still incomplete have been known to resist attempts to take them to the temple because "that is where you go to die." Despite this fact, sick adults are not only willing but eager to undergo the protracted ritual purification, if they can afford to do so. No matter how ill the supplicant or how grave the emergency, the guardians of many temples will not admit a client if he cannot give a rich gift to the custodian. Even after one has gained admission and survived the ceremonies, the guardians will not permit the neophyte to leave until he makes still another gift.

The supplicant entering the temple is first stripped of all his or her clothes. In everyday life the Nacirema avoids exposure of his body and its natural functions. Bathing and excretory acts are performed only in the secrecy of the household shrine, where they are ritualized as part of the body-rites. Psychological shock results from the fact that body secrecy is suddenly lost upon entry into the *latipso*. A man, whose own wife has never seen him in an excretory act, suddenly finds himself naked and assisted by a vestal maiden while he performs his natural functions into a sacred vessel. This sort of ceremonial treatment is necessitated by the fact that the excreta are used by a diviner to ascertain the course and nature of the client's sickness. Female clients, on the other hand, find their naked bodies are subjected to the scrutiny, manipulation and prodding of the medicine men.

Few supplicants in the temple are well enough to do anything but lie on their hard beds. The daily ceremonies, like the rites of the holy-mouth-men, involve discomfort and torture. With ritual precision, the vestals awaken their miserable charges each dawn and roll them about on their beds of pain while performing ablutions, in the formal movements of which the maidens are highly trained. At other times they insert magic wands in the supplicant's mouth or force him to eat substances which are supposed to be healing. From time to time the medicine men come to their clients and jab magically treated needles into their flesh. The fact that these temple ceremonies may not cure, and may even kill the neophyte, in no way decreases the people's faith in the medicine men.

There remains one other kind of practitioner, known as a "listener." This witch-doctor has the power to exorcise the devils that lodge in the heads of people who have been bewitched. The Nacirema believe that parents bewitch their own children. Mothers are particularly suspected of putting a curse on children while teaching them the secret body rituals. The counter-magic of the witch-doctor is unusual in its lack of ritual. The patient simply tells the "listener" all his troubles and fears, beginning with the earliest difficulties he can remember. The memory displayed by the Nacirema in these exorcism sessions is truly remarkable. It is not uncommon for the patient to bemoan the rejection he felt upon being weaned as a babe, and a few individuals even see their troubles going back to the traumatic effects of their own birth.

In conclusion, mention must be made of certain practices which have their base in native esthetics but which depend upon the pervasive aversion to the natural body and its functions. There are ritual fasts to make fat people thin and ceremonial feasts to make thin people fat. Still other rites are used to make women's breasts larger if they are small, and smaller if they are large. General dissatisfaction with breast shape is symbolized in the fact that the ideal form is virtually outside the range of human variation. A few women afflicted with almost inhuman hypermammary development are so idolized that they make a handsome living by simply going from village to village and permitting the natives to stare at them for a fee.

Reference has already been made to the fact that excretory functions are ritualized, routinized, and relegated to secrecy. Natural reproductive functions are similarly distorted. Intercourse is taboo as a topic and scheduled as an act. Efforts are made to avoid pregnancy by the use of magical materials or by limiting intercourse to certain phases of the moon. Conception is actually very infrequent. When pregnant, women dress so as to hide their condition. Parturition takes place in secret, without friends or relatives to assist, and the majority of women do not nurse their infants.

Our review of the ritual life of the Nacirema has certainly shown them to be a magic-ridden people. It is hard to understand how they have managed to exist so long under the burdens which they have imposed upon themselves. But even such exotic customs as these take on real meaning when they are viewed with the insight provided by Malinowski when he wrote (1948:70):

> Looking from far and above, from our high places of safety in the developed civilization, it is easy to see all the crudity and irrelevance of magic. But without its power and guidance early man could not have mastered his practical difficulties as he has done, nor could man have advanced to the higher stages of civilization.

Works Cited

Linton, Ralph. 1936. *The Study of Man.* New York, D. Appleton-Century Co.

Malinowski, Bronislaw. 1948. *Magic, Science, and Religion.* Glencoe, The Free Press.

Murdock, George P. 1949. *Social Structure.* New York, The Macmillan Co.

As you read this parody of American (*Nacirema* spelled backward) personal hygiene, you probably noticed how Miner's descriptions of everyday bathroom objects and grooming practices seemed like something you never before engaged in. He describes the medicine chest as a "shrine" that holds magic potions and "charms." The toothbrush is "a small bundle of hog hairs" for the application of "magical powders."

We laugh at Miner's parody because we see ourselves and our American obsession with cleanliness. This reading makes fun of our own cultural attitudes about bathing and cleansing habits, our American belief in dentists, doctors, and therapists, and our reliance on hospitals and diets. Miner defamiliarizes our everyday behaviors so that we can see ourselves as outsiders might describe us: a highly ritualized people who believe in magical customs and potions.

BOX 2
MAKING THE ORDINARY EXTRAORDINARY

Think of a routine in your everyday life that would seem extraordinary to someone from another culture or subculture. Try something simple like the way you fix your hair, listen to music, change a tire, take in the mail, or get ready for a sporting event. Make this routine unfamiliar as Rosaldo did when he described his family making breakfast. List the specific behaviors of your routine, and identify what might seem strange or extraordinary to others. Prepare your list to share with others, or write a short paragraph that describes the process.

Response

Ralph Beliveau writes of an experience that happens to most of us many times a day:

> The sound starts, loud enough to call for an action, not quite as jarring as a smoke alarm, but strong enough to disrupt what's already happening. Typically, X reads while Y searches through video images. Neither expects to always have to be responsible for stopping the noise. The negotiation begins with a glance. Mutual recognition that, yes, the noise is taking place. No, I'm not so involved in something as to ignore it. And no, I am not so angered by the interruption to refuse to respond. Past this glance, the next negotiated glare is proximity. Not just who is closer to the sound, but what obstacles are in the way between X and Y and the respective noise. The interrupted activities might prohibit motion—the need to keep a finger on a fast-forward button, or the size of the book opened in one's lap. These negotiations are influenced by a growing additional factor: time. The first noise induces anxiety. As each moment passes, the anxiety increases. At some point, self-consciousness adds its own voice. Am I being thoughtless by waiting? Is it fair to allow another to experience increased anxiety? Eventually, despite all these negotiations, it may be that the decision comes through default. "Hello? Uhhh, it's for you. . . ."

Posing Questions: Ethnographic and Journalistic

Miner's satire on American body rituals is a parody of the kind of traditional research that anthropologists have often published about foreign or exotic cultures. Nonfiction exposés, reports of personal experiences, and historical and documentary writings may read like fieldwork projects, but the difference lies in the research processes that led up to them. An ethnographer and a journalist may both gather information about the same event but write up their accounts very differently. A standard daily newspaper reporter, for example, conducts research in an attempt to be objective: to give the who, what, where, when, and why of an event for a readership that expects facts without too much interpretation. As a fieldworker, your purpose is to collect and consider multiple sources of information, not facts alone, to convey the perspective of the people about the culture you study.

The fieldworker asks big, open questions such as "What's going on here?" and "Where is the culture?" as he or she observes, listens, records, interprets, and analyzes. The journalist often writes from the outsider perspective, quoting insiders. The fieldworker must combine an outsider's point of view with an insider's perspective. Anthropologists use the term *emic* to mean the insider perspective and *etic* to refer to that of the outsider.

The following piece of front-page journalism from a small city's newspaper, "Church Opens Doors to Vietnamese," provides an example of reportage. But if we examine the article with an ethnographer's eye, we'll ask different questions that will help us examine information that a newswriter usually doesn't consider. To read for the complexity that this article implies, we need to uncover many layers of cultural meanings.

 Church Opens Doors to Vietnamese
St. Louis de Gonzague Holds First Mass in Vietnamese and Welcomes the Community to Its Parish

Byron Brown, Telegraph Staff

NASHUA—The one o'clock Mass at St. Louis de Gonzague Church was a little different Sunday. The choir and congregation sang "Meet Me in St. Louis" to greet its new minister, the Rev. Louis Nhien.

Nhien greeted his new parishioners by conducting Mass in Vietnamese.

Nhien's sermon was the first of what will be a weekly Vietnamese Mass at the church on West Hollis Street.

Before the 90-minute Mass, Nhien led about 200 Vietnamese worshipers into the church as hundreds of St. Louis' current parishioners stood and applauded. Nhien took a seat behind the altar alongside Pastor Roland Cote and Bishop Leo O'Neil of the Manchester diocese.

Older Vietnamese women wearing flowing silk blouses and pants, and younger Vietnamese families toting small children all filed into the pews in the center of the church.

There, they listened as O'Neil praised, with the help of an interpreter, the union of the Vietnamese community and the Roman Catholic Church.

"No matter what language we speak, no matter what country we come from, baptism has made us all brothers," he said. "We are one church as we profess one faith."

O'Neil spoke of St. Louis' history as a French-speaking church and how that had prepared its older parishioners for the new Vietnamese Mass.

"The French people of Nashua decided to build their own church where they could feel at home and speak their own language," he said. "The people of St. Louis want to welcome you here today, so you can feel at home."

Nhien then led the entire church in prayer and song.

Nhein, 38, was ordained last year and came to New Hampshire three weeks ago from Carthage, Mo. The New Hampshire Catholic Charities, led by Monsignor John Quinn, specifically brought him to the state to conduct Mass for the Vietnamese refugee community, which is centered in Greater Nashua and Manchester.

Older parishioners welcomed the Vietnamese worshipers and said their arrival makes St. Louis a stronger and more diversified church.

Veronica Barr, an Englishwoman who now lives in Nashua, said, "I'm excited. I think enthusiasm is an extension of us all being Catholic."

Ethnography and journalism differ, not only with respect to the writing process, but also with respect to depth of research, time allotted to it, and perspective represented. This journalist's responsibility was to report on that event—the special church service—as it happened at that church on that day, against a deadline and for a specific audience of newspaper readers. This journalist's goal was to gather the church's news, and his responsibility was to get it out quickly. But as a fieldworker, your responsibility would be to conduct research, to discover knowledge that may take months or even years to complete. Your commitment is an emic one—to capture the perspective of the insiders in the culture.

The newspaper account is the story of a Vietnamese priest from Carthage, Missouri, who has been invited to conduct a weekly Catholic Mass for Vietnamese refugees. The Mass takes place in a New Hampshire church whose pastor and parishioners are primarily French Canadian and whose bishop is Irish. The article connects the Vietnamese refugee community with the Catholic church. The article states that the choir sings a song from an American musical, "Meet Me in St. Louis," playing off the name of the church (St. Louis de Gonzague), its newest minister (Louis Nhien), and the state from which he has recently come (Missouri).

The article describes young Vietnamese women as "wearing flowing silk blouses and pants" and an Englishwoman as saying "I'm excited. I think enthusiasm is an extension of us all being Catholic." In the newspaper account, the bishop announces, "The people of St. Louis want to welcome you here today, so you can feel at home." The accompanying photograph shows an American flag, a bilingual banner that says "Welcome/Bienvenue," and a large stained-glass crucifix. Under these artifacts stand the three Catholic clergymen, posed before the congregation in their religious vestments. The caption reminds readers that the clergy recited the welcoming Mass in three languages: English, French, and Vietnamese.

As a fieldworker, you would ask focused questions of this cultural moment. You would emphasize issues that differ from the journalist's focus on the who, what, where, when, and why. You would ask questions like these: Who belongs to the Vietnamese refugee community? How do they see themselves here at this church? What languages do *they* speak? Do they define themselves as Catholic? Vietnamese? French? Americans? immigrants? settlers? Why are they associated with this French Canadian church? What is the history of French speakers in New Hampshire? What is the history of the French influence in Vietnam? Whether you choose the perspective of the Vietnamese priest, a non-Catholic Vietnamese refugee, the Irish bishop, or the mayor of Nashua, you will offer the insiders' perspective along with your own as you translate your cultural data into ethnographic text for your readers.

When Bishop O'Neil states in the article that he wants them to feel "at home," what does he mean by "at home"? Home to the people already in the church? to the Vietnamese refugee community of parishioners? to the other clergy? to the greater

Nashua community? The older Vietnamese women are reported to be wearing silk blouses and pants, but what were the younger women wearing? the men? the non-Vietnamese parishioners? Who was included in the "hundreds" who stood and applauded? Why did they applaud? Why was Veronica Barr specifically described as "an Englishwoman"? And how do we read her perspective, that "enthusiasm is an extension of us all being Catholic"? What, for example, would one of the Vietnamese parishioners say about the multicultural service?

As a fieldworker, investigating all these questions and trying to understand this cultural moment, you would collect more information (data) and do more field-work. You might, for example, gather artifacts (material objects that belong to and represent a culture): the printed service, prayerbooks and hymnals, documents or pamphlets describing the church and its programs—in any or all of the three languages. You might do some research at the library on the French occupation of Vietnam and on the history of the Catholic church in the United States, Canada, France, and Vietnam. Or you might go to the Nashua Historical Society to learn about the French Canadian settlers in Nashua. But you would not be able to write up your account until you had begun to decipher where the culture is.

One way you could begin would be to locate key informants to interview—a few people to help guide you and explain their culture. Such guides represent the "others," those who are different from the researcher. To describe their guides, field-workers use the terms *informants, consultants, subjects, natives, the other*, or *insiders*. Which term we use is our own decision, but since such descriptions reveal our attitudes toward the people we study, it is a crucial decision to make. Throughout this book, we use anthropology's term *informant* to refer to insiders in a culture. We realize that some readers may associate this term informant with police work (a "snitch," for instance). But we like this term because it emphasizes the knowledge—the *information*—that insiders have. For similar reasons, some fieldworkers like the term *consultant*.

So you will choose key informants in Nashua to interview, using a translator if necessary, holding conversations in homes and in other community settings as well as in the church. Your informants might offer different perspectives on the extent to which the church has welcomed the Vietnamese into its community. You might, for example, interview the three clergy, the Englishwoman Veronica Barr, one of the Vietnamese women, or even Byron Brown, the newswriter who wrote the account of the Sunday afternoon Mass. Other informants could include the church's choir director or Monsignor John Quinn, who brought Reverend Nhien to New Hampshire. You would tape your interviews and then transcribe them.

Throughout the process, you would keep careful fieldnotes describing the details in the places you go and the people you observe as they go about living in those places. You would also record your own subjective responses and feelings and how they affect your data: things that bother you, ideas you don't understand, events or comments that interest you. Looking over all this data, you would begin to formulate hypotheses about what is important in the culture of the St. Louis de Gonzague Church, Nashua's Vietnamese community, the larger refugee community, or the French Canadian Catholic community. As you think about your data, you must make choices about which part of it you will use to represent the people in the culture.

BOX 3
USING THE ETHNOGRAPHIC PERSPECTIVE

Find a news article in your local paper that shows a cultural moment and might challenge a fieldworker to do more research. A cultural moment need not be a major political or social event such as the dissembling of the Berlin Wall or the Million Man March on Washington. Local headlines often mark insider culture in smaller places: the opening of an ethnic restaurant, a local hero's action, or a community conflict. What cultural information does the article include? What kinds of questions might the fieldworker ask to uncover further the culture that the article describes? How would the fieldworker's questions differ from those of a newswriter? What information would the fieldworker want to gather to answer the question "What's going on here?" What other sources of information might the fieldworker use to penetrate the insider perspective? Where would you need to go to find them? Share the article and your answers to these questions with your colleagues.

Response

Here are some sample headlines our students chose from newspapers: "Amish Community Copes with Rare Murder," "Black Astronaut Carries Navajo Flag," "Korean University Professor Develops Education Program in Finland," "Art Teacher Saves Drowning Child in Treacherous River Dam," "Small Business Grant Slashed in Favor of Community Fireworks Display," "Kiwanis Club Donates Funds toward Little Juanita's New Kidney." Note that the headlines are specific, full of cultural details. Our students' analyses were twice as long as the news articles they chose. They asked more questions than they were able to answer as they peeled back layers of information to find out "Where is the culture?" An example follows.

BLACK ASTRONAUT CARRIES NAVAJO FLAG

CAPE CANAVERAL, Fla. (AP)—Before Bernard Harris Jr. was allowed to take a Navajo flag aboard Discovery, tribal medicine men had to bless it with corn pollen and make sure the space shuttle's path fit with their beliefs: It had to orbit clockwise.

When the Navajo decided that from their viewpoint, *Discovery's* orbit met the requirement, all signals were go for Harris to carry the first Navajo item to fly in space. NASA allows astronauts to carry up a few small belongings.

"I'm flying this flag for them because being there I could see their plight as the original Americans," said Harris, a 38-year-old black physician who lived on a Navajo reservation from ages 7 to 15. His mother taught at boarding schools run by the U.S. Bureau of Indian Affairs.

Harris, who today will become the first black to spacewalk, approached the Navajo in December about taking some tribal item with him on the mission.

Navajo Nation President Albert Hale decided on a flag after consulting with medicine men to make sure no spiritual traditions would be violated. The flag was blessed last month by Navajo medicine man Ross Nez.

Bernard Harris, Jr., an astronaut aboard the space shuttle Discovery.

Through a ceremony, Nez "was told by the Creator and the Holy People that it would strengthen the Navajo Nation for this flag to go around Mother Earth," Navajo spokeswoman Valerie Taliman said Wednesday.

"The flag is a symbol of our nation and reminds us of how we must live in balance with our Mother Earth to survive," Hale said.

Nez blessed the flag by sprinkling it with corn pollen, which has an importance for the Navajo roughly similar to holy water in the Catholic church.

Hale sent the blessed flag to NASA. A few days later, he said, a NASA official called: "We have the flag, but we have a question. What is this yellow stuff on it?"

Hale assured NASA the powder was sacred pollen used in prayers.

The Navajo flag depicts the four mountains that delineate traditional Navajo territory.

USING THE ETHNOGRAPHIC PERSPECTIVE

Steve Gates

"Black Astronaut Carries Navajo Flag," *Cedar Rapids Gazette*,
February 10, 1995

The article discusses Bernard Harris Jr.'s choice to carry a Navajo flag on board the NASA shuttle plane, *Discovery*. Harris is an African American who spent 8 years of his youth on a Navajo reservation. The article reveals general details about the circumstances and the way in which the decision was approved by Navajo tribal leaders.

Regarding the cultural issues, there are several things the article doesn't include. Why does Harris consider the Navajo the "first Americans," as he is quoted as saying? What daily interaction did Harris have with the Navajo during his youth, and what specific influence did they have on him? Why did he leave when he was 15? Did he maintain contact with the Navajo after he left the reservation? How much does he know about his African-American heritage compared to the Navajo culture? Did he also take an artifact from his African-American heritage? Why or why not? If so, what was it, and is there any connection to the Navajo flag?

Other questions worth pursuing might be knowing how Navajo officials and tribal leaders felt about Harris's choice for an artifact. Perhaps one could interview childhood friends of Harris's from the reservation to hear their reflections and opinions. Do they have the same opinion of him now that they did then? Why or why not? Did Harris actively participate in the Navajo culture and rituals as a young person? To what extent does his choice to carry their flag represent a sincere and genuine belief in their culture?

I would think tribal elders and the medicine man referred to in the article would be good sources for more insight into the cultural implications and details of this event. Another curiosity is the writer's choice to compare the use of corn pollen in Navajo rituals to the use of holy water in the Catholic church. This could be an example of a "mixed" metaphor since the frame of reference of the writer is the Christian church, and although there are some obvious general similarities (i.e., creation stories and the hereafter), there are many contradictions between the two, especially if one starts to pursue the concept of land ownership and its relationship to Christianity.

Obviously, an ethnographer could find numerous trails and sources to pursue.

FieldWorking with This Book

In the preceding section, as our imaginary fieldworker, you used one cultural moment at a church service to begin your field research. Researching involves making sense of cultural events. And to share your research with others, you'll need to organize your process as you work toward your final written project.

To help you organize, we've arranged this book around four learning strategies: reading, writing, fieldworking, and reflecting. Using these strategies will help you build two projects of your own: a research portfolio and a fieldwork essay or a series of shorter fieldworking pieces ("boxes"). To help you, we've gathered readings from a variety of genres, academic disciplines, and voices to show how to do fieldwork and how to write about it. Since writing is so integral to fieldworking, the boxes will help you develop the fieldworking skills you'll need. You may do the short exercises on topics that interest you and collect them in your portfolio. Or you may decide to build these pieces toward one fieldwork essay, as Rick Zollo does in his study of the truck stop in this chapter. In either instance, the writing you do becomes part of your research portfolio. The aim of a fieldworking portfolio is to develop personal insights and reflections on the research process as you go along, not just at the end of your project. We recommend that you share your work in progress several times during your research process. You may want to choose a portfolio partner among your colleagues to read your work regularly or form a research group to do the same.

With this book, you'll read published texts, but you'll also learn to "read" objects as cultural artifacts: baskets, buildings, quilts, clothing. And you'll learn to "read" places, events, and people: truck stops, restaurants and bars, mall stores, and town meetings. In the process of "reading" places and people, events and artifacts, you will dig into layers of meaning that lie inside language in words, expressions, stories, jokes, proverbs, and legends.

This book will initiate you into the gritty part of fieldwork. You will learn to keep researcher's notes, tape-record interviews with informants, collect material culture, gather multiple types of information (research data), develop questions and hunches, analyze patterns, and offer interpretations. A pencil and a notebook are your bare necessities, although you might consider other technologies (a camera, a laptop computer, a tape recorder). As a researcher, you'll need to develop a kind of bidirectional lens as you research, allowing you to look out at others and back at yourself. Far more important than the skills or the equipment you use for controlling your data, you will learn that *you are the main tool for your research.*

For example, as our imaginary fieldworker, if you were French Canadian and Catholic yourself you might not recognize the interesting collision of Asian, French Canadian, and Catholic cultures in a French Canadian Catholic church in Nashua. Or you might have a biased view of history because your own father was killed in the Vietnam War. Or you might not notice the significance of the song "Meet Me in St. Louis" and its connection to the name of the church, St. Louis de Gonzague. Through the process of writing and reflecting on your fieldwork, you'll become aware of the cultural lenses through which you look and how they affect what you understand, what you don't yet understand, and what you may never understand.

In this book, we'll review some of the basic writing strategies that fieldworkers use. Short writing exercises will help you hone your skills of description, specificity, mapping, organization, and analysis. You'll learn about constructing a researcher's voice in your ethnographic study and developing yourself as a narrator who guides your reader through your research. You will study and try out some of the aesthetic features of ethnographic writing: metaphors, sensory images, dialogue patterns, thematic structures. Particulars of audience, purpose, and focus will also help you shape your data for your reader.

Writing is both the process and the product of fieldwork. It is both the means for your thinking and the end result of your fieldwork project. All the writing you do—from brainstorming about possible research sites and topics through keeping fieldnotes, writing reflective memos to yourself, designing interview questions, and taking notes from other research sources to the drafts of your final fieldworking project—will become part of your research portfolio.

An Ethnographic Study: "Friday Night at Iowa 80"

We present here a fieldworking project completed by one of our students to give you a sample of the kind of research and writing we hope you'll be doing. We want to show you how a fieldworker "steps in" to a culture to investigate it, at the same time "stepping out" as he maintains the outsider's perspective while he observes. Rick Zollo wrote this study about a truck stop in Iowa as his major paper for a course centered on researching and writing ethnography. Rick is an older student, with a background in journalism, who is new to ethnographic research and has long been interested in truck drivers—so much so that he attended trucking school the summer after finishing his study. Though your own study will probably be shorter than Rick's, it will share many features of his approach, particularly the emphasis on the self as part of the research process.

You'll notice immediately that Rick's study of the truck stop is written as a narrative and reads like a nonfiction article from a magazine, a genre often called literary journalism or literary nonfiction. Seeing that he is a journalist now doing fieldwork, we'd like to distinguish the features of this study that make it ethnographic research and not journalism or reportage. As a reader new to ethnographic writing, you'll need to slip underneath Rick's smooth narrative line to see what goes into the fieldworking process. While reading it, you'll need to ask ethnographic questions like the ones we asked as we read the newspaper article: What were his sources of data? How does he confirm or disconfirm his ideas? What interpretations does he offer? What is the culture he describes? What makes it a culture? Does his writing convince you? Can you see the places and people he describes? Do you understand what it would be like to be an insider in this culture?

You'll need to keep in mind some background knowledge as you read Rick's interesting journey into the culture of truckers that he has captured by describing one truck stop, Iowa 80, on a Friday night. First, it's clear that although Rick writes about a single Friday evening, he's spent many Fridays and other days gathering data and working his way into this field site. He writes with the authority of having been there, and he makes us feel that we've been there too. It's also obvious that Rick has permission from the owner of the truck stop, Delia Moon, to hang out and interview truckers and staff members. Finally, it's also apparent from his study that Rick has read other articles and books about the trucking culture. He has knowledge about what he expects to see there. In some ways, this background information could put blinders on Rick as he sets out to confirm or disconfirm the ideas of other writers who claim that truckers form a community with shared interests, values, and language. Because, like Rick, you will be researching a place you are already interested in and want to know more about, you'll need to admit your possible biases about your topic and look to see how other researchers have written about it.

As you read Rick's study, make a list of questions about his research process so that you'll be prepared to discuss the piece from that point of view. We realize that Rick's research may be the first ethnographic study you've read, so we'd like you to recognize its form and content. For example, Rick provides headings to guide you through his study and help you organize the questions you may have. His form takes the shape of a journalistic essay, and his content focuses on the trucker subculture, but most of all, Rick describes his fieldworking process within the essay.

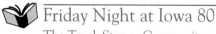

Friday Night at Iowa 80
The Truck Stop as Community and Culture
Rick Zollo

> Truck stops are the center of trucking culture. "Trucker Villages" . . .
> offer the driver an equivalent to the cowboys' town at trail's end or the
> friendly port to sailors.
>
> *James Thomas,* The Long Haul

A Modern Trucking Village

Friday nights are a special time all across America, for big and small towns alike, and it's no different at a "trucker town." Iowa 80 is advertised as "the largest Amoco truck stop in the world," and is located off Interstate 80 at exit 284, outside the small town of Walcott, about 10 miles from downtown Davenport and 40 miles from my Iowa City home.

I arrived at suppertime one fall Friday evening, with the intention of enjoying a meal in the full-service restaurant. But before I could even consider eating, I had to walk the grounds. In my experience, the best way to observe a community is with a walkabout, observing climate and current social interactions.

A huge hole occupied what had most recently been the south-side front parking lot. The hole was filled with a bright blue fuel tank roughly 40 by 60 feet in size, and topped by five large green plastic spirals. The operation was a result of another government mandate, concerning leaky fuel storage containers. Delia Moon, company vice president, told me this operation would cost Iowa 80 $180,000 ($40,000 to take out the old tanks and $140,000 for replacements), another example of "government interference." According to Delia, the tanks dug up so far were in good condition.

The truck stop is laid out in the form of a huge rectangle, taking up over 50 acres on the north side of the interstate exit. The first building facing incoming traffic is the main headquarters, which includes a restaurant at the front, video and game room next, a sunken shopping mall, and a stairway leading to second-floor corporate offices, hair salon, laundry room, movie theater (seats 40) and TV room, dental offices, exercise room, and private

(Photo: Susan Zollo)

shower stalls. The last renovations were completed in 1984, about the time I first began noticing the village, but Delia stated that a large building project was planned for 1994.

The evening had yet to begin, and the yard was only a quarter full, without that convoy pattern of trucks coming and going in single file, an orderly parade that in several hours would take on Fellini-like dimensions. I sauntered through the yard (in my usual loping stride), notebook in hand, making eye contact with truckers when they passed, not trying to act like one of them so much as feeling comfortable in their company.

Will Jennings, a former trucker and personal friend, talked about the insularity of the trucker community in Frederick Will's *Big Rig Souls*. "You go in truck stops and they have their own section. . . . Most of them [truckers] could tell from the minute you walk in the door you're not a driver. They hold most people who aren't drivers . . . with a good deal of disdain" (27).

I had already been spotted by employees of Iowa 80 as "not a driver," and in my many youthful years of hitchhiking around the country, I had been made to feel the outsider whenever I'd stumble into one of these trucking lairs. I had trouble understanding this resentment of outsiders, especially when I was on the road in need of a ride. But familiarity with the culture was bringing what scholar Sherman Paul calls "the sympathetic imagination," and I now felt I was beginning to understand.

On this late afternoon, the lot was rather calm, even though rigs waited in line to diesel up at the Jiffy fuel station, all four bays at the Truckomat truck wash were filled, and service was being rendered at the mechanics' and tire shop. The three buildings stood in a row on the north side of the lot, each about a third the size of the main complex and separated by several truck lanes for traffic.

(Photo: Susan Zollo)

The truckyard occupied the southern half of the property, with the interstate in its full glory to the south of that. Every time I stood in the middle of this immense yard, with truck traffic in full promenade, I'd experience a thrill. But for now, with walkabout complete, I doubled back to the restaurant. I was hungry.

Truck Stop Restaurant

By 6 p.m., Iowa 80's restaurant was full to capacity. Customers appeared to be divided equally between truckers and four-wheelers. After a short wait, I was led to a small table in the back section, where at an adjacent booth, a young waitress was serving supper to a grizzled veteran. I detected a mild flirtation passing between them.

The night's special was catfish, which I ordered. I ate heartily, fish fried light and crispy, a scoop of potatoes adorned with gravy, cole slaw, and a fresh warm roll. Every book on truckers I've read describes truck stop food as rich, plentiful, and greasy.

Ditto!

(Photo: Susan Zollo)

I sat opposite the veteran and watched him. He ate with gusto, enjoyed a smoke (truck stop restaurants are not smoke-free), and wrote in his logbook. Should I approach him? Why not.

"Excuse me, I'm doing research on truckers and truck stops. Can I talk to you?"

He looked up from his logbook and smiled. "Yeah, sure. I've got time."

I grabbed my gear and joined him. His name was Gordy,* and he drove out of Oklahoma City for Jim Brewer, a company that hauls racks of automobiles to dealerships. Gordy spoke with easy affability, and underneath his three-day growth of beard, I detected once boyish good looks reminiscent of the actor Lee Majors.

Gordy drove all over the country, hauling General Motors vehicles. He stopped at this truck stop often, but only because of the food. He made it a point to let me know that he generally didn't frequent truck stops.

"Your truck have a sleeper?"

"No. Wouldn't drive a truck that had one."

That was a surprise, since I thought that just about all long haulers used sleepers.

Gordy was a veteran, with 22 years of service on the road. "How does driving compare now with twenty years ago?"

"Worse. Things are worse now." So are the truck stops, he said, which are bigger, with more features, but run by national chains with no feeling for the trucker.

He blamed deregulation for today's problems. Before deregulation, freight rates were controlled, and a trucker knew what he could make from each delivery. Then came deregulation, and "all these fly-by-night companies" flooded the market. The power of the Teamsters was also curtailed, and Gordy, a union man, found his position threatened. "I'm real bitter about it."

He once owned his own truck, was out on the road for long periods of time, and made good money. Today, he drove only four-day runs, for a company that was the highest bidder for his services. He slept in motels and had his choice of destinations.

---

*The names of all truckers and employees, except those in management, have been changed.

(Photo: Susan Zollo)

As for the cursed paperwork that so many truckers complain about: "Hardly got any. Just this logbook. And they're fixin' to do away with that. By '96, they figure it'll all be on computer."

No issue galvanizes a trucker more than the logbook. Any time I wanted to test a trucker's spleen, I'd only have to mention the issue.

"I've been told that most truckers cheat on their logbooks." I said. "If they computerize it, you won't be able to cheat."

Gordy gave me a sly Lee Majors grin. "Oh, there'll be ways."

The Arcade

Fortified by a meal and a successful encounter, I ventured into the arcade area separating restaurant from shopping mall. The area was packed. During my hour with catfish and Gordy, many truckers had pulled off the road, and a handful of them were engaged in pinball games, laser-gun videos, a simulated NBA game, and in front of one large glass case with a miniature pickup shovel, a man and a woman were trying to win a pastel-colored stuffed animal. I stopped to watch. After several tries the man succeeded, and the couple rejoiced. I waited for their enthusiasm to wane and then introduced myself.

The driver's name was Morris, and he wasn't sure he wanted to talk to me. Like Gordy, he was middle-aged and grizzled, but where Gordy's three-day growth covered handsome features, Morris was a buzzard, with a hawk nose, a pointy chin, and a leather motorcycle cap pulled low over his forehead.

I assured him that my questions were for research purposes only, but he looked at me suspiciously, as if I were an authority sent to check on him.

Had he ever been at this truck stop before?

"First time, but I'm coming back. It's got everything."

How long had he been on this particular run? (Gordy was careful to emphasize that he made only four-day hauls.)

"Been home three and a half hours in the past four months."

Did he drive his own truck?

He was a lease operator (leasing his own rig to a company that moves furniture), presently hauling a load from Lafayette, Louisiana, to Cedar Rapids, Iowa.

How long did it take him to drive from Lafayette? (Knowing geography, I tried to calculate the time.) The question of time raised Morris's suspicions again, and instead of answering, he fixed me with a hard gaze. Sensing I had crossed some invisible boundary, I thanked him for his time. Obviously, my question related to logbook procedures, and I made a mental note to avoid that type of inquiry.

Also, I noticed that Morris and the woman for whom he had so gallantly won a prize were not together. Seeking a couple who actually drove in tandem, I walked into the mall area, past the cowboy boot display and chrome section ("the world's largest selection of truck chrome"), and spotted a couple with a baby moseying down the food aisles.

"Excuse me. I'm doing a research paper on truckers and truck stops. Are you a trucker?" I asked, directing my question to the presumed dad in the group.

"No, I'm not," he said emphatically.

Iowa 80 Employees

Truckers, four-wheelers (about 20% of the business at Iowa 80), and employees make up the truck stop community. The employees keep the community functioning, like municipal employees without whom towns and cities could not operate.

Two such employees stood at the end of one of the food aisles, stocking shelves. Sally and Maureen knew about me, thanks to a letter that General Manager Noel Neu had sent out a month ago, asking Iowa 80 workers to cooperate with my study. Sally was the shift manager of the merchandise area, and Maureen was one of her staff. I directed most of my questions to Sally.

How long had she been working at Iowa 80?

Eight years. Maureen had been with the company for only a year.

Which was the busiest shift?

"I think it's four to midnight, but if you ask someone on the day shift, they'd probably say their shift."

What did she most like about working four to midnight?

"The people. We get all kinds here. Down-to-earth people . . . crazy people." And she told me about a woman who several weeks ago came into the store ranting and raving, apparently in the throes of paranoid delusions. Authorities were called, and it was determined that "she was on some kind of bad trip—cocaine or something."

Sally mentioned that the police were out in the yard at this moment, making a drug bust. "How'd they know somebody was selling drugs?" I asked.

"A trucker reported it at the fuel center. Heard someone over the CB. We called the cops."

Apparently truckers police themselves. Sally also said that drivers will even turn in shoplifters. "They know if we get too much shoplifting, prices will go up."

I asked Sally about those prices, which I considered reasonable. She replied that they were cheap enough for most truckers, but there were always those who wanted to haggle.

"You're allowed to barter over costs?" I asked.

"Oh, yeah. Not as much as the day manager."

Sally came from a small town north of Walcott, and Maureen was from one of the Quad Cities*. Iowa 80 employed over 225 workers and was one of the largest employers outside of the Quad Cities municipal area.

"One of the things that most impresses me is how friendly the workers are here," I said.

"We try to be the trucker's second home," said Sally.

Talking to Truckers

Business continued to pick up. As with previous Friday night visits, I found much conversation in the aisles, as if the truckers could afford to be expansive, find community with colleagues, socialize at the end of a workweek. Many of these drivers, though, still had loads to deliver; others were settling in for the weekend, waiting for a Monday morning pickup.

I had hoped to talk to women and minorities. The popular image of the trucker is that of a Caucasian blue-collar male, and for the most part, that group represents the majority of the industry. But more women are entering the field, and from my observations, black men make up 10% to 20% of the population. Two black truckers stood behind displays of music tapes, engaged in spirited conservation. I didn't want to interrupt them. Near the cash register, I spotted another black trucker, a beefy 40-something fellow with flannel jacket and flat driving cap. He was reluctant and wary, but he agreed to answer questions.

Ronald was a long hauler from Detroit, making his third stop at Iowa 80. He had been driving for five years, after serving a 12-year hitch in the armed services. He drove all over the country, going out for three to five weeks at a time. He didn't mind sleeping in his rig. For every week on the road, he got a day off. He was presently hauling a load from Omaha to New Jersey, with plenty of time to get there. (I consciously steered my questions away from time lines.)

He wore a forced smile, which served as a shield, and any question that might seem personal made the smile stiffen. He didn't give off the scent of danger I detected from Morris, but he definitely eyed me more as an adversary than as a friendly interlocutor.

Our session was interrupted by a mid-sized white fellow, probably in his mid-thirties, sporting an orange pony tail, two diamond studs in his left earlobe, and several menacing facial scars.

"What you up to, man? Who you workin' for?" His voice had a manic edge that reminded me of Gary Busey in one of those action adventures they watched in the movie theater upstairs.

"I'm a researcher from the University of Iowa." I described my project.

"Oh, yeah?" he said, as if he didn't believe me. Then he turned his high-voltage attention on Ronald. They started talking about the rigs they drove.

Cal spoke so fast it was hard to keep up with him. He was telling Ronald that he had bought his own truck and would soon go independent, a status he encouraged Ronald to seek. Ronald's smile by this time had tightened like a band of steel. He was cornered by white guys, one with a notebook, the other a speed rapper with a pony tail. Ronald was clearly on guard.

Cal was from a nearby town, and he mentioned a motorcycle-driving buddy who was writing a book with help from someone in the Iowa Writer's Workshop. I dropped a few

---

*Bettendorf and Davenport, Iowa, and Moline and Rock Island, Illinois.

CHAPTER ONE   Stepping In and Stepping Out: Understanding Cultures

names Cal recognized, and he suddenly decided I was OK. When he couldn't convince Ronald to use his method to buy a truck, he ducked away to collar someone else. Ronald kept smiling and muttering, "Man, I don't want my own truck."

Before I could finish questioning Ronald, a well-built 30-something trucker with finely brushed hair and trimmed moustache jumped before me, arms folded, ready to unload his truck.

The atmosphere was getting uncomfortable. Who did these people think I was? I recalled a previous visit, when I was down at the truck wash. A woman named Connie, a road veteran who bragged of living on the highway for years as a hitchhiker, told me, "We thought you were a spotter."

Not knowing what that meant but reckoning that it couldn't be in my favor, I assured her I was only a writer. "What's a spotter?" I asked.

"They go around checking on company drivers, to see that they're not screwing up, taking riders, that kind of stuff."

My new friend's name was Dan, and he was at the truck stop because a trailer he was supposed to pick up at a nearby meat products plant was late being loaded. "Never come down here normally. Know why?" I sure didn't. "No counter in the restaurant. They took out the counter. And the food's greasy."

Dan presented me with a challenge. "Want to know what makes me mad? Want to know what pisses me off?"

A Trucker's Lament

Dan started in on his own speed rap. His eyes weren't glazed like Cal's but instead fixed on me, as if I were an authority he wanted to confront, an ear that would be judged by its sympathy or lack thereof.

I wanted Dan to know I was sympathetic. I'm all ears, good buddy.

As Dan began ticking off his grievances, I asked him the same questions I had asked the others. He didn't stop at Iowa 80 often. His schedule enlisted him on 3,000-mile hauls (however long they took—it varied, he said). He drove for a company, was non-union (didn't like the Teamsters but wanted to organize truckers into a national force), and had been driving for 12 years.

With that said, most of our conversation dealt with Dan's copious grievances, a litany other truckers voiced to various degrees.

Grievance number one: "I'm pissed about multiple speed limits. Iowa, the speed limit's the same, sixty-five for cars and trucks. In Illinois, it's sixty-five for cars but only fifty-five for trucks. Know why it's set up like that? Supposed to be for safety, have the trucks go slower, but it creates two flows of traffic, and that's a hazard. No, the real reason is revenue. Easier to give us a ticket."

Dan was angry, and I had trouble writing down all his words in a standing position. I suggested we go upstairs, where we found a spot by the shoeshine area just outside the movie theater, giving me a better position to get everything down. The Illinois complaint was not new; other truckers had sounded off about that state's split speed limit, as well as their war against radar detectors. The opinion in the trucker community was that the authorities in Illinois were against them.

Once we were seated in comfortable chairs, Dan went off on another tangent. "They take three million basically honest people and force us to break the law to make a living."

I assumed he was talking about the infamous logbook. I just so happened to have one with me. Dan grabbed it. "Know what we call this? A comic book. It's a joke!"

He proceeded to show me why. The logbook was symbol and substance of what was wrong with the industry, a monitoring device that was set up so it couldn't be followed except by lying. Once lawbreaking becomes institutionalized, other more serious laws become easier to break until the small man is truly the outlaw of romantic legend. And the trucker, in Dan's mind, at least, was a small man caught in the snares (Clifford Geertz's "webs of suspension") constructed by government and big business, a conspiracy of sorts designed to keep the proverbial small man down.

Dan opened the logbook and ran through a typical workweek. The trucker had two formats: 60 hours in seven days or a 70 hours in eight. Time frames are broken into four categories: off-duty, sleeper berth, driving, and on-duty. The last slot was what most agitated Dan. As he simulated a California run, he showed that loading and unloading is held against the trucker, since it is considered on-duty time. (Note that the trucker does have the option of leaving the site where his trailer is located, which is what Dan was doing when he met me, but that involves risk, especially in terms of truck hijacking and other forms of larceny.) "Sometimes we gotta wait eight hours before they load or unload our truck. That time is held against us, against our sixty- or seventy-hour week. We get paid by the mile. I don't make a cent unless my truck is moving."

Dan was convinced that big business and government were in a conspiracy. "Suppose I've got to deliver a load from Monfort [Illinois] to San Francisco. That's two thousand miles. Then they want me to turn around and bring a load back. How can I do it if I honestly report my hours?" He tapped the logbook nervously.

"You have to cheat." I said.

"Cheat or starve. Because if I follow the laws, I get no work. Company won't say anything. They'll just stop giving me orders."

"And if you get caught cheating, does the company back you?"

Dan's eyes lit up, and he gave me a manic half grin, half grimace, as if to say, "Now you're catching on."

"We get caught cheating, breaking the speed limit, you name it, the trucker pays all fines. Our fault, so we gotta pay."

Gripe number three: who is supposed to load and unload the truck? Dan waited for me to record this complaint. The company sells his services, which are to deliver meat products to supermarket warehouses. He's not paid to load and unload the truck. But the supermarket chains will not provide the service.

"I have a choice," he said. "Unload the truck myself, which I'm not supposed to do. Or hire a 'lumper.' "

Mere mention of the term lumper sent Dan into another paroxysm of indignation. Lumpers are scab laborers who hang around warehouses and get paid under the table ("out of my money!"). Dan was convinced that most of them were on welfare and made as much as $300 a day that they don't declare.

"I pay taxes on my wages. Lumpers get government welfare plus this other money." Another symbol and symptom of what was wrong with America. And who was to blame? The Department of Transportation.

"All the DOT does is drive up and down the highway busting truckers. They never go to the grocers and make sure we're not forced to unload our trucks." And the reason for the conspiracy? Simple. The supermarkets "get all this free labor."

The combination fuel tax and low-sulfur diesel oil requirement was another gripe. (A government-mandated low-sulfur fuel plus an additional 4 cents fuel tax had been imposed as of October 1.)

"Truckers are supposed to pay to clean up the air, but not airlines or bus companies or farmers. They all get exemptions. Farmers are exempt because of off-road use. Yet how many tractors we got running in this state?"

I asked if he thought conditions would improve. One trucker told me the split speed limits in Illinois were supposed to be abolished.

"Rumors. To keep truckers in line. They know if we organize a work stoppage, this nation'll stop running."

Dan believed in truckers organizing but felt that the trucker's independent nature prevented this from happening. He dismissed the Teamsters. "We need an organization run by and for truckers. Teamsters are not the answer, and this organization, the American Truckers Association, has sold us out, backing every law that's ever hurt us."

On and on. Dan's monologue was complicated by his nervously darting eyes, which kept sizing me up for sympathy. He talked about disparities in fines ($70 for a logbook violation in Nebraska; the same violation in California can cost you $1,500), unfriendly state police and DOT officials ("California, Ohio, and Virginia are the worst"), and big business and government collusion to keep the small man down.

"This country depends on truckers for survival. Trains and airplanes can't deliver like the truckers. Yet if this country is so dependent on us, why are we treated like scum?"

I could not adequately answer Dan's complaints, nor could I ascertain their complete veracity, except to say that similar complaints had been made by other informants. Yet even in the midst of these difficult working conditions, there was the sense that a living wage was being made. One particular trucker, who was vehement about the split speed limits and logbook absurdities (he drove from Omaha to Chicago and back twice a week), bragged that he made $600 to $1,000 a week.

Even Dan admitted to making more money driving a truck than he could ever earn in the small Iowa town where he lived when he wasn't on the road. His complaints were less about pay than about being forced to break the law to earn his living and about the lack of sympathy shown by greater society to this blue-collar occupation so responsible for America's land of plenty.

My sympathies were aroused. I've always felt sympathy for blue-collar concerns. My European forebears had fled to America for better jobs, freedom from persecution, rights to pursue an individual lifestyle. And I was nothing if not an advocate of individuality.

Dan and I traded addresses—he promised to send me a flyer for his own fledgling organization—and I thanked him for his time.

Town Meeting around the Cash Register

I wandered back downstairs and moved about the merchandise aisles, tired from my talk with Dan. Who did I meet in one of the back aisles but Cal, in the company of a tall, slender woman with a well-used look. He still had that manic glint in his eye. "Man, you're all right. You really are a writer. I thought you were government, but you're not."

My wandering brought me to the cash register, a good place to meet truckers. Drivers were either coming or going and were most receptive to exchange. I found a middle-aged driver paying for a purchase, and we passed pleasantries. No heavy conversations or even probing questions—Dan had exhausted me of that.

The woman working the register and the driver were comparing horror stories about truck stop robberies. I had noticed the woman before. She was one of the friendly employees who liked to talk to drivers. Many of the workers at Iowa 80 had this friendly conversational manner about them, and it always contributed to the atmosphere in the building.

The trucker knew a driver who had been robbed recently at a truck stop in Atlanta, where he was now heading. The woman told of another robbery at a truck stop outside Tampa. Both robberies occurred in the parking lot, and in both cases, the drivers were getting out of their rigs when someone stepped out of the shadows and robbed them at gunpoint.

The trucker left, and I lingered to talk to the woman. Her name was Bea. Her husband had been a trucker until last week, when he was involved in an accident outside Atlanta, caused by a drunk driver three cars ahead of his rig. Nobody was hurt, but there was $8,000 in damage. "Five years without an accident, and they fire him. I sent the guy who fired him a thank-you letter. We got two teenagers at home."

How was her husband taking his dismissal?

"He's broken up about it, but I'm glad."

What's he doing now?

"He's farming with relatives."

I pulled out my notebook and introduced myself. Bea knew about me, again thanks to Noel Neu's letter. She was convinced I had picked a great subject for research. She had been working for Iowa 80 part time, then left for a full-time job in Davenport. "But I came back because I missed it. Took a pay cut, but it's worth it to work here."

I mentioned my interview with Delia Moon and how many Iowa 80 employees seem to love the work atmosphere.

"Isn't Delia wonderful? I love this family." Bea told me a story about Bill Moon, founder of Iowa 80 and an empire builder in the truck stop industry. Years ago, Bea's son had a paper route in downtown Walcott. One morning, her son was stymied by a blizzard. Bill Moon saw the boy struggling to cover his route. The businessman got his car and helped her son finish the job. "That's the kind of guy he was."

Bill Moon died of cancer over a year ago. "You should have seen this place." said Bea. "Everyone was so sad."

Truck Yard at Night

Back outside, three hours after my arrival, I moved through the huge truck yard, filling my lungs with air and trying to catch a second wind. Trucks pulled in and out of the lot in promenade. Diesel fumes filled the air, and the lot was noisy with the sounds of transmissions shifting.

The yard was teeming. Large spotlights mounted on 50-foot poles outlined the scene. Puddles in the middle of the parking lot reflected blue and pink neon from the Jiffy Shop fuel center. A computerized sign facing the interstate spilled a cascade of shifting letters, advertising the night's menu, chrome supplies, free showers with tank of fuel, guaranteed scales to weigh freight.

I loped across the yard, tired but feeling fine, realizing that the more I learned about the trucking community, the more I would never know. I was a four-wheeler, a writer temporarily tangled in all these "webs of significance," an outsider whose sympathies could never connect all the many lives spent in forced but voluntary isolation. Long haulers were sentenced to a solitary voyage, and the truck stop was the oasis where they found temporary community.

Old-Timer at the Fuel Center

Inside the Jiffy Shop: quiet. Iowa 80's fuel center is built like your average convenience store, with fuel and sundries sold at a discount, except that here the fuel is diesel instead of gasoline and the sundries are marketed for truckers' needs.

A young black trucker was buying a sandwich at a back counter. Several of his white comrades were paying for their fuel up front. In one of the two-person booths that line the windows along the west wall sat an older gray-haired gentleman, resplendent in a green polo shirt and reading a trucker magazine.

I sat across from the old-timer in an adjoining booth and, after a few minutes of sizing up the situation, made my introduction. "May I ask you a few questions?"

He looked up from his magazine and admitted to being a trucker but added, "I don't like to get involved."

Fair enough. Still, we talked. Gradually he warmed up, and eventually I opened my notebook and began recording his remarks.

He had been driving trucks for some time but wouldn't say how long. He was at the truck stop getting an oil change for his tractor. He was primarily a short hauler, though he had done long hauls in his time.

I placed his age in the mid-sixties. Books I had read on over-the-road trucking mention how the long haul prematurely ages the driver. I could understand that this old-timer would change to shorter routes. As he warmed up to me, he revealed more information. He was articulate and had the face of a learned man. Perhaps he had retired from another profession. (More and more truckers were coming from other professions; many were veterans from the armed services.)

He asked me questions as well. His early pose of disinterest belied an avid curiosity. I soon had the impression that he would rather interview me.

He lived in the Quad Cites and had been a trucker all his life, starting at age 17 when he drove for construction outfits in the Fort Dodge area. He let slip that he was 60, an owner-operator of his own rig. Allusions to problems from years gone by hinted at previous financial difficulties.

Dan's populist appeal was still ringing in my ear, so I mentioned the rigors placed on truckers by big business and government. But the old-timer was not buying. True, big business and government put obstacles in the way, but there was a good living out there for anyone willing to put in the time. He told me a story similar to the fable of the tortoise and the hare. He always obeyed speed limits. He was in no hurry. Younger drivers would pass him, impatient with his caution. But the old-timer always got the job done on time. He clearly identified with the tortoise.

I found myself taking a shine to this man. There was something strong-willed and flinty about him, even in his refusal to give me his name. We talked about trucks, and he became a font of information. He pointed to his rig in the yard, a Ford. He would have preferred a Freightliner but couldn't get financing. He made disparaging remarks about Kenworths, called the Rolls-Royces of the profession, and about another highly rated competitor—"Why, I wouldn't even drive a Peterbilt. Cab's too narrow."

He was presently leasing his truck and services to a company that hauls general merchandise to stores like Pamida, K mart, and Sam's Warehouse. Earlier in the day, he had hauled 45,000 pounds of popcorn, but at present he had a trailer full of supplies for a Sam's Warehouse in Cedar Rapids. As for his earlier mention of being a short-hauler, well, that wasn't quite the truth. He tried to limit his runs to the Midwest—within the radius of Kansas City, Omaha, Fargo, and Youngstown—but sometimes he ventured as far as Atlanta or Dallas.

What about the complaint, first voiced by Gordy, that times were worse now than 20 years ago?

Yes in some instances, no in others. True, the logbook was a joke, especially concerning off-duty time. ("Why, when I hauled steel out of Gary, sometimes they made you wait 12 hours to get your load. That's all your driving time.") Yet the trucks these days were better, and the money was still good. ("I can drive from Kansas City to Des Moines without hardly changing gears. Couldn't do that 20 years ago." And, "I'm not saying I'm not making money. Making more money now than I was three years ago.")

He had to get back to his work, make his Cedar Rapids drop by 11. Otherwise he'd continue the conversation. I could tell he enjoyed our talk, and I had the urge to ask him if I could go out on the road with him. I was sure several weeks of riding with this old-timer would have given me an education.

But we parted as comrades, although when I asked again for his name, he declined to give it.

"I'll just refer to you as 'an esteemed older gentleman in a green shirt,'" I said. He enjoyed that description immensely and left me with a loud, ringing laugh.

Conclusion

My night at Iowa 80 was coming to a close. I had only to walk back through the truck lot and get into my little Japanese-made sedan. I was a four-wheeler, but that didn't stop me from making eye contact with the truckers in the yard, waving a hearty hello before I made my Hi-ho Silver.

What was I to make of this experience? I was exercising what Clifford Geertz calls "an intellectual poaching license" (*Local Knowledge* 12), engaging in what John Van Maanen terms "the peculiar practice of representing the social reality of others through the analysis of [my] own experience in the world of these others." (ix)

But had I truly experienced the community and culture? Had I penetrated the veils of unfamiliarity to become a reliable scribe of trucker life?

I had no doubts on that Friday night, as I returned to my car and drove home. I felt flushed. My informants, reluctant at first, had been forthcoming. Employees were friendly, and the truckers, although initially suspicious of my motives, spoke from both head and heart.

My experiences with the culture reflected what I had read by James Thomas and Michael Agar. I sensed a community that felt both proud and put upon, holding to perceived freedoms yet reined in by new regulations and restrictions. Some company drivers, like Gordy and Ronald, felt insulated from variables over which they had no control (fluctuating fuel prices), but others, like Dan, were angry about issues both on the road (DOT and highway patrolmen) and off (time and money constraints involving the unloading of deliveries). The owner-operator, my green-shirted older gentleman, did not feel like an endangered species, and the fact that Cal, however reliable his testimony might have been, was becoming an owner-operator attested to some of the virtues of that status.

The metaphor of the road cowboy certainly has significance. I surveyed the boot and shoe shop and found three varieties of cowboy boots (but not a loafer or a sneaker in sight), ranging from the economical $40 model with nonleather uppers to $150 snakeskin cowboy boots. Not far from the boot section were belts and buckles with a decidedly Western cast and enough cowboy hats to populate a Garth Brooks concert.

But connections to cowboys run deeper than clothes. Thomas writes that the "outstanding characteristics of both the trucker and the cowboy are independence, mobility, power, courage, and masculinity" (7). With all due apologies to the many women now trucking, that definition seems to apply. But it might be more mental than physical since, as my old-timer professed, driving a truck these days is not the physically rigorous activity it once was, and Dan's complaints about loading and unloading aside, truckers are not supposed to touch the product they deliver.

The cowboy element of the culture might seem like romantic accouterment rather than realistic assessment. Yet as Agar has pointed out, even romantic notions of the cowboy were more nonsense than truth, since that species in actuality "wore utilitarian clothes, engaged in long days of hard work, and ate boring and nutritionally deficient food" (*Independents Declared* 10), a description that sounds like trucker life.

I also found some agreement with Agar's assessment of present versus past times. The old-timer had a healthy attitude: "Some things are better, some things are worse." But for the most part, the veteran truckers I talked with see the past as "a better time . . . because regulations were simpler, enforcement was more lax, and fines were lower. Although the technology of trucks and roads has improved, the culturally spun webs of regulation have thickened into a maze" (44).

As for trucker grievances, one thing I found for certain, which Frederick Will documents in *Big Rig Souls*, is that "the trucker is condemned to rapid turnarounds after each load, to physical discomfort, to little or boring leisure, to being forever harried" (29).

I believe I found a community at Iowa 80. Delia Moon described the company's goal as turning the truck stop into a "destination." The dictionary defines *destination* as "the place to which a person or thing travels or is sent." Iowa 80, for all its scope and size, is still a truck stop. But a good many of my trucker informants were regulars, and the ones who were there for the first time were impressed by what they found.

Thomas states that "providing personal services for drivers is not where a truck stop gains most of its profits. The extras . . . are to lure truckers in from the road to the fuel pumps and service area" (17). Delia Moon supported this view. "We're working primarily to satisfy the . . . trucker. That's why you see the movie lounge and so much parking and chrome and everything" (interview, Oct. 7, 1993).

Yet in the process of giving truckers these amenities, as varied as a part-time dentist or a portable chapel for those needing to be born again, Iowa 80 is creating a context, setting up a multiplicity of complex structures that are both conceptual and real. A Friday night at this village is truly an adventure and, for those willing to engage experience as a form of education, an introduction into a dynamic community and culture.

Works Consulted

Agar, Michael. *The Professional Stranger: An Informal Introduction to Ethnography.* New York: Academic, 1980.

Agar, Michael. *Independents Declared.* Washington, DC: Smithsonian Inst., 1986.

Geertz, Clifford. *The Interpretation of Cultures.* New York: Basic, 1973.

Geertz, Clifford. *Local Knowledge.* New York: Basic, 1983.

Horwitz, Richard. *The Strip: An American Place.* Lincoln: U Nebraska, 1985.

Kramer, Jane. *Trucker: Portrait of the Last American Cowboy.* New York: McGraw, 1975.

Paul, Sherman. University of Iowa, English Dept., personal communication.

Thomas, James. *The Long Haul: Truckers, Truck Stops and Trucking.* Memphis: Memphis State U, 1979.

Van Maanen, John. *Tales of the Field.* Chicago: U Chicago P, 1988.

Will, Frederick. *Big Rig Souls: Truckers in the American Heartland.* West Bloomfield: Altwerger, 1992.

Wyckoff, D. Daryl. *Truck Drivers in America.* Lexington: Lexington, 1979.

Rick Zollo's research study has many features of a full-blown ethnography, which is a book-length study that often takes years to complete. Over the course of one semester, or even a year, neither Rick nor you could expect to write a complete ethnography of a subculture. Rick's study, however, includes most of the parts of a fuller piece of research: library and archival research, cultural artifacts, fieldnotes, photographs, interviews and transcripts, reflective memos, and multiple drafts of his writing. In his portfolio, he mentions having read Michael Agar's *Independents Declared*, an ethnography about truckers. In his reading at libraries and in private collections, he read Walt Whitman's poem "Song of the Open Road," Jack Kerouac's novel *On the Road*, and Woody Guthrie's road songs. He studied trucker magazines, truck school brochures from a community college, trucker trade journals, truck stop menus, and government regulations about the trucking industry. He also attended a two-day "truckers' jamboree," where he took more notes.

In "Friday Night at Iowa 80," Rick begins with thick and rich descriptions of both the inside and the outside of the truck stop, to establish a full sweep of the landscape. He starts by guiding his reader on a walk around the outside of the truck stop, moving from the huge unfilled hole that marks the uprooted fuel containers to the parking lot that holds 500 trucks. Once inside the mall-like complex, Rick shows us around the restaurant, where we watch him eat a meal of catfish and lumpy potatoes. We next accompany him into the arcade of pinball machines and laser-gun videos and then into the aisles of the convenience store, where employees are stocking shelves.

In addition to the sense of authority he gains through his physical descriptions of Iowa 80, Rick also collects an interesting range of interviews from both truckers and employees at the truck stop. Rick is able to get his informants to talk by hanging out and chatting with them. Sometimes informants don't talk to him because they're suspicious of him and think he is a "spotter" or some kind of spy from the Department of Transportation. Sometimes they don't trust him because he is a student-researcher. Other times that prompts a stream of valuable information. But because he persists and gathers a range of informants—male and female, black and white, trucker and nontrucker—weaving his interviews into the overall narrative, he advances his study toward an analysis of the information he's collected.

The data he relies on come mainly from informant interviews, but within these he sorts through a range of responses to his questions: insider terms, insider knowledge, and insider stories. Some informants supply insider terminology about the jobs, such as the words *lumper* and *spotter*. Others offer insider knowledge about how truckers do their jobs, answering questions about mileage, speed limits, logbooks, and truck preferences. From still others, he gathers occupational stories by inviting informants both to brag and to complain about their jobs.

After Rick has spent considerable time collecting this data about trucker beliefs and gripes, he introduces an unnamed informant who disconfirms and complicates much of what other drivers have said. Unlike the others, this lifetime driver felt trucking was a solid job and a good way to make a living and had little to complain about. Fieldworkers always try to disconfirm and complicate the theories that they are trying out. Rather than tossing out this interview data as something that doesn't fit, Rick includes it. An ethnography is compelling only when the author persuades us of his credibility. Rick does this by allowing the voices of his informants to speak. The fieldworker's obligation is both to inform and to persuade.

Rick's data analysis leads toward his initial hunch that the truck stop is a kind of community and a subculture for many of the truckers who spend time there. One of the Iowa 80 employees claims that the place is like the truckers' second home—a home away from home—which provides the central metaphor for Rick's paper. By the end of the study, Rick is able to link his own findings with other research that draws upon the image of the trucker as cowboy.

What makes Rick's study ethnographic, then, is the wide range and depth of description and interview data, the amount of time he spent gathering it, and his commitment to show the insider's perspective on the trucking culture. As a writer, Rick creates a "slice of time" device. He uses one Friday night at Iowa 80 to represent all the days and nights he's collected data there. In actuality, though, he spent weeks and months there. As a researcher, Rick writes himself into the study to show what he's in a position to see and understand, but he also points out what eludes him, who won't talk to him, and who walks away. All along, Rick reads and uses outside sources from other writers to test his own hunches about what trucking life and trucking culture are like. As a writer, Rick makes choices about how he will present his data from a wide range of options that are open to all contemporary ethnographers. But as a researcher, Rick conforms to the process of gathering, interpreting, and validating his data, which is what *doing* fieldwork is all about.

The Research Portfolio: Definitions and Purpose

During the course of his study, Rick kept a research portfolio, which we discuss further in each of the chapters in this book. We recommend developing working files for tracking your learning and documenting your work throughout the process. You might keep these files organized on your computer with backup disks or written out and stored in file folders or boxes. Once you have plentiful, accurate, organized working files, you can create a portfolio from them—not merely for final course evaluation or assessment but for your own self-reflection and evaluation. The working files will help you select documents to present in your portfolio so that you can lay out an array of your research in progress.

As you assemble and revise it, you'll develop a behind-the-scenes account of the story of your research, which you'll want to share with others. The research portfolio will house both the process and the product of your fieldwork. Naturally, it will include your final ethnographic essay, but your selections will also show the thinking process that led to this project. You'll want to represent selections from the reading, writing, and materials you've relied on along the way: writing exercises, fieldnotes, interview questions, charts, methods of analysis, and whatever helped you think your way through the final written report. You may include maps, transcripts, sketches or photographs, summaries of related reading materials (poems, songs, newsletters, advertisements), and any items unique to your study of a particular subculture. At the end of each chapter, we will offer ways to review the working files of your research to make selections for your research portfolio. In Chapter 3, we present Karen Downing's complete research portfolio, along with the full text of her field study.

To keep track of your project, you'll move back and forth among four key activities: collecting, selecting, reflecting, and projecting. Each time you work on the portfolio, and each time you share it with others, you'll be engaged in these processes.

At first, you might find it strange to **collect** wrinkled scraps of paper, lists on napkins, or dribbles of conversation you've overheard, but by gathering them in your portfolio, you'll see how they might fit into your larger project. In fact, the portfolio may look more like a scrapbook to you at first. But over time, you will see that it is a focused, not random, collection of artifacts and writing that lend shape to your fieldwork. Unlike a scrapbook, where the pieces are fastened down, in this portfolio you can move, remove, and replace your data to see potential patterns and structures. As you work with it, you'll move data around, determine other sources of evidence, and confirm or discard insights or hunches that you're making about your data. *The portfolio allows flexibility.*

Another advantage of a research portfolio is that you can **select** from parts of it for your final ethnographic writing. While your initial fieldnotes about the place you're studying may capture something different from the final report, you'll always be able to use some parts of your fieldnotes. If you've studied firefighters, for example, you may have collected pages and pages of fieldnotes describing the fire station even when your final project focuses on their language. In your final project, you'll still need to describe the firehouse before describing the words used there because your reader will need to understand the whole context of your field site before looking at specific parts of the culture. The skills of collecting and selecting, as you move between them, are important to your research portfolio.

At critical points during the fieldwork process, you will need to take time to **reflect** on the data in your portfolio—to look at your fieldnotes and informant interviews and begin to analyze and synthesize the data that are most important to your work. Every item that you include in the portfolio will require reflective writing on your part, from short fieldnote entries to longer memos to yourself. When you review your data alongside your thinking, you'll find options for further focus and analysis. Reflection is complex. As you look over what you've read, thought, said, written, and collected, you will begin to find meanings and patterns across your data that may surprise you and instruct you about where your work is headed. This reflective reviewing will enable you to **project**—to see your progress and form your goals: where you've been, where you are, and where you'll want to head next.

One of the most important parts of the portfolio process is to share your portfolio with others who are also conducting fieldwork. You may share it as hard copy or on-line through e-mail, or you may even want to create a listserv with colleagues whose interests match yours. Keeping a research portfolio makes little sense if it's relegated to the status of end-of-course activity. The major evaluation or assessment ought to be your own. We suggest that you choose a portfolio partner or a small group at the outset of your research and set aside regular times to meet and share your portfolios. At these meetings, you may ask your partner(s) to respond to your descriptions, offer ways of filling gaps in your data, suggest further resources for your research, point out themes or patterns in your data, or help verify your hunches. The process of talking about your data, your hunches, and your research plans and hearing those of others as you look through their portfolios in process will generate new ideas and strategies for your own fieldwork.

FieldWriting: Establishing a Voice

Research writing, like all good writing, has voice. And this voice should be yours—not that of a faceless third person, as in "it was determined" or "this researcher found." It's preferable, we believe, to use *I*, even in fieldwriting. *I* allows you to write with your own authority and with the authenticity of your own fieldwork, and it will ensure your credibility. Contemporary fieldwork, as a research methodology shared by anthropology, sociology, folklore, cultural studies, and linguistics, doesn't claim to be a totally objective social science, as either process or product, fieldworking or fieldwriting.

There's always been a vigorous conversation among scholars about "writing up" fieldwork—from notes to publication. Even several generations ago, during Hortense Powdermaker's time, fieldworkers debated how to incorporate their personal responses—feelings and emotions, sensory and aesthetic details—in their writing about others. In her classic book *Stranger and Friend*, from which we borrowed the idea of "stepping in and stepping out," Powdermaker writes about the similarity between fieldwriters and fiction writers:

> The novelist and the playwright, as well as the anthropologist, write out of their immersion and participation in a particular situation from which they have been able to detach themselves. But they write of the particular. . . . [T]he particular illuminates the human condition (296).

This conversation continues. Some scholars argue that social science field reports should be "scientific" and detached. They fear that blurring the boundaries between ethnography and journalism, fiction and nonfiction, the personal and the impersonal will weaken the credibility of their findings. But others, including ourselves, think that a distanced, objective stance would be dishonest. To ignore yourself as part of the data distorts your findings—you are the researcher who selects the particular details, records informants' particular voices, chooses what to leave in and what to take out, and decides how to write about the "particular" as it "illuminates the human condition" you studied. Your reader needs to know you as the person who has been there. To create a writing voice, you must invite yourself onto the page. To invite yourself onto the page means to ignore conventions that you've already learned—the formula for an essay, the passive voice, overuse of the third person, or the taboo against the personal pronoun *I*. Rather, the content and the language of your project should suggest its form as you shape it. The form should be an extension of the content. There is no fixed form for an ethnographic essay.

When we began to write this book together, one of our first challenges was to establish a common voice. There we sat, Macintosh Powerbooks side by side on an old dining room table, a small fan blowing cool air at us. Works by our favorite anthropologists and folklorists—fieldworkers who write well—lay in stacks, organized in our homemade library in the corner. Our students' and colleagues' writing hung in folders in a blue plastic file box. Our books, our own field experiences, and the research of our students and colleagues lent silent support to our project. And yet, even with all the data and support, we faced the problem that all writers face: how to create a voice for our reader to bring life to our pages. We were two separate writers, friends and colleagues who respected each other and shared similar training and philosophies about writing, teaching, and doing fieldwork. We knew the information we wanted to convey in this book. Our data were already collected and in order. But how to write the book?

We tried writing separately, thinking that that would be more efficient. But we kept looking at each other's screens, unable to ignore each other's texts. "Wait a minute," Elizabeth would admonish, "That's not what you mean!" Bonnie would peer over, shocked at what she read: "Don't you know about passive voice? You've robbed that sentence of all its action." Elizabeth teased Bonnie for her "baby sentences," which Bonnie claimed were for emphasis. Like this. Bonnie ribbed Elizabeth for getting so involved in her thoughts that her voice vacated the page entirely, disappearing into the words on the page. Soon we began to work on one computer, writing, rereading, and revising every line together.

We'd like to show you how we wrote the opening paragraph in this chapter. Elizabeth drafted long, complex sentences, junked up with scholarly phrases and extra jargon: "The anthropological fieldworker—one who has been trained to look through the eyes of the 'other'—positions herself three ways (textually, fixed, and subjectively), both in the field and on the page, to observe, listen, question, and interpret the behaviors and language patterns of those she is studying." Bonnie reacted, "Phew, Elizabeth! This sentence says everything we want to say in the first chapter—and even some stuff for the second. Actually, this sentence is the whole book. We may need to simplify this a bit." Bonnie would then begin to simplify by writing long strings of endless examples: "We question why someone would wear pig earrings, pierce her tongue, drive a certain kind of car, clench his fists, pick her fingernails, wear a rose or a snake or a dragon tatoo on a shoulder, a forearm, or an ankle." Elizabeth would read it and say, "This stuff is terrible. There are way too many examples, Bonnie. By the end of the example, the reader will forget what we're talking about."

After weeks of writing side by side, 12 hours a day, we've forged a collaborative writing voice that represents us both. Whether you choose to write with someone else or whether you write alone with your resources as colleagues, you'll need to think about and establish a voice for your fieldwriting. What we learned most, of great value to us as we developed our voice, was to write ourselves into our text, to be there on the page with the reader.

Similarly, writing research means first "being there"—in the field, as Rick Zollo was at the truck stop, and then on the page, as he is in his ethnographic study in this chapter. If you've never stopped at Iowa 80, Rick's research will take you there—

cruising the parking lot, eating fried catfish and potatoes, hearing the truckers' gripes and recording their lingo, reading their logbooks, and noticing their musical tastes. Rick shows that fieldworkers who care about their topics want their readers to learn as much as they did. He knew that his major challenge was to make the culture come alive for someone else. So he researched his field site and its background, established relationships with insiders, and thought hard about the data piled high on his desk and stuffed into boxes on his living room floor. As a researcher, he temporarily became a trucker, and through his writing, you, as his reader, become one, too. Here are some of the ways he did it:

1. *He begins by writing himself into his fieldnotes.* In this passage from his October journal, Rick contrasts his own mood as a researcher with the surroundings at the truck stop:

> When I hear that Mrs. Moon will be returning from a funeral, I feel uneasy, like perhaps I am partly responsible for this state of affairs, a harbinger of bad times. . . . That leaves me sauntering across the back lot heading for the Jiffy Shop and trying to shake off my uneasiness. The sun is high in the sky, giving no indication of the coming cold front. . . . Dark clouds slash in diagonals across the northwest and southeast skies, and I give silent thanks for this bit of good weather. . . . I am determined to get off my dime and get to work on this project. If it's going to amount to anything, I have to talk to *people.*

2. *He writes his interviews as dialogues, capturing both his own voice and that of his informants in his transcripts.* In his interview with Delia Moon, the founder's daughter and company vice-president, Rick records some company history. But he also records his own questions as part of the interview:

> Delia Moon has an office in back, parallel to the movie theater. She's brown-haired, fair-complected, in her late twenties, thin with nervously attentive features. Her office is crowded with a large desk and trucking industry mementos. . . . After a few introductory moments dealing with research objectives, we begin:

RZ: This truck stop was founded by your father?

DM: He worked for Standard Oil, in the engineering department, and when the interstate system was built, Amoco targeted places for stops, and my father would go in and buy the land and set up a dealer. He was responsible for setting up places all over the Midwest.

RZ: So he was a visionary? He had a vision of what truck stops in the future should be? Did he see it coming to this, places like Iowa 80 and Little America?

DM: I'd say it happened over time. Traffic here kept building. He was very . . . he really liked people, truckers. He'd sit in the restaurant and talk to them. The customers can always tell you how you can be better.

3. *He rejects his early drafts because his voice depends too much on other authorities.* In this short excerpt from the first paragraphs of a first draft of "Friday Night at Iowa 80," Rick cites two outside sources and even quotes the roadside sign he recorded in his fieldnotes. He struggles to balance his own voice with the recognized authorities from his reading. You might want to compare this early draft with the first few paragraphs of his final paper.

> "Truckstops are the center of the trucking culture," writes James Thomas in *The Long Haul,* and the new trucker villages "offer the driver an equivalent to the cowboys' town at trail's end or the friendly port to sailors" (111). One trucking village that exemplifies this roadside oasis is Iowa 80, "the largest Amoco truckstop in the world" (roadside advertisement), located off Interstate 80 in Walcott, Iowa, some dozen miles from Davenport and 40 miles from my Iowa City home.
>
> I spent selected days and evenings at this site during the fall of 1993, with hopes of discovering "those webs of significance" that make up the context of this very particular culture (Geertz, *Interpretation of Cultures* 5). I am interested in trucker life for a variety of reasons and have wanted to write about Iowa 80 since first noting its sprawling growth almost a decade ago. My time there was well spent, "sorting out the structures of signification" that I had to "first grasp and then render" (9–10).

4. *He experiments with another genre.* In a fiction-writing class he took while conducting his research, Rick began a novella about trucking that he describes as "pulp fiction." For this story, he invents a character, trucker Dick Deacon, and uses the setting he's learned about in his research. Sometimes fieldworkers discover that writing in another form—fiction, poetry, dramatic dialogue—helps them enter the worldview of their informants. When he later returned to the final draft of his ethnographic essay, Rick felt more confident that he transform his real-world data into an interesting text for his readers. Though an ethnographic essay is certainly not fiction, it relies on many of the techniques that writers use to craft other genres.

TRUCK DRIVIN' MAN
Rick Zollo

Chapter 1

"Ten-four, this is the Deacon on the Beacon."

> The sun was peeking over a small ridge of oak trees when Dick Deacon guided his '92 Peterbuilt conventional down Illinois I-88 and prepared to downshift for the turn-off onto I-80. He was heading for home, a free weekend in his home state of Iowa. He was tired and dragged out from twenty-one straight days of hauling, but he had to remind himself to look out for Smokies and watched ruefully as a comrade in an International cab-over hauling reefer blew by him.
>
> "Watch out, good buddy. This is Illinois," muttered Deacon, as he spotted a speed sign that said it all. "Sixty-five for automobiles, fifty-

five for commercial trucks"—one of those states with split limits. Illinois was not a favorite place of truckers. But Deacon took it all in stride. He was an over-the-roader, having taken to this way of life as soon as he could get his C.D.L. He drove tandem for five years with his Dad, then his Dad took sick. He missed his old man and was looking forward to their meeting later that evening.

5. *He combines some of these techniques in his ethnographic study.* Playing with technique, revising, and redrafting helped Rick establish his fieldworker's voice for "Friday Night at Iowa 80." In the final draft, his authority comes from combining his personal feelings and observations with those of his informants and of the texts he read.

The challenge in fieldwriting, as Rick learned, is to create a writer's voice that will engage a reader, based on the data gathered in the field. Often the most compelling techniques for writing up research are ones that fiction writers use. "As I undid necklaces of words and restrung them," writes anthropologist Ruth Behar, "as I dressed up hours of rambling talk in elegant sentences and paragraphs of prose, as I snipped at the flow of talk, stopping it sometimes for dramatic emphasis long before it had really stopped, I no longer knew where I stood on the border between fiction and nonfiction" (16). This borderland, where a fieldwriter experiments with voice, is an exciting place. It challenges us both as writers and as researchers. It is a borderland in which, as writers, we can step in and step out.

FieldWords

We'll end each chapter with a list of the key terms we've used and their definitions. Here is our first set of fieldwords.

Artifact: Any material object that belongs to and represents a culture.

Assumptions: Untested attitudes or theories you hold (based on your own experiences) about unfamiliar people, places, or ideas.

Colonization: The takeover of less powerful people by more powerful people who demand conformity to their group's ideas and values, as in a territory ruled or annexed by another country.

Culture: The invisible web of behaviors, patterns, and rules of a group of people who have contact with one another and share a common language.

Data: All the information, both written and material artifacts, that a researcher uses as the basis of evidence.

Ethnocentric: Projecting one's own cultural values onto others.

Ethnography: The study of people in other cultures and the resultant written text from that study. (Note that a fieldworker can adapt ethnographic methods for research and writing without producing a full-length ethnography.)

Fieldwork: The process of living and studying among other people in their own context, with their permission and cooperation.

Informant: A person who shares information about the meanings of his or her culture with a researcher; sometimes also referred to as a consultant, a subject, or "the other."

Insider/Outsider: The dialectical stance of detachment (outsider) or involvement (insider) that a researcher adapts toward the informants in the culture studied.

Portfolio: A collection of material artifacts that displays and explains a learning process, complete with a reflective analysis. Using it, the portfolio keeper can evaluate progress and accomplishments. When the portfolio is used as an instrument to look at others, as in a research portfolio, it becomes both reflective and reflexive. Building it, the portfolio keeper depends on four key recurring processes:

Collect. Gather data continually and organize it in your portfolio as you go along.

Select. Lay your data out in front of you, eliminate some of it, describe some of it, analyze the choices that you make, and weigh how the choices fit your current plans.

Reflect. Each time you work on your portfolio, write a one- or two-page reflection about the major items you include. In this reflective writing, address either yourself or your portfolio partner to explain and interpret your data. Discuss your choices and organizational patterns.

Project. Your reflective writing will point to gaps in your data, emerging patterns, and questions you might follow in further data collection and analysis. It will help you state a few goals for your project.

Reflection: The act of considering thoughtfully, looking back in order to gain insight.

Reflexivity: The process of self-scrutiny that results from studying others. To be reflexive demands both an "other" and some self-conscious awareness. Without the aid of an "other," the process is only self-reflective. To be reflective does not demand an "other."

Subjectivity: One's own personal inner feelings and attitudes toward a given subject or topic, as opposed to objective, verifiable, concrete, factual evidence.

Worldview: The perspective or point of view of any particular culture.

FieldReading

Anzaldua, Gloria. *Borderlands: La Frontiera: The New Mestiza*. San Francisco: Spinsters Aunt Lute, 1987.

Behar, Ruth. *Translated Woman: Crossing the Border with Esperanza's Story*. Boston: Beacon, 1993.

Benedict, Ruth. *Patterns of Culture*. New York: New American Library, 1953.

Fiske, John. *Understanding Popular Culture*. Boston: Unwin, 1989.

Goodenough, Ward. *Culture, Language, and Society*. Menlo Park: Benjamin, 1981.

Graves, Donald H., and Bonnie S. Sunstein. *Portfolio Portraits*. Portsmouth: Heinemann, 1992.

Hebdidge, Dick. *Subculture: The Meaning of Style*. New York: Methuen, 1984.

Moffatt, Michael. *Coming of Age in New Jersey: College and American Culture*. New Brunswick: Rutgers UP, 1989.

Peacock, James. *The Anthropological Lens: Harsh Light, Soft Focus*. Cambridge: Cambridge UP, 1986.

Powdermaker, Hortense. *Stranger and Friend: The Way of an Anthropologist*. New York: Norton, 1966.

Rosaldo, Renato. *Culture and Truth: The Remaking of Social Analysis.* Boston: Beacon, 1989.

Rose, Mike. *Lives on the Boundary: The Struggles and Achievements of America's Underprepared.* New York: Free, 1989.

Toth, Jennifer. *The Mole People: Life in the Tunnels of New York City.* Chicago: Chicago Review P, 1993.

Wolcott, Harry. *The Art of Fieldwork.* Walnut Creek: Altamira-Sage, 1995.

CHAPTER 2

Reading Self, Reading Cultures: Understanding Texts

The reader performs the poem or the novel, as the violinist performs the sonata. But the instrument on which the reader plays, and from which he evokes the work, is—himself.

Louise Rosenblatt

We all read differently. Literary theorist Louise Rosenblatt suggests that a reader's main instrument for making meaning is the self. And meaning is an intertwining of our past reading experiences, current tastes, attitudes about genres and forms, and history of teachers, mentors, friends, and relatives. No one reads exactly as you do. No one but you listened to your grandfather's stories on the front stoop. No one but you heard your second grade teacher read *Charlotte's Web* on the day you lost your first front tooth. No one but you searched the guide words in the phone book for the name of your boyfriend's family (and no one but you called him). No one but you has stayed up on a hot summer night finishing *To Kill a Mockingbird*. No one reads exactly as you do because no one has exactly the same experiences.

Your own choice of a good author is both personal and situational. For a plane trip, you may take Danielle Steele or John Grisham. Or you may be so frightened by flying that you read *Field and Stream* magazine or an economics text to keep your mind occupied. You may plow through the manual for your new Macintosh while your best friend ignores it and expects you to answer his constant questions. Yet this same person is willing to spend hours scrolling through America Online's restaurant guide to cities he has never visited. We read differently because we have different needs as readers.

We also read differently at different times in our lives. When you reread *Charlotte's Web* as an adult, you may not be as devastated for Wilbur, but instead you might notice that Charlotte the spider is a spiritualist and a philosopher. When Bonnie read *Little Women* to her daughter, she was surprised to find that she felt connected with the character of the mother "Marmee," although as a 10-year-old reading *Little Women*, she hadn't noticed the mother at all. We bring our current lives into the reading we do.

As a reader, you have formed tastes and predispositions from your many past experiences. What are your attitudes toward reading? Do you like to whip through a book quickly, or do you luxuriate in how an author uses words? Do you read novels differently than textbooks? Poetry differently than magazines and newspapers? What expectations do you carry for a bestseller? What behaviors do you engage in while you read? Do you like to mark your own comments in the margins? Do you respond to your reading in a journal? Do you like to talk with a friend about what you read?

Meaning itself is a process of negotiation among the reader, the text, and the writer. This negotiation takes place both on and off the page. *On the page* of your computer manual, for example, the text explains how to insert footers and page numbers. You take the technical writer's directions, negotiate them with your personal skills as a reader and a computer user, and carry that meaning directly to your keyboard to make footers and numbers on your page. You may find yourself rereading pages of a mystery novel for clues to the murder as you are reaching the conclusion of the book. But negotiation *off the page* is a less visible process. When you read a poem or hear a song, for example, the words on the page may have little meaning without your off-the-page experience. Sometimes it is through talk with others that you discover new meanings. At other times, knowing about the writer's background helps you negotiate meaning. Your understanding of a poem or song may come entirely through an emotional response. One metaphor may explode an entire image in your head. If no other person reads exactly like you do, it follows that no text has the same meaning for another reader. Meaning is a subjective experience.

Fieldworkers research cultures in the same way as readers approach novels. As you read the following excerpt from the opening of Gloria Naylor's *Mama Day*, we'd like you to "read yourself" into this text. This bestseller about the fictional sea island of Willow Springs invites you into an entire culture—one that you may approach by "stepping out," or one that you may already know by having "stepped in." You may know something about the novel's setting, the Georgia–South Carolina sea islands. You might think about Hilton Head, an island full of resort hotels, condominiums, and golf courses purchased (colonized) by land developers from the people born and raised there. Or you may have vacationed there with your family or worked at one of the hotels. You may think about the special Gullah dialect spoken there, which fascinates historians and linguists. You may have read or seen the movie based on Pat Conroy's book *The Water Is Wide*, another novel set in the sea islands. In other words, how do you situate yourself as a reader?

You probably approach any text with expectations based on your membership in different subcultures, including your readership preferences, which represent subcultures in themselves. For example, all of Linda Barnes's mystery readers belong to a subculture, as do all followers of James Morrow's science fiction novels, whether they know one another or not. Gloria Naylor is an African-American female novelist. What other writers does Naylor remind you of? William Faulkner, who created the fictional world of one county in the American South? Anne Tyler, who constructs characters enmeshed in complicated family situations? Ray Bradbury, whose fictional future worlds are filled with odd but familiar places and people? Does Gloria Naylor make you think of other African-American women writers, such as Alice Walker or Toni Morrison? If you're male, how will you approach a novel about a black female matriarch? Do you think your ethnicity and gender affect the way you read, or are they irrelevant?

We chose this excerpt from a novel because it depicts a fieldworker researching his culture. Reema's boy, though fictional, represents the novice fieldworker—a position you'll take when you enter your field site. He puzzles over an unfamiliar term he hears, "18 & 23," and tries to make sense of it. Notice both what he does as he researches this culture—in which he once lived—and what he forgets to do. As you read, use your subjective experiences to negotiate meaning—your personal background and your history as a reader. Add your response to that of the text. Take notes, pose questions, and write about your process of reading.

Mama Day
Gloria Naylor

Willow Springs. Everybody knows but nobody talks about the legend of Sapphira Wade. A true conjure woman: satin black, biscuit cream, red as Georgia clay: depending upon which of us takes a mind to her. She could walk through a lightning storm without being

touched; grab a bolt of lightning in the palm of her hand; use the heat of lightning to start the kindling going under her medicine pot: depending upon which of us takes a mind to her. She turned the moon into salve, the stars into a swaddling cloth, and healed the wounds of every creature walking up on two or down on four. It ain't about right or wrong, truth or lies; it's about a slave woman who brought a whole new meaning to both them words, soon as you cross over here from beyond the bridge. And somehow, some way, it happened in 1823: she smothered Bascombe Wade in his very bed and lived to tell the story for a thousand days. 1823: married Bascombe Wade, bore him seven sons in just a thousand days, to put a dagger through his kidney and escape the hangman's noose, laughing in a burst of flames. 1823: persuaded Bascombe Wade in a thousand days to deed all his slaves every inch of land in Willow Springs, poisoned him for his trouble, to go on and bear seven sons—by person or persons unknown. Mixing it all together and keeping everything that done shifted down through the holes of time, you end up with the death of Bascombe Wade (there's his tombstone right out by Chevy's Pass), the deeds to our land (all marked back to the very year), and seven sons (ain't Miss Abigail and Mama Day the granddaughters of that seventh boy?). The wild card in all this is the thousand days, and we guess if we put our heads together we'd come up with something—which ain't possible since Sapphira Wade don't live in the part of our memory we can use to form words.

But ain't a soul in Willow Springs don't know that little dark girls, hair all braided up with colored twine, got their "18 & 23's coming down" when they lean too long over them back yard fences, laughing at the antics of little dark boys who got the nerve to be "breathing 18 & 23" with mother's milk still on their tongues. And if she leans there just a mite too long or grins a bit too wide, it's gonna bring a holler straight through the dusty screen door. "Get your bow-legged self 'way from my fence, Johnny Blue. Won't be no 'early 18 & 23's' coming here for me to rock. I'm still raising her." Yes, the *name* Sapphira Wade is never breathed out of a single mouth in Willow Springs. But who don't know that old twisted-lip manager at the Sheraton Hotel beyond the bridge, offering Winky Browne only twelve dollars for his whole boatload of crawdaddies—"tried to 18 & 23 him," if he tried to do a thing? We all sitting here, a hop, skip, and one Christmas left before the year 2000, and ain't nobody told him niggers can read now? Like the menus in his restaurant don't say a handful of crawdaddies sprinkled over a little bowl of crushed ice is almost twelve dollars? Call it shrimp cocktail, or whatever he want—we can count, too. And the price of everything that swims, crawls, or lays at the bottom of The Sound went up in 1985, during the season we had that "18 & 23 summer" and the bridge blew down. Folks didn't take their lives in their hands out there in that treacherous water just to be doing it—ain't that much 18 & 23 in the world.

But that old hotel manager don't make no never mind. He's the least of what we done had to deal with here in Willow Springs. Malaria. Union soldiers. Sandy soil. Two big depressions. Hurricanes. Not to mention these new real estate developers who think we gonna sell our shore land just because we ain't fool enough to live there. Started coming over here in the early '90s, talking "vacation paradise," talking "pic-ture-ess." Like Winky said, we'd have to pick their ass out the bottom of the marsh first hurricane blow through here again. See, they just thinking about building where they ain't got no state taxes—never been and never will be, 'cause Willow Springs ain't in no state. Georgia and South Carolina done tried, though—been trying since right after the Civil War to prove that Willow Springs belong to one or the other of them. Look on any of them old maps they hurried and drew up soon as the Union soldiers pulled out and you can see that the only thing connects us to the mainland is a bridge—and even that gotta be rebuilt after every big storm. (They was talking about steel and concrete way back, but since Georgia and South Carolina couldn't claim the taxes, nobody wanted to shell out for the work. So we rebuild it ourselves when need be, and build it how we need it—strong enough to last till the next big wind. Only need a steel and concrete bridge once every seventy years or so. Wood and pitch is a tenth of the cost and serves us a good sixty-nine years—matter of simple arithmetic.) But anyways, all forty-nine square miles curves like a bow, stretching toward Georgia on the south end and South Carolina on the north, and right smack in the middle where each foot of our bridge sits is the dividing line between them two states.

So who it belong to? It belongs to us—clean and simple. And it belonged to our daddies, and our daddies before them, and them too—who at one time all belonged to Bascombe Wade. And when they tried to trace him and how he got it, found out he wasn't even American. Was Norway-born or something, and the land had been sitting in his family over there in Europe since it got explored and claimed by the Vikings—imagine that. So thanks to the conjuring of Sapphira Wade we got it from Norway or theres about, and if taxes owed, it's owed to them. But ain't no Vikings or anybody else from over in Europe come to us with the foolishness that them folks out of Columbia and Atlanta come with—we was being un-American. And the way we saw it, America ain't entered the question at all when it come to our land: Sapphira was African-born, Bascombe Wade was from Norway, and it was the 18 & 23'ing that went down between them two put deeds in our hands. And we wasn't even Americans when we got it—was slaves. And the laws about slaves not owning nothing in Georgia and South Carolina don't apply, 'cause the land wasn't then—and isn't now—in either of them places. When there was lots of cotton here, and we baled it up and sold it beyond the bridge, we paid our taxes to the U.S. of A. And we keeps account of all the fishing that's done and sold beyond the bridge, all the little truck farming. And later when we had to go over there to work or our children went, we paid taxes out of them earnings. We pays taxes on the telephone lines and electrical wires run over The Sound. Ain't nobody here about breaking the law. But Georgia and South Carolina ain't seeing the shine off a penny for our land, our homes, our roads, or our bridge. Well, they fought each other up to the Supreme Court about the whole matter, and it came to a draw. We guess they got so tired out from that, they decided to leave us be—until them developers started swarming over here like sand flies at a Sunday picnic.

Sure, we coulda used the money and weren't using the land. But like Mama Day told 'em (we knew to send 'em straight over there to her and Miss Abigail), they didn't come huffing and sweating all this way in them dark gaberdine suits if they didn't think our land could make them a bundle of money, and the way we saw it, there was enough land—shoreline, that is—to make us all pretty comfortable. And calculating on the basis of all them fancy plans they had in mind, a million an acre wasn't asking too much. Flap, flap, flap—Lord, didn't them jaws and silk ties move in the wind. The land wouldn't be worth that if they couldn't *build* on it. Yes, suh, she told 'em, and they couldn't build on it unless we *sold* it. So we get ours now, and they get theirs later. You shoulda seen them coattails flapping back across The Sound with all their lies about "community uplift" and "better jobs." 'Cause it weren't about no them now and us later—was them now and us never. Hadn't we seen it happen back in the '80s on St. Helena, Daufuskie, and St. John's? And before that in the '60s on Hilton Head? Got them folks' land, built fences around it first thing, and then brought in all the builders and high-paid managers from mainside—ain't nobody on them islands benefited. And the only dark faces you see now in them "vacation paradises" is the ones cleaning the toilets and cutting the grass. On their own land, mind you, their own land. Weren't gonna happen in Willow Springs. 'Cause if Mama Day say no, everybody say no. There's 18 & 23, and there's

18 & 23—and nobody was gonna trifle with Mama Day's, 'cause she know how to use it—her being a direct descendant of Sapphira Wade, piled on the fact of springing from the seventh son of a seventh son—uh, uh. Mama Day say no, everybody say no. No point in making a pile of money to be guaranteed the new moon will see you scratching at fleas you don't have, or rolling in the marsh like a mud turtle. And if some was waiting for her to die, they had a long wait. She says she ain't gonna. And when you think about it, to show up in one century, make it all the way through the next, and have a toe inching over into the one approaching *is* about as close to eternity anybody can come.

Well, them developers upped the price and changed the plans, changed the plans and upped the price, till it got to be a game with us. Winky bought a motorboat with what they offered him back in 1987, turned it in for a cabin cruiser two years later, and says he expects to be able to afford a yacht with the news that's waiting in the mail this year. Parris went from a new shingle roof to a split-level ranch and is making his way toward adding a swimming pool and greenhouse. But when all the laughing's done, it's the principle that remains. And we done learned that anything coming from beyond the bridge gotta be viewed real, real careful. Look what happened when Reema's boy—the one with the pear-shaped head—came hauling himself back from one of those fancy colleges mainside, dragging his notebooks and tape recorder and a funny way of curling up his lip and clicking his teeth, all excited and determined to put Willow Springs on the map.

We was polite enough—Reema always was a little addle-brained—so you couldn't blame the boy for not remembering that part of Willow Springs's problems was that it got put on some maps right after the War Between the States. And then when he went around asking us about 18 & 23, there weren't nothing to do but take pity on him as he rattled on about "ethnography," "unique speech patterns," "cultural preservation," and whatever else he seemed to be getting so much pleasure out of while talking into his little gray machine. He was all over the place—What 18 & 23 mean? What 18 & 23 mean? And we all told him the God-honest truth: it was just our way of saying something. Winky was awful, though, he even spit tobacco juice for him. Sat on his porch all day, chewing up the boy's Red Devil premium and spitting so the machine could pick it up. There was enough fun in that to take us through the fall and winter when he had hauled himself back over The Sound to wherever he was getting what was supposed to be passing for an education. And he sent everybody he'd talked to copies of the book he wrote, bound all nice with our name and his signed on the first page. We couldn't hold Reema down, she was so proud. It's a good thing she didn't read it. None of us made it much through the introduction, but that said it all: you see, he had come to the conclusion after "extensive field work" (ain't never picked a boll of cotton or head of lettuce in his life—Reema spoiled him silly), but he done still made it to the conclusion that 18 & 23 wasn't 18 & 23 at all—was really 81 & 32, which just so happened to be the lines of longitude and latitude marking off where Willow Springs sits on the map. And we were just so damned dumb that we turned the whole thing around.

Not that he called it being dumb, mind you, called it "asserting our cultural identity," "inverting hostile social and political parameters." 'Cause, see, being we was brought here as slaves, we had no choice but to look at everything upside-down. And then being that we was isolated off here on this island, everybody else in the country went on learning good English and calling things what they really was—in the dictionary and all that—while we kept on calling things ass-backwards. And he thought that was just so wonderful and marvelous, etcetera, etcetera . . . Well, after that crate of books came here, if anybody had any doubts about what them developers was up to, if there was just a tinge of seriousness behind them jokes about the motorboats and swimming pools that could be gotten from selling a piece of land, them books squashed it. The people who ran the type of schools that could turn our children into raving lunatics—and then put his picture on the back of the book so we couldn't even deny it was him—didn't mean us a speck of good.

If the boy wanted to know what 18 & 23 meant, why didn't he just ask? When he was running around sticking that machine in everybody's face, we was sitting right here—every one of us—and him being one of Reema's, we woulda obliged him. He coulda asked Cloris about the curve in her spine that came from the planting season when their mule broke its leg, and she took up the reins and kept pulling the plow with her own back. Winky woulda told him about the hot tar that took out the corner of his right eye the summer we had only seven days to rebuild the bridge so the few crops we had left after the storm could be gotten over before rot sat in. Anybody woulda carried him through the fields we had to stop farming back in the '80s to take outside jobs— washing cars, carrying groceries, cleaning house—anything—'cause it was leave the land or lose it during the Silent Depression. Had more folks sleeping in city streets and banks foreclosing on farms than in the Great Depression before that.

Naw, he didn't really want to know what 18 & 23 meant, or he woulda asked. He woulda asked right off where Miss Abigail Day was staying, so we coulda sent him down the main road to that little yellow house where she used to live. And she woulda given him a tall glass of ice water or some cinnamon tea as he heard about Peace dying young, then Hope and Peace again. But there was the child of Grace—the grandchild, a girl who went mainside, like him, and did real well. Was living outside of Charleston now with her husband and two boys. So she visits a lot more often than she did when she was up in New York. And she probably woulda pulled out that old photo album, so he coulda seen some pictures of her grandchild, Cocoa, and then Cocoa's mama, Grace. And Miss Abigail flips right through to the beautiful one of Grace resting in her satin-lined coffin. And as she walks him back out to the front porch and points him across the road to a silver trailer where her sister, Miranda, lives, she tells him to grab up and chew a few sprigs of mint growing at the foot of the steps—it'll help kill his thirst in the hot sun. And if he'd known enough to do just that, thirsty or not, he'd know when he got to that silver trailer to stand back a distance calling *Mama, Mama Day*, to wait for her to come out and beckon him near.

He'da told her he been sent by Miss Abigail and so, more likely than not, she lets him in. And he hears again about the child of Grace, her grandniece, who went mainside, like him, and did real well. Was living outside of Charleston now with her husband and two boys. So she visits a lot more often than she did when she was up in New York. Cocoa is like her very own, Mama Day tells him, since she never had no children.

And with him carrying that whiff of mint on his breath, she surely woulda walked him out to the side yard, facing that patch of dogwood, to say she has to end the visit a little short 'cause she has some gardening to do in the other place. And if he'd had the sense to offer to follow her just a bit of the way—then and only then—he hears about that summer fourteen years ago when Cocoa came visiting from New York with her first husband. Yes, she tells him, there was a first husband—a stone city boy. How his name was George. But how Cocoa left, and he stayed. How it was the year of the last big storm that blew her pecan trees down and even caved in the roof of the other place. And she woulda stopped him from walking just by a patch of oak: she reaches up, takes a bit of moss for him to put in them closed leather shoes—they're probably sweating his feet something terrible, she tells him. And he's to sit on the ground, right there, to untie his shoes and stick in the moss. And then he'd see through the low bush that old graveyard just down the slope. And when he looks back up, she woulda disappeared through the trees; but he's to keep pushing the moss in them shoes and go on down to that graveyard where he'll find buried Grace, Hope, Peace, and Peace again. Then a little ways off a grouping of seven old graves, and a little ways off seven older again. All circled by them live oaks and hanging moss, over a rise from the tip of The Sound.

Everything he needed to know coulda been heard from that yellow house to that silver trailer to that graveyard. Be too late for him to go that route now, since Miss Abigail's been dead for over nine years. Still, there's an easier way. He could just watch Cocoa any one of these times she comes in from Charleston. She goes straight to Miss Abigail's to air out the rooms and unpack her bags, then she's across the road to call out at Mama Day, who's gonna come to the door of the trailer and wave as Cocoa heads on through the patch of dogwoods to that oak grove. She stops and puts a bit of moss in her open-toe sandals, then goes on past those graves to a spot just down the rise toward The Sound, a little bit south of that circle of oaks. And if he was patient and stayed off a little ways, he'd realize she was there to meet up with her first husband so they could talk about that summer fourteen years ago when she left, but he stayed. And as her and George are there together for a good two hours or so—neither one saying a word—Reema's boy coulda heard from them everything there was to tell about 18 & 23.

But on second thought, someone who didn't know how to ask wouldn't know how to listen. And he coulda listened to them the way you been listening to us right now. Think about it: ain't nobody really talking to you. We're sitting here in Willow Springs, and you're God-knows-where. It's August 1999—ain't but a slim chance it's the same season where you are. Uh, huh, listen. Really listen this time: the only voice is your own. But you done just heard about the legend of Sapphira Wade, though nobody here breathes her name. You done heard it the way we know it, sitting on our porches and shelling June peas, quieting the midnight cough of a baby, taking apart the engine of a car—you done heard it without a single living soul really saying a word. Pity, though, Reema's boy couldn't listen, like you, to Cocoa and George down by them oaks—or he woulda left here with quite a story.

BOX 4
RESPONDING TO TEXT

We hope you found yourself reading this excerpt more than once. We did. When each of us first read it, we realized we needed to read it again. Bonnie's interest in the character of the bumbling young researcher, Reema's boy, focused her reading so that she excluded other characters. Elizabeth found herself looking at Naylor's map, imagining how close it might be to where she lives in North Carolina. She stared at Sapphira Wade's family tree and at the document that marked Sapphira's sale as a slave. As Elizabeth read the code word "18 & 23," she found herself trying to substitute other words each time she encountered it. But as we reread the text together for the purpose of writing this book, we talked about it and found ourselves discovering much more. We began to read the text in two

CHAPTER TWO   Reading Self, Reading Cultures: Understanding Texts ways: one as a parody of fieldworking and the other as a rich fictional account of a cultural group with its own codes, behaviors, stories, and rituals.

We'd like you to describe your own process of reading and rereading *Mama Day* in a page or two. If you're keeping a journal or a process log, you might want to use these questions to guide your response.

- What personal assumptions did you bring to this text? About this region's geography? This group of sea islanders? Rural families and their belief systems and values?
- What other books have you read or movies have you seen that this excerpt reminds you of? In what ways?
- How do your previous reading experiences affect the way you appreciate Naylor's writing? How would you describe Naylor's style?
- What was hard for you to understand in this text? Which words, phrases, or paragraphs made you stop and reread? How did you solve this problem?
- What stood out for you? Where in the text did you find yourself entertained? Immersed? Confused?
- What information was helpful as you read the first time? In your second reading, what did you discover that you missed the first time?
- Which of the characters interested you most, and why? Cocoa? Mama Day? Reema's boy? Sapphira Wade? The narrator?
- What details of the setting involved your imagination? When you share your response with your colleagues, notice how they might have read differently.

Response

Cheri Kreclic's response to this exercise looked like this:

> Reading *Mama Day*, I was reminded of the movie *Daughters of the Dust*, which is the story of the Gullahs on a very similar island during the early part of the twentieth century. This movie greatly influenced my visualization of the events in *Mama Day* and helped me understand the historical events and the writer's perspective. I am also acquainted with what happened to the Gullah people's redevelopment of their property in Hilton Head because of a series of programs on the subject on National Public Radio a few years ago. The dialect is also familiar since during a course called "The Black Experience," we listened to the language of the Gullahs.
>
> I was most intrigued with the character of Sapphira Wade. The narrator gives a very clear characterization of her, but I wanted to know more—how did she persuade Bascombe Wade to deed this land to the slaves, and how did she escape the hangman's noose? I had no trouble reading this excerpt and quickly fell into the rhythm of the words.

Brenda Yarish found herself less confused on each rereading:

> The first time I read *Mama Day*, I was so confused by the language that I completely missed the story. As I read it the second time, the language cleared up, and the third time, I finally grasped the story. The one thing in the language

that threw me was "18 & 23." It later became clearer when I started inserting other words to make the sentence have meaning for me. In the first paragraph where the narrator tells of Sapphira Wade's life, he says she "escaped the hangman's noose, laughing in a burst of flames." "Laughing in a burst of flames" still eludes me. I'm also still confused how Sapphira could have smothered a man, then married him, given him seven sons, then put a dagger through his kidney, then poisoned him, then bore him seven sons. Wow! She must have been quite a woman to have killed the same man so many times. The character that interested me the most was the narrator. He or she (not sure what gender) knew everything about the culture yet remains unidentified. My second favorite was Reema's boy. I related to him in his search for "culture" after having to write ethnographically. When you read ethnography, it seems so simple until you try it.

Reading Culture as Text and Text as Culture

We have suggested the kinds of questions that you might bring to any text you read. Reading any complex text can also involve reading a culture. In this text, we see culture's ordinary life—dailiness that fieldworkers always try to penetrate: catching crawdaddies, chewing tobacco, truck farming. But we also see this culture's uniqueness through Naylor's specific characters and setting.

Our own collaborative reading of Naylor's text helped us see the layers of culture she created. She begins with an omniscient insider narrator who takes us into Willow Springs, a place with its own folklore and folkways. Willow Springs is not easily accessible to outsiders; it even requires crossing a bridge between the mainland and the island. Crossing this bridge, as we read it, symbolizes the differences between mainland and island cultures, and many islanders are required to move back and forth between these two very different worlds, to be bicultural.

With the character of Reema's pear-headed nameless boy, Naylor offers us a parody of a field researcher. He is an insider, born on the island, and he returns from his fancy college, "dragging his notebooks and tape recorder and a funny way of curling up his lip and clicking his teeth, all excited to put Willow Springs on the map" (7). He conducts "extensive field work," which includes recording the sound of Winky Brown spitting tobacco and intensive interviews about "18 & 23." Reema's boy writes up his field study and gives it to his informants, who confess that they never even read the introduction, never mind the conclusions he makes about "18 & 23."

Reema's boy's college education had so shaped him that he was unable, even as an insider, to do what fieldworkers need to do: listen, observe, and participate in the life of the people he studied. Even the residents of Willow Springs knew more about how to do his fieldwork than he did: "If the boy wanted to know what 18 & 23 meant, why didn't he just ask?" The narrator concludes that a researcher who doesn't know how to form questions would never be in a position to understand answers. "But on second thought," the narrator reminds us, "someone who didn't know how to ask wouldn't know how to listen."

You'll need to think about how your background can affect what you see in another culture just as it does when you read a written text. What you see is affected by who you are. Your education, geography, family history, personal experiences, race, gender, or nationality can influence the way you do research. Learning to read a culture like a text is similar to learning to read a text like a culture.

Positioning: Reading and Writing about Yourself

As we conduct our fieldwork, we must be conscious of ourselves as the key instruments of the research process. When you begin to research a site, you will need to "read" yourself in the same way that you have deciphered texts, and you will want to write that perspective into your study. Had Reema's boy thought or written about his insider status, education and field training, family history, and geography, he might have asked different questions and gotten different answers. Instead of leaving out personal, subjective information, fieldworkers should write it in. The subjective perspective—as opposed to the objective one—admits the researcher's presence as she goes about her fieldwork.

Horace Miner's study of the Nacirema in Chapter 1 satirizes the so-called objective traditions of natural science that once dominated the field of anthropology by describing everyday routines such as brushing our teeth, as stylized ceremonies or rituals. Today, most contemporary scientists, in both the natural and the social sciences, realize that objectivity is not possible—that the observer is part of the person or culture observed.

In fieldwork, *positioning* includes all the subjective responses that affect how the researcher sees data. Readers of ethnography sometimes wonder how this kind of research could be considered social "science" if the researcher is not offering "objective" data. In fact, fieldworkers achieve a type of objectivity through *intersubjectivity*, the method of connecting as many different perspectives on the same data as possible. These multiple sources encourage the fieldworker to interpret patterns and interrelationships among various accounts alongside the researcher's own account and to leave other interpretations open as well.

Being the researcher so influences your fieldwork that it would be deceptive *not* to include relevant background information about yourself in your study. From our own experiences as fieldworkers, we believe that as a researcher you position or situate yourself in relationship to your study in at least three ways: fixed, subjective, and textual.

FIXED POSITIONS

Fixed positions are the personal facts that might influence how you see your data—your age, gender, class, nationality, race—factors that will not change during the course of the study but are often taken for granted and unexamined in the research process. Does it matter that you are middle-aged and studying adolescents? Or that you grew up on a kibbutz in Israel? Does being a middle-class African-American affect the way you interpret the lives of homeless African-Americans? How does being male affect your perspective?

In Elizabeth's research on college students' literacies, for example, her position as a woman was a key to understanding differences in the ways that men and women talk in college classrooms. Her gender helped her see why women were often silent in certain classrooms while male students dominated the talk. Being female enhanced her project and enabled her to see and record behaviors that might have been inaccessible to her had she been male. One of her male informants asked her, "What is this women's way of knowing?" implying that he just didn't understand how gender affected someone's knowledge and understanding. Rather than overlook the fixed positions of age, gender, nationality, class, or race, researchers need to reflect on these influences and include their reflections in their fieldnotes.

Our word *fixed* is problematic; nothing is truly "fixed." Sometimes fixed factors are subjected to change during the research process, and then that, too, demands the researcher's attention. If, for example, a male researcher looking at the play behaviors of preschool children becomes the father of a girl during his study, he may find himself looking at his field site data not only through his own eyes but also through those of his infant daughter. If what originally seemed a fixed influence in the researcher's position becomes more fluid, then that process of changed perspectives would become part of the researcher's data.

SUBJECTIVE POSITIONS

Subjective positions such as life history and personal experiences may also affect your research.

In Chapter 1, Renato Rosaldo's wife's death altered his perspective toward studying another culture. As he began to understand his grief and rage, he relied on his subjective feelings to understand the Ilongots. Living through a flood, an earthquake, or a hurricane may change your stance toward the world around you. But it does not take disaster, death, divorce, or illness to alter our perspective. Someone who grew up in a large extended or blended family will see the eating, sleeping, and conversation patterns of groups differently than someone from a small nuclear family. What seems to be a crowded room in a small household is not a crowded room in a home with extended family. Many people who grew up in large families confess that they learned to eat quickly at family meals because they wanted to get their fair share before the food disappeared. During their thirty-year marriage, Bonnie's husband, Drew, an electronics engineer with a history of "do-it-yourself" repairs, insisted on fixing their own appliances. For four years they lived with two jury-rigged interconnected TV sets—one for the picture and one for sound. Bonnie saw them both as broken, and Drew saw them both as usable. The children just watched the two sets.

TEXTUAL POSITIONS

Textual positions, the language choices you make to represent what you see, affect the writing of fieldnotes as well as the final ethnographic report. The way that you position yourself in the field with respect to the people you study—how close or how far away you focus your research lens—determines the kind of data you'll gather, the voice you'll create in your finished text, and to some extent your credibility as a researcher.

We assume, for example, that when Reema's boy gave the residents of Willow Springs his final field study, it was so distant and impersonal that they could not recognize themselves in the text. Positioning is a reflexive process. Through the "other," you look at yourself looking at your research. We caution you against standing back too far, as Reema's boy did, when you observe, participate, and record your experiences in your field site. Thinking about your positions makes you conscious of the ways you come to know *the way you know*.

BOX 5
POSITIONING YOURSELF

We urge you to uncover the assumptions, preconceptions, personal experiences, and feelings that influence you as a fieldworker by writing about them throughout your research process. When you enter a site prepared to "read" a culture, you learn to be conscious of your positioning as a researcher. Consider a site you might choose to research: a tattoo parlor, the lobby of a nursing home, a group of local musicians in a community theater production, a convenience store, a fingernail salon, a group of pheasant hunters, workers on break, an airport check-in desk. What are your reasons for choosing it? Which of your own fixed positions may affect what you see in that site? What subjective positions do you carry into your site? Write a short commentary describing how your positions might affect what you'll see in your field site. Writing short commentaries regularly will help you understand how these three positions affect your continuing research process.

Response

Rick Zollo, who wrote the ethnographic study in Chapter 1, "Friday Night at Iowa 80," wrote a personal commentary called "My Gig at the Truck Stop" while he was conducting his research. In this excerpt from his commentary, he discusses how his previous experience as a hippie and his own preconceptions about truck drivers initially affected his position as a researcher at Iowa 80. He is honest as he discovers his own subjective position, the baggage he carries into the research site from his past experiences. Writing short commentaries while he conducted his study enabled Rick to prepare for and think about the textual position he would take in his final study, which was one in which he kept himself very visible as the researcher guiding his reader throughout the text. In this early commentary, Rick writes:

> For many years, I enjoyed hitchhiking as a way to travel. Cheap and purposeful, it allowed me to wander when occasion arose, in a manner suiting my personality and economic means. These days it is no longer safe to hitchhike, and I lament this loss of engaged traveling, for every journey was an adventure and every ride was an existential meeting with new souls.
>
> During my so-called hippie days (I preferred to call myself a "freak"), I found a great unfriendliness toward me and people like me from the truck-driving community. Truckers would rarely pick up a long-haired hitchhiker, and whenever they did, it was usually because it was late at night and the

truck was without a C.B. radio or perhaps because the driver had a weirder personality than what hippie personalities were thought to be.

Visits to truck stops were always accompanied by a chill emanating from those so-called cowboys of the highway. I can remember vividly spending the greater part of one night—three hours at an Indiana interstate truckstop—begging truckers for a ride, their derision burning fires of indignation into my soul.

. . . Thus I had misgivings as I prepared to follow this truck stop gig along the line of a standard story: rising action, climax, falling action, and denouement. The trucking industry has undergone many changes since my last hitchhiking adventures. The redneck-versus-hippie tension has dissipated, as many of those truckers now wear ponytails and have pierced ears, the two classes of outlaws merging and mingling in the various contact zones of this great boiling pot of America.

Observing: "Look at Your Fish"

Reema's boy, the novice fieldworker, did not know how to listen, nor did he know how to look. He relied on a tape recorder instead of his own firsthand observations. Most of us need to train ourselves to become better observers of our surroundings by exercising our vision along with expanding other senses. In her book *A Natural History of the Senses*, Diane Ackerman writes that "seventy percent of the body's sense receptors cluster in the eyes, and it is mainly through seeing the world that we appraise and understand it" (230). Of course, seeing can also be deceptive; we can become overreliant on what we think we see, screening the world through predetermined filters.

Ethnographic fieldworkers teach themselves to see in new ways. They test what they think they see against their preconceptions and assumptions. Anthropologist Paul Stoller suggests that our experiences affect what we see and how we think. A good example of this happened when the two of us rented a house in Maine to work on this book and searched for the mailbox that the owner said was attached to the garage. Elizabeth returned empty-handed from her first mail run and reported to Bonnie that the only nearby box read "169." When we complained to the owner, she laughed and said, "Oh, that really means 199. The nine turned upside down into a six, and we never fixed it." "How very Maine," we both thought, as we reprimanded ourselves for not reading these numbers with the same "gaze" that the mail carrier, the owner, and perhaps all "Downeasterners" do.

Like student Samuel Scudder in the following reading, "Look at Your Fish," you may look and see nothing at first in your field site. But as art historian John Berger writes, "We only see what we look at. To look is an act of choice" (8). In your first trip to the field, details might seem so familiar that you do not lift your pencil to record a single thing. You don't record sounds or smells or textures; you passively wait. You're frustrated. You decide to change field sites. You have not yet learned to look. Seeing—establishing a gaze—requires receptivity, patience, and a willingness to penetrate the outer layer of things. In this short essay, Scudder, who aspired to study entomology (insects) in the nineteenth century, first learns to observe from his Harvard professor, Louis Agassiz, whose lessons in natural science are legendary.

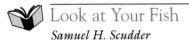

Look at Your Fish
Samuel H. Scudder

Samuel H. Scudder (1837–1911), a naturalist who specialized in the study of insects, wrote this amusing account for a Boston literary journal in 1873. He tells of enrolling at Harvard's Lawrence Scientific School and of his first lesson under the inspired teacher and popularizer of science, Louis Agassiz (1807–1873), then professor of natural history. After hours of detailed but unpatterned observation, Scudder let his problem incubate during an evening away from the laboratory.

It was more than fifteen years ago that I entered the laboratory of Professor Agassiz, and told him I had enrolled my name in the Scientific School as a student of natural history. He asked me a few questions about my object in coming, my antecedents generally, the mode in which I afterwards proposed to use the knowledge I might acquire, and, finally, whether I wished to study any special branch. To the latter I replied that, while I wished to be well grounded in all departments of zoology, I purposed to devote myself especially to insects.

"When do you wish to begin?" he asked.

"Now," I replied.

This seemed to please him, and with an energetic "Very well!" he reached from a shelf a huge jar of specimens in yellow alcohol. "Take this fish," he said, "and look at it; we call it a haemulon; by and by I will ask what you have seen."

With that he left me, but in a moment returned with explicit instructions as to the care of the object entrusted to me.

"No man is fit to be a naturalist," said he, "who does not know how to take care of specimens."

I was to keep the fish before me in a tin tray, and occasionally moisten the surface with alcohol from the jar, always taking care to replace the stopper tightly. Those were not the days of ground-glass stoppers and elegantly shaped exhibition jars; all the old students will recall the huge neckless glass bottles with their leaky, wax-besmeared corks, half eaten by insects, and begrimed with cellar dust. Entomology was a cleaner science than ichthyology, but the example of the Professor, who had unhesitatingly plunged to the bottom of the jar to produce the fish, was infectious; and though this alcohol had a "very ancient and fishlike smell," I really dared not show any aversion within these sacred precincts, and treated the alcohol as though it were pure water. Still I was conscious of a passing feeling of disappointment, for gazing at a fish did not commend itself to an ardent entomologist. My friends at home, too, were annoyed when they discovered that no amount of eau-de-Cologne would drown the perfume which haunted me like a shadow.

In ten minutes I had seen all that could be seen in that fish, and started in search of the Professor—who had, however, left the Museum; and when I returned, after lingering over some of the odd animals stored in the upper apartment, my specimen was dry all over. I dashed the fluid over the fish as if to resuscitate the beast from a fainting fit, and looked with anxiety for a return of the normal sloppy appearance. This little excitement over, nothing was to be done but to return to a steadfast gaze at my mute companion. Half an hour passed—an hour—another hour; the fish began to look loathsome. I turned it over and around; looked it in the face—ghastly; from behind, beneath, above, sideways, at a three-quarters' view—just as ghastly. I was in despair; at an early hour I concluded that lunch was necessary; so, with infinite relief, the fish was carefully replaced in the jar, and for an hour I was free.

On my return, I learned that Professor Agassiz had been at the Museum, but had gone, and would not return for several hours. My fellow-students were too busy to be disturbed by continued conversation. Slowly I drew forth that hideous fish, and with a feeling of desperation again looked at it. I might not use a magnifying-glass; instruments of all kinds were interdicted. My two hands, my two eyes, and the fish: it seemed a most limited field. I pushed my finger down its throat to feel how sharp the teeth were. I began to count the scales in the different rows, until I was convinced that that was nonsense. At last a happy thought struck me—I would draw the fish; and now with surprise I began to discover new features in the creature. Just then the Professor returned.

"That is right," said he; "a pencil is one of the best of eyes. I am glad to notice, too, that you keep your specimen wet, and your bottle corked."

With these encouraging words, he added:

"Well, what is it like?"

He listened attentively to my brief rehearsal of the structure of parts whose names were still unknown to me: the fringed gill-arches and movable operculum; the pores of the head, fleshy lips and lidless eyes; the lateral line, the spinous fins and forked tail; the compressed and arched body. When I finished, he waited as if expecting more, and then, with an air of disappointment:

"You have not looked very carefully; why," he continued more earnestly, "you haven't even seen one of the most conspicuous features of the animal, which is as plainly before your eyes as the fish itself; look again, look again!" and he left me to my misery.

I was piqued; I was mortified. Still more of that wretched fish! But now I set myself to my task with a will, and discovered one new thing after another, until I saw how just the Professor's criticism had been. The afternoon passed quickly; and when, towards its close, the Professor inquired:

"Do you see it yet?"

"No," I replied, "I am certain I do not, but I see how little I saw before."

"That is next best," said he, earnestly. "But I won't hear you now; put away your fish and go home; perhaps you will be ready with a better answer in the morning. I will examine you before you look at the fish."

This was disconcerting. Not only must I think of my fish all night, studying, without the object before me, what this unknown but most visible feature might be; but also, without reviewing my discoveries, I must give an exact account of them the next day. I had a bad memory; so I walked home by the Charles River in a distracted state, with my two perplexities.

The cordial greeting from the Professor the next morning was reassuring; here was a man who seemed to be quite as anxious as I that I should see for myself what he saw.

"Do you perhaps mean," I asked, "that the fish has symmetrical sides with paired organs?"

His thoroughly pleased "Of course! Of course!" repaid the wakeful hours of the previous night. After he had discoursed most happily and enthusiastically—as he always did—upon the importance of this point, I ventured to ask what I should do next.

"Oh, look at your fish!" he said, and left me again to my own devices. In a little more than an hour he returned, and heard my new catalogue.

"That is good, that is good!" he repeated; "but that is not all; go on"; and so for three long days he placed that fish before my eyes, forbidding me to look at anything else, or to use any artificial aid. "Look, look, look," was his repeated injunction.

This was the best entomological lesson I ever had—a lesson whose influence has extended to the details of every subsequent study; a legacy the Professor had left to me, as he has left it to many others, of inestimable value, which we could not buy, with which we cannot part.

A year afterward, some of us were amusing ourselves with chalking out-landish beasts on the Museum blackboard. We drew prancing starfishes; frogs in mortal combat; hydra-headed worms; stately crawfishes, standing on their tails, bearing aloft umbrellas; and grotesque fishes with gaping mouths and staring eyes. The Professor came in shortly after, and was as amused as any at our experiments. He looked at the fishes.

"Haemulons, every one of them," he said; "Mr.———drew them."

True; and to this day, if I attempt a fish, I can draw nothing but haemulons.

The fourth day, a second fish of the same group was placed beside the first, and I was bidden to point out the resemblances and differences between the two; another and another followed, until the entire family lay before me, and a whole legion of jars covered the table and surrounding shelves; the odor had become a pleasant perfume; and even now, the sight of an old, six-inch, worm-eaten cork brings fragrant memories.

The whole group of haemulons was thus brought in review; and, whether engaged upon the dissection of the internal organs, the preparation and examination of the bony framework, or the description of the various parts, Agassiz's training in the method of observing facts and their orderly arrangement was ever accompanied by the urgent exhortation not to be content with them.

"Facts are stupid things," he would say, "until brought into connection with some general law."

At the end of eight months, it was almost with reluctance that I left these friends and turned to insects; but what I had gained by this outside experience has been of greater value than years of later investigation in my favorite groups.

Scudder's observational training comes from Agassiz, a natural scientist, but it is equally important for the social scientist. Both researchers learn to gaze beyond the obvious, to look and then to look again. Scudder used many of the same skills that ethnographic researchers rely on—drawing pictures, asking focused questions, and "sleeping on the data."

The fieldworker can model Scudder's experience by looking at something unfamiliar, too. With time, knowledge, and familiarity, the fieldworker's boredom will turn to interest. With constant practice and attention, almost any field site and the people in it become fascinating. Scudder faced one of the most humbling experiences a fieldworker can have—to discover how little he actually saw after looking long and hard. Scudder also realized that the mere recording of data—"facts are stupid things"—is not important unless you connect it with some larger idea. Before you undertake fieldwork in your chosen site, it is good practice to observe an everyday object or event to consider its significance.

Here's what we've imagined Scudder might have written in his hours with the fish:

RECORD	RESPOND
First Ten Minutes	does yellow alcohol indicate old?
jar—yellow alcohol	is that its classification? phylum?
called a "haemulon"	kingdom? species?
"keep fish moistened?"	why keep it wet if it's dead?
Next 2 1/2 Hours	will it crumble? dry out? is it old?
dries after ten minutes	how much alcohol can a fish absorb?
all views the same (5 views:	why does it look ghastly from all
under, over, side, 3/4, behind)	positions, perspectives?
throat—teeth sharp	must eat hard things—shells, fish skin?
scales in rows	possible symmetry?
(sketch)	fish looks like a fish, but more
	complicated than at first

BOX 6
DOUBLE-ENTRY OBSERVATION

Select an ordinary object or event in nature to observe every day for a week. Record field-notes in double-entry format, using the left side of a page to list the specific details of the changes and the right side to reflect on the meaning of these changes. Your subject could be a fruit or vegetable, the moon or stars, or birds visiting your feeder. Your subject must be one that can alter within a week's time. At the end of the week, write a short reflection on what you learned by keeping these fieldnotes. Discuss what surprised you most and what you would do differently if you were to continue with this observation. How might you connect what you have seen with an overall hypothesis?

Response

Donna Niday observed one piece of bread exposed to the air for one week. These are her recorded notes and her reflective responses.

OBSERVATION OF ONE PIECE OF BREAD EXPOSED TO THE AIR FOR ONE WEEK

RECORD

1/7—Tues.
whole wheat—tan colored with flecks
  of darker brown
soft—indented impression made when
  pressed with thumb

no smell
4 x 4 1/2"

1/8—Wed.
no longer leaves an impression
  when pressed with thumb
drying is noticeable—feels tougher
softer in middle than edges
color doesn't change
when dropped, it thuds

1/9—Thurs.
left lower corner started to rise
looks shriveled and shrunk
very hard
when dropped, it bounces

1/10—Fri.
feels crunchy to touch
size looks more shrunken
brown crusts borders bread—
starting to curl

RESPOND

Prediction: Bread will become moldy.
Biblical: bread of life, communion,
  miracle of loaves and fishes
That's soft! Good for peanut
  butter, jelly, tuna fish, chicken
  salad, BLT, etc.
One food that doesn't smell!
It's like a square picture
  framed by crust.

Appropriate consistency for toasted
  cheese sandwich or French toast
Phrase: bread winner, "putting bread
on the table," bread as a staple
Why not?
A new toy!

Why the left lower corner first?
Reminds me of turkey stuffing
Types of bread—rye, whole wheat,
  tomato—cheese, pumpernickel, sour—
  dough, French bread, Italian
  bread, etc.
Other varieties—muffins, dinner rolls—
  bounce like baseballs

Looks like croutons
Realize to be moldy, needs moisture
  (inside a sealed plastic bag)
Think of bread's origins—wheat fields
  with wheat stalks waving in the wind
Imagine making bread—flour on fingers,
  sticky, gummy mixture of dough,
  rolling dough, forming balls, setting
  in pan
Bread shrinking makes me visualize
  the opposite—bread rising, expanding
  from yeast

(continued)

1/11—Sat.
has shrunk more
bottom half curling
in bottom half brown flecks in
 bread have gotten closer

Like European hard breads
Reminds me of science experiments—
 watching a corn seed germinate
Realize I should have placed the
 bread inside a baggie to obtain
 mold (would have been more fun
 to watch)

1/12—Sun.
now measures 3 1/4" x3 1/2"
all edges of bread are curling upward
feels solid
all bread flecks have gotten closer

Wow! I didn't think it would shrink
that much!
Think about how for bread to grow
mold, it needs other ingredients
such as moisture. For children's
language to grow, they need the
ingredients of role models and
encouragement or their minds may
shrink.

Since I don't often leave bread exposed to air, I hadn't really thought
about the factors in changing its appearance and structure. In fact,
I recalled throwing away moldy bread, so I created the hypothesis
that the bread would start to grow mold and that it would be fun to
observe the blue and green mold as it formed. However, the bread only
became harder and began to shrivel. I was surprised that the bread
shrank by 3/4 x 1".
I was also surprised by the many associations connected with bread. I
considered biblical references, common phrases, and a variety of uses.
As the days progressed, I considered bread in other contexts, such as
inside a toaster or inside a turkey. Overall, I continued to observe
the surface physical features while analyzing its possible contexts,
associations, and symbols.

Negotiating: The Ethics of Entry

When you enter a field site and make yourself known, you must follow many cour-
tesies to make yourself and the people you're observing feel comfortable. As a beginning researcher, don't enter a site where you feel at risk in the subculture. For the
kinds of projects this book suggests, you will not have adequate time to gain entry
or insider status in an intimidating group. One of our students, for example, wanted
to research a group of campus skinheads. They permitted Jake to hang out on the
edges of their subculture, even allowing him to read their "code of honor," which
included these statements:

- Be discreet about new recruits; check them out thoroughly.
- For prospects, we must have at least a ninety-day contact period in which we
can attest to your character. A probationary period and productivity report will
be given.

- Outsiders need no knowledge of what goes on or is said in our meetings
- No racial exceptions whatsoever! All members must be 100% white!

Early on, he began to realize that his research position was unworkable, that he was stuck. While the skinheads had let him into their subculture as a potential recruit, he could never fully enter their subculture or worldview. Their code of honor, which excluded minority groups, stood against his personal ethics. In an early portfolio reflection, Jake wrote, "I never hung out with them in public. I never went to an organizational meeting. I realized I was an outsider to this subculture."

Jake's negotiation experience was so dramatic that he was unable to gain full access, and so he was unable to collect the data he wanted. No matter how interested in and enthusiastic we are about a possible field site, we must be conscious of our own comfort levels and even potential dangers in investigating certain groups or places.

Harvey, another of our students, experienced difficulty negotiating entry due mainly to his own assumptions that it would be easy. He is a Native American, a Sioux, who wanted to research a gambling casino on another tribe's reservation. Because of his heritage, he assumed that he would be welcomed. But he wasn't. He had enormous difficulty finding people who were willing to talk to him, and he never really knew whether it was because of his Sioux background or because he was perceived as a student. Eventually, he had a conversation with the woman who ran the gift shop at the casino, and she introduced him to others. As his informant, she helped him gain an insider status in a place where he had assumed he already had it.

Any field site you enter requires that you be conscious of your own personal assumptions and how they reflect your ethics, but you must also be respectful of the people whose lives you are watching. All places in which you are a participant-observer involve an official process for "negotiating entry." And it is common courtesy for researchers to acknowledge time spent with informants with gestures as small as writing thank-you notes or as large as exchanging time (tutoring or babysitting, for example), or obtaining grant-funded stipends to pay them. As you work your way through this process, be sure to:

- Explain your project clearly to the people you will study, and obtain the requisite permissions from those in charge.
- Let your informants understand what part of the study you'll share with them.
- Think about what you can give back to the field site in exchange for your time there.

Some sites may require official documentation, as in the case two of our students who collaborated on a study of a day-care center. The center required them to have an interview, submit a proposal describing their project, and sign a document attesting that they had reviewed all of the center's rules and procedures. In other sites, when you think entry will be simple, it might be laborious. For this reason, it's important not to wait too long to make yourself visible to the insiders you study.

One student we worked with spent over a month in the field observing a Disney store. When she attempted to get official permission to write about this store, however, she was denied entry and could not continue her project.

Once you finalize your site, you might want to check with your instructor to find out your university's policy with respect to research on human subjects. For long-term projects, the human subjects review board usually requires that you file a proposal and submit permission forms from your informants. They are called "informed consent forms," and we present a sample of one of our own forms as a model. Universities usually have less formal procedures for the kind of short-term fieldwork that you might do for a one-semester course, and often there are no requirements for filing permissions. Fieldworkers, no matter what size their projects, are ethically responsible for accurately showing the voices of their informants on the page. We feel strongly that you should receive permission from all the informants whose work you tape as well as any official person at your field site, such as the manager in the following example.

Karen Downing, a high school teacher, chose to research "Photo Phantasies," a beauty photography studio at a suburban shopping mall. Her full-length study appears in Chapter 3, but in this section of her final project, she discusses the difficulties she encountered with the managers of the studio while she attempted to negotiate entry. Karen opens this section of her paper by narrating a telephone call she made to Photo Phantasies:

> "Hello, this is Photo Phantasies. My name is Mindy. Today's a great day." I am not calling Photo Phantasies to inquire about specials. I am not calling because I want to know if they have any free time today for a last-minute appointment. I am not calling to see if a $220 package of photographs has arrived. I am calling to speak to Ginny James, the manager. When I make this request and tell Mindy who I am, she says, "Oh. Hang on a sec," in a voice without intonation. Her hand covers the receiver, muffling sounds.
>
> When I talk with Ginny, I will not say that I have an aversion to her store and the whole Photo Phantasies concept. I will tell her I am fascinated by the photographs my high school students, always female, bring to school to show off. I will present myself as curious.
>
> "This is Ginny James. It's a great day! What can I do for you?" Her voice rises at the end of the question.
>
> I tell Ginny my name and ask her if she has received the letter I sent four days ago requesting to visit her store.
>
> "Letter? What letter are you referring to?"
>
> I am caught off guard by her response and feel slightly uneasy. I take a deep breath before explaining my "research project."
>
> Silence. And more silence. Finally, this from Ginny: "I'll need this in writing. Call me back after 11:30. That's when the mail comes. If there's no letter, you'll need to provide adequate documentation. You'll

Mary Smith

Dormitory Hall, State University, State
phone number

Date

I give my permission to Mary Smith to use my written and spoken words in her
research project written for "Advanced Composition/English 162" at State University. I
understand that I may read and approve the final draft of the material she uses about me in her
project.

Signature   _____

Address   _____

Phone number   _____

I prefer to use this pseudonym:

Informed consent form.

have to deliver it in person." Despite the mall noise in the background, I
sense immediately that Ginny is guarded with me. Her changed tone
results in sentences with periods, no longer exclamation points. I wait
until 12:30 and try again.

"Hello, this is Photo Phantasies. My name is Stacey! It's a great
day and we're searching for models! How may I help you?"

When I finally talk with Ginny during this second phone call, she
leaves out the conversational niceties. Yes, my letter had arrived in the

mail after all. "I'll have to clear this request with headquarters, which I can do tomorrow. I'm leaving for a Photo Phantasies meeting in Chicago. What kind of class is this for? Business? Sociology? I'll call you Wednesday night and leave a message about whether or not it's OK."

Wednesday night, no reply.

Friday morning, no reply.

My third call to Photo Phantasies is on Friday afternoon. "Hello, this is Photo Phantasies. My name is Ginny! Ask me about our model search! How may I help you?"

"Ginny, this is Karen Downing. You may help me by telling me that headquarters granted me permission to spend some time in your store." I try to be personable and charming.

"Karen Downing?"

"Yes, the one that sent the letter about doing research for . . ."

"Oh. Right. Well. Yes. You can come to the store, but I don't want an extra body around when customers are here. You could come to an in-store training session from 5:30 to 6:30 on Sunday night. And I have some material about Photo Phantasies that you could read."

"Huh. Well . . . huh. Ummm . . . when could I come out to pick up the material?"

"Saturdays are nuts. Sunday's the meeting day. Monday's my paper day . . . and I'm still catching up from Chicago . . ." She trails off into a sigh.

"How about today? This afternoon?"

"Fine." Click. When she hangs up, I realize that in three phone calls, I have never heard the official Photo Phantasies telephone goodbye.

I leave the house to go to the mall at 11:30, even though I know that, technically, it's not yet afternoon. But I have work to do in the afternoon and would rather not face more traffic and a busier mall. Before I leave, I think about what I am wearing. My standard look—black turtleneck and brown jeans, minimal gold jewelry, lipstick, powder, blush and eyeliner, curly and full hair tucked behind my right ear. I decide not to do anything differently to my appearance for this particular errand, but I am aware that I am thinking about how I look a lot more than I normally would. I hear the words of my mother, words I have grown up with: "You need more blush! And remember the lipstick! Without it, you don't look alive!" Today, I follow her advice, advice I usually ignore, and add just a bit more makeup to be sure it's noticeable.

Not only was Karen concerned about her attitude about Photo Phantasies; she was also concerned with how she presented herself. She thought about makeup more than usual because she wanted to fit into the culture she was seeking to enter. Her fieldnotes began long before she actually walked into the studio. She recorded her phone conversations, her impressions of how she was being interpreted by those she sought to interview, and her previous knowledge of the photos of her high school students. Karen was careful to monitor her feelings and her assumptions as she moved into her field site. She wrote, "I have an aversion to her store and the whole Photo Phantasies concept." She recorded feeling "caught off guard" and "slightly uneasy." She noted sarcastically that in three phone calls she never heard "the official Photo Phantasies telephone goodbye." She worries about makeup and thinks about her outfit, her jewelry, and her mother's advice. As an outsider stepping into a world in which she feels uncomfortable but to which she is nevertheless drawn, she is careful to be, in her own words, "personable and charming." But at the same time, she is honest about her own assumptions and attitudes toward Photo Phantasies and records these fieldnotes in a reflexive way. After negotiating with her subjective feelings and with her potential informants, she was ready to enter the studio.

Describing: Taking Fieldnotes

When you first enter your field site, sensory impressions surround you. You feel as if you'll never get them all down. One of our students tried to describe a band's outdoor concert in a New England harbor town, but there was so much to notice. Should she listen to the sounds of the band she came to hear? Try to eavesdrop on people's conversations about the band as they sat on their blankets? Describe the foghorn in the background? The drawbridge siren? Or should she focus on the outdoor smells? The flowers in the formal gardens surrounding the park? Hot dogs? Popcorn? Gyros? Calzones? Or the fishy harbor air? Her "gaze" expanded as she took more notes. The more she looked, the more she saw. She noted everything in order to capture the feeling of being at the harbor concert, even though she knew her research focus was the band itself, which had been playing together for 20 years.

To become a good fieldworker, you must observe closely and participate intimately, returning to your field site and informants again and again. And still again. As you take fieldnotes, you become better at appreciating what you initially took for granted. You start to gather a thick collection of notes, which will serve as a body of data. Later, you'll turn these notes into descriptions of your field site and your informants. You will take far more fieldnotes than you will ever use in your final description. It is common knowledge that professional writers publish only a fifth of the writing they do, and movies use only about a tenth of the footage they shoot. A few focused hours with a notebook, a pencil, and receptive senses will help you practice capturing good descriptive details. But for your final project, you'll need to plan many visits at different times to gather details, data, and materials before your writing begins.

Fieldworkers take notes in a variety of ways. Some find double-entry fieldnotes useful because they capture specifics as well as the researcher's reactions. Like Donna Niday's observation of the decaying bread, the left-hand column records observable facts and details in the field site, and the right-hand column monitors Donna's subjective, reflexive responses to those facts and details. On page 72 is a sample from Karen Downing's fieldnotes, taken in a stenographer's notebook, from Friday, April 7, at 11:45 a.m. In these notes, the manager claimed she was too busy to talk with Karen, rebuffed her, and asked her to return in the afternoon. At 1:30, Karen

fluffy boas—blue, pink

girl wants to be a psych major wanna be

peppermint candles

photos on calendars

track lighting, round

dressing room bulbs

curling irons, blow dr...

mousse, static guard

dressing rooms w/wh...

when I'm an old w...

setting goals 38 fo... 6 for

390 PP studios –

always in malls

main goals – retail.

product. Good work

People paid on ince...

Build self-esteem...

Team.   Manager

Coach, cheerleader,

Training camp – rew...

do make up, take p...

stresses, personal ch...

mall

the model wanna be
Hidden

very movie staresque
no mens' clothes
very feminine

Friday, April 6 1:30 in the store

women } giant pics of "wall of Fame"

couples }
     in separate room

fancy jackets—styds, gold, stars n' stripes

sequins, beaded corset things-stuffy old

never buy, hats, wardrobe racks

two video screens w/photo images

          sit on stool
          w/salesperson

Glamour, Elle, Mirabella on rack

pop music fairly lous. Not the radio though.

gray carpet w/muted pink

white walls

black modern furniture

notebook of thank you notes

sign "professional make-up artists"

large photos that look like movie reel

girl comes in to inquire about modeling

special: do you do it now?

      Not really.

    You have a really nice forehead.

    The competition – people are really

    excited about it. You could be a

    print model, runway model.

last apt. at 7:00

caramel corn smells

mall noise – footsteps on tile, children

crying of baby in mall

They look pretty darn good-are these
pics taken in this store?

Cheesey clothes! who picks these out?

where do they get it?

People probably want
to play dress up.

very clearly for women

age range 16-30ish

looks like a normal salon

! I need to read these.

how can we be sure?

"wall of Fame"

attractive, big eyes, dark hair, Italian
probably about 20.

Karen's fieldnotes.

returned to the store and took seven pages of fieldnotes on what she saw when she actually gained entry to Photo Phantasies for the first time. Page 72 shows two excerpts from these two visits on the same day.

Karen's fieldnotes show that she interpreted the right column later on after noting the details she saw. She lists, for example, the clothes in the left column: "fancy jackets with studs, gold stars and stripes, sequins, beaded corset thing, stuff you'd never buy, hats," and then in her reflection she asks, "Who picks these clothes out?" "Where do they get them?" And she begins to interpret, too: "People probably want to play dress-up." With this insight in her notes, Karen begins building a theory about why people are attracted to Photo Phantasies, a theory that she will need to test out through her entire research process. The interviews with staff and customers, collected artifacts like publicity brochures, and firsthand observations will furnish the data she'll need to confirm (or disconfirm) her initial thinking.

Like Karen, you should develop a personal, systematic way of taking fieldnotes. Your system should allow enough room to record details at the site, but it should also allow space to expand your initial impressions away from the site. Some people like to use spiral notebooks, some use three-ring binder paper, some use papers to be filed in folders, and some use laptop computers, keeping a separate file for each visit. Fieldnotes are your evidence for confirming theories you make about the observations you record. They are the permanent record of your fieldworking process, and they become part of your research portfolio. Without accurate fieldnotes, you have no project. Although each fieldworker develops his or her own system, any set of fieldnotes needs to include all of the following details:

- Date, time, and place of observation ("Friday, April 6, 11:45 in the store")
- Specific facts, numbers, details ("last appointment at 7 p.m.," "3 customers present," "sign: 'professional makeup artist' ")
- Sensory impressions: sights, sounds, textures, smells, tastes ("caramel corn smells, mall noise—footsteps on tile, children crying, pop music playing fairly loud, gray carpet with muted pink, white wails, black modern furniture, notebook of thank-you notes")
- Personal responses to the act of recording fieldnotes and how others watch you as you watch them ("giant pictures of Phantasy Phaces. They look pretty darn good—are these pics taken in this store?")
- Specific words, phrases, summaries of conversations, and insider language ("girl inquires about modeling special. Asks, 'Do you do it now?' Response: 'Not really, but you really have a nice forehead. You could be a runway model.' ")
- Questions about people or behaviors at the site for future investigation ("dressing rooms are small—they don't want you there for long")
- Continuous page-numbering system for future reference ("4/4 studio visit, page 5")

Rick Zollo's fieldnotes from his Iowa 80 project take the form of a narrative journal. Rick kept his truck stop journal in a spiral notebook and then expanded his notes into a computer journal that is 54 pages long. Here is one page from the journal, dated Friday, October 1, 11 a.m. Notice that in these expanded fieldnotes, he not only records but also reflects on what he's seen. We've italicized the reflective sections of his notes, in which he thinks about what he's observing and hearing.

My next stop is the truck wash, where lines of trucks wait at each bay. Business is booming on this sunny day, and I want to see how it's done.

Inside, a trucker waits at the counter to talk to a sales rep. The price of a truck wash is $43.95 for tractor and trailer, $26.95 or $24.95 for cab only, depending on the type of cab. The trucker is an old gent, gray hair covered by a black cowboy hat decked with pins and medallions, his rangy arms marked with faded tattoos. He talks over his shoulder to a woman drinking coffee and smoking a cigarette.

"Government pays real good. . . . It's just that you might have to wait six months to be paid." He then goes on to recount a story about a trucker he knows from Texas who's assembled millions in back pay that the government continues to owe in arrears. "He's retired now. Gets a check from the government every month."

The woman seems suitably impressed in her reply, but her tone betrays a bored casualness that hints at possible disbelief.

My notebook is open and I'm writing down information as fast as I can observe it. I'm still nosing around. I'm listening to these guys B.S.ing loudly. They want people to listen to them. I don't want to strictly be with just the colorful characters. I have a weakness for characters. I have to give voice to quiet people. They are the people who do all the work. The loud and noisy people are trying to sell you their con.

Past the office area, into the first bay, watching two workers in rubber boots steam spray both sides of an Atlas Van Line. A third worker stands on a moving platform and scrubs down the top of a cab with a brush broom. Overhead, a steamer runs along track and sprays the truck from above. A young worker in Bay 2 notices me and saunters over to talk.

"On a real good day we have four people to a bay, and we can wash twenty trucks a shift in each bay." Times four bays times three shifts tells me that on an ideal day, this truck-o-mat can clean 240 trucks.

I'm back outside looking at rigs and writing in my notebook when a woman trucker yells out, "Don't write my license plate down in that notebook!"

"I'm not writing down your license plate," I say defensively. "I'm doing research for the University of Iowa on this truck stop."

She looks at me like I'm crazy. She looks like she's interested in me, but she doesn't believe I'm doing a term paper. Truckers have a real "them-us" mentality. To them, I'm a real nerd. I'm driving a "Jap four-wheeler" and walking around with a notebook in my hand. I feel very existential, tentative—have to be circumspect. That sense of the "other." Polite.

Respectful. It's hard to make an introduction at a truck stop.

Few of Rick's notes from this truck-washing scene appear in his final paper, but his reflections become part of the theories about truckers that guide him throughout the project. As he began to see truckers as cowboys and outlaws, Rick sought to confirm (and disconfirm) this theory with his continued observations and interviews at Iowa 80. With each field visit, whether the specific facts became part of his final project or not, Rick became a sharper observer. He learned who would be a good informant and who wouldn't, and he came to feel more like an insider as he stepped further and further into the truck stop culture.

Professional fieldworkers take their notes, too, in a variety of ways, using codes and systems they've developed themselves. Here we present two samples of anthropologists' fieldnotes to give you further ideas.

ROGER SANJEK'S FIELDNOTES
*7 May 1988—Carmela George's Cleanup Day**

    Milagros and I arrived at 10 am, as Carmela told me, but 97th Street, the deadend, was already cleaned out, and the large garbage pickup truck, with rotating blades that crushed everything, was in the middle of 97th Place. I found Carmela, and met Phil Pirozzi of Sanitation, who had three men working on the cleanup, plus the sweeper that arrived a little later. The men and boys on 97th Place helping to load their garbage into the truck included several Guyanese Indians in their 20s, whom Carmela said have been here 2–3 years ['They're good.']; several families of Hispanics, and Korean and Chinese. They were loading TV sets, shopping carts, wood, old furniture, tree branches and pruning, and bags and boxes of garbage. Most houses had large piles of stuff in front, waiting for the truck. The little boys hanging on and helping were Hispanic, except for one Chinese. They spoke a mixture of Spanish and English together, when painting the LIRR walls.

    Carmela had put flyers at every house on Wednesday, and Police 'No Parkin Saturday' signs [D] were up on the telephone poles. A few cars were parked at the curb, but most of the curbside on the three blocks was empty so the sweeper could clean the gutters.

    The sweeper this year was smaller than the one in 1986, and there was no spraying of the streets, only sweeping the gutters. As before, people swept their curbs, and in some cases driveways, into the gutter. Carmela was a whirlwind. She asked her elderly Italian neighbor Jenny, who did not come out, if she could sweep the sand pile near Jenny's house in their common driveway. Jenny said don't bother, but Carmela did it anyway. She was running all around with plastic garbage bags, getting kids to help paint off the grafitti on the LIRR panels she had painted in the past, and commandeering women to clean out the grassy area near

---

*A page from Roger Sanjek's 1988 Elmhurst-Corona, Queens, New York, fieldnotes, printed from a computer word-processing program. (Size: 8.5 by 11 inches.)

the LIRR bridge at 45th Ave and National Street. She got a Colombian woman from 97th Place, and gave her a rake and plastic bag. She then rang the door bell across from the grassy area, behind the bodega, and an Indian-looking Hispanic woman came down, and later did the work with the Colombian woman.

Mareya Banks was out, in smock, helping organize and supervising the kids doing the LIRR wall painting. Milagros helped with this, and set up an interview appointment with Mareya. She also met a Bolivian woman, talking with Mareya, and sweeping her sidewalk on 45th Avenue.

Carmela also had potato chips and Pepsi for the kids, which the Colombian woman gave out to them, and OTB T-shirts.

Phil said this was the only such clean up in CB4. A man in Elmhurst does something like this, but just for his one block. The Dept. likes this, and hopes the spirit will be contagious. We like anything that gets the community involved. He said it began here because the new people didn't understand how to keep the area a nice place to live. Carmela went to them, and now they are involved.

Margery Wolf's Fieldnotes
March 5, 1960*
Present: 153 (F 54), 154 (F 31), 254 (F 53), 189 (F 50), 230 (F 17)

Yesterday 48 (F 30) was taken by her husband to a mental hospital in Tapu. 48I (F 12) told Wu Chieh that the woman ran out into the field, and her husband had to come to pick her up and take her to the hospital. The women were talking about this today and said that she was sent to a big mental hospital, and that her husband went there to see her but was not allowed to see her because she was tied up. The doctor said there was nothing else he could do with her. Someone told Wu Chieh that something like this had happened to 48 once before, but she was not hospitalized then. The women say that her illness this time came about as the result of her worrying about losing NTS90. She couldn't find the money and asked 49 (her seven-year-old son) about it, and he told her that his father took it to gamble. Her husband said that this was not true. They said that she may have known that she was going to get sick, because the day before she took her baby (3 months) over to her sister's house and asked her to take care of the baby. They said that 47 (her 32-year-old husband) was very dumb. If he knows that his wife has this kind of illness, he should not let her worry. He should have said that he had taken the money even if he didn't. Instead, when she started to get sick, he stood there and told everyone, "She is going to go crazy, she is going to go crazy." The women said that this

_____
*A page from Margery Wolf's fieldnotes taken in Taiwan. Wu Chieh is her informant/assistant, and she assigns numbers to other informants.

is the reason 47 is called "Dumb Tien-lai." 154: "When 492's (F 28) children and 48's children got into a fight and 48 went to talk with 492 about it, 492 scolded 48. She said: 'If children fight and kill each other it serves them right. If your children get killed, then you come and take your children home and bury them. You don't need to come and talk to me about it.' But once when 48's child hit 492's child, 492 went out and said something to 48, and she just said this back to her and then she had nothing to say." (All of the women agreed that 492 had said this to 48.)

Wu Chieh heard that 47 is going to go ask T'ai Tzu Yeh [a god] to help his wife get well. The women also said that when 48 fell into the field, she lay there saying: "Just because of children's things other people bully me, other people bully me just because of children's things. I won't forget this. I won't forget this." The women said that when a person is like this, you shouldn't let them worry and should encourage them to sleep a lot.

B O X 7
REFLECTIVE FIELDNOTES

You may need to spend some time at your field site making yourself feel at ease there before you begin taking notes. Record your experience as you negotiate entry at your site, even if there are no particular problems. Write about how you felt observing others and watching them observe you. Draw a few sketches, or map the space on paper. As you take notes, concentrate on the difference between verifiable information and your subjective responses to that information. Develop a note-taking scheme you'll be able to follow throughout the project. Create a consistent shorthand or code that you understand (spelling shortcuts like thru instead of through or ppl instead of people, for example). Once you have about 10 pages of notes, plan to share them with a partner. Here are some questions you and your partner may consider as you read and respond to one another's fieldnotes:

- Are the notes readable? Are the pages numbered and dated?
- What background material does someone need to understand the history and actual location of this place?
- Does the researcher include information about negotiating entry? About her own positioning? About her subjective feelings as she observes?
- What assumptions of her own does the researcher bring into this field site?
- What other details should she include so that another person could see, hear, and become immersed in the daily routines of this place?
- What details were most interesting? What would you like the researcher to write more about?
- What other data would you need to have in order to confirm some of the researcher's initial interpretations about this place?

Reading an Object: The Cultural Artifact

As you enter the field, you should train yourself to notice material objects—*arti-facts*—that represent the culture of that site. In his journal, Rick Zollo wrote about an "old gent's" black cowboy hat decked with pins and medallions." This artifact eventually connected with Rick's metaphor of the trucker as a cowboy. During his research, he became sensitized to truckers' musical tastes, cravings for home-cooked food, and their ways of passing time at the truck stop. To represent those features of the trucking culture, he collected trucking magazines, tapes and CDs of particular songs, menus from the diner, and pictures of the pinball machines. As he wrote about the truck stop later, he was able to include detailed descriptions of the artifacts he had collected. In his final project, the trucker's logbook became the primary cultural artifact that revealed values about the subculture. The logbook itself encouraged truckers to unveil their attitudes and politics about their jobs and the trucking industry as a whole. Researchers gather artifacts for what they reveal about subcultures. And researchers use artifacts to learn about insiders' perspectives on their subcultures.

Objects, then, are readable texts. As you read an object, your position as researcher affects your reading just as it affects the way you read a field site. You can investigate the surface details of an object, research its history, or learn about people's rules and rituals for using and making the object. Researchers—folklorists and anthropologists—use the term *material culture* to refer to those objects, personal artifacts loaded with meaning and history that people mark as special: tools, musical instruments, foods, toys, jewelry, ceremonial objects, and clothes.

Everyone wears jeans. But not all jeans convey the same cultural meanings. Some mean utility, some fashion, some status. Jeans that have been painted, beaded, patched, stone-washed, bleached, ripped, or tie-dyed by their owner (not purchased that way in a store) can be read as objects that mark the wearer's place in popular culture. But we cannot know the meaning of an object through observation alone because our eyes can deceive us and there are meanings that lie beyond the surface of an object. Japanese collectors, for instance, pay thousands of dollars for old pairs of American denim jeans. To search for the meanings of any cultural artifact, we need to look at the people who create, collect, and use it. The best way to learn about the meaning and value of an artifact is to ask questions about the object and listen carefully.

As you look at the photographs of the baskets on the following page, think about the kinds of questions you might want to ask the owner or the basketmaker. How is it made? How old is it? What is it used for?

On the surface, it is a woven basket with a lid. But the basket holds a coiled history, a collection of stories that belongs to its makers, its sellers, and its owners. The basket itself is an artifact produced by several interconnected cultures. It is made by African-American women on the coast of South Carolina, near the city of Charleston, not far from Gloria Naylor's fictional Willow Springs. The basketmakers use natural materials (coastal sweetgrass, palmetto fronds, and pine needles) found on the southeastern U.S. coast, much like the plants their ancestors knew on the

South Carolina Low Country coil basket. (Photos: Bruce Drummond)

western coast of Africa. These baskets come out of a strong craft tradition of using available materials to make everyday objects. It is a tradition that daughters learn from mothers, who learned it from their mothers, who learned it from their mothers. The basketmaking technique represents a long chain of informal instruction over many generations of craftswomen. And each generation—in fact, each basketmaker herself—adds her own technique and her own circumstances to what she has learned. During their years of American slavery, for example, African-American women modified kitchen implements, such as spoons, to create the tools they needed to continue making baskets according to their traditional designs.

But knowing the history of this craft and even holding the basket in your hand does not speak about the object the way the maker does. When Bonnie interviewed a basketmaker in the Charleston marketplace, a middle-aged woman named Wilma, she learned more than the observable and historical details we described here. Bonnie was already positioned by knowing the history of this craft from reading about the tradition and having heard a folklorist's lecture. So when she visited Charleston, she was eager to find a basketmaker who would talk about her craft. Bonnie wanted to buy one of Wilma's baskets, one with a beautifully tight-fitting top. As they examined it together, Wilma explained the challenge of pulling the fresh sweetgrass, weaving in palmetto fronds, and keeping the pine needles fresh enough to bend. After the basket is finished, Wilma said, it is important to coil it all carefully and work it with an awl-like tool made from a spoon. Bonnie complimented her on the top.

"Oh, I didn't make this," Wilma answered as she stroked the top that fit so well. "My cousin is the only person in the family who can make a tight top. My tops just float around. She's good at making tops. I'm good at selling them." This conversation contained important firsthand information about the stories that lie inside cultural objects. The information from Wilma—about her cousin, the awl-like tool made from a spoon, and the separate roles she and her cousin took—explained that the craft of basketmaking, like much folk art, is a collective endeavor that involves not only a long history of instruction but also a family of craftspeople who establish rules, determine roles, and invent new methods to carry on an old tradition.

Bonnie's subjective positioning from her knowledge of folklore and her history as a basket collector affected the way she "read" Wilma's basket. And Wilma's story of her family's craft unpacked another layer of meaning and cultural knowledge.

When researchers read an artifact, they try to unpack the stories that lie inside it and to understand the interplay between tradition and creativity. Objects carry traditions of form, function, and symbol: how they are made, how they are used, and what they mean to people. But while they carry on a cultural tradition such as making pottery, cooking foods, or working with wood, objects can also show how individuals digress from tradition. Each craftsperson remakes the object in a unique way according to what materials are available, what needs it must serve, and what the craftsperson's artistic sensibility brings to it. Wilma, her cousin, and her great-grandmother each had an opportunity to put their own creative mark on the basket-weaving tradition. They were reproducing an ancestral tradition in their culture, a stable core of purpose and technique. But at the same time, each had an opportunity to remake it as her own.

BOX 8
READING AN ARTIFACT

Try your fieldworker's gaze on an everyday object: a musical instrument, a tool, a piece of furniture, an article of clothing—something of everyday use. If you are already involved in your fieldwork, you'd probably want to choose something you've collected from your site for this exercise.

Observe it. Take fieldnotes while you study it. "Look at your fish." Then, with the help of your notes, try to describe the external details of the object. Sketch it, map it, or photograph it. If you can, read about objects like it in the library to learn about its history. If possible, interview the owner or the creator. Then make an interpretation. What does it say about the person who uses it? The person who made it? How are you positioned to see the object? What did you already know? Why did you choose it? Finally, what does the object teach about the culture from which it comes?

Response

Our colleague Jeanne Janson writes about the cotton quilt made by a Lakota woman on the reservation where Jeanne taught. Her positioning among Native Americans allowed her to read this quilt in ways that an outsider might not see. The quilt maker was the grandmother of one of Jeanne's high school students who was grateful for the extra help that Jeanne had offered her grandson. As Jeanne writes about this quilt as an artifact, she reads its history and culture, its tradition and creativity. Here is an excerpt from her written account.

> Even though this quilt was made on Standing Rock Indian Reservation in South Dakota, I suppose it does have much in common with the European and North American tradition of quilting. The materials and techniques used—the appliquéd scraps and the double layers of cloth with batting between—were no doubt borrowed from the European quilt tradition. But the designs the

Lakota Sioux star quilt. (Photo: Jeanne Janson)

Lakota Sioux women use go back in their own culture for at least a thousand years, long before the arrival of Columbus.

Originally the designs appeared in porcupine quillwork, which used either normal porcupine quills laid out and sewn into hide or flattened porcupine quills, which were dyed colors and were wound around cords to form intricate designs when the cords were sewn beside each other on the hide. When Queen Victoria made beads so popular in England and they spread to North America, Native Americans took to beadwork instead of quillwork because the beads were already dyed and were much more durable than the delicate porcupine quills. But the designs used for the beadwork remained the same as they had been for the porcupine quillwork.

I think the Lakotas' exposure to cotton quilts came a bit later—I'd guess the 1890s, when they were forced to stay on the reservation and use government-issue wool blankets—on beds in houses—instead of buffalo robes on hides in tepees. The Bureau of

Indian Affairs schools taught girls how to sew the "white man's way," so that was probably where they learned how to make quilts. But the designs they use today on the quilt covers are the same star designs used in the traditional quillwork and beadwork.

Reading Everyday Use: The Uses of Cultural Artifacts

Like Gloria Naylor's novel *Mama Day*, Alice Walker's short story, "Everyday Use," explores the theme of the college-educated insider returning to her own culture. In *Mama Day*, Reema's boy sought to decipher cultural codes of the citizens of Willow Springs. In "Everyday Use," Dee, the daughter of the narrator, places value on her family's artifacts without recognizing their cultural meanings or functions. Here are some questions to think about while you read the story:

- What are the different values the characters place on the cultural artifacts in the story? The butter churn and its dasher? The table benches? The food? The quilts?
- How are different characters positioned to value the cultural artifacts? What subjective history affects their positioning? How do the fixed positions of age, race, and gender affect the way they see these artifacts?
- Where are the indications of the interaction between tradition and creativity? Dee's old and new names, for example? The quilts?
- How does the narrator position herself in relationship to each of her daughters? What scenes show this?
- In what kind of culture do Maggie and her mother live? What everyday details stand out for you as they would for a fieldworker? The mother's outdoor work? The role of the church in the community? The use of snuff?

 Everyday Use

Alice Walker

for your grandmama

I will wait for her in the yard that Maggie and I made so clean and wavy yesterday afternoon. A yard like this is more comfortable than most people know. It is not just a yard. It is like an extended living room. When the hard clay is swept clean as a floor and the fine sand around the edges lined with tiny, irregular grooves, anyone can come and sit and look up into the elm tree and wait for the breezes that never come inside the house.

Maggie will be nervous until after her sister goes: she will stand hopelessly in corners, homely and ashamed of the burn scars down her arms and legs, eying her sister with a mixture of envy and awe. She thinks her sister has held life always in the palm of one hand, that "no" is a word the world never learned to say to her.

You've no doubt seen those TV shows where the child who has "made it" is confronted, as a surprise, by her own mother and father, tottering in weakly from backstage. (A pleasant surprise, of course: What would they do if parent and child came on the show only to curse out and insult each other?) On TV mother and child embrace and smile into each other's faces. Sometimes the mother and father weep, the child wraps them in her arms and leans across the table to tell how she would not have made it without their help. I have seen these programs.

Sometimes I dream a dream in which Dee and I are suddenly brought together on a TV program of this sort. Out of a dark and soft-seated limousine I am ushered into a bright room filled with many people. There I meet a smiling, gray, sporty man like Johnny Carson who shakes my hand and tells me what a fine girl I have. Then we are on the stage and Dee is embracing me with tears in her eyes. She pins on my dress a large orchid, even though she has told me once that she thinks orchids are tacky flowers.

In real life I am a large, big-boned woman with rough, man-working hands. In the winter I wear flannel nightgowns to bed and overalls during the day. I can kill and clean a hog as mercilessly as a man. My fat keeps me hot in zero weather. I can work outside all day, breaking ice to get water for washing; I can eat pork liver cooked over the open fire minutes after it comes steaming from the hog. One winter I knocked a bull calf straight in the brain between the eyes with a sledge hammer and had the meat hung up to chill before nightfall. But of course all this does not show on television. I am the way my daughter would want me to be: a hundred pounds lighter, my skin like an uncooked barley pancake. My hair glistens in the hot bright lights. Johnny Carson has much to do to keep up with my quick and witty tongue.

But that is a mistake. I know even before I wake up. Who ever knew a Johnson with a quick tongue? Who can even imagine me looking a strange white man in the eye? It seems to me I have talked to them always with one foot raised in flight, with my head turned in whichever way is farthest from them. Dee, though. She would always look anyone in the eye. Hesitation was no part of her nature.

"How do I look, Mama?" Maggie says, showing just enough of her thin body enveloped in pink skirt and red blouse for me to know she's there, almost hidden by the door.

"Come out into the yard," I say.

Have you ever seen a lame animal, perhaps a dog run over by some careless person rich enough to own a car, sidle up to someone who is ignorant enough to be kind to him? That is the way my Maggie walks. She has been like this, chin on chest, eyes on ground, feet in shuffle, ever since the fire that burned the other house to the ground.

Dee is lighter than Maggie, with nicer hair and a fuller figure. She's a woman now, though sometimes I forget. How long ago was it that the other house burned? Ten, twelve years? Sometimes I can still hear the flames and feel Maggie's arms sticking to me, her hair smoking and her dress falling off her in little black papery flakes. Her eyes seemed stretched open, blazed open by the flames reflected in them. And Dee. I see her standing off under the sweet gum tree she used to dig gum out of; a look of concentration on her face as she watched the last dingy gray board of the house fall in toward the red-hot brick chimney. Why don't you do a dance around the ashes? I'd wanted to ask her. She had hated the house that much.

I used to think she hated Maggie, too. But that was before we raised the money, the church and me, to send her to Augusta to school. She used to read to us without pity; forcing words, lies, other folks' habits, whole lives upon us two, sitting trapped and ignorant underneath her voice. She washed us in a river of make-believe, burned us with a lot of knowledge we didn't necessarily need to know. Pressed us to her with the serious way she read, to shove us away at just the moment, like dimwits, we seemed about to understand.

Dee wanted nice things. A yellow organdy dress to wear to her graduation from high school; black pumps to match a green suit she'd made from an old suit somebody gave me. She was determined to stare down any disaster in her efforts. Her eyelids would not flicker for minutes at a time. Often I fought off the temptation to shake her. At sixteen she had a style of her own: and knew what style was.

I never had an education myself. After second grade the school was closed down. Don't ask me why: in 1927 colored asked fewer questions than they do now. Sometimes Maggie reads to me. She stumbles along good-naturedly but can't see well. She knows she is not bright. Like good looks and money, quickness passed her by. She will marry John Thomas (who has mossy teeth in an earnest face) and then I'll be free to sit here and I guess just sing church songs to myself. Although I never was a good singer. Never could carry a tune. I was always better at a man's job. I used to love to milk till I was hooked in the side in '49. Cows are soothing and slow and don't bother you, unless you try to milk them the wrong way.

I have deliberately turned my back on the house. It is three rooms, just like the one that burned, except the roof is tin; they don't make shingle roofs any more. There are no real windows, just some 'holes cut in the sides, like the portholes in a ship, but not round and not square, with rawhide holding the shutters up on the outside. This house is in a pasture, too, like the other one. No doubt when Dee sees it she will want to tear it down. She wrote me once that no matter where we "choose" to live, she will manage to come see us. But she will never bring her friends. Maggie and I thought about this and Maggie asked me, "Mama, when did Dee ever *have* any friends?"

She had a few. Furtive boys in pink shirts hanging about on washday after school. Nervous girls who never laughed. Impressed with her they worshiped the well-turned phrase, the cute shape, the scalding humor that erupted like bubbles in lye. She read to them.

When she was courting Jimmy T she didn't have much time to pay to us, but turned all her faultfinding power on him. He *flew* to marry a cheap city girl from a family of ignorant flashy people. She hardly had time to recompose herself.

When she comes I will meet—but there they are!

Maggie attempts to make a dash for the house, in her shuffling way, but I stay her with my hand. "Come back here," I say. And she stops and tries to dig a well in the sand with her toe.

It is hard to see them clearly through the strong sun. But even the first glimpse of leg out of the car tells me it is Dee. Her feet were always neat-looking, as if God himself had shaped them with a certain style. From the other side of the car comes a short, stocky man. Hair is all over his head a foot long and hanging from his chin like a kinky mule tail. I hear Maggie suck in her breath. "Uhnnnh," is what it sounds like. Like when you see the wriggling end of a snake just in front of your foot on the road. "Uhnnnh."

Dee next. A dress down to the ground, in this hot weather. A dress so loud it hurts my eyes. There are yellows and oranges enough to throw back the light of the sun. I feel my whole face warming from the heat waves it throws out. Earrings gold, too, and hanging down to her shoulders. Bracelets dangling and making noises when she moves her arm up to shake the folds of the dress out of her armpits. The dress is loose and flows, and as she walks closer, I like it. I hear Maggie go "Uhnnnh" again. It is her sister's hair. It stands straight up like the wool on a sheep. It is black as night and around the edges are two long pigtails that rope about like small lizards disappearing behind her ears.

"Wa-su-zo-Tean-o!" she says, coming on in that gliding way the dress makes her move. The short stocky fellow with the hair to his navel is all grinning and he follows up with "Asalamalakim, my mother and sister!" He moves to hug Maggie but she falls back, right up against the back of my chair. I feel her trembling there and when I look up I see the perspiration falling off her chin.

"Don't get up," says Dee. Since I am stout it takes something of a push. You can see me trying to move a second or two before I make it. She turns, showing white heels through her sandals, and goes back to the car. Out she peeks next with a Polaroid. She stoops down quickly and lines up picture after picture of me sitting there in front of the house with Maggie cowering behind me. She never takes a shot without making sure the house is included. When a cow comes nibbling around the edge of the yard she snaps it and me and Maggie and the house. Then she puts the Polaroid in the back seat of the car, and comes up and kisses me on the forehead.

Meanwhile Asalamalakim is going through motions with Maggie's hand. Maggie's hand is as limp as a fish, and probably as cold, despite the sweat, and she keeps trying to pull it back. It looks like Asalamalakim wants to shake hands but wants to do it fancy. Or maybe he don't know how people shake hands. Anyhow, he soon gives up on Maggie.

"Well," I say. "Dee."

"No, Mama," she says. "Not 'Dee,' Wangero Leewanika Kemanjo!"

"What happened to 'Dee'?" I wanted to know.

"She's dead," Wangero said. "I couldn't bear it any longer, being named after the people who oppress me."

"You know as well as me you was named after your aunt Dicie," I said. Dicie is my sister. She named Dee. We called her "Big Dee" after Dee was born.

"But who was *she* named after?" asked Wangero.

"I guess after Grandma Dee," I said.

"And who was she named after?" asked Wangero.

"Her mother," I said, and saw Wangero was getting tired. "That's about as far back as I can trace it," I said. Though, in fact, I probably could have carried it back beyond the Civil War through the branches.

"Well," said Asalamalakim, "there you are."

"Uhnnnh," I heard Maggie say.

"There I was not," I said, "before 'Dicie' cropped up in our family, so why should I try to trace it that far back?"

He just stood there grinning, looking down on me like somebody inspecting a Model A car. Every once in a while he and Wangero sent eye signals over my head.

"How do you pronounce this name?" I asked.

"You don't have to call me by it if you don't want to." said Wangero.

"Why shouldn't I?" I asked. "If that's what you want us to call you, we'll call you."

"I know it might sound awkward at first," said Wangero.

"I'll get used to it," I said. "Ream it out again."

Well, soon we got the name out of the way. Asalamalakim had a name twice as long and three times as hard. After I tripped over it two or three times he told me to just call him Hakim-a-barber. I wanted to ask him was he a barber, but I didn't really think he was, so I didn't ask.

"You must belong to those beef-cattle peoples down the road," I said. They said "Asalamalakim" when they met you, too, but they didn't shake hands. Always too busy: feeding the cattle, fixing the fences, putting up salt-lick shelters, throwing down hay.

When the while folks poisoned some of the herd the men stayed up all night with rifles in their hands. I walked a mile and a half just to see the sight.

Hakim-a-barber said, "I accept some of their doctrines, but farming and raising cattle is not my style." (They didn't tell me, and I didn't ask, whether Wangero (Dee) had really gone and married him.)

We sat down to eat and right away he said he didn't eat collards and pork was unclean. Wangero, though, went on through the chitlins and corn bread, the greens and everything else. She talked a blue streak over the sweet potatoes. Everything delighted her. Even the fact that we still used the benches her daddy made for the table when we couldn't afford to buy chairs.

"Oh, Mama!" she cried. Then turned to Hakim-a-barber. "I never knew how lovely these benches are. You can feel the rump prints," she said, running her hands underneath her and along the bench. Then she gave a sigh and her hand closed over Grandma Dee's butter dish. "That's it!" she said. "I knew there was something I wanted to ask you if I could have." She jumped up from the table and went over in the corner where the churn stood, the milk in it clabber by now. She looked at the churn and looked at it.

"This churn top is what I need," she said. "Didn't Uncle Buddy whittle it out of a tree you all used to have?"

"Yes," I said.

"Uh huh," she said happily. "And I want the dasher, too."

"Uncle Buddy whittle that, too?" asked the barber.

Dee (Wangero) looked up at me.

"Aunt Dee's first husband whittled the dash," said Maggie so low you almost couldn't hear her. "His name was Henry, but they called him Stash."

"Maggie's brain is like an elephant's," Wangero said, laughing. "I can use the churn top as a centerpiece for the alcove table," she said, sliding a plate over the churn, "and I'll think of something artistic to do with the dasher."

When she finished wrapping the dasher the handle stuck out. I took it for a moment in my hands. You didn't even have to look close to see where hands pushing the dasher up and down to make butter had left a kind of sink in the wood. In fact, there were a lot of small sinks; you could see where thumbs and fingers had sunk into the wood. It was beautiful light yellow wood, from a tree that grew in the yard where Big Dee and Stash had lived.

After dinner Dee (Wangero) went to the trunk at the foot of my bed and started rifling through it. Maggie hung back in the kitchen over the dishpan. Out came Wangero with two quilts. They had been pieced by Grandma Dee and then Big Dee and we had hung them on the quilt frames on the front porch and quilted them. One was in the Lone Star pattern. The other was Walk Around the Mountain. In both of them were scraps of dresses Grandma Dee had worn fifty and more years ago. Bits and pieces of Grandpa Jarrell's Paisley shirts. And one teeny faded blue piece, about the size of a penny matchbox, that was from Great Grandpa Ezra's uniform that he wore in the Civil War.

"Mama," Wangero said sweet as a bird. "Can I have these old quilts?"

I heard something fall in the kitchen, and a minute later the kitchen door slammed.

"Why don't you take one or two of the others?" I asked. "These old things was just done by me and Big Dee from some tops your grandma pieced before she died."

"No," said Wangero. "I don't want those. They are stitched around the borders by machine."

"That'll make them last better," I said.

"That's not the point," said Wangero. "These are all pieces of dresses Grandma used to wear. She did all this stitching by hand. Imagine!" She held the quilts securely in her arms, stroking them.

"Some of the pieces, like those lavender ones, come from old clothes her mother handed down to her," I said, moving up to touch the quilts. Dee (Wangero) moved back just enough so that I couldn't reach the quilts. They already belonged to her.

"Imagine!" she breathed again, clutching them closely to her bosom.

"The truth is," I said, "I promised to give them quilts to Maggie, for when she marries John Thomas."

She gasped like a bee had stung her.

"Maggie can't appreciate these quilts!" she said. "She'd probably be backward enough to put them to everyday use."

"I reckon she would," I said. "God knows I been saving 'em for long enough with nobody using 'em. I hope she will!" I didn't want to bring up how I had offered Dee (Wangero) a quilt when she went away to college. Then she had told me they were old-fashioned, out of style.

"But they're *priceless*!" she was saying now, furiously; for she has a temper. "Maggie would put them on the bed and in five years they'd be in rags. Less than that!"

"She can always make some more," I said. "Maggie knows how to quilt."

Dee (Wangero) looked at me with hatred. "You just will not understand. The point is these quilts, *these* quilts!"

"Well," I said, stumped. "What would you do with them?"

"Hang them," she said. As if that was the only thing you *could* do with quilts.

Maggie by now was standing in the door. I could almost hear the sound her feet made as they scraped over each other.

"She can have them, Mama," she said, like somebody used to never winning anything, or having anything reserved for her. "I can 'member Grandma Dee without the quilts."

I looked at her hard. She had filled her bottom lip with checkerberry snuff and it gave her face a kind of dopey, hangdog look. It was Grandma Dee and Big Dee who taught her how to quilt herself. She stood there with her scarred hands hidden in the folds of her skirt. She looked at her sister with something like fear but she wasn't mad at her. This was Maggie's portion. This was the way she knew God to work.

When I looked at her like that something hit me in the top of my head and ran down to the soles of my feet. Just like when I'm in church and the spirit of God touches me and I get happy and shout. I did something I never had done before: hugged Maggie to me, then dragged her on into the room, snatched the quilts out of Miss Wangero's hands and dumped them into Maggie's lap. Maggie just sat there on my bed with her mouth open.

"Take one or two of the others," I said to Dee.

But she turned without a word and went out to Hakim-a-barber.

"You just don't understand," she said, as Maggie and I came out to the car.

"What don't I understand?" I wanted to know.

"Your heritage," she said. And then she turned to Maggie, kissed her, and said, "You ought to try to make something of yourself, too, Maggie. It's really a new day for us. But from the way you and Mama still live you'd never know it."

She put on some sunglasses that hid everything above the tip of her nose and her chin.

Maggie smiled; maybe at the sunglasses. But a real smile, not scared. After we watched the car dust settle I asked Maggie to bring me a dip of snuff. And then the two of us sat there just enjoying, until it was time to go in the house and go to bed.

In Walker's story, you may have noticed that Dee seeks to remove the cultural artifacts from the cultural site as she leaves her culture behind. Whereas Reema's boy saw himself as a fieldworker in training, Dee considers herself a sophisticated collector of valuable folk art. Neither was successful at listening or looking at the language, the rituals, or the artifacts of their home culture. Dee's desire to collect the quilt, perhaps even hang it, takes it out of its everyday context, distances it, and makes it more an object of art than of the living culture. In "Everyday Use," Dee's sister Maggie lives quietly inside the everyday community that her sister tries to interpret. Notice that the voice of this narrator, Dee's mother, is similar to the narrator in *Mama Day*, both full members of their communities, who already value and appreciate their culture.

These stories provide us with a contrast between "stepping in" and "stepping out." Dee and Reema's boy serve as both insiders and outsiders. Their misinterpretations of artifacts and rituals mark them as outsiders. Their histories and kinships mark them as insiders. Yet they have each left their home cultures and returned, no longer able to read the culture or its artifacts in the same way as the people who continued to live there.

Both this reading and the one that opened the chapter are reflective pieces of fiction intended to invite you into another distinct culture: its rituals, rules, behaviors, codes, and artifacts. Both Naylor and Walker illustrate culture as everyday lived experience that is not easily understood by outsiders. They show culture as more than kinship or geography, more than language and ways of behaving, but as a combination of all of these. And your own history as a close reader of texts has, we hope, taught you to enter fictional culture—to live within it and understand it from a character's point of view. Fictional worlds are both satisfying and neat for the reader. By starting and ending with fiction, we've drawn on your strengths as a reader, the same kinds of strengths you will need while you are reading and researching in the field.

The Research Portfolio: Options for Reflection

The portfolio is the site of your research reflections. It gives focus to a researcher's abstract thoughts and feelings. All your data—the writing you do, the artifacts you collect, and the readings you complete—are options for putting into your portfolio. The portfolio contains the artifacts, both the written and cultural material, of your work in progress. It records your fieldnotes: anxieties about looking at others and perhaps their anxieties about being researched. The portfolio captures both your fieldwork and your deskwork. And your written commentary about your ongoing research process reflects your positioning as a researcher. The key word in developing a research portfolio is *reflection*.

We hope you'll work with a portfolio partner or a small group to share your project in progress. This is a way to clarify your own ideas and get new ideas from other researchers who are working in sites and on projects different from yours. We've attended several professional ethnography conferences that hold a "Festival of Data" session where researchers share their work in progress. Sharing your portfolios can serve the same purpose. Our own students have found such data-sharing sessions useful and valuable.

ARTIFACT REFLECTIONS

Rick Zollo, for example, wrote several short reflections about his positioning as he researched Iowa 80. In them, he was able to explore how his own personal history linked with his research and affected his work in the field site. His portfolio included artifacts from the truck stop as well as his related reading and writing: a menu, a few brochures about trucking regulations, photocopies of articles he'd read about truckers, a trucker magazine, photographs he had taken at the truck stop, five writing exercises describing his field site, and a transcript of an interview with one of his informants. Each time he reviewed his portfolio, he wrote a short commentary about where he found himself in the research process. In one reflection about his position, he writes:

> This truck stop story has been gestating for years. I first conceived a project about truck drivers and their hangouts several years ago. The Iowa 80 truck stop became my place for planned inquiry, since it was along a major highway near my home, was practically in the center of our nation and its interstate highway system, and had grown into a strange (to my eyes, at least) little community that seemed to have its own life.

Researching another culture can be both messy and confusing, but if you reflect on the process, you'll find yourself sorting out the mess and clarifying much of the confusion. We believe that the process of reflecting is just as important as the final end product of an ethnographic study. For this reason, we want you to take time to think and write about what you've actually learned from each exercise you do at different stages of your research process. Get together with your portfolio partner, and share your work. Have your partner ask questions about your project and include those questions and responses in your portfolio as well: How does your own personal history affect what you've chosen? What does each artifact represent about a growing theme in your research? How do the artifacts connect to one another? In Rick's portfolio, he might look at the relationship between the menu, the trucking magazine, and his interview transcript, for example. With each reflective commentary, Rick has a chance to see the scope and depth of his project, and the reflection moves him toward the next phase of his research process.

READING REFLECTIONS

For your portfolio, you'll want to review each of the short readings you did and reflect on them: Samuel Scudder's essay "Look at Your Fish," Gloria Naylor's introduction to her novel *Mama Day*, and Alice Walker's short story "Everyday Use." Which of your responses do you prefer, and why? Which ones gave you more insight into researching another culture? Review the pieces you wrote on Scudder,

Naylor, and Walker, and choose one (or more) as an example of "reading culture" to place in your portfolio. You might also want to add other related readings you have done.

WRITING REFLECTIONS

This chapter has also started a few writing tasks for you as a fieldworker. So far, if you've completed the boxes, you have already

- Written about your positionality—the assumptions you carry into your field site
- Written about an everyday object or event using the double-entry format
- Started to take fieldnotes at your site
- Considered the process of negotiating entry
- Selected and "read" a cultural artifact

Review these writing exercises together, as a set, and look for common themes or concerns they represent. What is important about them to you as a writer, a researcher, and a beginning fieldworker? How have you have positioned yourself within your written responses? What have you left out, and why? If you've started to work in a field site or in a subculture that you want to continue with, compare your exercises to the actual fieldnotes you have started to take. Notice similarities and differences.

The portfolio itself is like a researcher's trips to the field. It shows the journey to the places you've observed and the people you've interviewed. It documents the resources you use throughout your field trips and the books and guides you've relied on to get there. When you see the evidence of your trip laid out in a portfolio, you can begin to reflect on what you've done and plan for the work that lies ahead.

FieldWriting: Published and Unpublished Written Sources

Fieldwriting depends far more on oral source material than written sources. Your informants, along with your fieldnotes, will contribute the most important data to your field projects. When fieldworkers write up their research, they treat informants' words in the same way that library researchers cite textual references. Because you'll need to cite their words as carefully as any written source, we include that information in a separate FieldWriting section in Chapter 4, which covers taping, transcribing, and presenting oral language on the page.

But to support your fieldwork's oral sources, you'll need to refer to written texts from both published and unpublished library and archival sources, as well as documents you've collected at your field site. As all research writers know, the basic role of documentation is to attribute ideas that are not your own to their original source. For example, when we use the phrase "stepping in and stepping out," we put quotation marks around it to indicate that it is not our original idea. We do this because we want to attribute this term to Hortense Powdermaker, whose quote from *Stranger and Friend* opens our book and whose idea has given us a new way to explain the insider-outsider researcher stance.

One exception to information that requires documentation is "common knowledge." Common knowledge refers to ideas that everyone might be expected to know, such as the presidents or the population of the United States, neither of which requires documentation of source material. A fieldwriter might consult an almanac, a map, a time chart, or an encyclopedia to verify such common knowledge, but she would not need to include that source in a final paper. Sometimes it's difficult to determine, however, what common knowledge particular readers will have. In this chapter, for example, we have assumed that our readers know that Gullah is an English dialect. However, they may not know that it is a creole form of English spoken in the South Carolina and Georgia low country of the United States; we write that information into our text in order to show this. We mention where Gullah is spoken and a novel and movie about people who speak Gullah. Writers who are unsure of their own readers' common knowledge should include contextual information, which itself often comes from published written sources.

Because this book is about fieldworking and the conventions associated with writing about it, we've limited our discussion of textual documentation to the issues directly related to writing about fieldwork. When you use documentation (published or unpublished) to support your fieldwork, you should refer to a more complete handbook or research manual. We like the Modern Language Association's *MLA Handbook for Writers of Research Papers*, fourth edition, because it illustrates how to cite movies, electronic publications, diskettes, tapes, and on-line databases, as well as personal interviews, letters, journals, e-mail, and more conventional text sources. Because we work in English departments, we follow the MLA documentation conventions; in other subject areas, your instructors may guide you toward equally thorough research manuals, such as the *Publication Manual of the American Psychological Association*, used in psychology and education; the *Chicago Manual of Style*, which many book publishers use; or one of the many other manuals of style specific to other disciplines, such as law, mathematics, science, medicine, linguistics, or engineering.

The current convention for documenting any source—informant or text, published or unpublished—is to give as much information about the source as possible within your actual written text. This is called intertextual citation, and it is a simpler convention than the older ones, which required footnotes, endnotes, and abbreviations of Latin phrases (*op. cit.* or *ibid.*, for example). Intertextual citation might include the author or informant's name and the book or document title, depending on how you introduce the material into your writing. Your first citation must always refer to the original source from which it came. For published sources, this would be the page number (for example, "Naylor 7" to "*Mama Day* 7"). For unpublished written sources, how you cite depends on the type of material you have collected. When you cite a written source intertextually, you must provide enough information so that a reader can find the complete citation in your "Works Cited" section—or "References," "Bibliography," or "FieldReading"—at the end. Intertextual documentation avoids interrupting the flow of your text and cluttering it with information that a reader can find elsewhere. Here are some of the many ways intertextual citation can be used. We draw our examples from this chapter.

INCORPORATING PUBLISHED SOURCES

In this chapter, we used intertextual citation when we quoted from writers John Berger and Diane Ackerman. When you want to cite only a sentence or two (no more than four lines), you try to weave someone else's words into your own text. Not only do you want to quote the source, but you also need to let your reader understand why you've called on it to support your own ideas. Include enough information about the citation for your reader to locate the source at the end of your work.

Although we are actually quoting from our own chapter here, we use quotation marks to indicate their use in an intertextual citation. Here is an example of a direct quotation from art historian John Berger. In this chapter, we used Berger's quote to amplify what we wanted to say about looking at Scudder's fish. It is a straightforward example of intertextual citation that identifies only the author and page number:

> But as art historian John Berger writes, "We only see what we look at. To look is an act of choice" (8).

The bibliographic entry would read:

> Berger, John. *Ways of Seeing*. New York: Penguin, 1972.

On page 230 of Diane Ackerman's book *A Natural History of the Senses*, she writes: "Seventy percent of the body's sense receptors cluster in the eyes, and it is mainly through seeing the world that we appraise and understand it." We wanted to use her words but incorporate them into a sentence of our own. Here's how we did that:

> Nonfiction writer Diane Ackerman emphasizes the importance of our sensory awareness: "Seventy percent of the body's sense receptors cluster in the eyes, and it is mainly through seeing the world that we appraise and understand it" (230).

Had we wanted to use only part of her sentence, we would have used ellipsis points to indicate the part that has been omitted:

> In her book *A Natural History of the Senses*, Diane Ackerman writes that "seventy percent of the body's sense receptors cluster in the eyes . . ." (230).

Note that capitalization of the first word of the quote matches the grammar of our sentence, not necessarily that of the original.

A quote of more than four lines of published text is called a *block quotation*. Instead of using quotation marks, a block quotation is set off by skipping a line and indenting both margins. Introduce a block quote by giving as much information about the source as possible. For example, to introduce Scudder, we wrote about his essay on studying entomology in the nineteenth century with his Harvard professor, Louis Agassiz. Here's a block quotation taken from Scudder's essay:

> It was more than fifteen years ago that I entered the library of Professor Agassiz, and told him I had enrolled my name in the Scientific School as a student of natural history. He asked me a few questions about my object in coming, my antecedents generally, the mode in which I afterwards proposed to use the knowledge I might acquire, and, finally, whether I wished to study any special branch. To the latter I replied that, while I wished to be well grounded in all departments of zoology, I purposed to devote myself especially to insects (1).

When a writer summarizes another person's words, there is no need to include quotation marks or page numbers as long as the reader can locate that information in your final list of references. If you've listed three books by Louise Rosenblatt, for instance, you would need to distinguish which book you were summarizing. We open this chapter with a quote from Louise Rosenblatt's book *Literature as Exploration* and follow it up immediately with our summary of her theory of reading. We write:

> Literary theorist Louise Rosenblatt suggests that a reader's main instrument for making meaning is herself.

In another part of this chapter, when we summarized parts of Gloria Naylor's novel *Mama Day* and also included directly quoted material, we indicated the page from which we took the quote. The combination of quoting directly and summarizing is yet another way of documenting written source material, just as it is when we cite our informants.

> With the character of Reema's pear-headed nameless boy, Naylor offers us a parody of a field researcher. He is an insider, born on the island, and he returns from his fancy college, "dragging his notebooks and tape recorder and a funny way of curling up his lip and clicking his teeth, all excited to put Willow Springs on the map" (56).

INCORPORATING UNPUBLISHED SOURCES

Many times in your fieldwork, you'll want to quote from your informants' unpublished written texts or from documents you collect at your field site. This might include, for example, journals, letters, diaries, photocopied documents meant for insiders, or notes written by informants that provide evidence you want to cite. Rick Zollo, for example, received a letter from one of his informants at Iowa 80 that illustrated the truckers' complaints about growing government regulations. Rick included this letter only in his research journal and decided not to use it in his final essay, but here's how he might have quoted from it. He could introduce the letter as follows:

> Dean Self, a truck driver who wanted his fellow truckers to organize, wrote this letter:
>
> Drivers:
> Enough is enough, we're finally fed up. We have shown unity through protest convoys and even a shutdown.
> No matter how much we protest, we will gain nothing due to the fact that we have no representation. We must have a national organization founded, funded, and operated by us drivers. With no outside interests. Then and only then will we be represented.

Another example of an unpublished written source in this chapter is Jake's photocopied "code of honor" from the skinheads he began to study. (We also present this material in a block quotation because it is over four lines.) Since it has no verifiable source, like Rick's letter from Dean Self, the full bibliographic reference for this code will indicate that it is unpublished. Here is the list of the skinheads' "Code of Honor" that Jake photocopied:

- Be discreet about new recruits, check them out thoroughly
- For prospects, we must have at least a ninety day contact period in which we can attest to your character. A probationary period and productivity report will be given.
- Outsiders need no knowledge of what goes on or is said in our meetings
- No racial exceptions whatsoever! All members must be 100% white!

Here's how these unpublished sources would be cited in the "Works Cited." For the first document, Rick Zollo knows the author of the letter and so places the entry among his references in alphabetical order like this:

> Self, Dean. Letter to the writer. October 1994.

By contrast, Jake has limited information about the original source of the skinheads' honor code. He would place this citation among his references in alphabetical order, and it would look like this:

> "Code of honor," unpublished document. 1993.

You'll notice throughout this book that fieldwriters draw from a wide range of unpublished materials that include flyers, brochures, menus, business statements, letters, signs, captions in family albums, xerography, photocopied or mimeographed pages meant for a group of insiders, and other kinds of personal and unpublished writing.

As a fieldwriter, your major responsibility in using your sources, both published and unpublished, is to amplify and support what you have to say by incorporating the written source material smoothly into your text. And you need to make it possible for another researcher to be able to locate whatever written resources you have cited, both by including information about the reference within your text and by making it available in your list of cited source materials.

FieldWords

Expanded fieldnotes: Additional comments and reflections made by the researcher, away from the research site.

Fieldnotes: Observations written by a researcher at a research site, during interviews, and throughout the data collection process.

Human subjects review board: An administrative department at a university that processes researchers' applications for conducting studies with people as their subjects. Its purpose is to protect human subjects from inappropriate or unethical projects. It also protects researchers by reviewing their project proposals and helping them anticipate any problems they may encounter in working with people.

Informed consent: The agreement between a researcher and his or her human subject (informant, consultant, collaborator) that gives the researcher permission to use the informant's observations, interview comments, and artifacts. Sometimes a researcher must also obtain such an agreement to enter a field site and conduct a study there.

Material culture: An accumulation of artifacts used by a group that represents meaning, history, values, and beliefs, including such things as tools, printed or written materials, musical instruments, foods, toys, jewelry, ceremonial objects, and clothes.

Participant-observer: The stance of a researcher who becomes involved in the daily life of a culture while observing it.

Positioning: The researcher's stance in relationship to the place and people studied, as well as its represention in a final written text. Positioning has fixed, subjective, and textual aspects.

Transcript: The official record of an interview or other oral event, put into print word for word.

FieldReading

Ackerman, Diane. *A Natural History of the Senses*. New York: Vintage, 1991.

Baldwin, James. *Nobody Knows My Name: More Notes of a Native Son*. New York: Dial, 1961.

Berger, John. *Ways of Seeing*. New York: Penguin, 1972.

Cary, Lorene. *Black Ice*. New York: Knopf, 1991.

Emerson, Robert M., Rachel I. Fretz, and Linda L. Shaw. *Writing Ethnographic Fieldnotes*. Chicago: U Chicago P, 1995.

Fitzgerald, Frances. *Cities on a Hill: A Journey through Contemporary American Cultures*. New York: Simon, 1986.

Lurie, Alison. *Imaginary Friends*. New York: Avon, 1991.

———. *The Language of Clothes*. New York: Random, 1986.

Naylor, Gloria. *Mama Day*. New York: Vintage, 1988.

Rosenblatt, Louise. *Literature as Exploration*. 5th ed. New York: Modern Language Association, 1995.

Sanjek, Roger. *Fieldnotes: The Makings of Anthropology*. Ithaca: Cornell UP, 1990.

Sims, Norman and Mark Kramer, Eds. *Literary Journalism*. New York: Ballantine, 1995.

Stoller, Paul. *The Taste of Ethnographic Things: The Senses in Anthropology*. Philadelphia: U Pennsylvania P, 1989.

Wolf, Margery. *A Thrice-Told Tale: Feminism, Postmodernism, and Ethnographic Responsibility*. Stanford: Stanford UP, 1992.

3

Researching Place:
The Spatial Gaze

"Gaze" is the act of seeing; it is an act of selective perception. Much of what we see is shaped by our experiences, and our "gaze" has a direct bearing on what we think. And what we see and think, to take the process one step further, has a bearing upon what we say and what and how we write.

Paul Stoller

The word *fieldworking* itself, of course, implies place. When researchers venture "into the field," they enter the surroundings of the "other." Researchers step out of familiar territory and into unfamiliar landscapes. But no matter where they conduct their research, they take their perspectives along. When you return to a place where you spent time in your early years, like your grandmother's apartment or a childhood playground, you're probably surprised that the place seems different, maybe smaller or larger than you imagined. And if you visit a kindergarten room, you notice that the scale is designed for smaller people: you bend down to look at the fish in the fishtank or the gerbils in their cages, you stuff yourself into a tiny plastic chair or fold your legs to your chin during rug time. Your spatial memory and your spatial assumptions depend on your past experiences and your present situation.

As anthropologist Paul Stoller implies in the opening quotation, what we see depends on how we filter or select what we see. What we see also depends on *how* we look—how we open ourselves to the acts of seeing. Just as we all read differently at different times in our lives, we also perceive differently. You might not have noticed that the antique stove in your grandmother's kitchen ran on gas until you started to cook yourself. Or as a child, you may not have realized the reasons for rug time in kindergarten often have more to do with the teacher's desire to establish community than to the fun you had leaving your desk. Stoller's expression "the spatial gaze" represents the fieldworker's stance and worldview. Anthropologists use the term *worldview* to encompass an informant's entire cultural perspective. Of course, how we understand an informant's worldview is dependent on our own.

This chapter is about researching place: remembering your personal geography and learning how to look at your field site, how to detail and map space, how to find unity and tension within a place, and how to locate a focal point. We are always part of the places we study. Whether they are familiar or unfamiliar, we always stand in relationship to those places. No matter how far outside we may situate ourselves, or how close-in, there can be no place description without an author. And authoring a place description requires personal involvement. Describing a place is much the same as choosing a perspective from which to take a picture.

You may have selected a field site by now and spent some time learning how to "read" it and some of its cultural materials. Researching place takes a long time; this chapter extends many of the skills of reading a cultural site that you tried in Chapter 2. Understanding how informants use the space in a field site constitutes the researcher's data. For this reason, fieldworkers train themselves to look through two pairs of eyes, as both insider (emic perspective) and outsider (etic perspective) at once, in order to include their own perspectives. Studying and writing about how informants interact in their spaces help the fieldworker learn the informants' perspective.

A Sense of Place: Personal Geography

Each of us has a sense of place, whether we've moved great distances or stayed within the same spaces all our lives. That sense of place evokes a kind of loyalty, linked to a familiar landscape that comforts us, even when it is not beautiful or particularly comfortable. Elizabeth grew up near strip-mined land in southern Ohio, which to most people is ecologically irresponsible. And yet that flat blackened landscape calls up strong and familiar sensations for her. Some of us, like Elizabeth, don't recognize our sense of place until we leave it, either by changing schools or homes, going to college, joining the service, traveling, or just growing up.

Even in a new place, something can evoke past sensations, uncovering a geographical memory and bringing with it a sudden surge of images. Ropes slapping against a flagpole in the Midwest may recall the sound of halyards slapping against an aluminum mast on a sailboat in the San Francisco Bay. The smell of a friend's skin cream on a winter day in Idaho can transport us to a searing beach on the New Jersey shore. Our personal geographies influence our spatial gaze; they influence how we look.

Bonnie grew up in Jenkintown, Pennsylvania, a suburb of Philadelphia. She remembers a tall bank clock next to the Snack Shop. With its black Roman numerals and latticed hands, it stood at the intersection where she learned to drive a car. The clock marks a flurry of adolescent images. Every morning, Miss Lobach, the ancient cross-eyed Latin teacher who lived above the drugstore, shuffled past that clock on her daily walk to school. Each afternoon, the Snack Shop sold cherry Cokes for a dime—and charged a penny for each straw to dissuade teenagers from blowing wrappers across the chrome counter at one another. Later, the clock became a gathering site for political rallies, with adults and teenagers chanting and waving handmade protest signs. Thirty years later and 1,200 miles away, in Iowa City, another bank clock reminds Bonnie of those memories, that intersection, and all that happened there.

In the following essay, Barry Lopez, a nonfiction and travel writer, calls for Americans to regain their sense of place, to become more conscious of their scenery, and to find local people who hold geographical knowledge. Such experts would make good research informants because they have, in Lopez's words, "a sense of memory over the land." Lopez claims that Americans are forfeiting their ecological integrity and sense of community by settling for a bland, calendar-like geography, in which one place looks pretty much like another. As you read his essay, "Losing Our Sense of Place," try to recall the large spaces that you remember with strong images like Elizabeth's scarred Ohio landscape or smaller ones that held significance in your mind like Bonnie's clock.

Losing Our Sense of Place

Barry Lopez

It has become commonplace to observe that Americans know little of the geography of their country, that they are innocent of it as a landscape of rivers, mountains, and towns. They do not know, supposedly, the location of the Delaware Water Gap, the Olympic Mountains, or the Piedmont Plateau; and, the indictment continues, they have little conception of the way the individual components of this landscape are imperiled, from a human perspective, by modern farming practices or industrial pollution.

I do not know how true this is, but it is easy to believe that it is truer than most of us would wish. A recent Gallup Organization and National Geographic Society survey found Americans woefully ignorant of world geography. Three out of four couldn't locate the Persian Gulf. The implication was that we knew no more about our own homeland, and that this ignorance undermined the integrity of our political processes and the efficiency of our business enterprises.

As Americans, we profess a sincere and fierce love for the American landscape, for our rolling prairies, free-flowing rivers, and "purple mountains' majesty"; but it is hard to imagine, actually, where this particular landscape is. It is not just that a nostalgic land-scape has passed away—Mark Twain's Mississippi is now dammed from Minnesota to Missouri and the prairies have all been sold and fenced. It is that it has always been a romantic's landscape. In the attenuated form in which it is presented on television today, in magazine articles and in calendar photographs, the essential wildness of the American landscape is reduced to attractive scenery. We look out on a familiar, memorized land-scape that portends adventure and promises enrichment. There are no distracting people in it and few artifacts of human life. The animals are all beautiful, diligent, one might even say well-behaved. Nature's unruliness, the power of rivers and skies to intimidate, and any evidence of disastrous human land management practices are all but invisible. It is, in short, a magnificent garden, a colonial vision of paradise imposed on a real place that is, at best, only selectively known.

The real American landscape is a face of almost incomprehensible depth and complexity. If one were to sit for a few days, for example, among the ponderosa pine forests and black lava fields of the Cascade Mountains in western Oregon, inhaling the pines' sweet balm on an evening breeze from some point on the barren rock, and then were to step off to the Olympic Peninsula in Washington, to those rain forests with sphagnum moss floors soft as fleece underfoot and Douglas firs too big around for five people to hug, and then head south to walk the ephemeral creeks and sun-blistered playas of the

Mojave Desert in southern California, one would be reeling under the sensations. The contrast is not only one of plants and soils, a different array, say, of brilliantly colored beetles. The shock to the senses comes from a different shape to the silence, a difference in the very quality of light, in the weight of the air. And this relatively short journey down the West Coast would still leave the traveler with all that lay to the east to explore—the anomalous sand hills of Nebraska, the heat and frog voices of Okefenokee Swamp, the fetch of Chesapeake Bay, the hardwood copses and black bears of the Ozark Mountains.

No one of these places, of course, can be entirely fathomed, biologically or aesthetically. They are mysteries upon which we impose names. Enchantments. We tick the names off glibly but lovingly. We mean no disrespect. Our genuine desire, though we might be skeptical about the time it would take and uncertain of its practical value to us, is to actually know these places. As deeply ingrained in the American psyche as the desire to conquer and control the land is the desire to sojourn in it, to sail up and down Pamlico Sound, to paddle a canoe through Minnesota's boundary waters, to walk on the desert of the Great Salt Lake, to camp in the stony hardwood valleys of Vermont.

To do this well, to really come to an understanding of a specific American geography, requires not only time but a kind of local expertise, an intimacy with place few of us ever develop. There is no way around the former requirement: If you want to know you must take the time. It is not in books. A specific geographical understanding, however, can be sought out and borrowed. It resides with men and women more or less sworn to a place, who abide there, who have a feel for the soil and history, for the turn of leaves and night sounds. Often they are glad to take the outlander in tow.

These local geniuses of American landscape, in my experience, are people in whom geography thrives. They are the antithesis of geographical ignorance. Rarely known outside their own communities, they often seem, at the first encounter, unremarkable and anonymous. They may not be able to recall the name of a particular wildflower—or they may have given it a name known only to them. They might have forgotten the precise circumstances of a local historical event. Or they can't say for certain when the last of the Canada geese passed through in the fall, or can't differentiate between two kinds of trout in the same creek. Like all of us, they have fallen prey to the fallacies of memory and are burdened with ignorance; but they are nearly flawless in the respect they bear these places they love. Their knowledge is intimate rather than encyclopedic, human but not necessarily scholarly. It rings with the concrete details of experience.

America, I believe, teems with such people. The paradox here, between a faulty grasp of geographical knowledge for which Americans are indicted and the intimate, apparently contradictory familiarity of a group of largely anonymous people, is not solely a matter of confused scale. (The local landscape is easier to know than a national geography.) And it is not simply ironic. The paradox is dark. To be succinct: The politics and advertising that seek a national audience must project a national geography; to be broadly useful that geography must, inevitably, be generalized and it is often romantic. It is therefore frequently misleading and imprecise. The same holds true with the entertainment industry, but here the problem might be clearer. The same films, magazines, and television features that honor an imaginary American landscape also tout the worth of the anonymous men and women who interpret it. Their affinity for the land is lauded, their local allegiance admired. But the rigor of their local geographies, taken as a whole, contradicts a patriotic, national vision of unspoiled, untroubled land. These men and women are ultimately forgotten, along with the details of the landscapes they speak for, in the face of more pressing national matters. It is the chilling nature of modern society to find an ignorance of geography, local or national, as excusable as an ignorance of hand tools; and to find the commitment of people to their home places only momentarily entertaining. And finally naive.

If one were to pass time among Basawara people in the Kalahari Desert, or with Kreen-Akrora in the Amazon Basin, or with Pitjantjatjara Aborigines in Australia, the most salient impression they might leave is of an absolutely stunning knowledge of their local geography—geology, hydrology, biology, and weather. In short, the extensive particulars of their intercourse with it.

In 40,000 years of human history, it has only been in the last few hundred years or so that a people could afford to ignore their local geographies as completely as we do and still survive. Technological innovations from refrigerated trucks to artificial fertilizers, from sophisticated cost accounting to mass air transportation, have utterly changed concepts of season, distance, soil productivity, and the real cost of drawing sustenance from the land. It is now possible for a resident of Boston to bite into a fresh strawberry in the dead of winter; for someone in San Francisco to travel to Atlanta in a few hours with no worry of how formidable might be crossings of the Great Basin Desert or the Mississippi River; for an absentee farmer to gain a tax advantage from a farm that leaches poisons into its water table and on which crops are left to rot. The Pitjantjatjara might shake their heads in bewilderment and bemusement, not because they are primitive or ignorant people, not because they have no sense of irony or are incapable of marveling, but because they have not (many would say not yet) realized a world in which such manipulation of the land—surmounting the imperatives of distance it imposes, for example, or turning the large-scale destruction of forests and arable land in wealth—is desirable or plausible.

In the years I have traveled through America, in cars and on horseback, on foot and by raft, I have repeatedly been brought to a sudden state of awe by some gracile or savage movement of animal, some odd wrapping of tree's foliage by the wind, an unimpeded run of dew-laden prairie stretching to a horizon flat as a coin where a pin-dot sun pales the dawn sky pink. I know these things are beyond intellection, that they are the vivid edges of a world that includes but also transcends the human world. In memory, when I dwell on these things, I know that in a truly national literature there should be odes to the Triassic reds of the Colorado Plateau, to the sharp and ghostly light of the Florida Keys, to the aeolian soils of southern Minnesota, and the Palouse in Washington, though the modern mind abjures the literary potential of such subjects. (If the sand and flood water farmers of Arizona and New Mexico were to take the black loams of Louisiana in their hands they would be flabbergasted, and that is the beginning of literature.) I know there should be eloquent evocations of the cobbled beaches of Maine, the plutonic walls of the Sierra Nevada, the orange canyons of the Kaibab Plateau. I have no doubt, in fact, that there are. They are as numerous and diverse as the eyes and fingers that ponder the country—it is that only a handful of them are known. The great majority are to be found in drawers and boxes, in the letters and private journals of millions of workaday people who have regarded their encounters with the land as an engagement bordering on the spiritual, as being fundamentally linked to their state of health.

One cannot acknowledge the extent and the history of this kind of testimony without being forced to the realization that something strange, if not dangerous, is afoot. Year by year, the number of people with firsthand experience in the land dwindles. Rural populations continue to shift to the cities. The family farm is in a state of demise, and government and industry continue to apply pressure on the native peoples of North America to sever their ties with the land. In the wake of this loss of personal and local knowledge from which a real geography is derived, the knowledge on which a country must ultimately stand, has come something hard to define but I think sinister and unsettling—the packaging and marketing of land as a form of entertainment. An incipient industry, capitalizing on the nostalgia Americans feel for the imagined virgin landscapes of their fathers, and on a desire for adventure, now offers people a convenient though sometimes incomplete or even spurious geography as an inducement to purchase a unique experience. But the line between authentic experience and a superficial exposure to the elements of experience is blurred. And the real landscape, in all its complexity, is distorted even further in the public imagination. No longer innately mysterious and dignified, a ground from which experience grows, it becomes a curiously generic backdrop on which experience is imposed.

In theme parks the profound, subtle, and protracted experience of running a river is reduced to a loud, quick, safe equivalence, a pleasant distraction. People only able to venture into the countryside on annual vacations are, increasingly, schooled in the belief that wild land will, and should, provide thrills and exceptional scenery on a timely basis. If it does not, something is wrong, either with the land itself or possibly with the company outfitting the trip.

People in America, then, face a convoluted situation. The land itself, vast and differentiated, defies the notion of a national geography. If applied at all it must be applied lightly, and it must grow out of the concrete detail of local geographies. Yet Americans are daily presented with, and have become accustomed to talking about, a homogenized national geography, one that seems to operate independently of the land, a collection of objects rather than a continuous bolt of fabric. It appears in advertisements, as a background in movies, and in patriotic calendars. The suggestion is that there can be national geography because the constituent parts are interchangeable and can be treated as commodities. In day-to-day affairs, in other words, one place serves as well as another to convey one's point. On reflection, this is an appalling condescension and a terrible imprecision, the very antithesis of knowledge. The idea that either the Green River in Utah or the Salmon River in Idaho will do, or that the valleys of Kentucky and West Virginia are virtually interchangeable, is not just misleading. For people still dependent on the soil for their sustenance, or for people whose memories tie them to those places, it betrays a numbing casualness, a utilitarian, expedient, and commercial frame of mind. It heralds a society in which it is no longer necessary for human beings to know where they live, except as those places are described and fixed by numbers. The truly difficult and life-long task of discovering where one lives is finally disdained.

If a society forgets or no longer cares where it lives, then anyone with the political power and the will to do so can manipulate the landscape to conform to certain social ideals or nostalgic visions. People may hardly notice that anything has happened, or assume that whatever happens—a mountain stripped of timber and eroding into its creeks—is for the common good. The more superficial a society's knowledge of the real dimensions of the land it occupies becomes, the more vulnerable the land is to exploitation, to manipulation for short-term gain. The land, virtually powerless before political and commercial entities, finds itself finally with no defenders. It finds itself bereft of intimates with indispensable, concrete knowledge. (Oddly, or perhaps not oddly, while American society continues to value local knowledge as a quaint part of its heritage, it continues to cut such people off from any real political power. This is as true for small farmers and illiterate cowboys as it is for American Indians, native Hawaiians, and Eskimos.)

The intense pressure of imagery in America, and the manipulation of images necessary to a society with specific goals, means the land will inevitably be treated like a commodity; and voices that tend to contradict the proffered image will, one way or another, be silenced or discredited by those in power. This is not new to America; the promulgation in America of a false or imposed geography has been the case from the beginning. All local geographies, as they were defined by hundreds of separate, independent native traditions, were denied in the beginning in favor of an imported and unifying vision of America's natural history. The country, the landscape itself, was eventually defined according to dictates of Progress like Manifest Destiny, and laws like the Homestead Act which reflected a poor understanding of the physical lay of the land.

When I was growing up in southern California, I formed the rudiments of a local geography—eucalyptus trees, February rains, Santa Ana winds. I lost much of it when my family moved to New York City, a move typical of the modern, peripatetic style of American life, responding to the exigencies of divorce and employment. As a boy I felt a hunger to know the American landscape that was extreme: when I was finally able to travel on my own, I did so. Eventually I visited most of the United States, living for brief periods of time in Arizona, Indiana, Alabama, Georgia, Wyoming, New Jersey, and Montana before settling 20 years ago in western Oregon.

The astonishing level of my ignorance confronted me everywhere I went. I knew early on that the country could not be held together in a few phrases, that its geography was magnificent and incomprehensible, that a man or woman could devote a lifetime to its elucidation and still feel in the end that he had but sailed many thousands of miles over the surface of the ocean. So I came into the habit of traversing landscapes I wanted to know with local tutors and reading what had previously been written about, and in, those places. I came to value exceedingly novels and essays and works of nonfiction that connected human enterprise to real and specific places, and I grew to be mildly distrustful of work that occurred in no particular place, work so cerebral and detached as to be refutable only in an argument of ideas.

These sojourns in various corners of the country infused me, somewhat to my surprise on thinking about it, with a great sense of hope. Whatever despair I had come to feel at a waning sense of the real land and the emergence of false geographies—elements of the land being manipulated, for example, to create erroneous but useful patterns in advertising—was dispelled by the depth of a single person's local knowledge, by the serenity that seemed to come with that intelligence. Any harm that might be done by people who cared nothing for the land, to whom it was not innately worthy but only something ultimately for sale, I thought, would one day have to meet this kind of integrity, people with the same dignity and transcendence as the land they occupied. So when I traveled, when I rolled my sleeping bag out on the shores of the Beaufort Sea, or in the high pastures of the Absaroka Range in Wyoming, or at the bottom of the Grand Canyon, I absorbed those particular testaments to life, the indigenous color and songbird song, the smell of sun-bleached rock, damp earth, and wild honey, with some crude appreciation of the singular magnificence of each of those places. And the reassurance I felt expanded in the knowledge that there were, and would likely always be, people speaking out whenever they felt the dignity of the Earth imperiled in those places.

The promulgation of false geographies, which threaten the fundamental notion of what it means to live somewhere, is a current with a stable and perhaps growing countercurrent. People living in New York City are familiar with the stone basements, the cratonic geology, of that island and have a feeling for birds migrating through in the fall, their sequence and number. They do not find the city alien but human, its attenuated natural history merely different from that of rural Georgia or Kansas. I find the countermeasure, too, among Eskimos who cannot read but who might engage you for days on the subtleties of sea-ice topography. And among men and women who, though they have followed in the footsteps of their parents, have come to the conclusion that they cannot farm or fish or log in the way their ancestors did; the finite boundaries to this sort of wealth have appeared in their lifetime. Or among young men and women who have taken several decades of book-learned agronomy, zoology, silviculture and horticulture, ecology, ethnobotany, and fluvial geomorphology and turned it into a new kind of local knowledge, who have taken up residence in a place and sought, both because of and in spite of their education, to develop a deep intimacy with it. Or they have gone to work, idealistically, for the National Park Service or the fish and wildlife services or for a private institution like the Nature Conservancy. They are people to whom the land is more than politics and economics. These are people for whom the land is alive. It feeds them, directly, and that is how and why they learn its geography.

In the end, then, if one begins among the blue crabs of Chesapeake Bay and wanders for several years, down through the Smoky Mountains and back to the bluegrass hills, along the drainages of the Ohio and into the hill country of Missouri, where in summer a chorus of cicadas might drown out human conversation, then up the Missouri itself, reading on the way the entries of Meriwether Lewis and William Clark and musing on the demise of the plains grizzly and the sturgeon, crosses west into the drainage of the Platte and spends the evenings with Gene Weltfish's *The Lost Universe,* her book about the Pawnee who once thrived there, then drops south to the Palo Duro Canyon and the irrigated farms of the Llano Estacado in Texas, turns west across the Sangre de Cristo, southernmost of the Rocky Mountain ranges, and moves north and west up onto the slickrock mesas of Utah, those browns and oranges, the ocherous hues reverberating in the deep canyons, then goes north, swinging west to the insular ranges that sit like battleships in the pelagic space of Nevada, camps at the steaming edge of the sulfur springs in the Black Rock desert, where alkaline pans are glazed with a ferocious light, a heat to melt iron, then crosses the northern Sierra Nevada, waist-deep in summer snow in the passes, to descend to the valley of the Sacramento, and rises through groves of the elephantine redwoods in the Coast Range, to arrive at Cape Mendocino, before Balboa's Pacific, cormorants and gulls, gray whales headed north for Unimak Pass in the Aleutians, the winds crashing down on you, facing the ocean over the blue ocean that gives the scene its true vastness, making this crossing, having been so often astonished at the line and the color of the land, the ingenious lives of its plants and animals, the varieties of its darknesses, the intensity of the stars overhead, you would be ashamed to discover, then, in yourself, any capacity to focus on ravages in the land that left you unsettled. You would have seen so much, breathtaking, startling, and outsize, that you might not be able for a long time to break the spell, the sense, especially finishing your journey in the West, that the land had not been as rearranged or quite as compromised as you had first imagined.

After you had slept some nights on the beach, however, with that finite line of the ocean before you and the land stretching out behind you, the wind first battering then cradling you, you would be compelled by memory, obligated by your own involvement, to speak of what left you troubled. To find the rivers dammed and shrunken, the soil washed away, the land fenced, a tracery of pipes and wires and roads laid down everywhere and animals, cutting the eye off repeatedly and confining it—you had expected this. It troubles you no more than your despair over the ruthlessness, the insensitivity, the impetuousness of modern life. What underlies this obvious change, however, is less noticeable pattern of disruption: acidic lakes, the skies empty of birds, fouled beaches, the poisonous slags of industry, the sun burning like a molten coin in ruined air.

It is a tenet of certain ideologies that man is responsible for all that is ugly, that everything nature creates is beautiful. Nature's darkness goes partly unreported, of course, and human brilliance is often perversely ignored. What is true is that man has a power, literally beyond his comprehension, to destroy. The lethality of some of what he manufactures, the incompetence with which he stores it or seeks to dispose of it, the cavalier way in which he employs in his daily living substances that threaten his health, the leniency of the courts in these matters (as though products as well as people enjoyed the protection the Fifth Amendment), and the treatment of open land, rivers, and the atmosphere as if, in some medieval way, they could still be regarded as disposal sinks of infinite capacity, would make you wonder, standing face to in the wind at Cape Mendocino, if we weren't bent on an errand of madness.

The geographies of North America, the myriad small landscapes that make up the national fabric, are threatened—by ignorance of what makes them unique, by utilitarian attitudes, by failure to include them in the moral universe, and by brutal disregard. A testament of minor voices can clear away an ignorance of any place, can inform us of its special qualities; but no voice, by merely telling a story, can cause the poisonous wastes that saturate some parts of the land to decompose, to evaporate. This responsibility falls ultimately to the national community, a vague and fragile entity. to be sure, but one that, in America, can be ferocious in exerting its will.

Geography, the formal way in which we grapple with this areal mystery, is finally knowledge that calls up something in the land we recognize and respond to. It gives us a sense of place and a sense of community. Both are indispensable to a state of well-being, an individual's and a country's.

One afternoon on the Siuslaw River in the Coast Range of Oregon, in January, I hooked a steelhead, a sea run trout, that told me, through the muscles of my hands and arms and shoulders, something of the nature of the thing I was calling "the Siuslaw River." Years ago I had stood under a pecan tree in Upson County, Georgia, idly eating the nuts, when slowly it occurred to me that these nuts would taste different from pecans growing somewhere up in South Carolina. I didn't need a sharp sense of taste to know this, only to pay attention at a level no one had ever told me was necessary. One November dawn, long before the sun rose, I began a vigil at the Dumont Dunes in the Mojave Desert in California, which I kept until a few minutes after the sun broke the horizon. During that time I named to myself the colors by which the sky changed and by which the sand itself flowed like a rising tide through grays and silvers and blues into yellows, pinks, washed duns, and fallow beiges.

It is through the power of observation, the gifts of eye and ear, of tongue and nose and finger, that a place first rises up in our mind; afterward, it is memory that carries the place, that allows it to grow in depth and complexity. For as long as our records go back, we have held these two things dear, landscape and memory. Each infuses us with a different kind of life. The one feeds us, figuratively and literally. The other protects us from lies and tyranny. To keep landscapes intact and the memory of them, our history in them, alive, seems as imperative a task in modern time as finding the extent to which individual expression can be accommodated, before it threatens to destroy the fabric of society.

If I were now to visit another country, I would ask my local companion, before I saw any museum or library, any factory or fabled town, to walk me in the country of his or her youth, to tell me the names of things and how, traditionally, they have been fitted together in a community. I would ask for the stories, the voice of memory over the land. I would ask about the history of storms there, the age of the trees, the winter color of the hills. Only then would I ask to see the museum. I would want first the sense of a real place, to know that I was not inhabiting an idea. I would want to know the lay of land first, the real geography, and take some measure of the love of it in my companion before I stood before the painting or read works of scholarship. I would want to have something real and remembered against which I might hope to measure their truth.

BOX 9
RECALLING A SENSE OF PLACE

We carry our sense of place, our personal geography, into our fieldwork. Before we research place, it is important to retrieve and record our own internal landscape and make it explicit to ourselves. What images do we remember from particular landscapes? What details do we recall about places we've visited? Why do these sensations return to us at particular moments in time? Why those images, details, and sensations and not others? Lopez suggests that the intimate link between landscape and memory comes through the act of writing and

> . . . through the power of observation, the gifts of eye and ear, of tongue and nose and finger, that a place first rises up in our mind; afterward, it is memory that carries the place, that allows it to grow in depth and complexity. For as long as our records go back, we have held these two things dear, landscape and memory.

Choose a spot that brings back a rush of sensory details: sights, sounds, smells, textures, and tastes. It doesn't need to be an enormous natural wonder like the Grand Canyon or the Cascade Mountains; it can be a much smaller place. Try describing a private spot—a certain tree in your backyard, a basketball court, a relative's dining room, the corner of a city lot, the interior of a closet, or a window seat that catches the sunlight. As you think about the specifics of this place, its details and sensations, you'll probably retrieve a dominant impression, a cluster of images, or some person connected to the memory. These are all part of your internal landscape. Write a few short descriptive paragraphs with as many details as you can to share with your writing partner.

Response

Harvey Du Marce wrote about his home, a Sioux reservation in South Dakota. To write his paragraph, he first made a list of sensory details and then added a column of personal reflections based on his memories:

Sensory Detail	Reflections
hot, August, 90 degrees	burned out landscape—a symbol?
dry brown prairie grass	familiar landscape
buzzing crickets	comforting sound of home
distant hills	childhood imagination, excitement
mother—white patch in dark hair	quiet affection
soft voice, fixes food	regret, guilt for going away to school
small, cool living room	neatness, comfort, welcoming
clinging vines on windows	brings nature in
star quilts to keep out sun	traditional design—both craft and utility
corn soup, fry bread, chokecherries	nostalgic childhood foods

Harvey's descriptive details evoke a strong sense of place, of both the prairie and the interior of his childhood home. These paragraphs illustrate his spatial gaze as he sweeps across the land around the reservation, moving in closer to his mother's house. In these short paragraphs, he combines both the large and small details of his own internal landscape:

> I came home to the reservation that August. The weather was hot and dry. The green grass around my mother's house had burned brown and crisp. A pulsating buzz of crickets caught my ear. The sound came from behind the house; it would rise collectively and then slowly fade in the tree line. My mother intuitively sensed my return as she stood on the porch. She looked the same from a distance; I imagined her gentle open face still had a smooth quality. I thought I saw a small patch of white in her short black hair.
>
> I could not reconcile myself with this landscape, which was once a part of my life, and perhaps it would always be part of me. I momentarily forgot who I was. Could I be the restless young man who left the reservation ten years ago? Was I really the educated college person? The crickets and my mother's soft voice merged somewhere in the back of my mind.
>
> When I walked into the house, she greeted me with affection. My long absence did not seem to matter to her, but it mattered to me. Two star quilts hung over the living room windows to keep out the heat of the day. No air conditioner hummed, but inside, the house was cool and comfortable. The living room was small. A thick green strand of clinging vines covered the west window, turning the room into a blend of shade and light. I noticed that my mother's cherished and manicured vines had finally reached the roof of the house.
>
> When I sat down on the old sofa, I looked out the south window and saw a range of dark blue hills in the distance. The hills were old and eternal like the earth. As a child, those hills stirred my imagination the way a wind lifts an eagle. Over the years, my imagination had eroded and decayed until only its root still existed in a far corner of my soul. My dreams were now ordinary.
>
> Homemade corn soup and fry bread smells wafted out of the kitchen. I turned away from the window. Mother put a bowl of the steaming soup and two pieces of fry bread on the table and called to me to come and eat. We would talk later.

A Sense of Place: Selective Perception

Most anthropologists begin their fieldwork in distant places, teaching themselves how to see the local landscape through the eyes of the people in the culture. Folklorist Henry Glassie's *Passing the Time in Ballymenone* is a full-length ethnographic study (10 years, 852 pages) of storytelling, conversation, and music making in a small community in Northern Ireland. While he passed the time at the evening *ceili* (their term for these fireside sessions), Glassie also learned how to look at the northern Irish landscape. Over time, his gaze expanded to include evenings spent inside the neighbors' cottages as he farmed with them during the day and researched their geography, genealogy, local and national history, politics, economics, and cultural values. He came to see the influences of their daily living on their verbal art of "ceiliing." Gradually, Ballymenone's landscape took hold of him, drawing him into the study of his informants' world. In this short excerpt, which introduces a ceili session at the Flanagans', Glassie begins with a verbal snapshot of the landscape, a wide-angle sweep of the hillside, and ends with a close-up of the neighbors as they gather around the hearth.

The house cattle should have been onto the hillsides early in April, but summer came lashing wet winds down the brown hedges and through bleak fields. Across the bog and over the hills, air lay bone cold. Some of the cows, they say, starved in their byres, dying on beds of sodden rushes, and into the minds of men waiting for the sun blew years when black frost shriveled the spuds on the ridges, years when turf lay on the spread through the summer, and winter closed down without food for the belly or fuel for the hearth. The bright, warm days expected in May and June never came. In running gray skies, in the dank sloughs of the gaps, summer broke, damp, chilled.

Now it is calm. Fat cattle move slowly in the blue harvest evening. Lush grasslands swell and fold in the haze. Some of last year's potatoes and turf and hay remain, heaped into pits on the moss ground, thatched in lumps on the bog, piled in haysheds, built into rotund pecks along the lanes. Old defenses against hard times, displays of industry cover the land.

A month ago summer ended in a blaze of sunshine and a frenzy of work. Hay was rooked, turf was clamped. Sun and warm winds drove out the wet. Once built into rounded conical rooks, and clamps the shape of ancient oratories, hay and turf are considered won. That is their word for victory in the cyclical war fought with the hand-tools they call weapons: the pitchfork and the spade.

Now it is quiet, an interlude in work and worry. The main crop potatoes are not yet ready to dig, nor is it time to transplant winter cabbage, shear the corn, or drive the cattle onto the sweet aftergrass of the meadows. Work slows but does not stop. It is a time for gathering in the spoils of war, drawing turf and hay home, and it is time to hack back hedges with billhooks and cart broken turf to gardens built on barren land. Gently, the next campaign begins.

Turf and hay are won. For a month the new potatoes, the Epicures, have been boiled for dinner. It is a time, too, for mild extravagance. This year's potatoes are boiled in lavish numbers, fires built of this year's turf are unnecessarily hearty. Winter's word is bitter. In its depths, when winds pound at the walls of home, potatoes will be sparingly spent and the fire will be stretched with gathered sticks, but today victory expands in little luxuries.

Joe Flanagan turns from the sack of turf next to the open front door. Damp green and blue melt behind him. He cradles an armload. Peter lifts a violin from its case in the corner and settles on a stool by the hearth. Dinner is done, the hens are fed, empty teacups sit on the floor. Joe tongs live coals from the fire, lines them in front of the hearthstone, and sweeps the ashes off to his side with a besom of heather bound round with twine (95–96).

In this short passage, Glassie writes from the stance of the Ballymenone residents, capturing the lilting rhythms of their language, seeing what they would see, using words they would use to describe the setting. His first line describes a history of recent weather conditions, noting that the "cattle should have been on the hillside in April," that summer "came lashing wet winds," that the "bright, warm days in May and June never came," and when summer finally came it was damp and chilled. He writes not only with the knowledge of how weather has affected the current daily lives and livelihoods of the villagers but also its importance in the past when harsher weather affected the potato harvest: "years when black frost shriveled the spuds," "when turf lay on the spread," and "when winter closed down without food for the belly or fuel for the hearth." His description focuses on the features of the landscape that the villagers themselves would notice: bog, rushes, spuds, turf and hay, cattle. His eye rests on the things their eyes would rest on.

Just as Harvey described his own personal spatial memories, Glassie's description also begins with a large but detailed sweep of the landscape—fattened cattle moving on lush grasslands in a hazy blue harvest evening—into the small space of the Flanagan hearthstone with empty teacups sitting on the floor. His spatial gaze moves from outside to inside, creating a mood and a setting for the ceili (storytelling session). Though Glassie writes using the third-person point of view, this description is not objective. In fact, some scholars believe that Glassie romanticizes the Irish culture in descriptions such as this. Like all of us, Glassie operates with a spatial gaze framed by his own biases, assumptions, and cultural baggage. He might ask himself these questions about his descriptions, as all of us should about our field sites:

- Why do I focus on this element of the landscape and not that?
- What is my reason for narrowing my gaze to any specific place?
- What spaces have I rejected as I've narrowed my gaze?
- Why do I use the metaphors and descriptions I do?
- Which metaphors and descriptions did I abandon as inappropriate?
- Where in my fieldnotes do I find evidence for this description?
- What have I rejected, and why?

Spatial details are an important part of the fieldworker's data. All fieldworkers describe their informants in a setting, working from an abundance of evidence: fieldnotes, photos, maps, and background history gathered over time. Researchers cannot lean entirely on visual details; the ethnographic eye should also include sounds, textures, tastes, and smells. Important details also come from noticing and documenting, as Glassie does, conditions of color, weather, light, shape, time, season, atmosphere, and ambiance. Choosing details is an act of selective perception. As we write, we revise our worldviews. The point of doing fieldwork is to learn to see not just the other but ourselves as well. The spatial gaze demands that we look—and then look back again.

BOX 10
WRITING A VERBAL SNAPSHOT

Your fieldnotes are a rich source of data from which you can select key details to begin to create verbal snapshots for your project. Choose a small portion of your field site to describe for this exercise. Whether you have recorded your data as a list, as Harvey did, or as a narrative, read and review those fieldnotes and underline, tag, or highlight 5 to 10 details that stand out at your field site. What did your informant call to your attention that you might not have noticed? What is the most typical? The most unusual? Which one stood out for you?

Comb through the data to determine categories of sights, sounds, smells, textures, and tastes; weather, atmospheric conditions, colors, light, shapes. Categorizing will help you write your description, and it will also help you fill in the missing data in your fieldwork. Noticing the gaps helps you determine where or in what ways your data might be incomplete. Do you need different sensory details? More about the setting at different times of day? Do you want to focus on a certain spot in this place where there's important activity going on? What details do you need more of? What did you forget to take in? Asking these questions helps you decide if you want to return to your field site to gather more evidence.

Writing a place description involves more than making an inventory or listing details. Your description needs to suggest the overall sense of place you are trying to understand and should mirror your informants' perspective as well. Sometimes, one small detail from your data can expand into a rich image that reflects a dominant theme within the culture. For example, Glassie gives us the image of Joe sweeping the hearth with a "besom of heather bound round with twine," which evokes the poetic and domestic sides of Irish culture. The effect would have been quite different had he written, "Joe swept the floor with a homemade broom." Since one of the goals of fieldworking is to include your informant's worldview, field site descriptions should ring true to both outsiders and insiders.

After writing a short description based on your notes about setting details, share a page or two with a colleague to see if you've successfully created a sense of place and to discuss what you might do in further research. As you respond to your partner, help point out the most telling details. Which details evoke larger images? Which details uncover cultural information about the place? Which details seem to represent the informant's perspective? Are there any specific words that seem like insider language?

Response

For this response, we return to Karen Downing, the English teacher whose fieldnotes from Photo Phantasies we discussed in Chapter 2. You've read the section where she struggles to negotiate access into the store. Karen's entire study, "Strike a Pose," along with her research portfolio appear later in this chapter. She opens her research essay about the mall store that sells glamorized photographs with the section "Smiling Women." She selects details to represent the contemporary American mall culture: a Chinese restaurant that uses plastic forks instead of chopsticks, a gang of middle schoolers with Disney bags that read, "Take home a little magic," and Photo Phantasies employee and promoter Bettie, who slumps against a display rack picking her fingernails. The exterior details describing mall life will set the scene for the interior of Photo Phantasies. The details Karen chooses come from her fieldnotes.

As I pull open one of the heavy glass doors at Forum West Mall, a medium-sized suburban shopping mall, I am overwhelmed by sensations. Bells and laughs and sirens from the Fun Factory layer on top of piped-in Muzak. Large, colorful movie posters advertise *Man of the House*, *A Goofy Movie*, and *The Pebble and the Penguin*. People are everywhere—men and women in business suits eating lunch, several teenagers smoking by the reflecting pond, mothers running errands with babies in tow, older people exercise-walking in fitness gear. The smells of freshly baked bread from Subway, sugary caramel corn, greasy pizza, and fried tacos hang in the air. There are yellow benches and tables and leafy trees reaching toward skylights and winding staircases and two automatic teller machines and a lingerie store and a department store and an engraving stand. I experience all of this just 10 feet inside of the mall.

As a teenager, I would spend hours at Forum West each weekend, roaming through the stores with various best friends. Now, as woman in my twenties, when I go to the mall, I go with a purpose. Today I am in the mall to look for tennis shoes. To get to Durham's Discount Sporting Goods, I must pass two food stands and three other shops. I walk quickly, head down, thinking about walking shoes versus cross-trainers, Reeboks versus Nikes. I pass Chopstixs, an Asian fast-food restaurant that provides plastic forks instead of chopsticks. Up ahead I see the Disney Store, or rather I hear the Disney Store—strains of the *Little Mermaid* soundtrack carry out into the mall. To my right, a group of middle school girls are huddled together, each clutching shopping bags that encourage "Take home a little magic—take home Disney." They giggle as they try on Mickey Mouse ears. I pull closer in toward the storefronts. Durham's is only 12 feet away.

"Hi, let me tell you about Photo Phantasies. My name is Bettie. What's yours?" This woman was slumped against a display rack, picking her fingernails, until she saw me. I smile at Bettie and try to pass, but she keeps speaking to me.

"Look, 'Somewhere in America, a new model is waiting to be discovered. It could be you! Just ask how. Today!' " Bettie reads the words in bold print on the display as I note the photograph under the words. It is of a girl who is possibly in her late teens or early twenties. She is smiling at the camera. Her brown hair cascades around her face and rests on her shoulders. Her brown eyes and lipsticked mouth reflect a glimmer of light.

"The Photo Phantasies process is simple and fun! It's a celebration! And you could be chosen to be a model. With those eyes, I think you'd stand a good chance! We may just have openings right now. At least take a brochure home. Talk to your friends! You should do it! It's fun! . . ."

I take the brochure, smile again, and walk away. She calls out these parting words: "You'd look great! Just great! I promise." I hear these words as I see an image on the television monitor. The woman is smiling at me. She is wearing a red hat that fans out from her face. Gold and rhinestone earrings dangle from her ears. She looks as if she's posing for a camera, but I can't actually see the camera. She drops her shoulder and tilts her head to one side. Then the photographer steps into the image on the monitor. He lowers the woman's chin with his hand. He adjusts the bustier that she is wearing by tugging it down on the right side, his hands close to the woman's waist. He steps out of the picture. She's still. She looks right at me and smiles. I fold the Photo Phantasies brochure and put it inside my coat pocket and walk into Durham's.

Learning How to Look: Mapping Space

As a researcher, like Karen, you'll teach yourself how to look, how to "read" a space. Make lists, for instance, of sensory details at your site, interior and exterior, paying attention to more than just visual impressions. Track who goes in and out of the field site at different times of day and how they use different areas. Draw actual maps or diagrams, which give you information that would be difficult to get merely through observation. Research the space further by talking to informants or by studying documents that describe it. As you take notes, record your assumptions about how the space is used. As you follow up on these initial notes, you will discover surprising information about the place. Through recording, listing, mapping, and researching, you'll learn about how the people you're studying use their space.

Henry Glassie, in his study of the ceili sessions, mapped the visiting patterns among four houses in Ballymenone to determine how the neighbors' and families' relationships interconnect, how his informants' stories influence each other, and how the evening visits between houses mirror their work during the day. By mapping the space, Glassie obtained information that would be difficult to understand any other way. Fieldworkers who study cultures for long periods of time make extensive inventories of household goods and cultural artifacts; study kinship patterns, genealogies, and family records; sketch and photograph buildings, implements, and topography; categorize local flora and fauna; and conduct surveys among the locals. Sometimes a culture's archives—old records such as diaries, journals, and albums; photos; church histories; and architectural documents—can assist the fieldworker in developing a sense of place.

Karen Downing, who studied the Photo Phantasies subculture for a much shorter period of time, takes advantage of many of these fieldworking skills and displays artifacts from her research in her portfolio. She includes cover pages from glamour magazines and books about the beauty culture, a marketing flyer and promotional package for customers of Photo Phantasies, a company document for employees called "Business Culture" that outlines its beliefs and values, and the manager's favorite poem, which hung in her office. These are the archives of the business, which help Karen understand more fully how the space represents the glamour photography culture. Using these archival records and the lists of details

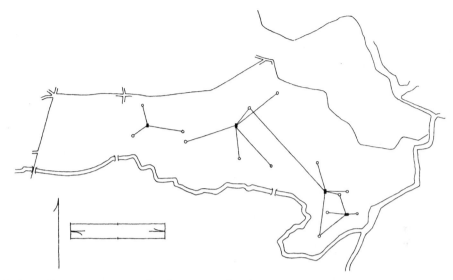

Ceiliing. Customary patterns of night-visiting to four houses.

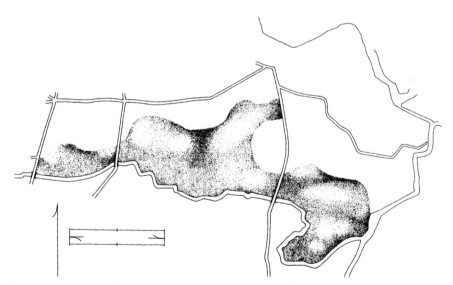

The Community. The shape of the community, "our district of the country,"
shaded to indicate topography.

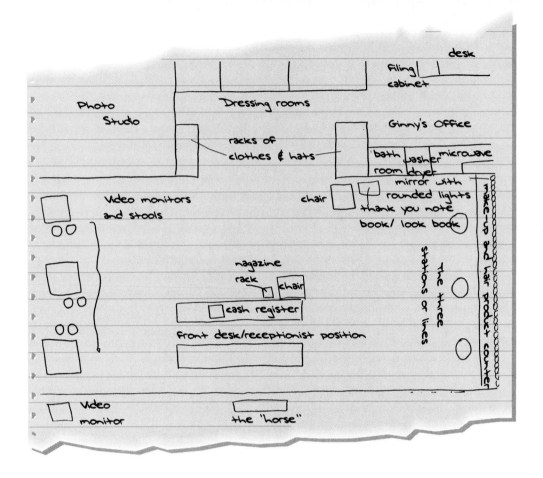

desk

Filing cabinet

Photo Studio

Dressing rooms

Ginny's Office

racks of clothes & hats

bath room

washer dryer

microwave

Video monitors and stools

chair

mirror with rounded lights

thank you note

book/ look book

make-up and hair product counter

the three stations or lines

magazine rack

chair

cash register

front desk/receptionist position

Video monitor

the "horse"

Karen Downing's map of the Photo Phantasies store.

from her fieldnotes as background, Karen sketched a map of the store itself. Her map eventually helped her understand the use of space at Photo Phantasies and its relationship to the business as a whole. She learned that the store organized its layout so efficiently that the customer would be unconscious of either the small size of the store or the underlying hard sell. In her portfolio, Karen reflects on her map: "A map of the PP store (very much not in scale!). What my drawing doesn't show is just how small this store actually is. The layout reflects the theme that efficiency equals greater sales. Everything moves in a progressive way, from one step to the next, like a well-orchestrated dance."

The following section from her final essay describing Photo Phantasies draws from all of her background research, her map, and her fieldnotes to create a verbal snapshot of the store. In this excerpt, as Karen waits for her appointment with Ginny James, the manager, she pulls out her research journal and records fieldnotes about what she sees, worried, at the same time, that the receptionist might be watching her. Here's her place description:

The store is perhaps 30 feet by 30 feet, but each inch of space is used. There are three black vinyl chairs facing a mirrored wall and a counter where I assume makeup and hair are done. A sign hanging above this area reads "Professional Makeup Artists." I look around for these people, but no one is working near the three chairs, nor is anyone in the store but the receptionist. Surrounding the 4-foot-high mirror on the wall are round light bulbs that remind me of movie stars' dressing rooms. On the counter, an array of curling irons, blow dryers, Q-tips, mousse, static guard, and hair spray joins tray after tray of makeup. Above the mirror is the wall of "Phantasy Phaces": Photo Phantasies photographs, each measuring 3 feet on a side, arranged to look like film coming off a movie reel. All of the photographs are of women, except for two little girls and one couple.

In front of my chair are racks of clothing—denim jackets with gold studs, gold lamé blouses, a coat with red, white, and blue stars and stripes, sequined blazers, beaded bustiers, blue and pink boas, and shelves of hats. Beyond the wardrobe selections, there are three dressing rooms without mirrors or seats inside. Each one has a white mesh hamper for clothes and a white hook on the wall and a black curtain that can be pulled over the opening to the dressing room.

Next to the racks of clothes is the photography sitting room. I cannot see much of that room because the door is only halfway open, but I can see part of a royal blue background and a black vinyl stool. I can only assume that the camera is in there somewhere. On the other side of the photography sitting room are three computer monitors. The computer monitors, placed in a straight row, are off to the right of the receptionist desk and the cash register. My high school students who have been to Photo Phantasies tell me that after they have had their pictures taken, they change back into their street clothes and meet a salesperson who uses the computer monitor to display the proofs. There is no wait time—a customer can see her photographs on the monitor seconds after the pictures have been taken.

After 15 minutes, the receptionist touches me on the shoulder. She looks down at the notes in my journal as I look down at the floor, feeling like I have just been caught doing something inappropriate. "Cool handwriting! It kinda looks like calligraphy! Ginny's ready for you now." She points toward the back of the store, past the racks of clothes to a door near the dressing rooms. The door is open. I stand there, waiting for Ginny to look up. After several moments, I knock and say hello.

BOX 11
MAPPING SPACE: A MEAL IN THE MAKING

This is a version of a mapping exercise we completed in our own training as fieldworkers and have since adapted for our classes. The point of the exercise is to record and gather observations during a half-hour of an everyday routine. We suggest watching people making a meal, but you can choose any daily routine that involves at least two people. It is best to work collaboratively so that you and your partner can collect a range of data. For example, one person can focus on body language and use of space while the other focuses on spoken language. You and your partner can compare the preresearch assumptions you bring to the site and discuss possible conclusions as you work through your data together. Here are some things to consider:

1. *Obtain access.* Choose a site in which at least two people are engaged in the daily mealtime routines—children and parent, housemates, spouses, friends. Choose people who will feel comfortable being watched, as this exercise demands such close observation that you will not be able to help make the meal or set the table. Of course, if your informants choose to invite you to eat it with them, that's another choice. Be sure, as any good guest would, to offer something in return. You might bring flowers or dessert.

2. *Record your assumptions.* Speculate on what you think you'll see. What do you already know about these people and their relationship? Their kitchen? Their lifestyle?

3. *Take notes on the overall setting.* What details of place seem relevant? How does the eating area fit into the overall plan of the home? Is it casual or formal? Be sure to be specific with relevant details. Note "8 hand-painted Delft plates" rather than "pile of plates."

4. *Map the space.* Draw a diagram of the kitchen or the place where the meal is being prepared. Use it to show where your informants move within the space. Colored markers or pencils can be useful to designate each informant's movements.

5. *Describe the activities.* Develop a system for recording the movements of each informant. What are the meal makers doing? Pay attention to what's going on: phone interruptions, neighbors' and children's visits, other incidents that break the flow of the activity. What utensils and objects do they use? How do they use them? Make a time line, noting how long each activity takes.

6. *Tape-record the conversation or take notes by hand.* How much of talk is related to the meal-making interaction itself? How much is everyday talk? What talk is related to the power relationships among the meal makers? Who initiates talk? Who is silent? Who interrupts? Who gives directions and who follows? If males and females are involved, are there gender-related issues or differences?

7. *Talk with your partner.* Expand your fieldnotes together, talk about your findings, and speculate on what your conclusions might be. What do you agree on? What do you see differently?

8. *Write up the data collaboratively (two to three pages).* Attach to this description the fieldnotes, the transcripts, your map, and notes from your

discussions with your partner. It is rewarding to see the amount of data two researchers can collect in a half-hour's time.

Response

While she was researching her Photo Phantasies project, Karen did this exercise to learn more about observing and mapping space. The first part of this exercise represents the data Karen and her partner gathered in the field. Her written commentary represents the reflexive analysis they did away from the field.

With a colleague, Liesl, Karen spent a half-hour at the home of Ellen Friar, watching Ellen and her daughter, Paula, prepare dinner. Together, Karen and Liesl gathered over 12 pages of fieldnotes, transcripts, and maps. After their observation, they collaborated on the following set of notes. In looking over their data, they found that their map provided the most important information about the use of space.

Date:	February 13
Time:	5:45 p.m.
Participants:	Ellen (E)—mother, Paula (P)—20-year-old daughter
Nonparticipating characters:	Bill (B)—Ellen's husband and Paula's father, Frank (F)— Paula's boyfriend, Liesl (L) and Karen (K)—observers

1. *Obtain access.* We called Ellen and explained the dinner exercise. She was curious and willing to allow us to observe. She explained that her husband, Bill, and Paula's boyfriend, Frank, would not be part of the preparation but would be eating the dinner. She asked us to come on a Wednesday, when Paula was home from work and would be teaching Ellen how to make fajitas, a meal she had learned from a family in Arizona. "It will be a nice change for me to let Paula cook," she told us, inviting us to eat with them afterward. On Wednesday afternoon, we stopped at Dot's Flower Shop to pick up some red carnations as a small gift of appreciation.

2. *Record your assumptions.* We entered with very different assumptions because Liesl knew the family and Karen didn't. Liesl assumed that Ellen would prepare most of the meal. Liesl also felt that Ellen would be very curious about our observation because she's a teacher herself. Karen felt she would make a good collaborator as she carried no preconceptions about the family, but she had more speculations. Karen wondered, though, how much their researcher presence would affect the preparation. She speculated about how typical this half-hour would be. Would sitting in their kitchen with a tape recorder and two notepads make the family self-conscious? Would the mother and daughter behave normally with two researchers watching their every move?

3. *Take notes on the overall setting.* The house is about three years old, and the Friars are the first family to live there. . . . We note that the kitchen is an alcove, or C-shaped room, that opens to the dining room. It includes a counter or bar area with stools that look into the kitchen from the dining room side. . . . The kitchen has green marble-patterned countertops and light pine cupboards. Appliances are all white (refrigerator, stove, microwave, dishwasher, coffeepot) and match the white wall paint and white floor tile. A matching green rug is

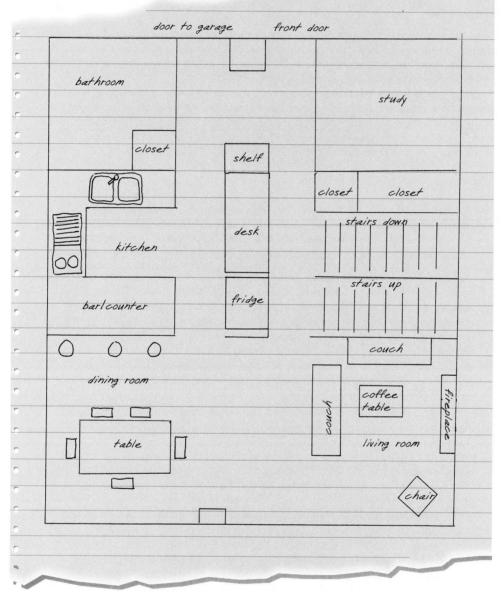

Map A

CHAPTER THREE   Researching Place: The Spatial Gaze

placed to one side. The electric griddle, chicken, onions, condiments, and utensils ready and waiting on the counter space suggest that they have prepared for us. On the desk near the fridge, a small portable radio is tuned softly to National Public Radio. E wears a red sweatshirt with valentine hearts, matching sweatpants, socks, and slippers. She is small (approx 5'3"/110 lbs), thin face, dark brown hair. P is dressed in a navy blue sweatshirt and stretch pants with socks. She is larger than E (approx 5'6"/160 lbs), full face, blonde hair.

4. *Map the space* (see Map A).

5 and 6. *Describe the activities and record the conversation.*

5:48 p.m.
E asks "What do I do?" She stands idly waiting in the middle of the kitchen for Paula to give her directions.
P points to the chicken and E begins to slice it very thin with an enormous knife.
P begins chopping onions on plastic cutting board, away from E.
E says "We don't usually cook this way—you know, make this food like this. I just didn't cook when you weren't here, not just for Bob and me. Now that you're here, we're cooking more." E explains that it is hard to plan ahead. She stops chopping and waves the knife. She turns to P. "I come home from work, feed the dog, then get dinner—it's rush rush. You know, rush in, rush out." E begins chopping again. "I want you to notice that your father scrubbed the burner and got all that gunk off." E points to the burner. P does not respond. "He did a good job. It's pretty clean. Can you see?" P does not respond.

5:55
P puts tortilla chips on table and returns to kitchen, where she throws the chicken onto the griddle.
"It's almost done." E says, "Hmmm, good."
E is cleaning all utensils, cutting boards, and dishes. E rinses everything thoroughly and places it all in the dishwasher.

6:03
E says "OK, I think we're about ready." She takes six brown dishes from the cupboard and sets them at each place at the table.
F enters the kitchen and whispers something in P's ear. P rolls her eyes, and F leaves the kitchen-dining area.
E says "Maybe we should have some salad, or I could cut up some fruit?"
P says "Mom. . . . no, it's fine."
E says "Well, the table looks so sparse! There's hardly a thing on it! Oh! Wait! I do have some fruit bars!" E takes a small plastic container from the cupboard. She removes some lemon squares from it and places them on a plate.
P asks "When did you make those?"
E laughs "That's right! If you had known about them, there would be none for dinner!"

7. *Talk with your partner.* Afterward, since there was such little talk, we wondered how each person knew what duties to perform. We thought P and E negotiated the tiny space fairly well without getting in each other's way or being confused over their duties. E remained mostly stationary or in one immediate area, while P moved about. Were we imagining a tension between P and E? E seemed to

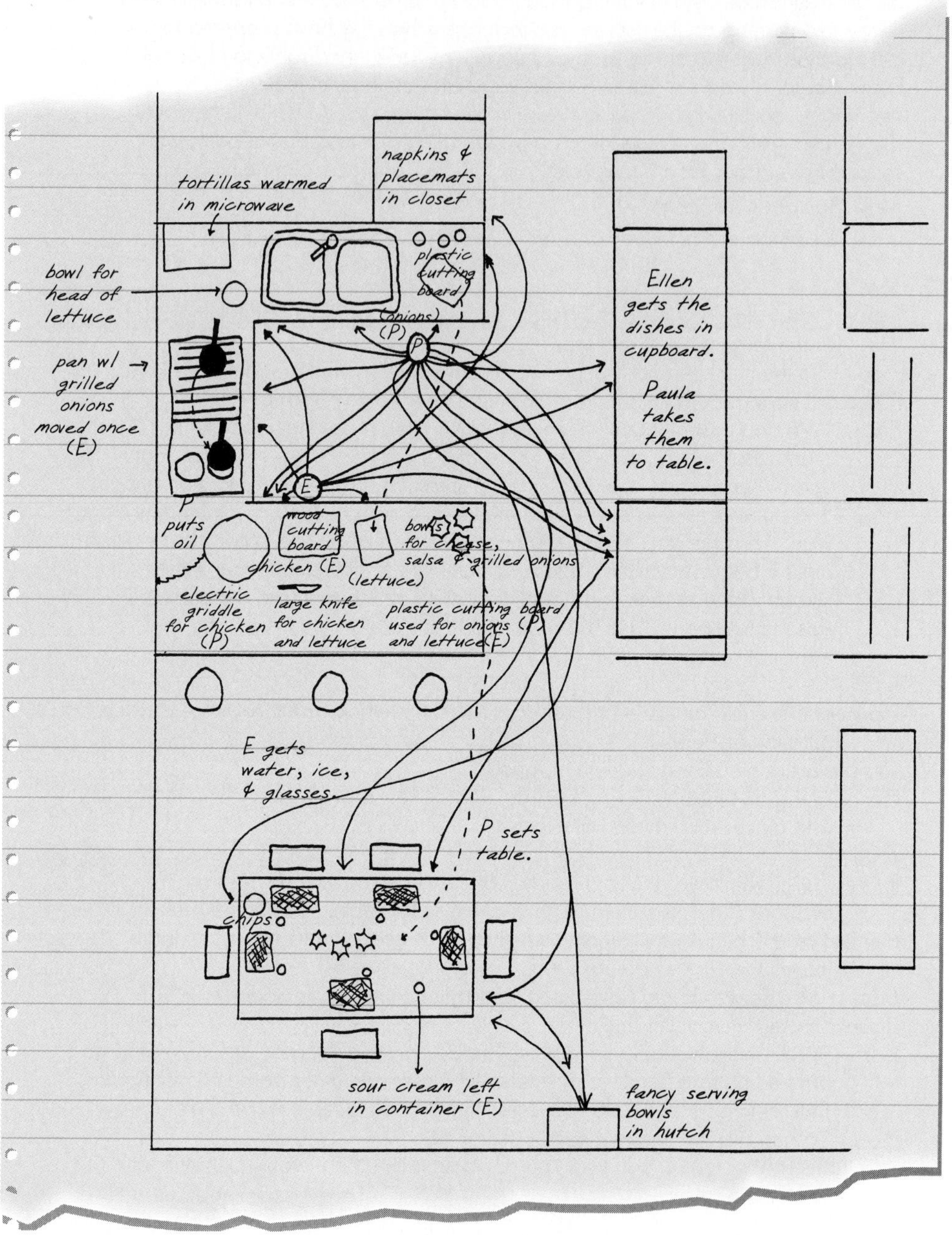
tortillas warmed in microwave
napkins & placemats in closet
bowl for head of lettuce
plastic cutting board
(onions) (P)
P
Ellen gets the dishes in cupboard.
Paula takes them to table.
pan w/ grilled onions moved once (E)
E
P puts oil
wood cutting board
chicken (E)
(lettuce)
bowls for cheese, salsa & grilled onions
electric griddle for chicken (P)
large knife for chicken and lettuce
plastic cutting board used for onions (P) and lettuce (E)
E gets water, ice, & glasses.
P sets table.
chips
sour cream left in container (E)
fancy serving bowls in hutch

Map B

be the outgoing director of the action and P the quiet subversive follower. There seemed to be real control issues between them. Even though P was teaching E how to make the dinner, E seemed to control P's actions. As Map B shows, P moved in and out of the kitchen area twice as often as E, who worked mostly in one place. E seems concerned about neatness and cleaning up after a mess is made. The kitchen may be a haven or sanctuary for her. E struck us as a great talker, a facilitator of conversation but not the best listener. What did F whisper to P that caused her eyes to roll? Would he have done that if we weren't there? Or would he have spoken instead of whispered? We wondered what E really thought about P's live-in boyfriend. Did our presence seem to interrupt any of their movements? Our follow-up questions would consider the themes of power relationships and spatial ownership.

8. *Write up the data collaboratively.*

DINNER EXERCISE—FINAL DRAFT

Liesl Fowler and Karen Downing

Families are complex systems that operate with many unstated rules and roles for their members. We each know this from our experiences within our own family units. Familiar familial settings often reveal the most about family members because feelings of comfort and safety are inherent in an intimate setting. Perhaps no more comfortable setting exists for this group than the dinner table.

An aspect of family of continual issue is power and control among the various members of the group. Simple dinner conversation can be very telling about the roles each plays in the family unit. Dinner preparation also can distinguish between real and perceived control of the family. This moment of preparation is where we focused our study.

The Friar home is less than three years old; they are the first family to occupy it. Inside, the decor was white and utilitarian. Everything has a purpose and a place—newspapers are folded and put inside a basket by the couch and a blanket is squarely folded and placed symmetrically across the back of the couch. The downstairs consists of a small bathroom across the main entry from an unused study. The kitchen, dining room, and living room are open-air rooms in an L-shape arrangement. Ellen (51) and her daughter Paula (21) prepared the evening meal in the small C-shaped kitchen. Paula, a college student still living at home, was wearing an oversized Yale sweatshirt and white sweatpants. Her mother was dressed similarly, although Ellen's red sweats outfit matched her earrings, socks, and slippers, with a Valentine theme. Upon first appearance the two look strikingly different: Paula's long, blonde hair and large size is contrasted by Ellen's short, dark hair-style and slight frame. Two family members not present were Frank, Ellen's husband and Paula's father, and Paula's boyfriend, who shares a bedroom with Paula in their family home.

The main dynamic we observed was a dichotomy of power. Overtly, Ellen attempted to dominate the advance preparations for the meal: she had fewer duties during the meal preparation, but those duties were essential;

she maintained a constant level of talk during the preparation; and she kept her work in the focal point of the kitchen. Covertly, Paula controlled the conversation through passivity. While she moved from the kitchen to the dining room during the meal preparations, Paula's contributions were extraneous. The wrestling back and forth between mother and daughter over control was central to their relationship. Although this would seem to be a conflict, their interaction was synchronized and familiar. The differences between mother and daughter serve as the foundation for their relationship.

"We're having FRA-heet-as!" Ellen announced as the preparation began. The fact that she mispronounced the dish shows that, although she made the decisions about the meal, she wasn't familiar with what was being prepared. In fact it was Paula who discovered this recipe when she stayed with her uncle. However, when asked who had decided what they would eat, Ellen commented, "Well, . . . I guess, I did." Ellen also did the shopping for the grocery items needed, although Frank did accompany her to the store, against his wishes. She laughs, "I made him go," again exhibiting her desire to control family situations.

Paula and Ellen navigated the small kitchen despite their size differences and the many preparational tasks. Neither ever stated who was going to undertake each task. Peripheral duties—cutting onions, taking food out of the refrigerator, setting the table, transferring food from container to serving dishes—were Paula's responsibilities. Paula was in constant motion from kitchen counter to sink to refrigerator to dining room. Ellen cut the chicken carefully and deliberately; each piece was nearly identical in size. Her chopping of the lettuce was done in much the same fashion. Ellen remained very much in one section of the kitchen cooking the chicken in the skillet and the onions on the stove. She frequently cleaned Paula's work-stations with a damp cloth as Paula moved on the other tasks. They seemed to never be in each other's way. If Paula entered Ellen's "space," Ellen silently shifted to another area momentarily, and vice versa.

The conversation between mother and daughter floated from the tasks before them to work and family. The dialogue was dominated by Ellen's questions about Paula's job and friends and boyfriend. Paula's responses were either short or nonexistent. Paula made no verbal response to statements her mother made about Frank but met the remarks with eye-rolling and sighing behind her mother's back. Ellen either seemed oblivious to this behavior or accepted it as a characteristic of the way they communicate. Ellen functioned as the vehicle for conversation keeping the spaces filled with speech. On the rare occasion that Paula would verbally respond, Ellen responded vaguely or in a noncommittal way:

E: So you don't work all week?

P: All week?! I work on Sunday! With the high school chick. I'll have to do everything!

E: Hmmmmm . . . Paula generated only one topic for discussion:

P: They [onions] aren't cooking, it isn't hot enough here.

E: (*Exerting her control*) Yes it is now. But I'll move them over to the small burner.

Our final excerpt is the only example of unmasked tension. Ellen's desire to control the meal preparations, her brush-off of Paula's comment and Ellen's joking assumptions about Paula's potential behavior indicate the struggle between mother and daughter:

E: (*Gesturing toward the table*) Maybe we should have some salad or I could cut up some fruit?

P: (*Rolling her eyes*) Mom, no, it's fine.

E: Well, the table looks so sparse. There's hardly a thing on it . . . Oh, wait! I do have some bars! (Ellen takes a small plastic container from cupboard and removes several dessert-like bars and places them on a plate.)

P: (*Whirling around with glasses in her hands*) When did you make those?!

E: (*Laughing*) That's right! If you had known about them, there would be none for dinner.

P: (*Rolling her eyes and quickly turning her back on her mother*) You mean, if ANYONE had known about them!

At that point in the conversation, Paula's boyfriend entered the kitchen and the focus switched to his being in the way when he dropped his backpack in the middle of the meal preparation.

From our observations of the Friars' meal preparation, we feel that the synchronized wrestling of power between this mother and daughter is indicative of their complex relationship.

Learning How to Look: Finding a Focal Point

Mapping places is one of the first ways researchers learn how informants in a culture see and use their space. Glassie's map helped him understand the visiting patterns among the Irish neighbors, Karen's map showed her how the Photo Phantasies management used space, and Karen and Liesl's map highlighted dinner making as the playing field for a power struggle between a mother and a daughter.

By looking at how space is used, fieldworkers come to understand the field site—not just what it looks like but also how their informants inhabit it. Mapping helps researchers lay out masses of data that might otherwise be overwhelming. Studying field site maps alongside other information about the culture and its informants can help you find a focal point within data. Mapping helps you see as a researcher, and your narrative description of the space helps the reader see what you've seen.

Sometimes by mapping the field site, you locate a focal point in the space you're studying. A focal point is a spot, an area, or a place where the insiders' activities cluster. In the dinner exercise, all of the important activities take place within the kitchen counter space, with fewer steps taken outside toward the dining room. Researchers often comb their data looking for focal points in their field sites.

In Barbara Myerhoff's full-length ethnography *Number Our Days*, she describes the researcher's problem of how to select a focal point from masses of data. In this passage, she explains her organizational dilemma as well as her solution:

> The amount and variety of information accumulated in a field study is overwhelming. There is no definite or correct solution to the problem of what to include, how to cut up the pie of social reality, when precisely to leave or stop. . . . Of the three hundred center members, I met and talked with about a half. . . . Of these, I knew eighty personally, and interviewed and spent my time with thirty-six. I tape recorded extensive interviews with these, ranging from two to sixteen hours, visited nearly all in their homes, took trips with them from time to time outside the neighborhood—to doctors, social workers, shopping, funerals, visiting their friends in old age homes, following my subjects to convalescent homes and hospitals; I went to many funerals and memorial services. Apart from these excursions and my interviews with outsiders who knew Center people well—teachers, rabbis, local politicians, volunteers—I concentrated on the Center and its external extensions, the benches, boardwalk, and hotel and apartment lobbies where they congregated (28,29).

Myerhoff's study is of elderly Jews, many of them Holocaust survivors, who spend their days at the Aliyah Senior Citizens' Center in Venice, California, but live independently in apartments. The center elders are immigrants who raised their families into mainstream America; most of them are now forgotten and in poverty. She follows them around the community, tracking their daily routines to and from the center and into their homes. From the data that Myerhoff collected, she selected the Senior Center and its external extensions—a set of benches near the beach and the boardwalk—as her focal points.

When Myerhoff takes her readers on a tour around the center, she notes the cacophony of verbal data that characterizes the culture of the place. She chooses advertisements and posters that proclaim " 'Hot Kosher Meal—Nutritious—65 cents," signs in both Yiddish and English, "Today at 2:00 Jewish History Class. Teacher, Clara Shapiro. *Very educational.*" "Sunday at 1:00. Special Event: Films on Israel. *Refreshments. Come. Enjoy.*"

Myerhoff also describes the walls, decorated by center elders, that slide us through their cultural history: paintings of traditional ceremonies and life in the European shtetl, portraits of Jewish heroes, and artifacts like "a large wooden Star of David illuminated by a string of Christmas lights." A wall-length mural, painted by the elders, portrays "their common journey from the past to the present," a shtetl street scene, a boat full of immigrants arriving at Ellis Island, picketers bearing signs such as "Protest Treatment." Finally, the walls return us to the seniors' everyday life with two pictures of themselves, celebrating the Sabbath inside the center and seated on benches along the boardwalk.

While most of her study's data revolves around the activities inside the Senior Center, Myerhoff pulls her reader toward her other focal point—the benches outside, which face both the ocean and the boardwalk. She uses these benches as her vantage point, as her informants do, to survey the surrounding cultural scene.

Myerhoff observes that the benches serve as a village plaza, a public place for social interaction. In the following description, she analyzes the seniors' bench behavior—and what the behavior represents—as an outside extension of the Center.

As the morning wears on, the benches fill. Benches are attached back to back, one side facing the ocean, one side the boardwalk. The people on the ocean side swivel around to face their friends, the boardwalk, and the Center.

Bench behavior is highly stylized. The half-dozen or so benches immediately to the north and south of the Center are the territory of the members, segregated by sex and conversation topic. The men's benches are devoted to abstract, ideological concerns—philosophical debate, politics, religion, and economics. The women's benches are given more to talk about immediate, personal matters—children, food, health, neighbors, love affairs, scandals, and "managing." Men and women talk about Israel and its welfare, and about being a Jew and about Center politics. On the benches, reputations are made and broken, controversies explored, leaders selected, factions formed and dissolved. Here is the outdoor dimension of Center life, like a village plaza, a focus of protracted, intense sociability.

The surrounding scene rarely penetrates the invisible, pulsing membrane of the Center community. The old people are too absorbed in their own talk to attend to the setting. Surfers, sunbathers, children, dogs, bicyclists, winos, hippies, voyeurs, photographers, panhandlers, artists, junkies, roller skaters, peddlers, and police are omnipresent all year round. Every social class, age, race, and sexual preference is represented. Jesus cults, Hare Krishna parades, and sidewalk preachers jostle steel bands and itinerant musicians. As colorful and flamboyant as the scene is by day, it is as dangerous by night. Muggings, theft, rape, harassment, and occasional murders make it a perilous neighborhood for the old people after dark (4–5).

In these paragraphs, Myerhoff observes her informants enacting their engendered and cultural roles within the setting. She documents months of recorded conversation by noting men's and women's separate topics but also the topics—critical to their cultural history—that they share. Myerhoff sees these cultural roles acted against the backdrop of the benches as part of the boardwalk's staged setting outside the center.

Not only does she gaze outward at the landscape, but she also looks inward with a reflexive gaze at her own internal landscape to examine how she is affected by the place she studies. As a Jewish woman of a younger generation and an ex–social worker, perched on the benches that define the boundaries between inside and outside, she acknowledges her role as researcher within this social drama. Myerhoff uses the benches to meditate on her own relationship with the seniors; she uses the benches as her informants do:

I sat on the benches outside the Center and thought about how strange it was to be back in the neighborhood where sixteen years before

I had lived and for a time had been a social worker with elderly citizens on public relief. Then the area was called "Oshini Beach." The word "shini" still made me cringe. As a child I had been taunted with it. Like many second-generation Americans, I wasn't sure what being a Jew meant. When I was child our family had avoided the words *Jew* and *Yid* (11).

Myerhoff's reflexivity on the place she is researching becomes an integral part of the text, linking her informants' lives with her own internal landscape and personal memory. The reflexive researcher includes herself as part of the data, not just to draw attention to herself, but to draw attention to the fact that she is the one looking at this place, telling this story, and writing these descriptions.

B O X 1 2

FINDING A FOCAL POINT

In this box, we'd like you to review the data you've collected about your field site: field-notes, descriptive paragraphs, cultural artifacts, archival documents, and maps. As you read through your material and reflect on what you have gathered, look for the focal points of your site, either from your vantage point or that of your informants. Are they the same perspective, like Myerhoff's benches? Or are there any contradictions? Write a description of one focal point you find in your setting. Consider whether there are any ways in which your own perspective influences you to see what you do see in this site. Share a draft of your focal point description with a colleague to see if it creates the image you're after.

Response

Karen Downing, for example, finds a contradiction when she matches her fieldnotes with the map of the space and the cultural artifacts she gathered. This contradiction is in the image of its "hostesses," who stand outside the door greeting customers with compliments but are trained in hard-sell tactics for roping customers into the store. In her field-notes, she describes the "horse," a sitting area and display table that is used to promote the Photo Phantasies business and to solicit customers. In Karen's reflective fieldnotes, she suggests that the horse serves "to take 'em for a ride," admitting her cynicism and her feminist perspective toward the beauty culture. After viewing a 12-step training video that outlines the company's customer service policies, she summarizes the purpose of the "horse":

> . . . A Photo Phantasies hostess should man the horse, the brochure stand out-side the store, at all times, particularly when the mall is busy. The hostess should greet the people in the mall as they pass and tell them about the pro-fessional makeup salon and photo studio. She should show them the "Look Book" with the before and after pictures of previous customers, give them a brochure, take them on a tour of the store, explain the Photo Phantasies

process, and work to get an appointment set up on the spot. "Yes or no" questions should be avoided—the focus is on selling the concept.

The "horse" is a place detail that illuminates the values of the beauty culture; the illusion of beauty can be sold to any customer. A salesperson posts herself at the "horse," ready to rope in her customer and tie up the transaction with the biggest package of photos she can sell.

Learning How to Look: Identifying Unity and Tension

Karen's description of the "horse" and the "hostesses" who "man" the sales table serves to confirm other details she's already accumulated about her Photo Phantasies field site and the beauty business it represents. Her interview with Ginny the manager, her description and map of the store's space, and the training videos she watches unify Karen's growing skepticism.

At the Sunday evening sales meeting, Karen records details that further confirm the contrast between the company's beauty sell and the everyday reality of this mall business. As she sits in the meeting, forgotten in the black chair, she takes fieldnotes about the employees who present themselves in rather ordinary ways. She writes, "While I understand this is after-hours, I have a hard time believing these are the same people who are responsible for creating beauty and self-confidence in others. Their appearance contrasts with the prototypical image of the Photo Phantasies employee I saw in two videos." She also notes three slumped women picking at their nail polish and chewing gum, a one-armed photographer who smells of body odor, and a make-up artist eating frozen yogurt who scrapes the bottom of her cup with a plastic spoon as she balances a sleeping child in her lap.

The store manager's pep talk to her staff confirms Karen's growing insights about Photo Phantasies' daily work. The manager points out the uses of the space that Karen has already mapped, that different areas of store space have entirely different purposes. Ginny reminds her staff about one simple rule for using those areas: "We praise each other in front, and we talk about bad things in back. That's what my office is there for." This guideline is such a major part of the business policy that whenever employees begin to say something negative, they are instructed to "touch the red heart on your name tag."

In order to write about the culture you've researched, you must look, as Karen did, for a unifying perspective. Much of fieldwork involves confirming unity—unity of themes and patterns that hang together in the data. Disparate data sources—maps, interviews, observations, and reflections—accumulate to form a coherent whole. Looking for unity in masses of data is much like Samuel Scudder looking at the fish. At first, you'll see very little, but over time and with close study, important unifying details will come together, like the symmetry of the fish, which took so long for Scudder to see.

But it is equally important for a researcher to locate disconfirming data, discontinuity, and tensions. Tensions show up in data at moments of contradiction when multiple or opposing perspectives collide. For Karen, the first tension in her study arises when she realizes that not all people share her attitude toward having beauty pictures taken. After Karen spends $60 on a pair of Reeboks at the mall and $10 on a bouquet of irises at the grocery store, she holds a conversation with a checkout clerk over what it means to "treat yourself." Karen is jarred when she realizes that for some people, having their pictures taken at Photo Phantasies might be a treat. Here is part of her short exchange with Darlene, a familiar clerk who's never talked with her before. In this passage, Karen begins to recognize the discontinuities between her own values and those of others. In a way, this moment serves as a disconfirming source of data. Whenever a researcher senses tension, she needs to recognize and record it.

"God, these are beautiful. How much?" The woman on the other side of the counter smiles as she picks up my flowers and brings them close to her face. I have been checking out movies here for ten years, and she has never asked me anything other than perfunctory information.

"Uh, ten dollars, I think. Aren't they great? And not really all that expensive. I bought them as a treat." I grin at her with my lips pressed together.

"Are there any left? I just may get some. A treat, like you said. It's either flowers or Photo Phantasies. I've been wanting to do that for so . . ."

"Photo Phantasies?" I raise my eyebrows at this notion.

"God, yes." As she turns to retrieve my movie, I see her name tag reads "Darlene." "I mean, what could be a better treat? I wanna go in there, have 'em do up my hair and my makeup, put on all those cool clothes, take a whole bunch of pictures, and then go out on the town lookin' so hot! I'd leave my kids with my mother and stay out as late as I wanted. Hopefully, plenty of men would be willin' to buy me drinks."

"Yeah. Hmmm." I don't know how to respond to this because Darlene's version of a treat or an indulgence is not mine. I hate the idea of having my picture taken. Period. And having my picture taken in clothes and hair and makeup that turn me into someone I'm not? Never! I know the feminist rhetoric—a woman's body is hers to do with as she pleases. And I think I believe this feminist rhetoric, or I would like to think I do. But a Photo Phantasies makeover? What a waste of money for something that won't last.

"We'll see. Maybe someday." As Darlene says this, she pushes up the sleeves of her white uniform and sighs. Her two-inch red nails with chipped polish click the price of my movie into the cash register. I am on the verge of suggesting that Darlene get a massage instead of a makeover when I stop short. I see a smudged blue pen mark on her cheek and the trace of dark circles under her eyes.

"No, not someday. Now. Why wait?" Suddenly, I want Darlene to leave the grocery store this instant and drive straight to Forum West

[Mall]. I am surprised by my encouragement, but I empathize with her, despite our different ideas of indulgence. "This is weird, but here, look what I just happen to have." I reach into my coat pocket and take out the Photo Phantasies brochure. "I was just at the mall. They gave me this. Here. You can have it. I think they're doing some kind of model search. You should go. Give it a try." It did not escape me that I sounded just like Bettie from the Photo Phantasies store. . . .

"A model search? Wow. No way. That's so cool! I can have this? Really? Cool! Thanks. I just may go. I just may." Darlene tucks the hot pink brochure into the front pocket of her white uniform and hands me the movie.

"Do it!" I say, smiling. "And remember me when you get discovered."

Darlene smiles, showing the white of her teeth. "Maybe when you come back, I'll have pictures to show you." I think about her comment while I wait in the checkout line to pay for my $10 flowers, which I know won't last a week. I buy them anyway.

It is this conversation with Darlene that causes Karen to unpack the personal "baggage" about beauty photography that she brings to her project and to examine her assumptions. Her encounter at the checkout is a moment of insight in which Karen sees Photo Phantasies through the eye of the "other." This tension prompts her to reflect on her own investments of time and money—Reeboks and a bunch of irises—which show her that she's guided her study with her own values, not those of the "other." She realizes she must now research Photo Phantasies from the insider's position.

If Karen had continued to look only for unity by just interviewing customers who shared her perspective, she might have discarded her encounter with Darlene as data. After interviewing customers who were, in fact, proud and satisfied with their beauty photographs, she understood the value of beauty photography through their eyes, not just her own. In spite of her own resistances throughout the project, Karen reaches a dramatic and ironic conclusion about the subculture of Photo Phantasies. At the end of her paper, she writes, "Sometimes things are not what they seem."

Karen's reflexive conclusion about Photo Phantasies invited layers of insights: that a hard-selling business meant to create illusions could, in fact, build self-esteem in customers and that her own negative attitude about the beauty culture almost blocked her understanding during her research. In her portfolio reflection, she writes about starting the project "very smug and haughty . . . I scoffed at the notion and I scoffed at the women who swallowed the absurd 'Model for a Day' rhetoric Photo Phantasies features in their ads. I was out to prove myself right." As the research continued, however, and she began to interview customers, she found herself "championing their desires and validating their experiences" from their perspective. When she stepped back to consider her own values, such as a gym membership and new exercise clothes, she saw "a level of vanity and indulgence inherent" in her own choices. And finally, she accepted Photo Phantasies as "not *my* way, but *a* way," and she admits that the culture of Photo Phantasies could be viewed "as a microcosm for a much larger female culture" to which she also unavoidably belongs.

Karen's study shows us that researchers can impose their own values on the places they study unless they are reflexive about the process of their own fieldwork. As educated middle-class American women, Karen and her informants exercised personal choices about ways to join or not join the dominant American beauty culture. To indulge herself, Karen chooses Reeboks, exercise clothes, and health clubs over beauty photos, and she admits this in her writing. All researchers need to explain—to themselves and to their readers—the differences between their values and those of others they study, separating their attitudes and assumptions both on and off the page. And her readers can sense Karen's tension as they read her writing. One reader, Andrew Platt, who never met Karen, responded to a draft of her project. Andrew asks two questions, "Is anyone else really being hurt here?" and "So what else is new?" He writes:

> "Humankind cannot bear very much reality," said T. S. Eliot. We all need fantasy. Without it, reality is far too great for us to even remotely handle. Some pull or buy themselves out of it, but aren't they just buying themselves into a new nonreality? What I mean to say is, the customer in this situation buys into a fantasy, the salesperson promises it, the makeup artist creates the illusion, the photographer captures it. The store manager proves to his/her employees that a group effort is necessary to fulfill their obligation to keep America beautiful. The store manager, herself a product of manipulation, lives within a fantasy that all anybody truly wants is to be physically pleasing. The big man at the top has spent a lifetime convincing himself that all he really needs is more money to find happiness, regardless of how many he may deceive in order to do so.
>
> So who's being hurt? We all are continuing that age-old fallacy that love and happiness can be found in exterior beauty. But can we ever imagine that to change? I don't think so. I honestly wish I could say I don't care, say, "Let them throw away their money. Let them buy their temporary luxury," but I cannot do without feeling a snapping at my heart and a voice snatched up in the back of my throat wanting to scream, "No, please, no."
>
> It's wonderful the distance that Karen places herself at. She too is attracted to the beautiful. She too worries about her appearance, but with a cynical eye, or I should say, a cynical mind still inhabiting a very human body. She is affected—both repulsed and amused.

Learning How to Look: Colonized Spaces

Fieldworkers look for the tension in the way informants inhabit their spaces because sometimes informants inhabit spaces not of their own choosing. Andrew recognizes the tensions Karen writes about: between her own attitude toward the beauty culture and that of her informants, between the management and the customers. Her affect is one of amusement and repulsion at the same time. If Karen had researched even further some of the employees she observed, she might have found that they, too, feel tensions in their everyday jobs of creating glamour. The Photo Phantasies photographer, for example, may have preferred to be outside shooting pictures of the natural landscape rather than the artificial images he was paid to create for customers. The woman with the baby on her lap at the employee sales meeting might prefer to stay at home with her child rather than work in a cramped store at the mall. While these people may disagree with the Photo Phantasies dogma, may prefer to be working elsewhere, or may feel oppressed by their economic situation, they do have choices. They have some control over the spaces they inhabit every day.

But lack of control in cultural spaces can present itself on a much larger scale. When people inhabit spaces over which they have no control, they are considered to be *colonized*. In particular, when a dominant or powerful culture forces itself upon a less powerful group, assuming control over its territories and people, this constitutes *colonization*. Researchers must recognize the vantage point of their own dominant culture and guard against describing others in terms that belong solely to their own culture's values and belief systems. Colonization can involve imposing your own culture's sense of time, place, religion, food, rituals, hygiene, education, morals, and even story structures. Descriptive words about other places and people, like *quaint, picturesque, simple, primitive, native*, or *backward*, imply cultural value judgments. When researchers write about cultures other than their own, they must try to separate their belief systems from those they study. This is a difficult—and sometimes impossible—task.

For example, about a century ago, anthropologists who studied religion in cultures that practiced witchcraft and sorcery needed to acknowledge how their own Judeo-Christian backgrounds influenced what they saw, as well as how they wrote about it. Many did not. One anthropologist whose cultural background guided her study of the spiritual practices of hoodoo was Zora Neale Hurston, whose work you'll read in Chapter 4. Hurston was among the first American fieldworkers to return to her own home culture, study oral storytelling and other folk practices there, and write about herself as she did it. She was a trained anthropologist who focused on the orality of her own people while weaving herself deftly into her field-writing account. Contemporary fieldworkers who study marginalized groups such as the homeless, gang members, immigrants, or the elderly must be careful not to let their value systems dominate their fieldwork. One way they guard against ethnocentrism is to write about their personal reactions and their belief systems throughout the research process, sometimes in their journals, sometimes in double-entry field-notes, and sometimes in letters to their colleagues. Writing about it doesn't solve the problem of colonization, but writing can expose it.

In this book, you will read the fieldwork of many researchers who faced the challenge of writing about subcultures with very different value systems. For example, in Chapter 4, you'll read two studies of waitresses' joking, gossip, and stories in which the researchers were careful not to impose any occupational stereotypes on their informants. And in Chapter 5, Paul Russ, who conducted interviews with AIDS survivors, had to recognize his assumptions about the people who contracted the disease as he worked with them. Cindie Marshall admits how her own white-collar background influenced how she saw the biker bar culture that she writes about in Chapter 5.

Colonization can take place both in the field and in the writing process. In the field, it happens when researchers don't adopt the informants' perspective. Karen Downing, for example, had to recognize that her own value system made her prefer Reeboks and irises over a Photo Phantasies package. In the writing process, colonization happens when we use our own language rather than allow our informants' language to describe their spaces. Henry Glassie's description of the broom as a "besom of heather bound round with twine" is the phrasing of his Northern Irish informants, not his own.

In all the studies we've mentioned, informants exercised choice within their field sites over whether or not to allow researchers to study there. In a few cases, researchers were denied full entry, as in Jake's study of the skinheads, or the access involved sticky negotiations, as in Karen's at Photo Phantasies. But in all cases, the informants had the power to offer or deny access to the fieldworker. When informants inhabit spaces that are not of their own choosing, as in studies of institutions such as prisons, hospitals, or even schools, researchers may have to leave out some of their best information to protect the privacy and safety of their informants.

Barbara Myerhoff's elderly Jews, for example, found themselves at the end of their lives in sometimes cramped and uncomfortable spaces, not by their own choice, but because of economics, family transience, and an inadequate social welfare system. Although Myerhoff realizes that the Senior Center provides the elderly with a safe community, her freedom as a researcher and control of her own cultural space is far greater than that of her informants. In her book, she reflects on her informants' lack of power and her own sense of guilt. She fears that her research and writing will colonize them because she holds so much more power within the culture than they do.

> I had become a tasteless ethnic joke, paralyzed by Jewish guilt: about my relative youth and strength, about having a future where they did not, about my ability to come and go as I chose while they had to await my visits and my convenience, when I relished food that I knew they could not digest, when I slept soundly through the night warmed by my husband's body, knowing the old people were sleeping alone in cold rooms . . . (27).

Myerhoff is very sensitive to the possibility that unconsciously and unwillingly, a researcher can colonize her informants and their space. And unconsciously and unwillingly, too, informants can allow themselves to be colonized. To illustrate from an informant's point of view how it feels to be colonized, how another country's dominant values and belief systems can overtake an entire community's perspective on itself, we share Jamaica Kincaid's nonfiction essay "On Seeing England for the First Time." This reflective memoir is about growing up on the island of Antigua, a British colony in the West Indies. As a child, Kincaid did not realize that England's cultural values overtook her Caribbean island life, but as an adult she writes about its domineering influences on her childhood. As you read her essay, notice how many of the British cultural practices and values she mentions are shaped by the dominant English culture—an ocean away from Antigua.

On Seeing England for the First Time
Jamaica Kincaid

> *Jamaica Kincaid was born in St. John's, Antigua, and lives in Vermont.*

When I saw England for the first time, I was a child in school sitting at a desk. The England I was looking at was laid out on a map gently, beautifully, delicately, a very special jewel; it lay on a bed of sky blue—the background of the map—its yellow form mysterious, because though it looked like a leg of mutton, it could not really look like anything so familiar as a leg of mutton because it was England—with shadings of pink and green, unlike any shadings of pink and green I had seen before, squiggly veins of red running in every direction. England was a special jewel all right, and only special people got to wear it. The people who got to wear England were English people. They wore it well and they wore it everywhere: in jungles, in deserts, on plains, on top of the highest mountains, on all the oceans, on all the seas. When my teacher had pinned this map up on the blackboard, she said, "This is England"—and she said it with authority, seriousness, and adoration, and we all sat up. It was as if she had said, "This is Jerusalem, the place you will go to when you die but only if you have been good." We understood then—we were meant to understand then—that England was to be our source of myth and the source from which we got our sense of reality, our sense of what was meaningful, our sense of what was meaningless—and much about our own lives and much about the very idea of us headed that last list.

At the time I was a child sitting at my desk seeing England for the first time, I was already very familiar with the greatness of it. Each morning before I left for school, I ate a breakfast of half a grapefruit, an egg, bread and butter and a slice of cheese, and a cup of cocoa; or half a grapefruit, a bowl of oat porridge, bread and butter and a slice of cheese, and a cup of cocoa. The can of cocoa was often left on the table in front of me. It had written on it the name of the company, the year the company was established, and the words "Made in England." Those words, "Made in England," were written on the box the oats came in too. They would also have been written on the box the shoes I was wearing came in; the bolt of gray linen cloth lying on the shelf of a store from which my mother had bought three yards to make the uniform that I was wearing had written along its edge those three words. The shoes I wore were made in England; so were my socks and cotton undergarments and the satin ribbons I wore tied at the end of two plaits of my hair. My father, who might have sat next to me at breakfast, was a carpenter and cabinetmaker. The shoes he wore to work would have been made in England, as were his khaki shirt and trousers, his underpants and undershirt, his socks and brown felt hat. Felt was not the proper material from which a hat that was expected to provide shade from the hot sun should have been made, but my father must have seen and admired a picture of an Englishman wearing such a hat in England, and this picture that he saw must have been so compelling that it caused him to wear the wrong hat for a hot climate most of his long life. And this hat—a brown felt hat—became so central to his character that it was the first thing he put on in the morning as he stepped out of bed and the last thing he took off before he stepped back into bed at night. As we sat at breakfast, a car might go by. The car, a Hillman or a Zephyr, was made in England. The very idea of the meal itself, breakfast, and its substantial quality and quantity, was an idea from England; we somehow knew that in England they began the day with this meal called breakfast, and a proper breakfast was a big breakfast. No one I knew liked eating so much food so early in the day; it made us feel sleepy, tired. But this breakfast business was "Made in England" like almost everything else that surrounded us, the exceptions being the sea, the sky, and the air we breathed.

At the time I saw this map—seeing England for the first time—I did not say to myself, "Ah, so that's what it looks like," because there was no longing in me to put a shape to those three words that ran through every part of my life no matter how small; for me to have had such a longing would have meant that I lived in a certain atmosphere, an atmosphere in which those three words were felt as a burden. But I did not live in such an atmosphere. When my teacher showed us the map, she asked us to study it carefully, because no test we would ever take would be complete without this statement: "Draw a map of England." I did not know then that the statement "Draw a map of England" was something far worse than a declaration of war, for a flat-out declaration of war would have put me on alert. In fact, there was no need for war—I had long ago been conquered. I did not know then that this statement was part of a process that would result in my erasure—not my physical erasure, but my erasure all the same. I did not know then that this statement was meant to make me feel awe and small whenever I heard the word "England": awe at the power of its existence, small because I was not from it.

After that there were many times of seeing England for the first time. I saw England in history. I knew the names of all the kings of England. I knew the names of their children, their wives, their disappointments, their triumphs, the names of people who betrayed them. I knew the dates on which they were born and the dates they died. I knew their conquests and was made to feel good if I figured in them; I knew their defeats.

This view—the naming of the kings, their deeds, their disappointments—was the vivid view, the forceful view. There were other views, subtler ones, softer, almost not there—but these softer views were the ones that made the most lasting impression on me, the ones that made me really feel like nothing. "When morning touched the sky" was one phrase, for no morning touched the sky where I lived. The morning where I lived came on abruptly, with a shock of heat and loud noises. "Evening approaches" was another. But the evenings where I lived did not approach; in fact, I had no evening—I had night and I had day, and they came and went in a mechanical way: on, off, on, off. And then there were gentle mountains and low blue skies and moors over which people took walks for nothing but pleasure, when where I lived a walk was an act of labor, a burden, something only death or the automobile could relieve. And the weather there was so remarkable because the rain fell gently always, and the wind blew in gusts that were sometimes deep, and the air was various shades of gray, each an appealing shade for a dress to be worn when a portrait was being painted; and when it rained at twilight, wonderful things happened: People bumped into each other unexpectedly and that would lead to all sorts of turns of events—a plot, the mere weather caused plots.

The reality of my life, the life I led at the time I was being shown these views of England for the first time, for the second time, for the one hundred millionth time, was this: The sun shone with what sometimes seemed to be a deliberate cruelty; we must have done something to deserve that. My dresses did not rustle in the evening air as I strolled to the theater (I had no evening, I had no theater; my dresses were made of a cheap cotton, the weave of which would give way after not too many washings). I got up in the morning, I did my chores (fetched water from the public pipe for my mother, swept the yard), I washed myself, I went to a woman to have my hair combed freshly every day (because before we were allowed into our classroom our teachers would inspect us, and children who had not bathed that day, or had dirt under their fingernails, or whose hair had not been combed anew that day might not be allowed to attend class). I ate that breakfast. I walked to school. At school we gathered in an auditorium and sang a hymn, "All Things Bright and Beautiful," and looking down on us as we sang were portraits of the queen of England and her husband; they wore jewels and medals and they smiled. I was a Brownie. At each meeting we would form a little group around a flagpole, and after raising the Union Jack, we would say, "I promise to do my best, to do my duty to God and the queen, to help other people every day and obey the scouts' law."

But who were these people and why had I never seen them? I mean, really seen them, in the place where they lived? I had never been to England. England! I had seen England's representatives. I had seen the governor-general at the public grounds at a ceremony celebrating the queen's birthday. I had seen an old princess and I had seen a young princess. They had both been extremely not beautiful, but who among us would have told them that? I had never seen England, really seen it. I had only met a representative, seen a picture, read books, memorized its history. I had never set foot, my own foot, in it.

The space between the idea of something and its reality is always wide and deep and dark. The longer they are kept apart—idea of thing, reality of thing—the wider the width, the deeper the depth, the thicker and darker the darkness. This space starts out empty, there is nothing in it, but it rapidly becomes filled up with obsession or desire or hatred or love—sometimes all of these things, sometimes some of these things. That the idea of something and its reality are often two completely different things is something no one ever remembers; and so when they meet and find that they are not compatible, the weaker of the two, idea or reality, dies.

And so finally, when I was a grown-up woman, the mother of two children, the wife of someone, a person who resides in a powerful country that takes up more than its fair share of a continent, the owner of a house with many rooms in it and of two automobiles, with the desire and will (which I very much act upon) to take from the world more than I give back to it, more than I deserve, more than I need, finally then, I saw England, the real England, not a picture, not a painting, not through a story in a book, but England, for the first time. In me, the space between the idea of it and its reality had become filled with hatred, and so when at last I saw it I wanted to take it into my hands and tear it into little pieces and then crumble it up as if it were clay, child's clay. That was impossible, and so I could only indulge in not-favorable opinions.

If I had told an English person what I thought, that I find England ugly, that I hate England; the weather is like a jail sentence; the English are a very ugly people; the food in England is like a jail sentence; the hair of English people is so straight, so dead-looking; the English have an unbearable smell so different from the smell of people I know, real people of course, I would have been told that I was a person full of prejudice. Apart from the fact that it is I—that is, the people who look like me—who would make that English person aware of the unpleasantness of such a thing, the idea of such a thing, prejudice, that person would have been only partly right, sort of right: I may be capable of prejudice, but my prejudices have no weight to them, my prejudices have no force behind them, my prejudices remain opinions, my prejudices remain my personal opinion. And a great feeling of rage and disappointment came over me as I looked at England, my head full of personal opinions that could not have public, my public, approval. The people I come from are powerless to do evil on a grand scale.

The moment I wished every sentence, everything I knew, that began with England would end with "and then it all died, we don't know how, it just all died" was when I saw the white cliffs of Dover. I had sung hymns and recited poems that were about a longing to see the white cliffs of Dover again. At the time I sang the hymns and recited the poems, I could really long to see them again because I had never seen them at all, nor had anyone around me at the time. But there we were, groups of people longing for something we had never seen. And so there they were, the white cliffs, but they were not that pearly, majestic thing I used to sing about, that thing that created such a feeling in these people that when they died in the place where I lived they had themselves buried facing a direction that would allow them to see the white cliffs of Dover when they were resurrected, as surely they would be. The white cliffs of Dover, when finally I saw them, were cliffs, but they were not white; you could only call them that if the word "white" meant something special to you; they were steep; they were so steep, the correct height from which all my views of England, starting with the map before me in my classroom and ending with the trip I had just taken, should jump and die and disappear forever.

Kincaid depicts herself in this essay as a colonized child who, later as an adult, breaks away from the dominant English culture and grows to understand its enormous influence on her worldview. The British controlled not only these Caribbean islanders' government, economics, and political practices, as she shows us, but also their personal geography, their everyday cultural practices, and even their spatial gaze—the way they viewed their surrounding landscape. In this essay, Kincaid takes us into her home, her school, and her island surroundings so that we can see through her eyes what it meant to be overtaken by another culture.

She uses the map of England as a concrete image to show us how the spatial gaze restricts her ability to see and be heard. English cultural values seep through her descriptive language: the map looks like a leg of mutton with squiggly veins of red; the shades of pink and green are unfamiliar. The idea of England itself is a special jewel for only special people, echoing its well-known crown jewels. When Kincaid is asked in school to draw a map of England, she feels conquered and erased. Her spatial gaze is both symbolic and concrete as she describes the tension between a concept, her ideas of England, and its reality, which she eventually encounters. Kincaid suggests the mysterious space between her childhood image of England and its actualization in her adulthood: "The space between the idea of something and its reality is always wide and deep and dark. The longer they are kept apart—idea of thing, reality of thing—the wider the width, the deeper the depth, the thicker and darker the darkness . . . and so when they meet and find that they are not compatible, the weaker of two, idea or reality, dies." In Kincaid's case, it was the idea of England that died when she finally chose to go to England on her own and saw its reality: "not a picture, not a painting, not a storybook, but England for the first time." To her, the real England was an ugly place—from the white cliffs of Dover to the food and weather to the dead-looking, smelly English who had imposed their values on her people.

The British spatial gaze had been instilled in her as a child. She grew up feeling a tension between what she actually saw and what she was told to see. Her internal landscape was based on her everyday experiences living on Antigua, but the landscape she read about, sang about, and learned about was based on a more powerful island in an entirely different geography. While she sang "When Morning Touched the Sky," she lived a life "where no morning touched the sky." "The morning where I lived," she writes, "came on abruptly, with a shock of heat and loud noises" and where "the sun shone with what sometimes seemed to be deliberate cruelty . . ." Kincaid finds dissonance between the English literary images of gentle mountains and moors "where people took walks for nothing but pleasure" and her local knowledge that where she lived, "a walk was an act of labor"; her people did not take strolls but trudged in hot fields and had no leisure time.

There is not only a mismatch in the spatial gaze and the personal landscape Kincaid describes but also a mismatch between the English cultural practices imposed on Antiguans and what might have been more appropriate ones for their island lives. One focal point she uses is the big English breakfast with grapefruit, eggs, cheese, porridge, oatmeal, and cocoa made in England. This breakfast, along with her hair ribbons, socks, and cotton underwear, her father's khaki shirt, and his brown felt hat, forced upon her family the daily practices of the British culture. While these practices were all unconscious, she understood even as a child that they were inappropriate. Islanders, for example, felt sleepy from eating "so much food" early in the hot morning, and she instinctively knew that her father's brown felt hat, which he had selected from a picture of an Englishman wearing one, should have been a hat more suited to the Caribbean climate. All these practices, she suggests, were " 'Made in England' like almost everything else that surrounded us."

Kincaid achieves this powerful portrait of a colonized child with expert writing. She evokes a sense of place and brings us into that childhood landscape, making us as readers feel colonized too, and perhaps a little guilty. She selects sensory details of time, place, weather, color, smells, textures, sounds, tastes, and sights, creating verbal snapshots of both Antigua and England, real and imagined. Through her descriptive language, we learn to map the space that she has mapped as a child. She uses as her focal point an actual map of England forced upon her at her British-run school and carries this focal point throughout her memoir until she reaches the real England in her adulthood, when she is no longer colonized by British practices.

We don't need to be living in a colonized country to experience colonization. Within our own dominant American culture, many subgroups unconsciously colonize others. In fact, Karen's study of Photo Phantasies gives a clear example. American women—customers, employees, managers, mall shoppers, and even skeptics like Karen—find themselves accepting, and sometimes even internalizing, the values of beauty, costumes, jewelry, and makeup as represented in the glamour photography business. What's important about researching place is to understand how we acquire our spatial gaze, how that gaze informs our look at others, and what's behind the gaze of others who look back at us.

The Research Portfolio: Learning from Your Data

Many portfolios are meant primarily for display, summaries of what you've accomplished, designs to present to someone for an assessment. Artists submit their portfolios to juries for art shows or to gallery owners and private customers. Financiers such as stockbrokers present portfolios as options for their clients' investment possibilities and potentials. Students often find themselves assembling portfolios of written products to fulfill course requirements or institutional evaluations.

But your research portfolio can serve a very different purpose. It becomes a tool for documenting your learning and analyzing your research process. Think of your portfolio as a cultural site—in this case, your personal field site—and the artifacts you choose to place in your portfolio as data that teaches you about your own fieldworking process. The reader of your portfolio (which, of course, includes you) needs to know why you have collected and selected the cultural artifacts you display. Your portfolio might include, too, a representation of what data you've rejected, what you've left out, or what data you might collect more of in the future. Your own reflections on your portfolio artifacts need to accompany the selections to document your learning process. By writing reflections about each artifact, you'll learn about your unifying themes and be able to find tensions and notice gaps in your data.

As the researcher, then, you are an intimate part of your data, and yet you can learn from it. In Chapter 2's portfolio suggestions, you reflected on how you read and write, how you select and position yourself in the field. In this chapter, we'd like you to think about what you can learn from laying out your data, looking at the range and depth of artifacts and information from the field and from your background research from maps, archives, documents, and books.

Karen Downing's portfolio contains 12 artifacts, her complete study, and a reflective essay based on her analysis of her process. She presents each artifact in a plastic slipcover and writes a reflection about it on a Post-it note attached to each.

ARTIFACTS

1. A typed page, labeled "Assumptions" (p. 139).
2. A map of the store (p. 140).
3. A promotional flyer for Photo Phantasies (not pictured): "This came in the mail in a mailing of coupons and real estate options. On the back of this is an ad for 'Long John Silver's Big Fish Deals, $3.99 for combination platter #4.' both ads prey on getting a good deal for a small price. The text of the PP ad indicates the model theme prevalent in PP rhetoric.
4. A bright pink promotional checklist for customers to pick up in the store (p. 141).
5. The three-page business statement for employees, printed on fax paper (p. 142).
6. A copy of the poem that Ginny James had posted in her office (p. 143).
7. A list of guiding questions for interviewing informants (p. 144).
8. The transcript of a conversation with Mrs. Conway, a customer (p. 145).
9. A set of notes torn out of her fieldnotes from a stenographer's notebook (p. 146).
10. Collage of fashion words (p. 147).
11. Cover from the bestselling book *Backlash: The Undeclared War against Women* by Susan Faludi (not pictured).
12. A photo of Karen, her friend Amy, and Amy's husband (p. 148).

Assumptions

I should start first with the whole mall culture. I spent many weekend hours
circling that place with Carolyn. We would poke around the stores, fingering the
clothes, knowing we would rarely make a purchase. We would then go downstairs and
each order a piece of pizza and a Coke at Scottos or whatever it was called. We had
no P.P.-that hadn't made its way to __ yet. I doubt very much that I would have
been going to it even if it were in the mall. I could picture certain girls--Jill Jacobs,
Sundi Geisler, Nikki Hampton--going for the big photo shoot and then bringing the
pictures into school to pass around or making up a cute little gift package for their
boyfriends. Maybe since I never had a serious boyfriend, I had no compelling reason
to go.

Ok, now I'm on to something here. I associate P.P. with a certain kind of woman,
of which I am not one. It's not even necessary that this imaginary woman be
beautiful, but she would be someone who has her bedroom done in matching patterns,
believes in window treatments, has coordinating clothes for workouts, and lives in a
new apartment. I see these women in the making in some of my students, the ones
that bring in their P.P. pictures to school and ask me which one is my favorite. The
other students in the class will flock around and ooh and ahhh and say how wonderful
this girl looks as I stand by and wonder just what the heck all this attention means.

There is something quite overwhelming to me about getting my picture taken. I cried
for five years straight growing up each time my parents assembled us in August to pose
for the annual Christmas card wearing our coordinating wool sweaters with our white dog.
My parents were out of town during my senior pictures, and to this day my mother
still laments how bad the shots are because she didn't get to pick out my outfit
of advise me on hair and make-up. What I remember about sorority pictures is pretty
limited, although I was one of the few girls that only had one half-way decent proof to
choose from. My tongue always poked out between my lips and my smile had a way of
sloping quite unattractively. My hair was always a crap shoot--would or wouldn't the
curls cooperate at that particular moment.

So for me to hear the woman behind the pharmacy counter tell me that she's
thinking of going to treat herself, I don't quite get it. It was my bunch of irises
that spurred her into sharing this with me. "I just want to do it, w
those pictures. I want to find a babysitter, have everything poss
 then go out for the evening and have a great time. God, what
myself encouraging this woman to do just that, giving her t
short line" and all that other Hallmarky stuff. As I wa
had a feminist dilemma on my hands. Part of me knew it w
the physical appearance bit. Maybe I should have told he
white grocery store uniform--that she would look just gre
she believed it. But the other part of me thought, right
and treat yourself. And if make-up and hairstyling and p
gosh darn, you go right ahead. Inspires a muddle of thin
strong emotions. I'd love to say that looking good doesn
but it does. I choose to shape my look through exercise
that's me. Where do I get off being holier than thou? Bu
That combines two things that I can't stand.

My assumptions, written
before I began the research
process. I "discovered" this
on my disk late last
week-interesting that I
"forgot" about this. My
dilemma about PP is evident
here.

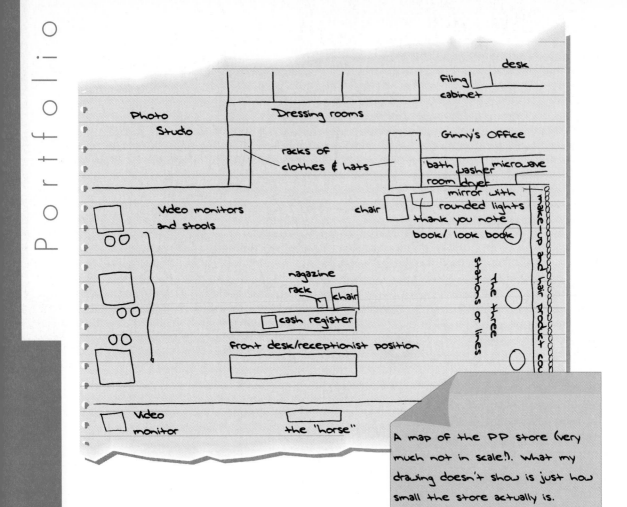

desk

Filing
cabinet

Photo
Studio

Dressing rooms

Ginny's Office

racks of
clothes & hats

bath washer microwave
room dryer

Video monitors
and stools

chair

mirror with
rounded lights
thank you note
book/ look book

make-up and hair product cou...

magazine
rack

chair

cash register

the three
stations or lines

Front desk/receptionist position

Video
monitor

the "horse"

A map of the PP store (very
much not in scale!). What my
drawing doesn't show is just how
small the store actually is.
The layout reflects the theme
of efficiency: greater sales.
Everything moves in a progessive
way, from one step to the next,
like a well-orchestrated dance.

140

CHECKLIST

HIGH FASHION PHOTOGRAPHY

HAVE YOU THOUGHT OF EVERYONE?

Husband ☐
Wife ☐
Mom ☐
Dad ☐
Grandparents ☐
Children ☐
Uncle ☐
Aunt ☐
Brother/Sister ☐
Cousin ☐
Friend ☐
Boyfriend/Girlfriend ☐
Wedding Attendants ☐
Classmates ☐
In-laws ☐
You ☐

REMEMBER THESE PHOTOGRAPH GIVING OCCASIO

Birthdays
Valenti
Chr
Anni
We
Grad
Mother's Da
Secret
Tha
Engagem
E
Su
Housewarming

A "needs" sheet from PP. The purpose is to have the customer begin thinking about buying photos right when she comes in for her appointment. "Suggestion selling in pretty pink." (A Ginny James quote.)

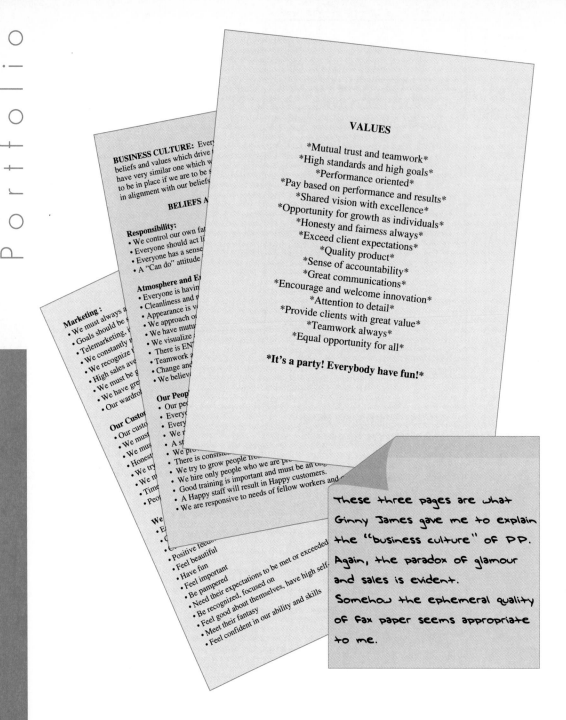

VALUES

Mutual trust and teamwork
High standards and high goals
Performance oriented
Pay based on performance and results
Shared vision with excellence
Opportunity for growth as individuals
Honesty and fairness always
Exceed client expectations
Quality product
Sense of accountability
Great communications
Encourage and welcome innovation
Attention to detail
Provide clients with great value
Teamwork always
Equal opportunity for all

It's a party! Everybody have fun!

BUSINESS CULTURE: Every
beliefs and values which drive
have very similar one which w
to be in place if we are to be s
in alignment with our beliefs

BELIEFS A

Responsibility:
• We control our own fa
• Everyone should act li
• Everyone has a sense
• A "Can do" attitude

Atmosphere and E
• Everyone is havin
• Cleanliness and
• Appearance is v
• We approach o
• We have mutu
• We visualize
• There is EN
• Teamwork a
• Change and
• We believe

Our Peop
• Our pe
• Every
• Every
• We
• A st
• We pro
• There is consiste
• We try to grow people fro
• We hire only people who we are pr
• Good training is important and must be an on
• A Happy staff will result in Happy customers.
• We are responsive to needs of fellow workers and

Marketing :
• We must always a
• Goals should be s
• Telemarketing, i
• We constantly p
• We recognize
• High sales ave
• We must be g
• We have gre
• Our wardro

Our Custo
• Our custo
• We must
• We must
• Honest
• We try
• We m
• Time
• Peo

We
• E
• C
• Positive feed
• Feel beautiful
• Have fun
• Feel important
• Feel pampered
• Be pampered
• Need their expectations to be met or exceeded
• Be recognized, focused on have high self-
• Feel good about themselves, have high self-
• Meet their fantasy
• Feel confident in our ability and skills

These three pages are what
Ginny James gave me to explain
the "business culture" of PP.
Again, the paradox of glamour
and sales is evident.
Somehow the ephemeral quality
of fax paper seems appropriate
to me.

Warning
Jenny Joseph

When I am an old woman I shall wear purple
With a red hat which doesn't go, and doesn't suit me.
And I shall spend my pension on brandy and summer gloves
And satin sandals, and say we've no money for butter.
I shall sit down on the pavement when I'm tired
And gobble up samples in shops and press alarm bells
And run my stick along the public railings
And make up for the sobriety of my youth.
I shall go out in my slippers in the rain
And pick the flowers in other people's gardens
And learn to spit.

You can wear terrible shirts and grow more fat
And eat three pounds of sausages at a go
Or only bread and pickle for a week
And hoard pens and pencils and beermats and things in boxes.

But now we must have clothes that keep us dry
And pay our rent and not swear in the street
And set a good example for the children.
We must have friends to dinner and read the papers.

But maybe I ought to practise a little now?
So people who knew me are not too shocked and surprised
When suddenly I am old, and start to wear purple.

A copy of a poem Ginny James had in her office. She had it next to her witch picture and her PP photo. The sentiment expressed in the poem seems so contrary to the PP philosophy. This is just one of the many paradoxes I encountered there.

Questions for informants who have been to Photo Phantasies

1. How did you decide to go?

2. Who went with you?

3. How did you feel before the appointment?

4. Tell me about the process in the store—what parts did you like, dislike?

5. What did you talk about with the stylists?

6. What clothes did you pick out?

7. What was it like to have your picture taken?

8. Watching the video images, did you feel any pressure to make a purchase? Did you feel pressure before that?

9. Did you like the pictures?

10. How have you used the photos?

11. Would you go again?

The two interviews I did with informants who had been to PP gave me a feeling of control over the material. While I did ask all of these questions, the conversations with these two women really opened up and quickly became centered on much larger issues, like marriage and family.

transcription of a conversation with Mrs. Conway
place--her house on the east side of town
date and time--April 24, 1995 2:00 on Monday afternoon

I have never met Mrs. Conway before, but I know her daughter-in-law who is my mother's cleaning lady. I spoke with Mrs. Conway on the phone about setting up an interview time and she gave me directions to her house. When I arrived, the first thing she did was show me the photographs of her family members and tell me a little about each of them. In her description, she talked mainly about how each of them looked, what things she thought stood out about them physically. Mrs. Conway is 76 years old and has permed gray hair ("It's thick, feel it!"). She is wearing glasses with pink and green and blue flecks of color on blue frames. She offered me coffee and we began talking about how she decided to go to Photo Phantasies. Her husband had always wanted her to go to PP. Mrs. Conway saw that they were having a special and decided to go. Her husband drove her to the mall and waited for her in the store during the process.

K:	So you went out without make-up on...
Mrs. C.:	Uh huh.
K:	...and you just washed your hair...
Mrs. C.:	Yes, I was petrified that someone might see me without my face on at the mall.
	Yep, I was walking around the mall without my face.
K:	Ah!!
Mrs. C.:	And you know, they do your hair and your make-up.
K:	So you got right in, and what did they do first? Hair?
Mrs. C.:	They do the make-up, I think. Here, do you want to see the pictures?
K:	Absolutely!
	Mrs. C. gets up from the couch and walks into the kitchen. From the other room:
Mrs. C.:	Do you know Michael? (Her son.)
K:	Yes, I love Mike. In fact Robin (her future daughter-in-law) told me that Mike has offered to give her and Joel $2,000 if they would elope to Las Vegas instead of having a wedding. That sounds like Mike...
Mrs. C.:	Oh, yes (still in the other room)
K:	That sounds just like him.
	Mrs. C. returns to the living room and hands me two wallet size photos of the same PP. In the photographs, she is wearing a satiny pink drape around her shoulders, pearl earrings and a pearl necklace. Her make-up and hair looks much the same as it does today in her house.
K:	Ah. These are gor-geee-ous!
Mrs. C.:	Thanks. (She giggles.)
K:	Oh, my word!
Mrs. C.:	Boy, I'll tell you, they're expensive.
K:	That's kind of what I thought, too.
Mrs. C.:	They are. Let me tell you, you don't get them for $14.95 like the ad promises.
K:	That's sort of the trick. That price might get you in there, but that doesn't get you anything. Sure, you could walk away without ordering anything, but...
Mrs. C.:	Well, they snap a picture of everything that you have on, everything they put on you, and then they show you the pictures on one of those screens.
K:	One of those video screens?
Mrs. C.:	A video screen. They put all these things on you. Finally after they tried a bunch o̶f̶ ... I asked for something to be put on me that is pastel?"
K:	Where they doing you up in glitter?
Mrs. C.:	Everything. Cowgirl, hats...
K:	Cowgirl?
Mrs. C.:	...gloves, but...it wasn't me.
K;	So you didn't get to pick your clothes?
Mrs. C.:	No, I only asked for something soft and feminine and pastel.
K:	And these are absolutely perfect. How about the jewelry? Did you do̶ ...
Mrs. C.:	No, they did that.
K:	Are these the only ones that you bought?
Mrs. C.:	I bought eight so the kids could each have one.
K:	So you didn't buy any with the dangly stuff?
Mrs. C.:	No, I just went for that one cause...It's me, more me.
K:	Yeh, that's what you want.
Mrs. C.:	It's me.

A copy of my transcript from a conversation with Mrs. Conway. This was the only time I was able to use a tape recorder when gathering information. I like re-reading this. It reminds me of how affirming I am about her pictures. It shows a real genuine connection to her.

Composing An Image: After
-describe store
-contrast with descrip. of office
-Ginny mixed me
    - selling v
    - artists
    - create
    - custom
    - phone

Playing Your Part
-describe sales vi
-describe employm
[-describe thank
[-describe staff m

Putting On Your
    -interview
    -me

map of pp
make-over pic.
Vogue cover

Talking with customers. M/F managers.
Bright star stores.
Ads in paper-rigorous test taking
Process, references, 90 days prob.
All in white.
Extensive training now—prob. in the
past
"On-board" since Feb. 6.   Ast. buyer
for Yonkers, worked at MH— more
than selling underwear. wanted to
give something back to society.
Worked at Science Center Shop—
Turned it around.
Christmas w/5 kids—3 step and
marriage.
-How the phone is answered.
-Party atmosphere.
"Not hype."
Artists.
My eye color is my best feature.
Mother-daughter. Look at features.
Ancestral pictures.
"I see my mother"-grateful to
age that way. She's beautiful.

One of my many organizational
attempts done throughout the
"writing up" process. I've
included this as a reminder of
how a researcher shapes her
text.

Not even two months, yet she acts
so confident, knowledgeable

What? making people feel better
about themselves?

This is a treat, special occasion
Oh really? What about the handout
on the closest door which seemed
to suggest that compliments sell.

I blush. Feel embarrassed and
flattered. "I could do such good
things w/those eyes."

emphasis on photos as keepsake

That's a selling pt. in their eyes. How
Ginny felt when she saw her pictures.

A collage of words from the fashion magazines I look at. This shows my lookist side. Ahh!
I know I shouldn't enjoy all this—the ole feminist voice comes out—but I do love the self-indulgent quality of these magazines.

147

During the time I was working
on this assignment, I visited
my friend, Amy, in California.
She is an education trainer for
a make-up company. This
picture shows the results of a
make-over she gave me. She
thought I looked much better
than usual. This is as close to
Photo Phantasies as I'll
probably get.

COMPLETED STUDY

Here is Karen's study, "Strike a Pose," in its entirety.

 Strike a Pose
Karen Downing

> It's not easy to create a myth and to emulate it at the same time. . . . What is ultimately clear is that even the attempted myth must be made a model for imitating, a drama to be tried on for fit. . . . It is a mold, a prescription of characters, a plot.
>
> *Jerome Butler in* The Beauty Myth

Smiling Women

As I pull open one of the heavy glass doors at Forum West Mall, a medium-sized suburban shopping mall, I am overwhelmed by sensations. Bells and laughs and sirens from the Fun Factory layer on top of piped-in Muzak. Large, colorful movie posters advertise *Man of the House, A Goofy Movie,* and *The Pebble and the Penguin.* People are everywhere—men and women in business suits eating lunch, several teenagers smoking by the reflecting pond, mothers running errands with babies in tow, older people exercise-walking in fitness gear. The smells of freshly baked bread from Subway, sugary caramel corn, greasy pizza, and fried tacos hang in the air. There are yellow benches and tables and leafy trees reaching toward skylights and winding staircases and two automatic teller machines and a lingerie store and a department store and an engraving stand. I experienced all of this just 10 feet inside the mall.

As a teenager, I would spend hours at Forum West each weekend, roaming through the stores with various best friends. Now, as a woman in my twenties, when I go to the mall, I go with a purpose. Today I am in the mall to look for tennis shoes. To get to Durham's Discount Sporting Goods, I must pass two food stands and three other shops. I walk quickly, head down, thinking about walking shoes versus cross-trainers, Reeboks versus Nikes. I pass Chopstix, an Asian fast-food restaurant that provides plastic forks instead of chopsticks with their meals. Up ahead I see the Disney Store, or rather I hear the Disney Store—strains of the *Little Mermaid* soundtrack carry out into the mall. To my right, a group of middle school girls are huddled together, each clutching shopping bags that encourage "Take home a little magic—take home Disney." They giggle as they try on Mickey Mouse ears. I pull closer toward the storefronts. Durham's is only 12 feet away.

"Hi, let me tell you about Photo Phantasies. My name is Bettie. What's yours?" This woman was slumped against a display rack, picking her fingernails, until she saw me. I smile at Bettie and try to pass, but she keeps speaking to me.

"Look! 'Somewhere in America, a new model is waiting to be discovered. It could be you! Just ask how. Today!' " Bettie reads the words in bold print on the display as I notice the photograph under the words. It is of a girl who is possibly in her late teens or early twenties. She is smiling at the camera. Her brown hair cascades around her face and rests on her shoulders. Her brown eyes and lipsticked mouth reflect a glimmer of light.

"The Photo Phantasies process is simple and fun! It's a celebration! And you could be chosen to be a model! With those eyes, I think you'd stand a good chance! We may just have openings right now. At least take a brochure home. Talk to your friends! You should do it! It's fun!" Although Bettie does not have a southern accent, I hear her words and cannot resist adding a slight twang to her speech.

I take the brochure, smile again, and walk away. She calls out these parting words: "You'd look great! Just great! I promise!" I hear these words as I see an image on a television monitor located at the far left side of the store, just an inch or two from the threshold. The woman on the monitor is smiling at me. She's wearing a red hat that fans out from her face. Gold and rhinestone earrings dangle from her ears. She looks like she is posing for a camera, or so I assume, although I can't actually see a camera. She drops her shoulder and tilts her head to the right. She smiles. And then she moves. This time, the photographer steps into the image on the screen. He lowers the woman's chin with his hand. He adjusts the bustier that she is wearing by tugging it down on the right side, his hands close to the woman's waist. He steps out of the picture. She's still. Ready. Looking right at me, this woman on the television monitor smiles. I fold the Photo Phantasies brochure, put it inside my coat pocket, and walk into the sports store.

After I buy my $62.00 Reebok cross-trainers from a man dressed in an umpire's uniform, I drive to my grocery store. I pick up some bananas and 12 long-stem irises before checking out a movie to watch that night with my husband. I take the movie to the pharmacy counter and put the flowers down while I search for my rental card.

"God, these are beautiful. How much?" The woman on the other side of the counter smiles as she picks up my flowers and brings them close to her face. I have been checking out movies here for ten years, and she has never asked me anything other than perfunctory information.

"Uh, ten dollars, I think. Aren't they great? And not really all that expensive. I bought them as a treat." I grin at her with my lips pressed together.

"Are there any left? I just may get some. A treat, like you said. It's either flowers or Photo Phantasies. I've been wanting to do that for so . . ."

"Photo Phantasies?" I raise my eyebrows at this notion.

"God, yes." As she turns to retrieve my movie, I see her name tag reads "Darlene." "I mean, what could be a better treat? I wanna go in there, have 'em do up my hair and my makeup, put on all those cool clothes, take a whole bunch of pictures, and then go out on the town lookin' hot! I'd leave my kids with my mother and stay out as late as I wanted. Hopefully, plenty of men would be willin' to buy me drinks."

"Yeah. Hmmm." I don't know how to respond to this because Darlene's version of a treat or an indulgence is not mine. I hate the idea of having my picture taken. Period. And having my picture taken in clothes and hair and makeup that turn me into someone I'm not? Never! I know the feminist rhetoric—a woman's body is hers to do with as she pleases. And I think I believe this feminist rhetoric, or I would like to think I do. A Photo Phantasies makeover? What a waste of money for something that won't last.

"We'll see. Maybe someday." As Darlene says this, she pushes up the sleeves of her white uniform and sighs. Her two-inch red nails with chipped polish click the price of my movie into the cash register. I am on the verge of suggesting that Darlene get a massage instead of a makeover when I stop short. I see a smudged blue pen mark on her cheek and the trace of dark circles under her eyes.

"No, not someday. Now. Why wait?" Suddenly, I want Darlene to leave the grocery store and this instant drive straight to Forum West. I am surprised by my encouragement, but I empathize with her, despite our differing ideas of indulgence. "This is weird, but here, look what I just happen to have." I reach into my coat pocket and take out the Photo Phantasies brochure. "I was just at the mall. They gave me this. Here. You can have it. I think they're doing some kind of model search. You should go. Give it a try." It did not escape me that I sounded just like Bettie from the Photo Phantasies store. I fought off the southern twang.

"A model search? Wow. No way. That's so cool! I can have this? Really? Cool! Thanks. I just may go. I just may." Darlene tucks the hot pink brochure into the front pocket of her white uniform and hands me the movie.

"Do it!" I say, smiling. "And remember me when you get discovered."

Darlene smiles, showing the white of her teeth. "Maybe when you come back, I'll have pictures to show you." I think about her comment while I wait in the checkout line to pay for my $10 flowers, which I know won't last a week. I buy them anyway.

Composing an Image: Before

"Hello, this is Photo Phantasies. My name is Mindy. Today's a great day." I am not calling Photo Phantasies to inquire about specials. I am not calling because I want to know if they have any free time today for a last-minute appointment. I am not calling to see if a $220 package of photographs has arrived. I am calling to speak to Ginny James, the manager. When I make this request and tell Mindy who I am, she says, "Oh. Hang on a sec," in a voice without intonation. Her hand covers the receiver, muffling sounds.

When I talk with Ginny, I will not say that I have an aversion to her store and the whole Photo Phantasies concept. I will tell her that I am fascinated by the photographs my high school students, always female, bring to school to show off. I will present myself as curious.

"This is Ginny James. It's a great day! What can I do for you?" Her voice rises at the end of the question.

I tell Ginny my name and ask her if she has received the letter I sent four days ago requesting to visit her store.

"Letter? What letter are you referring to?"

I am caught off guard by her response and feel slightly uneasy. I take a deep breath before explaining my "research project."

Silence. And more silence. Finally, this from Ginny: "I'll need this in writing. Call me back after 11:30. That's when the mail comes. If there's no letter, you'll need to provide adequate documentation. You'll have to deliver it in person." Despite the mall noise in the background, I sense immediately that Ginny is guarded with me. Her changed tone results in sentences with periods, no longer exclamation points. I wait until 12:30 and try again.

"Hello, this is Photo Phantasies. My name is Stacey! It's a great day and we're searching for models! How may I help you?"

When I finally talk with Ginny during this second phone call, she leaves out the conversational niceties. Yes, my letter had arrived in the mail after all. "I'll have to clear this request with headquarters, which I can do tomorrow. I'm leaving for a Photo Phantasies meeting in Chicago. What kind of class is this for? Business? Sociology? I'll call you Wednesday night and leave a message about whether or not it's OK."

Wednesday night, no reply.

Friday morning, no reply.

My third call to Photo Phantasies is on Friday afternoon. "Hello, this is Photo Phantasies. My name is Ginny! Ask me about our model search! How may I help you?"

"Ginny, this is Karen Downing. You may help me by telling me that headquarters granted me permission to spend some time in your store." I try to be personable and charming.

"Karen Downing?"

"Yes, the one that sent the letter about doing research for . . ."

"Oh. Right. Well. Yes. You can come to the store, but I don't want an extra body around when customers are here. You could come to an in-store training session from 5:30 to 6:30 on Sunday night. And I have some material about Photo Phantasies that you could read."

"Huh. Well . . . huh. Ummm . . . when could I come out to pick up the material?"

"Saturdays are nuts. Sunday's the meeting day. Monday's my paper day . . . and I'm still catching up from Chicago . . ." She trails off into a sigh.

"How about today? This afternoon?"

"Fine." Click. When she hangs up, I realize that in three phone calls, I have never heard the official Photo Phantasies telephone goodbye.

I leave the house to go to the mall at 11:30, even though I know that, technically, it's not yet afternoon. But I have work to do in the afternoon and would rather not face more traffic and a busier mall. Before I leave, I think about what I am wearing. My standard look—black turtleneck and brown jeans, minimal gold jewelry, lipstick, powder, blush and eyeliner, curly and full hair tucked behind my right ear. I decide not to do anything different to my appearance for this particular errand, but I am aware that I am thinking about how I look a lot more than I normally would. I hear the words of my mother, the words I have grown up with: "You need more blush! And remember the lipstick! Without it, you don't look alive!" Today, I follow her advice, advice I usually ignore, and add just a bit more makeup to be sure it's noticeable. I am glad my husband is at work. Although he would not come right out and say I am wearing too much makeup, he would give me the slightest hint of a goodbye kiss and then say, "Lipstick." I know just what he means.

Once inside the mall, I walk through a lunchtime crowd of over 100 people who fill the tables and wait at the food stands. Most of the people are dressed in business clothes; some carry briefcases and cellular phones and Gap bags. I round the bend beyond the food court and am practically inside Photo Phantasies before I know it.

"Hi! May I help you?"

I wonder if this is Mindy or Sharon or Ginny or some employee I have yet to talk with on the phone. There are three other people behind the counter besides the receptionist—two women and one man. I glance at them, noting only that they all wear either black or white clothes. I introduce myself and say I have come to the store to pick up some material from Ginny James. At the sound of her name, three of the people behind the counter stop what they are doing, move over to the right side of the counter, and begin organizing and sorting papers, their bodies still half-turned in my direction.

"I'm Ginny. I thought you said you would be by this afternoon." This from one of the women behind the counter, dressed all in white, probably in her early to mid-forties. She has glasses on, and her brown hair is pulled back into a ponytail tied with a white fabric bow. She glances up at the wall behind me, where I assume she reads a clock.

"Is this too early?"

"Yep." She taps her pen against her chest and continues to stare behind me, eyes lifted, toward the wall.

"When would be better for you?"

"This afternoon. Like I said, 1:30." And with that her eyes leave the wall, pass over me, and return to the papers in front of her.

At exactly 1:30, I return to Photo Phantasies for a second time. I am told by the receptionist that Ginny is busy. I ask if I may take a seat while I wait. She points to a black vinyl chair in the corner. Sitting there, I hear crying children and Disney music and footsteps on tile, even though my back is to the mall. I am almost thankful that Ginny is busy; I have a chance to look around. I pull out my journal, glancing behind to see if the receptionist is watching. Thankfully, she is examining the face of a teenage girl under the bright lights of the makeup station's mirror. I look around the store. Next to my chair is a black magazine rack with *Glamour* and *Elle* and *Mirabella*. I have already read the first two magazines, but I don't mind the chance to page through *Mirabella*. The walls of the store are white and the carpet is gray with muted lines of rose running throughout in a zigzag pattern. Pop music, loud enough to cover some of the mall noise, comes from overhead speakers.

The store is perhaps 30 feet by 30 feet, but each inch of space is used. There are three black vinyl chairs facing a mirrored wall and a counter where I assume makeup and hair are done. A sign hanging above this area reads "Professional Makeup Artists." I look around for these people, but no one is working near the three chairs, nor is anyone in the store but the receptionist. Surrounding the 4-foot-high mirror on the wall are round light bulbs that remind me of a movie star's dressing room. On the counter, an array of curling irons, blow dryers, Q-tips, mousse, static guard, and hair spray joins tray after tray of makeup. Above the mirror is the wall of Phantasy Phaces—Photo Phantasy photographs, each measuring 3 feet on a side, arranged to look like film coming off a movie reel. All of the photographs are of women, except for two little girls and one couple.

In front of my chair are racks of clothing—denim jackets with gold studs, gold lamé blouses, a coat with red, white, and blue stars and stripes, sequined blazers, beaded bustiers, blue and pink boas, and shelves of hats. Beyond the wardrobe selections, there are three dressing rooms without mirrors or seats inside. Each one has a white mesh hamper for clothes and a white hook on the wall and a black curtain that can be pulled over the opening to the dressing room.

Next to the racks of clothes is the photography sitting room. I cannot see much of that room because the door is only halfway open, but I can see part of a royal blue background and a black vinyl stool. I can only assume that the camera is in there somewhere. On the other side of the photography sitting room are three computer monitors. The computer monitors, placed in a straight row, stand off to the right of the receptionist desk and the cash register. My high school students who have been to Photo Phantasies tell me that after they have had their photos taken, they change back into their street clothes and meet a salesperson who uses the computer monitor to display the proofs. There is no wait time—a customer can see her photographs on the monitor seconds after they have been taken.

After 15 minutes, the receptionist touches me on the shoulder. She looks down at the notes in my journal as I look down at the floor, feeling like I have just been caught doing something inappropriate. "Cool handwriting! It kinda looks like calligraphy! Ginny's ready for you now." She points toward the back of the store, past the racks of clothes to a door near the dressing rooms. The door is open. I stand there, waiting for Ginny to look up. After several moments, I knock and say hello.

"Oh, right. Sit here. 'Scuse the mess. I'm still not caught up from Chicago. Let's see, you want to know about Photo Phantasies. Well, here's some information." Ginny continues without waiting for me to look through material.

"There are 390 Photo Phantasies studios in the United States. Our corporation's name is Bright Star. Our main goal is retail. We sell an excellent product. We believe in a good work environment and pay our employees well, based on a series of incentives. I'm a manager, coach, cheerleader, and toilet cleaner. Here at Photo Phantasies we have a team philosophy. I'm here to make sure we're victorious." Ginny leans back in her chair, away from me. She holds a pen in her hand that she points in my direction when she wants to stress a point. She looks right at me and does not pause to allow me time to get her words into my notes. I feel like I am listening to a well-rehearsed speech. When she stops to swallow, I ask her how long she has been with Photo Phantasies.

"I've been on board since February 6. I used to be an assistant buyer at another store, and then I single-handedly turned around the gift shop at the museum. But I reached a point where I wanted to do more than sell underwear or stuffed dinosaurs. I wanted to give something back to society. Here I am, managing a Photo Phantasies."

When I ask her about what she thinks Photo Phantasies gives back to society, Ginny does not hesitate, "Self-confidence. An escape. An opportunity to feel good about who you are. It all starts with the initial call to the store. From there on out, this place is about a party atmosphere. And that's no hype. Those of us that work here are artists, waiting to transform."

She stops speaking for a moment and studies my face. "Your eyes. That's what I would concentrate on if I were going to do you. They're your best feature. I'd play those up for sure."

Part of me resents the fact that this woman who has just met me thinks she has the authority to point out my best feature; the other part of me shamelessly succumbs to her comment with a blush.

"We fulfill dreams at Photo Phantasies. Everyone wants to enter a modeling contest. We make it happen. The ol' Miss America dream—it comes alive here. I know, there's all this talk about how that can be damaging, but I put that aside because we're in the business of making people—everyone—beautiful."

I ask her if there has ever been a customer who has presented a challenge. She looks away and smiles. "I probably shouldn't tell you this, but oh well. One day, right after I started, we were short a makeup artist. I had to run the show. So this woman comes in and wants a Photo Phantasies experience. Yeah. Well, let me just say, she was Irish. You know what I mean when I say that? She had that skin that looked like she'd spent too much time out tending sheep. She had wrinkles and a sunburn, and she was broken out, plus she had a cold sore."

I find myself laughing aloud at this, but I wonder if Ginny views my response as laughing at the woman. What I think I am laughing at is the contrast between the woman described and the woman pictured in Photo Phantasies advertisements.

"She was a tough one to build up, but I did it. I looked at her like she was a lump of clay. As an artist, it was my job to shape her. See that angel up there?" She points to an angel figurine, dressed in a white robe with gold glitter on her face and in her hair. "I made that to watch over the place. And just like I made that, I made this Irish woman. I put so much base makeup on her, she looked flawless. And you know what? Those pictures turned out great, and she was thrilled. I think she spent over $100 on a package. And why not? When would she ever look as good?

The receptionist has been standing in the doorway, waiting for Ginny to finish talking. She walks over to Ginny and whispers something in her ear. Ginny says in my direction, "One moment, I've got to take this call. 'Hello, this is Ginny! It's a great day at Photo Phantasies. How may I help you?' "

With the receiver cradled between her head and her shoulder, Ginny shuffles the papers around on her desk and says a few "uh huhs" into the phone.

"No, there's no problem at all! Let me put you on hold for just one moment, and I will consult the scheduling book, just to make sure! Thanks so much for your patience!" As she puts the phone down, she rolls her eyes at me. "Hang on. I've gotta sort this person out."

Alone in her office, I have the chance to look around. She is right. The office is a "mess," and it probably does not help matters that it looks to be no larger than an oversized closet. On one side of the office, there is a stacked washer and dryer. Lint from previous loads gathers on the floor in front of the machines. On the counter, cleaning supplies, Big Gulp cups, and empty cans of diet soda surround a microwave. On the wall are two calendars labeled "Sales Goals" and "Sales Reality." I am too far away to read the numbers that are penciled on each date. Next to this on the wall is a plaque recognizing achievement in regional sales gift certificates. Underneath this, an article from a London newspaper about the "Queen for a Day" concept in England, the Anglo version of Photo Phantasies, I assume.

Underneath Ginny's desk are five purses of varying sizes. I gather that the people who work here use Ginny's office for their belongings, too. On the top of the desk are stacks of paper, notebooks, Post-it notes, and a fax machine. Ginny has her own Photo Phantasies photograph, taken with her wearing a straw hat and a denim jacket with sunflowers embroidered on the collar. Right beside this photograph is a picture of a witch, complete with broom and black cat. Above the witch picture, a Post-it note reads "Before." Above the Photo Phantasies photograph, a Post-it note reads "After." Next to these pictures is the poem "Warning" by Jenny Joseph. "When I am an old woman I shall wear purple . . ." To the left of my chair is a black storage cabinet about six feet in height. On it is a sign-up sheet for employee meetings with Ginny, as well as some promotional material and sales material. From the latter, I read, "Remember, you need to celebrate the perfect pose. When you look at the pictures with the customer, pick out a specific feature to celebrate. Tell her that her hair is gorgeous in that pose. Celebrate! Celebrate! Celebrate!" The sales tip is stuck to the storage cabinet with a magnet that advertises a local group of surgeons specializing in plastic and reconstructive surgery.

Playing Your Part

Before I leave Photo Phantasies, Ginny gives me two company videos. Not until the day I need to return the tapes do I finally watch them. Somehow, having the videos in my home makes me feel oddly connected to the store, as if I work there and am watching these videos to improve my job performance.

Still in my pajamas at 10:00 Sunday morning, I settle in on the couch to see just how Photo Phantasies presents itself. The first video is titled *Photo Phantasies' 12 Steps of Customer Service*. To illustrate each of the 12 steps, several employees of the Bright Star Corporation act out a skit. Dressed in black T-shirts and khaki pants, the employees first model the wrong way to serve a customer before proceeding to the right way, making constant reference to the "before and after" theme.

After watching the first couple of steps to effective customer service, I realize that "customer service" is actually a Photo Phantasies euphemism for "increasing sales." The 12 steps of customer service are as follows:

1. *The horse.* A Photo Phantasies hostess should man the horse, the brochure stand outside the store, at all times, particularly when the mall is busy. The hostess should

greet people as they pass and tell them about the professional makeup salon and photo studio. She should show them the "Look Book" with the before and after pictures of previous customers, give them a brochure, take them on a tour of the store, explain the Photo Phantasies process, and work to get an appointment set up on the spot. "Yes or no" questions should be avoided—the focus is on selling the concept.

2. *The photo inquiry.* When the customer calls to set up an appointment, the receptionist must be sure to use the client's name whenever possible during the phone call. Explain the Photo Phantasies process thoroughly, reminding the customer to arrive for the appointment without makeup and with clean, unstyled hair. Receptionists should tell callers about specials, remind them to bring credit cards for immediate photo purchases, and secure all appointments with credit cards in case the customer cancels a scheduled appointment.

3. *Booking the appointment.* The video recommends that appointments be booked within seven days of a customer's phone call so that there is less time for a change of mind. Appointments should first be scheduled during slow hours, like weekdays and mornings. Suggestion selling is important. The customer should be reassured that her pictures will look great and that she will want to buy enough for everyone she knows.

4. *The confirmation call.* Forty-eight hours in advance of an appointment employees are encouraged to contact the customer just to say how much the staff is looking forward to the appointment. The customer should be encouraged to bring a friend and share the experience. And again, the client should be reminded that she will want to purchase pictures the day of her appointment.

5. *The front counter greeting.* This step urges employees to use customers' names immediately, for they are likely to embarrassed, particularly if they arrived without makeup and are nervous about the unfamiliar situation. The front counter greeting should involve filling out a bio card so that employees can get to know customers better and make them feel at ease.

6. *In the makeup chair.* This step involves compliments. "You're going to look absolutely beautiful." The employee is encouraged to build up rapport so that the customer shares feelings. Makeup artists should write down two things about each customer and pass that note along to the photographer. That way the photographer will know what to say to increase sales. "What kind of look do you want? Something sexy?" If the customer feels like she has been listened to, she will buy more. The makeup artists should point out their own photos on their name tags and talk about how much fun the process was for them.

7. *Transition to photo.* Everyone in the store should affirm how attractive the customer looks once she has put on her wardrobe selections. "You look absolutely gorgeous. What a great color for you!" The makeup artist should introduce the customer to the photographer. The photographer should say, "It will be so much fun to be a model!" and play this opportunity up as every woman's fantasy.

8. *The photo session.* During this step, the model theme continues with comments like "You're a natural for this" and "You look like you could be a model. Have you ever been one before?" Suggestions sell with comments like "This shot would be perfect for your husband. You look sexy!"

9. *The video sale.* The salesperson should tell the customer she is pretty. With each picture, the sales person needs to make a specific suggestion to the customer, for

instance, by telling the customer how she might use this photograph for display at work or that photograph for gifts.

10. *Ringing the sale.* The receptionist should tell the customer that her pictures are great and tell her how much fun the experience must have been for her. In addition, the receptionist should encourage customers to upgrade to a higher-priced photo package or to buy the proofs, too.

11. *Exiting the customer.* It is recommended that employees use customers' names when mentioning how much they look forward to seeing the proofs.

12. *Delivering the order.* The final step involves opening up the photo package and looking at the pictures. Employees should be excited because excitement is contagious. Customers should be told that they can order more photographs now that they see how good the results are. Again, employees should use customers' names as much as possible.

The second video, *Preemployment screening*, lasts only about 15 minutes. This is the video a potential employee would watch before a job interview. I am still in my pajamas on the couch and have now been joined by my husband, who stretches in the living room before his jog. Together, we talk back to the video, offering sarcastic responses to the information provided.

Preemployment Screening is composed of a series of quick images set to fast-paced music. It begins with a testimonial from a Photo Phantasies manager about how employees change lives and attitudes and have a good time doing it. Customers, according to this manager, can go anywhere to have their pictures taken, but they come to Photo Phantasies for the magic. It is this atmosphere that makes them want to order pictures. Images of stores are flashed on the screens with voice-over testimonials from customers.

Next, a narrator talks to the camera. She is probably in her late twenties, southern, and wearing a dress. She is filmed inside stores and inside the company's central photo processing lab. Using the "before and after" theme, the video shows what bad employees do and what good employees do. A gum-chewing, magazine-reading employee turns into a complimentary, smiling hostess. Star performers at Photo Phantasies make $7 to $9 an hour, based on a set rate plus commission. They are expected to look the part, which means wearing makeup, doing their nails, styling their hair, and wearing fashionable black or white clothing. Male employees must have a neat appearance and wear a tie. There are parties and trips for employees, but before any fun can be had, duties must be done. All employees clean, vacuum, wipe, dust, and scrub equipment. Teamwork is the key. If one person succeeds, then everyone in the store is successful. The goal of a Photo Phantasies employee is to bring out a customer's potential. When the customer feels beautiful, she is self-confident. She will want to buy the image that reflects that self-confidence. Before closing with "From all of us at Photo Phantasies, keep smiling!" the narrator asks the viewer if she has what it takes to be part of the magic, to be a part of the Photo Phantasies team. Not everyone, she reminds us, is cut out for the part.

Sunday evening at Photo Phantasies. Thirty minutes after the mall has closed and only a few people pass outside the steel gate that now separates the store from the mall, I have again arrived early, this time for the staff in-service meeting. Just as before, I am pointed to the black vinyl chair in the corner and forgotten. I page through the book of thank-you notes on display next to the "Look Book." The black notebook holds at least a dozen thank-you notes from students in local small-town high schools who appreciate the store's donation to after-prom parties. The donations are always the same—free sittings but never free photographs. There are a few letters from organizations like dieters' clubs and girl scout troups. Each thanks Photo Phantasies for a free sittings donation. I am struck by the method behind Photo Phantasies' generosity. The audience appears, always, to be female, and the donation appears, always, to be made with the potential for profit. Only one letter comes from an individual. It is handwritten on stationery headed "From the desk of someone waiting to be DISCOVERED." Sheila O'Riley's note reads, "My customers asked if I was going to Hollywood. They thought I looked like a model. It was a special experience. I was able to live my childhood dream. Thank you!" I speculate about Sheila O'Riley's occupation and wonder if any of the "Phantasy Phaces" photographs that gaze down on me is of her.

At 5:50, the staff in-service gets under way. Ginny is seated on a stool at the front counter, this time dressed in a blue print outfit. There are seven staff members present, both men and women, some of whom I recognize from my two previous visits to the store. One person is eating a waffle cone, another has a large serving of frozen yogurt, and two people are drinking out of the Big Gulps I saw in Ginny's office. The employee "look" for this meeting is jeans or leggings, tennis shoes, and sweatshirts. While I understand that this meeting is after-hours, I have a hard time believing that these are the same people who are responsible for creating beauty and self-confidence in others. Their appearance contrasts with the prototypical image of the Photo Phantasies I saw in the two videos.

Ginny begins the meeting. "This won't take long if we concentrate. First of all, I want to remind all of you of a very simple rule. We praise each other in front, and we talk about bad things in back. That's what my office is there for. Pass this around to those people who aren't here. Naturally, they're the ones that need to hear it the most."

The employees show no reaction to her words. Three women slump in the chairs their customers sat in just an hour ago. Now the employees pick at their nail polish and chew gum. A photographer seated near me smells of body odor.

The rest of the meeting focuses on how to make the Photo Phantasies team more efficient. Ginny gives the employees an assignment for the next meeting. "Think about ways that other areas can help you. How can the photographer help the sales folks? Let us know. We need to pay attention to each other's needs. Communicate. If we communicate, we're more likely to work on schedule. Maybe we need to get stopwatches at each station. Remember, this is supposed to be a two-hour process for the customer. If we're efficient, we serve more customers. If we serve more customers, our sales average puts money in our paycheck."

"Yeah, well, I have a question," a man with blond hair who looks to be in his early twenties interjects. "Corporate's always talking about role playing. Role playing will make us more efficient, blah, blah, blah. When are we supposed to do this? We just don't have time. 'Oh, excuse me, customer, we're going to role play now.' "

"Sunday nights," Ginny responds immediately. "Sunday nights, like right now, is the time to practice for the real thing. That's what these meetings are for." Her comments meet with no response from the group. A child, under a year old, sleeps on her mother's lap. The mother, a professional makeup artist I saw in the store before, continues eating her frozen yogurt, scraping at the bottom of the cup with a plastic spoon.

After glancing down at a clipboard, Ginny continues. "OK, we have an opportunity to have a whole bunch of fun on Tuesday. It's a power day. I've made up copies of lists of customers who bought pictures in December 1992 who were born between 1939 and 1972. We'll call all of these people. It'll be telemarketing all day long. Each of you will have a booking sheet. Our goal is to set up fifty to a hundred appointments. You will all be given scripts for telemarketing. This is a Corporate idea. Seventy percent of our customers said they would return in one to five years. Only five percent have."

Again, no response from the employees, except for the same blond man who spoke earlier. "Cool idea! The people we call will be customers that have been here and liked it." Ginny turns toward this man.

"You know, you're doing a great job! Last week, you were one of the Booksey Twins. And we know who the other one was!"

Everyone looks now at the woman with the baby. She half-smiles while looking down at the carpet. Ginny says, "Keep it up!" She pauses for a moment and then finishes. "That's what I mean. That's the kind of stuff we need to be saying to one another on the floor. The other stuff—back in my office."

She finishes her agenda by telling the employees about the Easter parade theme that kicks off next week. Instead of black and white, the employees will be allowed to wear pastels for the week. They will wear Easter bonnets or bunny ears. Parade music will be played in the store. Children will get Easter candy, and adult customers will be given plastic Easter eggs with slips of paper announcing the current special inside the egg. A few plastic eggs will have coupons for free sittings. A customer appreciation table will be set up in the front of the store with Irish linens and finger sandwiches and fruit and coffee. In the back in Ginny's office, the employees will have their own table with veggies, dip, and pretzels. The employees will get grab bag prizes for the most bookings or the most sales during the Easter parade. But before the fun happens, some work needs to get done. The clothes need to be arranged, the phone stations need to be organized, and makeup and hair stations need to be cleaned.

It is 6:30 p.m., the official end of the meeting, when the first employee leaves the store with his portable phone that never rang. Several clusters of employees are talking among themselves about bunny ears and what to do if the makeup artists take too long and throw off the time schedule. Ginny gives the group one more assignment. "Those of you who are successful, if you have any tips, share them with the rest of us. That's the way our paychecks will increase."

This assignment seems to spark something in the employees. They begin calling out ideas.

"If we confirm appointments correctly, they should be ready to buy."

"Keep it rolling—that will eliminate objections."

"It's not a negative that they pay for their pictures at the time they're taken because the pictures come in a week. Just tell them, 'You'll really like the pictures. They'll be great!' "

Why should they bring in a friend? Because it's more money for us? No, because it's more fun for the customer." This tip meets with laughter by the whole group, even Ginny.

"Remember, attitudes mean everything. When you're about to say something negative, touch the red heart sticker on your name tag. Come out smiling, and you'll feel better."

"It's a party-party atmosphere here. That's with the customer, now with one another."

"Here's my tip. Pretend you're the customer. What would tick you off? What would make you feel great?"

As I get up to leave, I pass by Ginny and whisper a "thank you" in her direction. She asks me what I think. I hesitate before responding and then opt for something as neutral as possible. "It sounds like a lot of hard work."

"As a customer, you'd never guess what goes on behind the scenes, would you?"

As I tell people about my research project, I hear this time and time again. "Oh, Photo Phantasies. My mom (sister, aunt, best friend, neighbor) went there. She loved it!"

It seems there is no shortage of possible informants I could talk to about their Photo Phantasies experiences. I end up speaking with two women, both of whom are connected to Lynn, my mother's friend. The first, Robin, will soon be Lynn's daughter-in-law, and the second, Norma, is Lynn's mother-in-law.

I call Robin on the telephone, my list of questions by my side. At last I feel like I have some control over my research process. If Photo Phantasies will not allow me to be in the store when customers are there, I will find my own customers to interview. I manage to catch Robin between her two jobs, full time at the post office and part time at a lumber store. She went to Photo Phantasies a year ago with her mother, her aunt, and her cousin on the occasion of her mother's 48th birthday. Robin was nervous about the appointment before she went because she did not really know what to expect, but she tells me now it was a lot of fun being pampered. She notes that the makeup people asked her a lot of questions, trying hard to make her comfortable with the look they created. They "glitzed her up," but Robin was already comfortable wearing a fair amount of makeup, so this did not bother her. When I asked her if she had concerns about anything during the process, she admitted she did.

"Before I went, I was concerned about the size of the clothes. You see, I'm not exactly petite. I worried that nothing would fit me. But they had thought about that and with zippers hidden in the back of the tops and those loose drapes, they get around the size issue. I worried about my double chin in the pictures but the photographer told me she would take care of that. I also didn't like having to wear a tube top underneath the clothes. When you do the wardrobe changes, that's all you're in. Because the photographer was a woman, I felt OK about it."

Robin liked her pictures when she saw them on the video screen. She bought her proofs, two 8 × 10s, four 5 × 7s, and two or three sets of wallet-size pictures. She also paid for her mother's pictures as her birthday present. Lynn brought Robin's pictures to the house, so I had seen the photographs. I remember Robin's brown eyes and one picture of her in which she wore a gold lamé drape and gold earrings. I ask her if she thinks the pictures look like her. "Yes, I'm comfortable with them. They do look like me, in a different way. I do myself everyday, so I wasn't surprised by a glitzed-up version of what I see all the time. Sometimes people will look at the pictures and tell me that they don't think it looks like me at all. I tell them that it does. What I say to myself when I hear those comments is that they don't know the real me."

I conduct my interview with Norma, Lynn's mother-in-law, in person. I arrive at her house at 2:00 on a Monday afternoon. She has sent her husband away "so we can girl-talk in private." Before I set my bag and tape recorder down, she takes me over to the bookshelf and talks me through the 20 or so photographs of her family that line the shelves. She tells me who everyone is and points out a physical characteristic in each person she thinks stands out. "I know you aren't supposed to have pictures of your family in the living room," she tells me, "but they're all so beautiful. I just have to."

She asks me to sit in the recliner, gives me a cup of coffee, and settles in on the couch. She tells me she is 76 years old, a fact I have a hard time believing. Her skin has only a few wrinkles. She has permed gray hair ("It's thick, feel it!"), and she wears glasses with pink, green, and blue flecks of color on the blue frames. I ask her what prompted her to go to Photo Phantasies, and she tells me it was her husband who encouraged her to go. She saw an advertisement on television about a Photo Phantasies special, so she made an appointment, and her husband drove her to the mall.

"I went without my face to the mall. I was petrified that someone might see me. I looked like a real hag. Yep, I was walking around the mall without my face on. Every morning, my husband tells me to put on my face. That day, I had an excuse why I couldn't."

Norma rises from the couch and goes into the other room to look for her pictures. She returns with one wallet-size photograph. In the picture, her hair and makeup look much the same as they do today. She is wearing the same glasses, and she has a satiny pink drape around her shoulders, plus pearl earrings and a pearl necklace.

"They snap a picture of everything that you have on, everything they put on you. Finally, after they tried a bunch of things on me, I said, "Would you mind if I asked for something to be put on me that is pastel?" They had me in cowgirl clothes and hats and gloves. It wasn't me. I felt like a little girl dressing up. Finally, I asked for something soft and feminine and pastel. I bought eight wallet-size photos so my kids and grandkids could each have one. I didn't buy any of the ones with dangly stuff, just this one. It's me, more me. It's me."

I tell Norma how nice her pictures are. And I mean it. They are beautiful, and they do look just like her. After I leave Norma's house, I have a two-hour drive to the university. For miles, I think about Norma's comment, "putting on my face." Surrealistic, sci-fi images come to mind, images of faceless women waking up in the morning and groping around the nightstand for their faces. I am reminded of an old roommate of mine. The first thing she did when she woke up in the morning was put on her glasses, which she always kept by her alarm clock. Without those glasses, she could not see well enough to get out of bed safely. She wore her glasses for the 10-step walk to the bathroom, where she would immediately put in her contact lenses. Her glasses went into a case for the day, until the 10-step walk to the bedroom at night.

I always felt a surge of tenderness when I saw my roommate in her glasses. I was struck by the vulnerability and honesty of her situation in those moments. In much the same way, I feel this about Robin and Norma when they are without "their faces." I talked to each of them for 45 minutes with perhaps only a quarter of our conversations dealing with Photo Phantasies. In each interview, what began with makeup, hair, and photos quickly moved into more personal territory. Robin told me about working two jobs while trying to plan a wedding. We swapped wedding horror stories about insensitive grooms, difficult mothers, and demanding bridesmaids. Norma told me about her family and about God. She talked about her grandson, who is giving his parents a hard time right now, and about a letter she wrote to him that included passages of Scripture. I told her about some times when I was nasty with my parents and why I may have behaved the way I did. These women allowed me to question them about Photo Phantasies, and in a short time, they revealed much more to me. They revealed to me the part of them that is always there, underneath "the face." In the short time I spoke with them, I moved from researcher to female, quickly putting aside any academic concerns about Photo Phantasies that I may have had at the beginning of the conversation. We moved past surface differences to a common ground our gender shares.

Before Norma left the room to get her Photo Phantasies photo, she gave me a joke to read, one she carries around in her wallet. Cut out from *Redbook* years ago, the joke concerns a school psychologist's visit to a teacher's classroom. The psychologist is convinced that the students are not paying attention to the teacher. When the students leave for recess, the psychologist informs the teacher he plans to conduct an experiment after the students return. When the students come back to the room, the psychologist asks the students to call out a number and tells the students he will write the number on the chalkboard. One student calls out "14," and psychologist writes "41." None of the students says anything. Another student volunteers "56," and the researcher writes "65" on the chalkboard. Again, no reply. Another student says "88," and then pauses. The same student says to the psychologist, "See what you can do with that." Norma chuckled over the joke and said, "Guess that little boy showed the smart psychologist just how to look at things." I smiled back, knowing just how the psychologist feels. Sometimes things are not what they seem.

Works Cited

Faludi, Susan. *Backlash: The Undeclared War against American Women*. New York: Crown, 1991.

Joseph, Jenny. "Warning." *When I am an Old Woman I Shall Wear Purple*. Ed. Sandra Martz. Watsonville, CA: Papier-Mache, 1987.

Wolf, Naomi. *The Beauty Myth: How Images of Beauty are Used Against Women*. New York: Morrow, 1991.

PORTFOLIO REFLECTION

Karen wrote a reflection on her final project after its completion. She compiled this reflection on the basis of other reflective notes written throughout the process.

 Portfolio Reflection: A Pose on "Strike a Pose"

When I think back over this research process, I'm reminded of something Professor Richard Horwitz said when he spoke to our class. About selecting subjects for ethnography, Horwitz advised, "Think about an experience that is really moving to you, an experience that brings out strong conflicting emotions, possibly within yourself, possibly in relation to yourself and others." That, in a pithy quote, is just what Photo Phantasies is for me.

When I started this project, I was very smug and haughty about PP. I scoffed at the notion, and I scoffed at the women who swallowed the absurd "model for a day" rhetoric PP featured in their ads. I was out to prove myself right. I had a heck of a time gaining access to the kind of information I thought I both wanted and needed. From the beginning, I felt off balance and not in control when dealing with Ginny James, the manager of the PP store at the Forum West Mall. But as the research process went on, I learned that the story I was getting—restricted access and all—was indeed a story, and a very compelling one at that. I was amazed by the conflicting messages embedded in the PP dogma, like saying "customer service" when they actually mean "things we need to do to increase sales." I could laugh at the videos, roll my eyes at some of the things the receptionist said about being an artist, and sit in the corner at the staff in-service meeting furiously scribbling away in my journal. But as soon as I started talking with women, women who either wanted to go to PP or who had experienced PP, I was surprised by my reaction. Not only could I understand their desire to go; I found myself championing their desires and validating their experiences after very brief conversations with them.

When I stepped back from my initial stance, I began to see PP as a way for women to treat themselves. Not *my* way, but *a* way. I started thinking about the things I do to treat myself—haircuts and a gym membership and new exercise clothes—and had to admit to the level of vanity and indulgence inherent in my own choices.

The PP topic was so full of metaphors. Early on, it became easy for me to see how the metaphors could shape my text. And not surprisingly, the metaphors I came up with seemed applicable to the paradoxes within myself as well as within PP. So the outsider was an insider, and before I knew it, the lines started intersecting all over the place, just like the metaphors. That's probably because the culture of PP could be viewed as a microcosm for a much larger female culture, something I'm naturally a part of, like it or not.

If I had more time with this project, there are other areas I'd want to explore. I would do more readings and interviews on the subject of beauty. What little reading I did made me all the more curious about other sources and other ideas. I would interview women of diverse backgrounds who had been to PP. That way, I would have a more complete picture than my two interviews provided. Believe it or not, I now feel like I could go for the PP experience. (Easy to say after the project is turned in!) It wasn't until I talked with Robin and Norma that I began to feel I could handle immersing myself that completely in the culture, photo session and all. (Mind you, it would only be for the sake of the project!) Finally, I would want more time to simply "look at my fish." Because my research took a while, I found I had very little time to let all of this soak in. Consequently, my final few pages of my piece, which I view as very important, feel tacked on and not as insightful as I would like. In truth, though, PP touches on some issues I could spend a lifetime sorting out and still never be satisfied with the insight I have.

FieldWriting: The Grammar of Observation

As a fieldwriter, your job is to describe your site as accurately as you can, combining your informants' perspectives with your own. Writers in other genres, like Barry Lopez and Jamaica Kincaid, can create place descriptions based on their own spatial gazes, influenced by their political perspectives and their personal passions. Kincaid writes as a colonized islander, with an antagonistic stance toward the British influence over her culture. Lopez writes with a naturalist's gaze, taking a stance against Americans' ignorance of their diverse geographical inheritance. For both of these writers of nonfiction, their responsibility was to render their versions of reality—of that place and its people—for their readers.

But the fieldwriter has a double responsibility. You must represent your own perspective at the same time you are representing your informants' perspectives of the field site. And through reflection, you must discuss your role as constructor of this doubled version of reality. Karen, for example, enters Photo Phantasies with a cynical attitude toward the glamour industry. But as she takes fieldnotes, she records her informants' enthusiastic perspectives, and in the end, her fieldwork documents her own changed attitude toward beauty photography. Neither Kincaid nor Lopez conducted fieldwork, and although they make us feel intimately connected with the places they write about, neither is trying to write ethnographically. For this reason, Kincaid, for example, doesn't need to interview her father to get his perspective on his brown felt hat or her mother about her big English breakfasts. But Karen Downing, as a fieldwriter, is responsible for representing the satisfied Photo Phantasies customers, for including their spatial gazes along with her own.

Fieldwriting places special demands on us as writers. We write on the basis of our collected data—our fieldnotes, expanded versions of them, and reflections about them. When we assemble and draft our final researched account, we revise it many times because fieldwriting, like all writing, is a recursive process. But fieldwriters must return often to their evidence—fieldnotes, transcripts, artifacts, reflections—to verify the account. For example, you may have noticed that many words and phrases Karen jotted into her fieldnotes appear in her final paper. Throughout our drafts, we must be aware of the words we choose. The special demand of fieldwriting is that descriptive material must have corresponding verification in the data. That's why it's called field research.

Over the years, as we and our students have conducted research, we've developed some strategies specific to fieldwriting, what we call the "grammar of observation." Here are a few ways we help our students revise their field projects, based on working with four elementary parts of speech.

NOUNS

Fieldwriters write from an abundance of detail, making lists in their fieldnotes of actual people, places, and things that both they and their informants observe. Sometimes these lists appear in a final text, such as Myerhoff's description of Venice, California, from the benches where the seniors sit:

> Surfers, sunbathers, children, dogs, bicyclists, winos, hippies, voyeurs, photographers, panhandlers, artists, junkies, roller skaters, peddlers, and police are omnipresent all year round. Every social class, age, race, and sexual preference is represented. Jesus cults, Hare Krishna parades, sidewalk preachers jostle steel bands and itinerant musicians.

But more often, fieldwriters cull such lists for strong, telling nouns that will organize a description or provide a focal point. Karen Downing focused on the "horse" outside Photo Phantasies, Myerhoff on the benches, Glassie on the hearth. And in Kincaid's nonfiction essay, she used the same technique with her description of the map of England. A focal point is often a noun, a concrete object in the informants' space that represents even more than it actually is. A focal point can serve as a metaphor, a frame to set off more complex cultural themes. The horse outside Photo Phantasies "took the customers for a ride," Myerhoff's benches held the elderly at the boundary between their outside and inside worlds, and Glassie's hearth was a space for storytelling and music making among neighbors. An effective fieldwriter searches through fieldnotes to identify important nouns that hold cultural meanings in those spaces and uses them to write up the research study. Sometimes these nouns are also metaphors, like the horse, the benches, and the hearth, that can be linked to larger cultural themes.

VERBS

Strong verbs assist all writers because they bring action to the page. A strong verb can capture motion in one word. From the list *walk, saunter, lumber, dart, toddle, slither, sneak, clomp, traipse, schlep, dawdle*, and *pace, walk* is obviously the weakest but the one that would most readily come to mind. Forcing yourself to find the right verb makes you look more closely at the action in your field site so that you can describe it. Finding the right verb makes you a more accurate fieldwriter. But finding the right verb may not happen until you've drafted and redrafted.

In many passages of this book, we struggled to use lively verbs that would pace our writing and free it of clutter. For instance, in the opening of this chapter, we replaced ordinary verbs with stronger ones like *bend, stuff, filter, select, evoke, recall, trigger, slap, transport*, and *retrieve*. Sometimes we even invented verbs, as when we used *junked* to describe Elizabeth's drafting process at the end of Chapter 1.

As we wrote, we alerted ourselves to passive verb forms and reworked those sentences. For example, one sentence included two passive verb constructions: "The spatial gaze *is enhanced* by the fieldworker's ability *to have been taught* to be a good observer." Our polished version was shorter and moved forward: "The spatial gaze demands that we look—and then look again." Cleaning your sentence of verb clutter is actually a challenging task.

Try what we call a "verb pass." Scan through your text, and highlight or circle the tired, flabby, and overused verbs that flatten prose. Most often, these are forms of the verb *be* or passive voice constructions. Excise these with no remorse. Substitute more precise and more interesting verbs to describe the actions you've observed. Haul the action forward with active, not passive, verbs. Locate focal points, metaphors, and cultural themes in your data to get ideas for new verb choices. For example, when we wrote about Karen's image of the Photo Phantasies "horse" and her idea that it "took customers for a ride," we couldn't resist adding that the horse was ready to "rope in" its customers and "tie up" the transactions.

ADJECTIVES AND ADVERBS

Cultural assumptions can hide inside the adjectives and adverbs you use. When you write "The dinner table was arranged *beautifully*" or "The *perky* dog greeted me with a *frenzied* lick" or "The *very sultry* atmosphere was *warm and friendly*" or "The *dull, dirty* apartment was crammed with *cheap blue* pottery," the qualifying words convey value judgments that are not verifiable because they belong to you. As a fieldwriter, let your reader make the judgment from the material you present. And let your informants and your other data contribute that material.

Karen Downing is a high school English teacher and a student of writing herself working toward her Master of Fine Arts degree in nonfiction. She found fieldwriting challenging because she wrote—and she taught her students to write—with lots of adjectives and adverbs to add color and "texture." When she realized that fieldwriters must question each qualifier they use, she knew she'd need to pay particular attention to how she wrote about Photo Phantasies. As you can see, her study offers very sharp and close observations, which are expressed with strong nouns and verbs.

She reserved her assumptions and value judgments for portions of the paper devoted to discussing them.

With Karen's permission, we have altered a portion of her study, in which she describes Ginny James's office, by stuffing adjectives and adverbs into her clean sentences. We loaded up these paragraphs to show how a writer can bury attitudes under adjectives and adverbs. To see how qualifiers impose a researcher's value judgments and hide cultural assumptions, compare our versions of her description with Karen's on page. Each of our versions emphasizes a different set of assumptions.

VERSION 1

Underneath Ginny's untidy desk, there are five bulging purses of varying sizes, from sleek, expensive leather clutches to cheap plastic bags. I gather from this backstage mess that the disorganized people who mechanically work here also need to use Ginny's sleazy office for their unprofessional belongings. On the top of Ginny's trashy desk, there are sloppy stacks of paper and torn notebooks and curled Post-it notes and a noisy, out-of-date, obsolete fax machine. She has her own ridiculously posed Photo Phantasies photograph, taken hurriedly, with her wearing a yellowed straw hat and a faded denim jacket with garish sunflowers embroidered haphazardly on the collar. Right beside this tacky photograph is a picture of an old haggy witch complete with bent broom and a wicked scraggly black cat.

VERSION 2

Underneath Ginny's meticulous desk, there are five neatly arranged purses of varying sizes, organized carefully from large to small. I gather that the efficient, tidy people who cheerfully work here need to use Ginny's neat office for their modest personal belongings, too. On the top of Ginny's antique cherry desk, there are straight stacks of brightly colored paper and well-organized matching burgundy notebooks and recently purchased Post-it notes and a quiet, understated fax machine. She has her own sedately posed Photo Phantasies photograph, taken carefully with her wearing a jaunty straw hat and an imported denim jacket with delicate sunflowers hand-embroidered on the dainty collar. Right beside this elegant photograph is a picture of a spiritual witch, complete with hand-crafted broom and a sleek, assured black cat.

The grammar of observation is really just the grammar of good writing: strong specific nouns, accurate active verbs, and adjectives and adverbs that add texture without masquerading cultural bias. All writers face a responsibility to bring their observations—as they see them—to the page. But fieldwriters face a doubled ethical challenge: to translate their informants' voices and perspectives for their readers yet still acknowledge their own presence in the text. This challenge requires careful observation, focused selection and verification of detail, and a deep awareness of the role of the self in writing about the other.

FieldWords

Dominate: To control, govern, or rule.

Focal point: A central place in the field site where ideas, artifacts, or people converge that sometimes provides a guide for writing field studies.

Mainstream: The prevailing or dominant influence within a culture.

Marginalization: The process of pushing nonmainstream people toward the edges of society to prevent their access to power.

Perception: Taking in information, observing, or understanding by means of the senses.

Perspective: A point of view; an angle of vision (the "spatial gaze," the "ethnographic ear").

FieldReading

Baldwin, James. "Stranger in the Village." *Notes of a Native Son*. Boston: Beacon, 1955.

Glassie, Henry. *Passing the Time in Ballymenone: Culture and History of an Ulster Community*. Philadelphia: U Pennsylvania P, 1982.

Goffman, Erving. *Behavior in Public Places*. New York: Free, 1963.

Guterson, David. "Enclosed. Encyclopedia. Endured. One Week at the Mall of America." *Harper's* (Aug. 1993): 49–56.

hooks, bell. "Choosing the Margin as a Space for Radical Openness." *Yearning: Race and Gender in the Cultural Marketplace*. Boston: South End, 1990.

Horwitz, Richard P. *The Strip: An American Place*. Lincoln: U Nebraska P, 1985.

Jacobs, Jane. "The Uses of Sidewalks: Control." *Death and Life of Great American Cities*. New York: Random, 1961.

MacLeod, Jay. *Ain't No Makin' It: Aspirations & Attainment in a Low-Income Neighborhood*. 2nd ed. Boulder, CO: Westview, 1995.

Marshall, Paule. *The Chosen Place, The Timeless People*. New York: Vintage, 1992.

Moore, Alexander. "Walt Disney World: Bounded Ritual Space and the Playful Pilgrimage Center." *Anthropological Quarterly* 53.4 (1980): 207–18.

Morris, Desmond. "Territorial Behavior." *Manwatching. A Field Guide to Human Behavior*. New York: Abrams, 1977.

Morris, Mary. *Nothing to Declare: Memoirs of a Woman Traveling Alone*. Boston: Houghton, 1988.

Myerhoff, Barbara. *Number Our Days*. New York: Touchstone-Simon, 1978.

Naipul, V. S. *A Turn in the South*. New York: Knopf, 1989.

Rose, Dan. *Black American Street Life: South Philadelphia, 1969–1971*. Philadelphia: U Pennsylvania P, 1987.

Stack, Carol B. *All Our Kin: Strategies for Survival in a Black Community*. New York: Harper, 1974.

Stoller, Paul. *The Taste of Ethnographic Things: The Senses in Anthropology*. Philadelphia: U Pennsylvania, 1989.

Whyte, William Foote. *Street Corner Society: The Social Structure of an Italian Slum*. 4th ed. Chicago: U Chicago P, 1993.

CHAPTER 4

Researching Language: The Cultural Translator

. . . [T]he simple act of listening is crucial to the concept of language, more crucial even than reading and writing, and language in turn is crucial to human society. There is proof of that, I think, in all the histories and prehistories of human experience . . .

M. Scott Momaday

It is difficult to realize how language both shapes and reflects our culture because it's so intrinsic to our everyday lives. As Scott Momaday reminds us, listening is a crucial skill that both builds and binds cultures. This chapter is about listening to language and translating what it has to say about culture. You'll read, write, and research language and language events—the use of words in everyday talk. You'll also research more formal oral "performances": jokes, stories, sayings, and legends.

Although some linguists claim that there is no thought without language, we think much of daily life moves along *without* the language of *words*. The visual and musical arts, dance and athletics, and scientific notation are all examples of nonverbal languages with which we communicate. Fieldworkers notice and record a culture's *nonverbal* languages in an attempt to learn more about the people they study. But they depend on *verbal* language as an intricate tool for at least three purposes. First, as a tool for the mind, verbal language brings nonverbal thoughts to the surface of consciousness. Second, for some fieldworkers, language becomes the topic of their research, illustrating how a culture shares knowledge through words. Finally, because researchers write, language provides them with the means to communicate knowledge about others.

Language, then, shapes the thoughts in your mind, can provide a subject for your research, and communicates your ideas to others. This tool we call language is equipped with a kind of filter. It filters out cultural specifics, keeping outsiders away from understanding. You've probably felt outside the range of some groups' languages, like being with a group of musicians, nurses, computer technicians, or athletes who talk their own insider language.

In the same way, a language can clarify a culture for the insiders, reminding them of their membership. Institutional language, for example, provides insider communication among people who work for the company. Without knowing it, a college uses terms to construct the insider business of being a student, and it filters that role from outsiders. The terms *credit hours, drop-adds, GPA, major,* and *minor* are more than a familiar vocabulary; they form a set of terms displaying insider membership in the subculture of academics. And as students know, these terms are all but incomprehensible to the outsider hearing them for the first time. When taking a general education course, you're introduced to the vocabulary of that field. In a music appreciation course, for example, you learn new meanings for familiar words: *score, signature, beat, measure, repeat.*

As you pay attention to the way language serves as a tool with an inside-outsider filter, you'll learn about your informants' perspectives. Listening to language will help you move further inside a culture and become intimate with it. You'll introduce yourself to a subculture as you describe its settings, daily events, and behaviors and learn more by examining its histories and artifacts. But it's not until you listen to and record its language that you'll become familiar enough to understand the connection of language to a culture's way of being. Even though you are using your own language to capture your informants' language, your job is to listen for theirs. You serve, in a way, as a cultural translator, always placing the insider's perspective in the foreground and your outsider's perspective in the background.

Researching Language: Linking Body and Culture

Your earliest attempts at recording and questioning the language of informants will probably involve description of their *body language* and reflection on it. When we think about human expression, we often think first, and perhaps only, of speech. But fieldworkers often learn early in their work that speech, or verbal communication, is only one of several modes that communicate individual and collective meaning about a culture. Early in his study, Rick Zollo felt the significance of body language. Asking questions of Morris, a lease operator of his own rig, Rick sensed he had asked one question too many. In his final project Rick writes, "The question of time raised Morris's suspicions again and instead of answering, he fixed me with a hard gaze. Sensing I had crossed some invisible boundary, I thanked him for his time. Obviously my question related to log book procedures, and I made a mental note to avoid that type of inquiry."

By being attentive to body language, Rick realized his intrusion and backed off, respecting Morris's need for privacy. At the same time, Rick made mental notes that deepened his understanding of his subject. The sooner and the more sensitively you discover, interpret, and use the non-verbal conventions of the culture you're studying, the more successful you'll be.

Since the 1950s, anthropologists, folklorists, linguists, and rhetoricians have contributed much to our understanding of the body as a means of nonverbal expression. With Ray Birdwhistell's 1952 *Introduction to Kinesics,* researchers began to study body communication (kinesics)—how individuals express themselves through body position and motion (facial expression, eye contact, posture, and gesture). Of course, we all engage in this kind of study informally, particularly in college classrooms, when we notice someone who slumps over her desk, puts her feet on another chair, or refuses to make eye contact with others. Still other researchers extended the study of individual body communication to spatial relationships (*proxemics*)—how individuals communicate nonverbally when in groups. Members of sports teams are experts at proxemics, communicating meaning constantly with their bodies as they strategize together throughout a game. And so do the fans watching from the stands. If you have ever entered an unfamiliar coffeehouse or bar, you may find yourself startled by how people use that public space to send messages. There is a stance that some men and women adopt that means they are "available." No words are used, but the meaning is communicated as clearly as if they were wearing signs. On airplanes, people signal whether they want to talk to their seat companions or remain silent merely by the way they hold a book or a folder. If you have ever ventured into a culture to find yourself startled by unfamiliar uses of personal or public space, you know the significant role that body language plays in human expression.

Through the physical display of our bodies to others, we signal not only who we are but also who we are in relation to those who "read" us. The body is not just a physical object; it is a social object. For this reason, studying how your informants dress or "adorn" their bodies and how they use them will tell you much about how they see themselves and their cultures. In Jake's participation with the skinheads (Chapter 2), one of the most obvious features that linked this group together was that every member of the group had a shaved head. This common marking for skinheads, Jake discovered, meant that they did not want their membership to be secret or underground.

Understanding the language of the body can come about in at least two ways. First, you can document body language in fieldnotes (this is better than waltzing up to informants and asking questions that will leave you sorry and them feeling awkward or abused). Early in your fieldwork, you might decide to observe and describe how members of the culture adorn their bodies—features of clothing, accessories, and body decoration like makeup, tattoos, piercings, and hairstyles). Rick Zollo's study of the truck drivers in Chapter 1 considered the "cowboy" dress of truckers and how that shaped their image of themselves.

Of course, one way to build reflexivity into your fieldnotes is to consider your own body in relation to the people you study. What sense do you get of their perceptions of your adornment? What, in terms of body language, is the relationship of self and other? In Chapter 3, Karen Downing reflected on her own makeup habits as she prepared to meet the manager of Photo Phantasies. Her thoughts were prompted entirely by being in the gaze of a differently madeup group of women—as well as her mother's voice inside her head.

From this initial focus on adornment, you might next begin to consider a person's body as a kinesic form of expression. Reflect on the patterns of movement you observe and what these patterns communicate, not just to outsiders (in this case, you), but also to other members of the culture—to the insiders. Had Karen Downing spent a bit more time reading the body language of her informants at Photo Phantasies, she would have additional data, information that might help us understand to what degree employees of the store "buy into" the images they sell. And if Karen had posed for Photo Phantasies herself, she might have added another dimension of feeling about herself in that space.

Finally, you might broaden your study of the body to consider how the people you study share and possess space. In other words, what do you notice about the proxemics of the culture? In Chapter 3, we discussed the importance of describing spaces. Now we hope you can discover strategies that will help you document how your informants inhabit space. As you take fieldnotes and reflect on them, you may come to discover underlying reasons why people in the location you've chosen move and communicate as they do. Perhaps these reasons have something to do with informants' "fixed positions" (gender, race, class, or age); perhaps they do not. Elizabeth's longest field study, a book called *Academic Literacies*, shows one of her informants, Nick, a college student, as he stretches himself over three chairs when he works in a writing group with three women—a kind of defense against them because he was afraid they would assault his text. And it was a "male thing" to take more space than was allotted to him. Had she not noticed this silent body language, Elizabeth might have never discovered this important dimension of Nick's work with his female peers.

As an interpreter of body language, your job as fieldworker is to discover not just what bodies "say" but why they say what they do. Another way, of course, to elicit information about body language is to ask informants themselves. Keep in mind that questions about body language require a good deal of rapport, particularly if your informant (or the culture) views the body as a taboo subject. But if it strikes you that an informant might ponder your questions without taking offense, think about the observations and ask for an insider's perspective. For instance, Elizabeth, merely by asking Nick, "Why did you need three chairs?" learned a lot about how he felt having three women read drafts of his writing. If your informant is willing to think consciously about his or her adornment, movement, and use of space, you will have a wonderful opportunity to test and revise your thinking.

Researching Language: Linking Word and Culture

Listening to the spoken language of your informant is an important way to learn about a culture. One key word, like one key piece of clothing or a gesture, can unlock information about the habits and beliefs, geography and history of a whole group of people. Your job as a fieldworker is to act as a cultural translator, recording and questioning the meanings of key words, phrases, and ideas that might serve as clues to "step in" to your informant's culture.

A fieldworker questioning our colleague Danling Fu, who grew up in the People's Republic of China, might be astonished to discover the array of Chinese words for silk. There are over 20 words that refer to how silk is made: words that denote shininess, smoothness, thickness, weight, and purity. Learning that there are so many silk words would be a signal to a fieldworker to investigate more about the cultural significance of silk. As Danling's friends, we knew only two things: that there were many words for silk in Chinese and that she had kept pet silkworms as a child. We wanted to see how these two facts might show us more about Chinese culture, so we interviewed her as a fieldworker would. We indicate our research strategies in italics.

B&E: Were you unusual, or do all Chinese children keep pet silkworms?

(We wanted to start with what we knew—that she had a pet silkworm when she was a child.)

D: Our relationship with worms is like yours with cats and dogs. I grew up in Jiangsu province, a silk-producing place, and all children kept silkworms. Every family does it. The full name we use is "baby silkworms." We care for them, keep them clean, learn to hold them tenderly, and watch the whole life cycle process.

B&E: How do you care for them?

(Although we were looking for language—words and stories—we wanted to give her time to remember details about keeping silkworms. We also wanted to hear more about the process because we knew that would illustrate more about the whole culture.)

D: In early spring, we put eggs—thousands of little eggs, laid by the silk moth the year before—on little squares of paper in a shoebox. We put them in the sun for warmth. Sometimes we start them in school, like American children grow seeds in paper cups or chicken eggs in incubators. Eventually, a worm hatches—so tiny, so black, smaller than an ant. As the leaves come out, we feed them to the little worms. Day by day, we watch them grow bigger, as thick as a little finger, in different shades of white and black.

B&E: Do children compete over how many silkworms they have?

(We wondered if Chinese children keep pet silkworms, whether they have rules for ownership, if they trade or have contests, and if that would suggest anything more about the culture itself. We weren't prepared for her answer, because our thinking was so American, so based on our sense of competition.)

D: Yes, but only because we all want a few to live so we can care for them. They eat a lot of leaves, and we don't have enough of them. In cities, families protect their trees because children steal each other's leaves. Sometimes I would buy extra leaves from farmers to feed my worms. Each year, if I had a ten percent survival rate, I would consider it a victory.

B&E: So where does the silk come in? What do you do with the silk?

(The discussion was beginning to move in a different direction. We wanted to know about silk; she wanted to talk about keeping pets. We tried to redirect it.)

D: Until their last moment of life, they produce silk. These worms are hard workers, a good image for Chinese people. When they are ready to build the cocoon in the summer, they become transparent—they look like the silk itself. And we build little hills for them with straw. The cocoons are red and pink and yellow—so beautiful on the straw hills. My mother used them as decorations in the house.

B&E: But then what? How do you get the silk out of the cocoon?

(*It was fun to visualize those little straw mountains with the colorful cocoons. But we hoped that she'd describe a very specific cultural practice here, that it might lead to more interesting insider knowledge. She did, and it did.*)

D: We put the cocoon in hot water. And then we pull out a silk thread, very carefully. You wouldn't believe how long it is. One cocoon makes one very long silk thread—yards and yards of silk. We wrap it around a bamboo chopstick, and then we have the thread to play with.

B&E: Do you play games with the silk thread? Weave with it?

(*The silk thread and bamboo pole sounded like the beginning of a children's game. Would children's games tell us more about the culture? Again, we were biased by our own culture and surprised at her answer.*)

D: Not really. It's only just a part of watching the whole process and learning about life and production. Life and productivity are the main parts of our culture. Such a little body, so much hard work. It just gives and gives and gives until the moment it dies. You know, we use every part of the process.

B&E: What do you mean by "every part of the process"?

(*Her answer takes an interesting direction. Games with silk aren't as important to her as learning about the life cycle and how production is tied to life.*)

D: Well, besides the silk, we watch the males and females produce the eggs together. We even use the waste. We dry it and stuff pillows. We eat the cocoon.

B&E: Yuk! Ugh! Are you kidding? You eat the cocoon?

(*We laughed as we teased our friend. We recognized our own assumptions about acceptable food and saw that the message was still tied to productivity—the Chinese don't want to waste anything*).

D: Yep. It's good. We deep-fry the inside. Tastes like a peanut.

B&E: So the silkworm is a pet, but you use so much of it to learn about other things.

(*We wanted to see what other insider cultural information might come when we asked what they learned from keeping these pets.*)

D: The worm is so soft, so tender. That's why we call it "baby silkworm"; we learn to care for it like a baby. These worms live really clean lives. We change the papers and the boxes. We scrape the leaves and the waste when we feed them. We need cheap pets, you know, in China. We cannot feed them our food like you do with your pets because we don't even have enough for ourselves.

(Without realizing it, she offers an important insight—that Chinese pets must not threaten human needs but must offer children a chance to learn about life.)

B&E: So children learn about the life cycle with these pets? And you have all those words about how silk is made: texture, shininess, thickness, weight. It's about life and production, as you said?

(We wanted to summarize what we had already heard her say, reemphasize why we interviewed her to begin with, and offer her an opportunity to elaborate, hoping we'd hear more about how silk and silkworms figure into Chinese language. We were hoping for more, but we couldn't force it.)

D: Yes, we have a children's song. It says "Be faithful. Even when you die, you can still contribute without taking anything. Like a silkworm." The silkworm gives us songs, metaphors, and images of our culture.

(Aha, a song! The song holds many of the very values she's been describing: economy, production, collaboration, and the cycle of life. And she recognizes it as she tells us.)

B&E: Wow, all those images of production. Bet that worked well during the Cultural Revolution.

(We knew Danling had been a teenager during the Cultural Revolution.)

D: *(laughs)* Yes, there are a lot of revolutionary songs with silkworms in them.

(If it had a song, would a culture that keeps silkworms and has many words for silk also have other forms of "verbal art"—stories, proverbs, and the like—that revealed its beliefs? She was telling us more about exactly what we wanted to know. This was exciting data.)

B&E: Are there any legends or proverbs about silkworms?

D: Well, not proverbs, exactly, but there are many stories. There's an image-story like "The Tortoise and the Hare." We say that to get something done with patience and consistency, it's like a silkworm, eating a leaf bit by bit, little by little. That little mouth eats so quietly, so fast. Overnight it can consume so many leaves.

(Ah, a relevant saying: to live a productive life takes patience and consistency. A cultural truth with a silkworm as the main character.)

B&E: And are there other sayings about the silk itself?

D: A silk thread, when it's in a cocoon, is so long, so intricate, so soft, and so tangled. It is difficult to figure out where the beginning is and where the end is. When we have a complicated problem, we say we are "tangled by a silk thread."

(And the silk thread even figures into explaining problems—another indicator of its importance in the culture.)

B&E: So there's the silkworm as a pet and so many words about silk. Language and learning and life.

(She was really remembering, and we didn't want to stop or redirect her line of thought. But we wanted her to know we were interested. So we offered another summary. Her own lovely statement summarizes—from her own perspective—better than we ever could from ours.)

D: With silkworms, we see the whole process. We see how silk comes into our lives—not only how we wear it, but how we live with it.

This interview taught us much about Chinese culture—not only how Chinese wear silk, as Danling put it, but also how they "live with it." Two key words that were far more important in her language than in ours, *silk* and *silkworm*, show the extent to which thought determines language—how a culture creates the words it needs. Our focus on these words unleashed information about Chinese history, metaphors, images, sayings, and songs. Danling's digressions on the care and feeding of pet silkworms revealed the cultural values of hard work, sacrifice, and productivity, not to mention the practice of eating cocoons. Because Danling is bilingual and bicultural, she assisted in our cultural translation.

Because Danling is our friend and fellow researcher, we felt comfortable interviewing her, and we were able to explore information more easily than an outsider might. We want our interview with Danling to serve as a model for you, but we realize that she was able to translate as many insiders cannot do. Most of us begin as outsiders who don't know our informants, nor do we have key words in mind when we begin our interviews. Outsider status is the point of entry for all fieldworkers, and practice in listening to insider language is a good way to "step in" toward the inside.

BOX 13
LISTENING FOR "THE WORD": CREATING A GLOSSARY

This exercise asks you to listen for key words in your field site and create a glossary of insider language. It will be important to get informants' permission to take fieldnotes or tape-record your conversation. As you listen, you may want to repeat what you hear so that your informants can add to, correct, or respond further to the insider language they are sharing with you. Later, you will also need to confirm your list of terms with informants in your field site. Try to collect as much insider language as you can. Do you notice certain everyday words being used in new ways? Are there names for things that are entirely new to you? In this exercise, we want you to sharpen your listening skills to make yourself alert to language at your research site.

Here is a section from Rick Zollo's much longer glossary, gathered from two instructors at the trucking school he attended. Rick first heard these words at Iowa 80, but it wasn't until he sat through some of the formal instruction, read the written material, and interviewed these truckers that he could confirm the meanings of a trucker's vocabulary. Notice that Rick has organized the glossary in alphabetical order and that his definitions are short, concise, and parallel in structure.

Bear bait: A truck driving faster than the flow of traffic.
Bear trap: A radar trap.
Chicken coop: A truck-weighing station.
Chicken lights: Flashy lights surrounding a trailer.
Comic book: A trucker's log, required by the U.S. Department of Transportation.
Double nickel: 55 mph speed limit for trucks.
Kojak with a Kodak: Police with radar.
Lot lizard: Woman who frequents truck stops selling favors.
Parking lot: A trailer transporting motor vehicles.
Ratchet-jawing: Talking on a CB radio.

Response

Cheri Krcelic researched the subculture of freestyle bikers, a group of people who share interests in inventing, practicing, and performing tricks with customized bikes. Cheri writes, "The parts of the freestyle bike are bought separately and assembled by the owners, allowing the riders to build the bike that suits them best. Freestyle bikers have a common interest but allow the rider to express individuality." In her research, Cheri discovered that most freestylers display their tricks informally. But freestyling is also an organized sport with competitions and exhibitions sponsored by clubs, magazines, and bike shops. Cheri divides her glossary into two categories: the important attachments to the bicycle and the tricks performed with the bicycle:

IMPORTANT ATTACHMENTS TO THE BICYCLE

Gyro: A device located underneath the handlebars, pulling the cables through one place. It allows the rider to turn the handlebars completely around without tangling the cables.
Pegs: Round, cylindrical metal rods attached at a 90-degree angle to the front and rear wheels of the bike. They provide built-in platforms for the biker to stand on.

TRICKS PERFORMED WITH A BICYCLE

Decade: An easy trick. Popping up on the back wheel, jumping off the frame, over the top of the bike, landing on the other side of the frame, and riding off.
Wheelie: An easy trick. Riding for a long distance with the front wheel off the ground.
Whiplash: A difficult trick. Rolling on the front wheel while standing on the front pegs, while the rest of the bike is spinning around. The biker steps over the frame each time it spins around.

After you've gathered and alphabetized a list, try clustering words into categories as Cheri did. She learned through her categories that the freestyle biking culture had two major concerns: the construction of the bike and the invention and display of tricks. The excerpt from Rick's list showed that truckers use familiar words in unfamiliar ways to develop important insider understandings. The terms *silk* and *baby silkworms*, in the interview with Danling, signaled cultural meanings about life cycles and the value of productivity. Categorization is the beginning of analysis.

Researching Occupation: Recording Insider Language

Anthropologists, sociologists, and folklorists have always been interested in the language of occupations. They have studied and written about, for example, flight attendants, police, cab drivers, bartenders, nurses, farmers, fishermen, factory workers, and waitresses. To research insider occupational language, you cannot be merely an observer, but you must become a participant-observer, asking questions. As you read these short studies of waitresses, notice that a few phrases of occupational language reveal entire sets of rules, rituals, and ways of thinking. Insider language—a word, a term, or a phrase—can trigger whole stories that illustrate the perspective inside a subculture.

In her full-length ethnography called *Dishing It Out*, anthropologist Greta Foff Paules includes a list of waitresses' insider terms, which includes "the floor," "call out," "walk out," and "pulling bus pans" as grass-root expressions coined by the workers themselves to discuss their own work situations. This is not officially sanctioned language that we would find in a manual, guidebook, or even a photocopied set of rules for working in a restaurant. It's interesting, though, that occupational terms are stable. Whether you are a waitress in California, Texas, or New Jersey, you'll know that a "station" is a waitresses' service area and that to be "stiffed" by a customer means that you've been left no tip.

Here are two "stiffing" stories from two different fieldworkers. They both show how waitresses, when stiffed, retaliate. Our colleague Donna Qualley, who was a part-time waitress herself for many years, studied the way waitresses talked among themselves about their work at Norton's Seafood restaurant. Donna recorded this dialogue, shared between an older waitress named Rae, her younger coworker Erin, and herself:

"I had this young couple"

"How old?" Erin interjects.

"In their twenties I would guess. They order two fish and chips and two glasses of water."

"Cheap. I'm surprised they didn't ask to split one meal," Erin mumbles.

"When they are done I put the check on the table and tell them I will be right back to collect it for them. I go into the kitchen and when I come back, there is a ten-dollar bill, a dime, a nickel, and a penny on the table."

"How much is the bill?" I ask.

"That makes me so mad . . ." Erin begins.

"But," Rae smiles, "the woman had left her coat on the chair. They were in such a hurry to get out she forgot her coat! I grab the coat, check, and money. and then I see her coming back for her coat . . ."

"I hope you kept it until they left a better tip," I laugh.

"I said to this woman, 'Oh, did you come back for your change?' "

"You really said that? How much was the bill again?" Erin asks.

"Ten fifteen, and they left me ten sixteen. Well, this woman turns all red and apologetic and says, 'We didn't have any money—we thought this was a takeout place.' Yeah, right. They knew what they were doing."

This conversation, taken from long transcripts of recorded waitress talk, is part of Donna's fieldwork study, which shows how talk and gossip bind waitresses as they work. Waitresses, an occupational group that can be oppressed at times, retaliate with gossip against the rude behavior of customers who stiff them.

Greta Paules's study of waitressing, this one conducted at Route, a family-style chain restaurant, illustrates a waitress's outrage at being "stiffed." This waitress, in an attempt to cut her losses, resists waiting on regular customers who previously left without tipping her:

This party of two guys come in and they order thirty to forty dollars' worth of food . . . and they stiff us. Every time. So Kaddie told them, "If you don't tip us, we're not going to wait on you." They said, "We'll tip you." So Kaddie waited on them, and they tipped her. The next night they came in, I waited on them and they didn't tip me. The third time they came in [the manager] put them in my station and I told [the manager] straight up, "I'm not waiting on them . . ." so when they came in the next night . . . [they] said, "Are you going to give us a table?" I said, "You going to tip me? I'm not going to wait on you".(31)

Both of these stories center around the insider term *stiffing*, which means "leaving no tip." In the context of waitressing, the stories that surround the term convey a whole set of behaviors and attitudes toward the occupational term and the event itself. Out of context the occupational term does not convey the waitresses' worldview in the same way that the story, which includes the event, does.

Another insider expression used at Norton's Seafood refers to a waitress who is "in the weeds," which means extremely busy. A waitress who is "in the weeds" might do something extraordinary under such pressure. In Donna's fieldwork, Carrie's story is an example of what happens to a waitress in this context:

I was carrying this huge oval tray, and it was filled with food. And a man stood up right in front of me and said, "I want my beer now." So I handed him the tray and went and got his beer. He stood in the aisle holding the tray. He didn't know what to do. I thought, "If anyone sees this, I'm going to get fired." But it was just "I want my beer now" and me with fifteen dinners on my tray. "OK sir," I said, set the beer on the table, and took the tray. I didn't know what else to do. I didn't want to yell at him—I wanted to throw the tray at him.

Occupations that form subcultures, like waitressing, often convey their insider terms through stories, words, and phrases. Like Carrie's being stuck "in the weeds," too tangled and overwhelmed to get out, insider terms sometimes serve as metaphors. Occupational folklorists have suggested that the relationship between job terms and a group's cultural worldview is so strong that the terminology literally shapes the perspective of the workers. Most waitresses agree that to be busy feels like being caught "in the weeds" and to be insulted by a customer evokes retaliation against those who "stiff" them. Learning occupational terms and swapping stories shape behaviors and values. In the case of these waitresses, the incidents were reminders of caution against customer disrespect and efficiency in the face of customer demands. The occupational language and its accompanying stories help initiate new waitresses into the profession and reaffirm seasoned waitresses' experience. Occupational language reflects an insider's perspective.

In this chapter, we've offered two very different models for listening to language. We set up our interview with Danling with specific questions about language use in her culture. We directed questions toward our goal, but we didn't stop her when she seemed a little off the track. Because informants know more than outsiders do about their own culture, researchers must trust that digressions may lead to important knowledge.

In Donna Qualley's study of waitresses, the best stories came when she just hung out and listened. Although she had worked in the restaurant herself, she had never stopped to listen in quite that way. When Donna set out to identify occupational terms through the stories she heard, she made field notes of waitresses' talk and began to sift out the categories of insider language that she hadn't even noticed as a member of the culture.

Whether you are an insider or an outsider to the subculture you study, whether you conduct a formal interview or collect words, phrases, and stories informally, you can learn much from listening to language. Your goal is to try to describe language from your informant's perspective and analyze what it tells you about the occupation it represents. If you choose to tape-record, you will need the information we provide at the end of this chapter about taping and transcribing oral language.

BOX 14
DESCRIBING INSIDER LANGUAGE: OCCUPATIONAL TERMS

In your field site, select an occupation to study, or someone who uses specific occupational language. Spend some time watching the work and listening to the workers and their language. Record fieldnotes or tape insider language, if possible. Once you've gathered some terms or phrases, words or unfamiliar usages, arrange to interview an informant. From your informant, find out as much as you can about the history and uses of these occupational terms or phrases. Try to get your informant to tell a story that illustrates a certain term. Ask, "What do you mean by X?" "Tell me how Y works?" "How do you use Z?" You may find your informant wanting to explain techniques, rules, rituals, or processes of the occupation. Or, like the researchers who studied waitresses, you may hear a good story. The best way to get a good story, of course, is to hang out long enough to hear one.

Response

In this reflective response, Donna Qualley writes about how she gathered the waitresses' stories. She acted as a kind of cultural translator between the waitresses' lives and her academic life as college student, instructor, and waitress:

> In a sense, I think I had earned the right to consider myself bicultural since I had worked in that place for eight years. I had not only witnessed but also participated in the kind of cathartic talk I describe, weekend after weekend and summer after summer. What set me apart was my double perspective— my academic take on everything. I could take these conversations and place them in other arenas, adding new layers of meaning. My part-time status at the university was always recognized, so I was not one of them completely. And yet when waitresses told their stories, I recognized them as my own. For in the eyes of the customer, we were all the same. Particularly, when I was a student and literally needed Norton's to survive, . . . being stiffed was a very serious story. We all felt each other's situation keenly. We recognized the type of tale we were telling.
>
> What was different is that when I actively began to do research, to take notes both on the job and at times when I wasn't working, just the act of writing, of actively looking, of fleshing out my notes as fieldnotes at the end of a shift caused me to see more connections than previously and to articulate them more fully. And I suppose in a way it was different for the waitresses, too, in that I was making their lives matter to someone else. And when I interviewed several waitresses alone, I think this also made them feel their lives were important. People came up to me with their stories. "Put this in your book," they would say. Interestingly, the cooks and the busboys got snippety when they found out they weren't going to be in it. They had an idea of something like "Nortons: The Untold Story." But my research project was to focus on the gossip and stories of waitresses and what that revealed about the occupation of serving others.

Researching Verbal Performance: The Curse and the Culture

Our waitress stories fit the category of occupational folklore, but they are also what folklorists and anthropologists call "performance events" or examples of "verbal art." Performance events include a wide range of expressive art, from informal to formal: the telling of jokes, proverbs and taboos, songs and chants, urban legends, curses and spells, myths and tales, traditional stories, and entire ceremonies complete with storytelling and ritual verbal behaviors (like weddings, initiations, retirements, and seasonal celebrations). These performances use spontaneous verbal art; they are unrehearsed, unscripted, and not often staged. This concept of verbal performance comes from folklore and depends on three features: a performer who is an insider to the culture, a recognizable oral performance, and an audience of insiders.

As the waitresses told their stories, away from customers, they engaged in the performance event of occupational storytelling. Their stories were spontaneous and unrehearsed. Audience, storyteller, and researcher understood this performance event. The performers were waitresses who signaled to the insider audience with their shared terms—"I got stiffed last night"—that they were about to offer a story. The researchers who collected those stories were insiders to the occupational culture and understood the key terms, which alerted them to turn on the tape recorder.

In the same way that a folk object, like the basket or quilt we described in Chapter 2, is an expressive art form that blends cultural tradition with individual creativity, so does a verbal performance. A joke, for example, has a traditional core—either of content (the chicken crosses the road) or of form, ("Knock, knock!" "Who's there?"). But jokes and stories have variants; they change according to the performer's creativity, personal history, and culture ("Oh, I heard a different version of that where I lived").

So the twin laws of folklore—tradition and creativity—are present in our verbal performance events, although we are not consciously aware of them. Telling a joke or gossiping, both verbal performances, are so automatic and integrated into our conversational lives that we don't often stand back to analyze them. But we all know someone who is a good joke teller, and we depend on certain people to give us the latest gossip. We also notice when an outsider "doesn't get" a joke—"You had to be there." Only insiders to a subculture have the cultural knowledge to "get it."

Like a joke or a story, a curse is a kind of verbal performance that exists in many cultures. It is closely connected with other verbal arts in a culture: songs and chants, for example. Looking at the curses of a culture helps us understand its taboos, history and geography, values and beliefs. Zora Neale Hurston, an anthropologist working in the 1930s, was one of the first ethnographers to study the folk tales and magic practices of her own culture, recounted in her book *Mules and Men*. Unlike the insensitive researcher Reema's boy in Willow Springs, Hurston traveled to her native Eatonville, Florida, knowing that there was a rich collection of folk tales to gather there among her people. She used her status as an insider to work her way towards New Orleans in order to study hoodoo, a uniquely American practice, blended from a mixture of African and Haitian black magic (voodoo) and New Orleans French Catholic religious beliefs.

Hurston learns a curse from hoodoo doctor Luke Turner, who agrees to take her on as a pupil, having himself learned hoodoo from an infamous conjurer named Marie Laveau. From Turner, Hurston also learns the process for putting a curse on someone: sending the names of your enemies to their house sealed with the wax from a porcupine plant, and mixing a package of damnation powders for them. Then the conjurer etches the enemy's name with a needle on a black candle dressed in vinegar and sets it on the altar, pays 15 cents to the spirit of Death, and invokes this curse-prayer:

> To the Man God: O Great One, I have been sorely tried by my enemies and have been blasphemed and lied against. My good thoughts and my honest actions have been turned to bad actions and dishonest ideas. My home has been disrespected, my children have been cursed and

ill-treated. My dear ones have been backbitten and their virtue questioned. O Man God, I beg that this that I ask for my enemies shall come to pass:

That the South wind shall scorch their bodies and make them wither and shall not be tempered to them. That the North wind shall freeze their blood and numb their muscles and that it shall not be tempered to them. That the west wind shall blow away their life's breath and will not leave their hair grow, and that their finger nails shall fall off and their bones shall crumble. That the East wind shall make their minds grow dark, their sight shall fail and their seed dry up so that they shall not multiply.

I ask that their fathers and mothers from their furthest generation will not intercede for them before the great throne, and the wombs of their women shall not bear fruit except for strangers, and that they shall become extinct. I pray that the children who may come shall be weak of mind and paralyzed of limb and that they themselves shall curse them in their turn for ever turning the breath of life into their bodies. I pray that disease and death shall be forever with them and that their worldly goods shall not prosper and that their crops shall not multiply and that their cows, their sheep, and their hogs and all their living beasts shall die of starvation and thirst. I pray that their house shall be unroofed and that the rain, thunder and lightning shall find the innermost recesses of their home and that the foundation shall crumble and the floods tear it asunder. I pray that the sun shall not shed its rays on them in benevolence, but instead it shall beat down on them and burn them and destroy them. I pray that the moon shall not give them peace, but instead shall deride them and decry them and cause their minds to shrivel. I pray that their friends shall betray them and cause them loss of power, of gold and of silver, and that their enemies shall smite them until they beg for mercy which shall not be given them. I pray that their tongues shall forget how to speak in sweet words, and that it shall be paralyzed and that all about them will be desolation, pestilence and death. O Man God, I ask you for all these things because they have dragged me in the dust and destroyed my good name; broken my heart and caused me to curse the day that I was born. So be it. (197–198)

This curse, collected by Hurston, is a good example of verbal performance art. As a fieldworker, she tries to capture the performer's oral style in her writing. If you read this curse aloud or to a friend, you would understand the full force of its performance features, which link it closely to a wide range of spiritual traditions that invite audience participation. It opens with an evocation "To the Man God: O Great One," and ends with the closing "So be it."

Anthropologists would recognize this curse and its African-American, French Creole, and Haitian voodoo roots, as many verbal art forms share traditional and universal features. The hoodoo curses the enemy's most basic cultural elements: disease and death, crops and weather, fertility and birth. The variations on this curse (the "creative spin" or "variant"), specific to these conjurers, includes creative use of language that shows the voice and rhythms of this New Orleans subculture: "their finger nails shall fall off and their bones shall crumble," "their house shall be unroofed and the rain, thunder and lightning shall find the innermost recesses of their home."

This culture may seem foreign, exotic, and removed from our own. But in fact, the following piece of short fiction written by our colleague Rebecca Rule uses the curse as the central structure to write about the subculture of New Englanders in the setting of a town meeting. Whether she means to do so or not, Becky draws on the verbal curse tradition: the main character, Miranda, identifies her enemy at the outset and concentrates on him throughout the story. Like Hurston's hoodoo curse, Miranda's curse is repetitive, and she, too, draws on universal features of weather and crops, fertility, home, and family. As you read this story, look for the creative ways that Becky represents a uniquely New England perspective. As the storyteller, she puts her own creative spin on the tradition of the curse.

The first time we heard this short story, it was an act of performance. Becky read it aloud to a group of New Englanders in a setting much like the one she describes. Because they were insiders, they howled with laughter at the outrageous curses Miranda wishes on her enemy. The story was in draft form, and Becky enjoys "trying her writing out" on an audience. In fact, she often revises according to her audience's reactions. She reworked this story and had it performed as a play two years later in her rural New Hampshire hometown. Her fiction, then, even though it's written, is coupled with her oral storytelling performance. It has characteristics similar to traditional folkloric performance: a performer, an insider audience, and a performance with traditional elements. Like a traditional oral storyteller, Rebecca Rule shifts her creative spin—creates a new variant—each time she reads her stories to an audience.

Yankee Curse
Rebecca Rule

At the School District Meeting, Miranda knits.
May your neighbors steal from your wood pile, Mort Wallace.
The points of her flexi-needle slide in and out of the heavy burgundy wool.
May they incinerate their garbage in a barrel at your property line. And may the wind blow in your direction.
She counts seventeen stitches. She recounts, eighteen stitches. She remembers the musk of burning garbage, the red smoke blowing over, ash falling like snow.
May you choke on the smoke.
She maintains tension with her right index finger. That's the trick of it, isn't it, the pressure against callused flesh of wool flowing over.
May the ashes fall hot on your bald head.
Miranda's thick hair—bands of gray and white—beehives in mysterious swirls that amaze the young parents sitting one row behind her. When she lifts her chin, the back of her neck straightens, and the lines of her jaw smooth into youth.

She knits. Yarn loops her forefinger like a bloody slice.

Mort Wallace stands, but not to speak. He sidles to the PTA concession for a refill from the coffee urn—his fifth since the meeting started. The PTA volunteers are beginning to look at him strangely. He throws coins on the counter, then opens his lips to suction in the hot liquid—black and rainbow skimmed.

At the front of the gym Kaye Elbow, school board chair, speaks . The microphone amplifies the quaver in her voice. Mort Wallace will destroy this young woman if he can: Miranda has seen that in his cold, deep-set eyes—eyes that, over the years, seem to have sunk deeper and deeper into his skull. His hand tests the strength of the Styrofoam cup. His nostrils take in the steam.

Miranda knits faster, drops one stitch, corrects, knits on, drops another. She has hated Mort Wallace since childhood. Her parents hated his parents, so she in turn hated him. That is the way of it in these small towns—to hate by tradition. But make no mistake, Mort Wallace has earned his share. Even Miranda's Aunt Lou (who had a kind word for everyone) said of having been Mort's Red Cross swimming instructor when he was a boy: "I should have drowned him when I had the chance."

She was referring to Mort's meanness. He is an opinionated man. Everyone in town has opinions, most of them set in granite. Mort's opinions, though, are veined with meanness. He stands *against* on every issue; *against*, vehemently and with nothing but contempt and harsh words for those who who stand *for*. He is a mean man. See it in his face. Hear it in his voice. Know it in the way his children leave home as soon they graduate high school and never come back.

May your children spite you with with their choices. May they abandon you in old age.

Know it in the way his first wife disappeared without warning—leaving her own babies, as though she saw in them what she loathed in her husband.

Know it in the way his followers—he has a few—peck at the grains of his meanness like chickens following the feeding pail.

May your chickens lay thin-shelled eggs, Mort Wallace. May skunks nest under the hen house. May raccoons scream at midnight in the pine tree that scratches your bedroom window.

Miranda does not invoke rabies—nor does she ever wish, even in the secret pocket of her heart, for the death of her enemy. "Curse them in this life," said her Gramma Annie, from whom she learned the art of the well-directed curse. Gramma Annie, whom Miranda much admired, said death was an evil call and unworthy.

Though they've never spoken, Miranda has admired Kaye Elbow from the first time she saw her smiling down a heckler, too naive it seemed even to realize she was being heckled. Miranda admires Kaye Elbow's broad dark face and the way emotions skitter across it like bird shadows on the water. Miranda, who has no children, has long been ripe with maternal instincts, which come on strong for Kaye Elbow (her heart quickens, her mouth tastes metal) when Mort Wallace's hand shoots up, raised stiff-armed from the shoulder, like a school boy in need of a bathroom pass. His shoulders round forward. His chest—under thin checked flannel—appears to fold in on itself, yet there is enough air in those folded lungs to give his voice a boom that turns all heads: "Yes, I *do* have a question for you, Madam Chairman."

Miranda's husband Everett, God rest his soul, said this about Mort Wallace: "He's got two gears—neutral and steaming mad." When Mort speaks in public, it is always in anger. Some in the crowd lower their heads, embarrassed, hoping the storm will blow through quickly. Some exchange gleeful looks: *Mort's gonna give it to 'em now!* Some want to fight back. Some want to shoot him down and watch him, winged, spiral splat into the water.

Miranda expects Mort acts even worse at home. She pities his second wife—the nonentity, step-mother to his grown and gone children. They say she is an active alcoholic who never leaves the house after 6 p.m. Of course, Mort is out practically every evening; stirring up trouble at selectmen's meetings, budget committee, planning board, Save-Our-Wetlands. (He opposes wetlands.) Wherever there is trouble to be stirred, he stirs it.

In summer, Mort Wallace's second wife tends a garden of annuals along the walkway in front of the house: ageratum, marigold, cleome, and masses of white petunias. Walking by, Miranda sometimes sees her kneeling on the bricks, dragging at the weeds with eager hands.

"Hello," Miranda says if their eyes meet. "Hello," Mort Wallace's second wife says back.

Miranda knits to the rhythm of her curse.

May your second wife find a sharp tongue in the bottle she loves and slice you with it.

Miranda knits the left sleeve of a burgundy cardigan for the man in the old-folks-home who is still her father though he no longer knows her. This is a curse she would never levy, not even on Mort Wallace: to live too long. The rhythm of her stitches falters when she thinks of her good-hearted father, beyond suffering they say, but *they* don't know, do they? The rhythm of her stitches falters when she thinks of her own strong, kind Everett struck down by a weak heart before his time, and Mort Wallace, who never did a bit of good for anybody in this town, living on and on like some tough old bramble dug in so deep you can't kill it no matter how many times you mow it down.

"Mort Wallace was a bully as a child and he's still a bully," Aunt Lou said.

"Just like his old man," her father said.

"He's a phenomenon," Everett said.

Mort Wallace didn't much bother Everett, not even during Everett's four terms on the Board of Selectmen. Though once, when Mort accused him outright and in public of fraud, Everett did get riled. "You do get some funny ideas, Mr. Wallace," Everett said, out of his chair and advancing. "I'm not much of a one for lawyers and lawsuits, but you say that again, and I'm on the phone, misterman." Everett's thick finger pushed into Mort's concave chest, "And I'm going to find me a lawyer."

It hurt her to see Everett attacked, especially with his dying so soon after. It hurt her too deep to forgive. She curls her knitting in her lap and lowers her head. So far the discussion at this School District Meeting has been civil, back-and-forth talk among good people trying hard to come to terms, trying to find a balance. Mort Wallace will try to change all that with his old trick of setting neighbor against neighbor.

May your neighbor's children BB your windows, cherry-bomb your mailbox, siphon your gas, and deflate your tires. May the little ones pierce your rest with their shrieks.

She studies the rich color of the sweater that will eventually be her father's but remains hers until the last tail is tied off.

May your dog bark on and on. May she someday turn on you without warning. May she haunt your dreams when she's gone.

Miranda studies the fine, even stitches, row upon row, interlocking like the fingers of clasped hands.

May the words you are about to fire at Kate Elbow turn like a boomerang stick and strike you between your cold, depthless eyes.

Mort's voice carries, loud and sharp as gunfire.

May your shingles curl and your clapboards peel.

Miranda lets the hum in her head turn Mort Wallace's words to gibberish. *May your sills rot under your feet.* She fingers her knitting, hefts accomplishment. She holds the sleeve out for scrutiny, a sharp eye for flaw. But sees no flaw. She sees a perfect burgundy plain. *May carpenter ants turn your beams to powder.* A stranger in the next chair pokes her and whispers, "That's coming along good?" Miranda meets the stranger's eyes, and he is struck by how beautiful her eyes are, like clear water flowing over mica-flecked ledge.

Kaye Elbow smiles at Mort Wallace, a tense dark figure leaning hard into the cement-block wall. His arms are crossed so tight it looks painful. For Kaye, a smile is her first line of defense. She is new to the board, chair by default (no one else would take the job), and has been warned about this man and how he would try to influence the vote with a hard, fast twist of reality. "What gives you people the gall," Mort Wallace says, "to ask us hard-working taxpayers to cough up more money? You didn't manage your budget—plain and simple. Maybe you didn't know how. Maybe you didn't want to. Maybe you didn't care. Maybe you're stupid. I won't say you're a bunch of crooks—I'd like to but I won't."

"I'm sorry, sir," Kaye Elbow says. "Would you state your name for the record?"

"You don't know who I am? Tell her who I am, Robert," he says to one of the other school board members.

"You tell her," Robert says.

May a rat die between the studs of your bedroom wall.

Everett always said, "Mort Wallace has his followers, but they're none too many and none too bright." When Everett chaired the Board of Selectmen, he knew how to handle Mort's kind: "Sit down," he'd say, "we've heard enough," with a rap of the gavel. And if they didn't sit down, he'd suggest, mildly, "You want to step outside then, and settle it in town hall yard?" No one ever took him up on the offer, especially not Mort.

"For the record, my name is Morton Wallace. Is that clear enough for you, honey?"

Kaye Elbow says in a high, steady voice (she is no longer smiling): "Quite clear, honey. Now let me clarify something." She holds one white index card in her hand. She reads from it. The School District, she explains, is not in deficit and cannot, by law, enter into deficit. The board is simply presenting the facts so voters can decide how to proceed, considering the special education overrun, the hike in insurance, and the fact that the furnace is so far gone it can't be fixed and winter coming on.

She looks straight at Mort Wallace, tilts her head sweetly: "And by the way, I don't feel that any particular gall is required to stand before you. I'm just doing the job I was elected to do."

Mort Wallace hates to be checked by a woman. His eyes darken. They are as dark as scorched pine. His face is gray, the hard lines deepened by his freshly inflamed anger and the artificial light.

Miranda watches the pulse in the cording of his throat. She sees how the cuff of his shirt hangs at his wrist, how his belt is freshly notched. He has smoked too many cigarettes and slipped too many shots of whiskey into his bottomless cup of coffee. More importantly, a terrible backwash of his own venom has poisoned him, is punishing him more than her mild curses ever could.

Now, she raises her hand, full of knitting. An umbilical cord of burgundy yarn trials into the tapestry bag at her feet. The sleeve is a burgundy flag. Recognized by the chair, Miranda stands: "Mrs. Coffey—Miranda Coffey—some of you know me." She reminds herself to speak right up. "I realize you folks are doing the best you can. You're working awful hard and you've got figures to back up what you're saying. So I'm going to vote the money you asked for."

From the corner of her eye, she sees Mort with his hand in the air again. She turns to face him. She addresses her kind lie directly to him: "Mort Wallace, I know you mean well," she says. She holds her knitting tight to her chest, and takes a long breath. "But there's no need for you to be talking that way to these good people. Sit down, now; we've heard enough."

Since he has no chair, Mort can't sit down. But Miranda sees that he would if he could. She sees it in the way his mouth opens and closes, in the way he flattens into the cement-block wall and fades like old paint. Everett would approve.

Miranda sits down. The stranger next to her touches her elbow. The young mother behind her leans forward and whispers: "I'm glad you spoke up."

Miranda knits.

Curses and spiritual performances, like seances, tarot readings, and fortune telling—even religious sermons—reveal aspects of a culture's belief system. Less formal oral performances like proverbs, jokes, and sayings reveal the everyday rules and rituals that a culture lives by. All cultures and subcultures have sayings, which are often not only entertaining but also didactic—they teach youngsters and newcomers the values and traditions that a culture holds true. Even though there is a traditional core (form or content), each culture's proverbs and sayings are creative and unique. Verbal art is valued in a culture because its shared oral tradition allows each person to bring creativity to each rendering of the performance.

BOX 15
GATHERING VERBAL ART: PROVERBS, JOKES, AND SAYINGS

Try researching a form of verbal art: jokes, proverbs, sayings, or perhaps even curses or chants. If you are working on a major project, you may want to relate this exercise to your fieldwork. Begin data collection by choosing a form and a theme: a certain type of joke, proverbs about a certain theme, childhood chants. This is a good exercise to supplement with library research. There are lots of collections of proverbs and jokes, for example. You will find chants and curses in studies about specific cultures. The folklore section in your library holds a treasury of many forms of verbal art. You might even want to look in the reference room for Stith Thompson's *Motif Index of Folk Literature* and *The Types of the Folk-Tale: A Classification and Bibliography* by Antti Aarne, two valuable resources that categorize types and themes of folk narratives around the world and throughout history. Of course, you may be able to collect quite a few pieces of verbal art just by requesting it from the people around you. Once you've gathered your data, cluster it into a list.

Here are some questions that might help you analyze your list: What are the common themes? What words reappear in different ways? What do the variations tell you about the unique features of culture from which it came? What behaviors does it encourage or discourage? If you were an outsider to this culture, what could you learn?

RESPONSE

One class put together this group of proverbs about talk:

1. Put up or shut up.
2. Silence is golden.
3. Talk is cheap.

4. Loose lips sink ships.
5. Do as I say, not as I do.
6. Talk softly and carry a big stick.
7. Sticks and stones will break my bones, but names will never hurt me.
8. Children should be seen and not heard.
9. If you can't say anything nice, don't say anything at all.
10. The best answer to anger is silence.

After you have collected a list of items and named the category ("proverbs about talk"), you can begin to interpret them. For example, this group of proverbs carries American assumptions about speaking—its rights and responsibilities. Note that children have fewer speaking rights (8) than adults and that silence is valued over talk (2, 4, 9, 10). The stance of *action* being more important than *words* is an American value (1, 5, 6, 7). Note, too, that proverb 4, "Loose lips sink ships," has a historical origin. In World War II, the government warned citizens to guard their talk carefully because anyone might be a spy.

Another class collected five proverbs from different countries that have the same core theme but transformed with their cultural perspectives:

1. Variety is the spice of life (English).
2. Ten men, ten minds (Japanese).
3. The clock strikes differently every hour (Hindustan).
4. Whatever is natural possesses variety (French).
5. No two things are exactly alike (West African).

Each of these proverbs shares the theme of human difference, but with its own cultural variant. If you already know something about the country's history, you may be able to describe the features of the culture that the proverb suggests.

Sara Simonson collected these descriptions of beliefs and some of their accompanying sayings, shared by what she calls "good ole boy farmers" in Illinois:

- The color of the coat or stripes of wooly bear caterpillars indicates the severity of the upcoming winter.
- If leaves on hedge trees are as big as squirrels' ears, spring is here.
- If you did a good job harvesting beans without leaving many on the ground, neighbors might say, "You could starve a rooster out here."
- Corn should be "knee high by the fourth of July."

These beliefs about agriculture are shared by people who depend on the weather and the seasons for their livelihoods. Any farming subculture has beliefs and sayings about natural conditions and animals that affect the growth of their crops. Proverbs serve multiple, even conflicting functions in a culture. For example, "the early bird catches the worm" refers on the surface to having efficient work habits, but its hidden or implied meaning refers to an individual's ability to compete in capitalist culture where everyone is out to get as much as they can. Danling agrees that no such proverb would exist in China, where the community is more important than the efficient individual.

Researching Verbal Performance:
Urban Legends

You've been collecting performance events: everyday stories of a subculture and more ritualized language events (jokes, curses, proverbs) that fall into the category of lore. We are just as unconscious of our folklore as we are of our everyday language. The lore we pass along in our culture, like curses, stories, tales, and songs, is much more than mere superstition. Our folklore serves to control our anxieties, explain our deepest fears, and teach us how to go about living in our cultures. Like the waitresses' gossip and the conjurers' curses, lore conveys a traditional core as well as variants, depending on the teller.

A culture's myths, one form of lore, are never taken as truth, whereas legends and tales have enough truthful elements to serve as what we might consider folk history. We hear American lore without recognizing it: about dead ancestors (your uncle who almost made a fortune), about famous historical figures (George Washington wouldn't tell a lie), and cultural heroes (John Henry built the railroad and Rip Van Winkle awoke to a changed world after 20 years asleep). We retell legends without consciously recognizing the cultural belief systems they symbolize: capitalism, honesty, hard work, progress.

One class of folklore narrative is the *urban legend*, set in contemporary times, including elements that are believable to us. Like other verbal art, urban legends encompass belief systems and can also be considered cautionary tales for ways of behaving in our modern life. Urban legends, like ghost stories, are told in places where people come together to eat and sleep temporarily, as in a camp or a dorm. Like all folklore, urban legends travel from one site to another. We have found from our students that a legend told in Des Moines, Iowa, may have a variant in the outer banks of North Carolina. Wherever you grew up, you probably heard about a woman with a ribbon around her neck, a haunted family tombstone, a bloody hook, or rat meat in a fast-food hamburger.

Jan Brunvand, a famous folklorist, has collected examples of urban legends, weird and macabre tales that often feel like truth. Here is an excerpt from his book *The Vanishing Hitchhiker*, which describes many variants of the urban legend that folklorists call "The Roommate's Death."

The Roommate's Death
Jan Harald Brunvand

Another especially popular example of the American adolescent shocker story is the widely-known legend of "The Roommate's Death." It shares several themes with other urban legends. As in "The Killer in the Backseat" and "The Baby-sitter and the Man Upstairs," it is usually a lone woman in the story who is threatened—or thinks she is—by a strange man. As in "The Hook" and "The Boyfriend's Death," the assailant is often said to be an escaped criminal or a maniac. Finally, as in the latter legend, the actual commission of the crime is never described; only the resulting mutilated corpse is. The scratching sounds outside the girl's place of refuge are an additional element of suspense.

Here is a version told by a University of Kansas student in 1965 set in Corbin Hall, a freshman women's dormitory there:

> These two girls in Corbin had stayed late over Christmas vacation. One of them had to wait for a later train, and the other wanted to go to a fraternity party given that night of vacation. The dorm assistant was in her room—sacked out. They waited and waited for the intercom, and then they heard this knocking and knocking outside in front of the dorm. So the girl thought it was her date and she went down. But she didn't come back and she didn't come back. So real late that night this other girl heard a scratching and gasping down the hall. She couldn't lock the door, so she locked herself in the closet. In the morning she let herself out and her roommate had had her throat cut and if the other girl had opened the door earlier, she [the dead roommate] would have been saved.

At all the campuses where the story is told the reasons for the girls' remaining alone in the dorm vary, but they are always realistic and plausible. The girls' homes may be too far away for them to visit during vacation, such as in Hawaii or a foreign country. In some cases they wanted to avoid a campus meeting or other obligation. What separates the two roommates may be either that one goes out for food, or to answer the door, or to use the rest room. The girl who is left behind may hear the scratching noise either at her room door or at the closet door, if she hides there. Sometimes her hair turns white or gray overnight from the shock of the experience (an old folk motif). The Implication in the story is that some maniac is after her (as is suspected about the pursuer in "The Killer in the Backseat"); but the truth is that her own roommate needs help, and she might have supplied it had she only acted more decisively when the noises were first heard. Usually some special emphasis is put on the victim's fingernails, scratched to bloody stumps by her desperate efforts to signal for help.

A story told by a California teenager, remembered from about 1964, seems to combine motifs of "The Baby-sitter and the Man Upstairs" with "The Roommate's Death." The text is unusually detailed with names and the circumstances of the crime:

> Linda accepted a baby-siting job for a wealthy family who lived in a two-story home up in the hills for whom she had never baby-sat for before. Linda was rather hesitant as the house was rather isolated and so she asked a girlfriend, Sharon, to go along with her, promising Sharon half of the baby-sitting fee she would earn. Sharon accepted Linda's offer and the two girls went up to the big two-story house.
>
> The night was an especially dark and windy one and rain was threatening. All went well for the girls as they read stories aloud to the three little boys they were sitting for and they had no problem putting the boys to bed in the upstairs part of the house. When this was done, the girls settled down to watching television.
>
> It was not long before the telephone rang. Linda answered the telephone, only to hear the heavy breathing of the caller on the other end. She attempted to elicit a response from the caller but he merely hung up. Thinking little of it and not wanting to panic Sharon, Linda went back to watching her television program, remarking that the caller had dialed a wrong number. Upon receiving the second call at which time the caller first engaged in a bit of heavy breathing and then instructed them to

check on the children, the two girls became frightened and decided to call the operator for assistance. The operator instructed the girls to keep the caller on the line as long as possible should he call again so that she might be able to trace the call. The operator would check back with them.

The two girls then decided between themselves that one should stay downstairs to answer the phone. It was Sharon who volunteered to go upstairs. Shortly, the telephone rang again and Linda did as the operator had instructed her. Within a few minutes, the operator called back telling Linda to leave the house immediately with her friend because she had traced the calls to the upstairs phone.

Linda immediately hung up the telephone and proceeded to run to the stairway to call Sharon. She then heard a thumping sound coming from the stairway and when she approached the stairs she saw her friend dragging herself down the stairs by her chin, all of her limbs severed from her body. The three boys also lay dead upstairs in their beds.

Once again, the Indiana University Folklore Archive has provided the best published report on variants of "The Roommate's Death," Linda Dégh's summary of thirty-one texts and several subtypes and related plots collected since 1961. The most significant feature, according to her report, is the frequent appearance of a male rescuer at the end of the story. In one version, for example, two girls are left behind alone in the dorm by their roommate when she goes downstairs for food; they hear noises, and so stay in their room all night without opening the door. Finally the mailman comes around the next morning, and they call him from the window:

> The mailman came in the front door and went up the stairs, and told the girls to stay in their room, that everything was all right but that they were to stay in their rooms [sic]. But the girls didn't listen to him 'cause he had said it was all right, so they came out into the hall. When they opened the door, they saw their girlfriend on the floor with a hatchet in her head.

In other Indiana texts the helpful male is a handyman, a milkman, or the brother of one of the roommates.

According to folklorist Beverly Crane, the male-female characters are only one pair of a series of significant opposites, which also includes home and away, intellectual versus emotional behavior, life and death, and several others. A male is needed to resolve the female's uncertainty—motivated by her emotional fear—about how to act in a new situation. Another male has mutilated and killed her roommate with a blow to her head, "the one part of the body with which women are not supposed to compete." The girls, Crane suggested, are doubly out of place in the beginning, having left the haven of home to engage in intellectual pursuits, and having remained alone in the campus dormitory instead of rejoining the family on a holiday. Ironically, the injured girl must use her fingernails, intended to be long, lovely, feminine adornments, in order to scratch for help. But because her roommate fails to investigate the sound, the victim dies, her once pretty nails now bloody stumps. Crane concluded this ingenious interpretation with these generalizations:

> The points of value implicit in this narrative are then twofold. If women wish to depend on traditional attitudes and responses they had best stay in a place where these attitudes and responses are best able to protect

them. If, however, women do choose to venture into the realm of equality with men, they must become less dependent, more self-sufficient, more confident in their own abilities, and, above all, more willing to assume responsibility for themselves and others.

One might not expect to find women's liberation messages embedded in the spooky stories told by teenagers, but Beverly Crane's case is plausible and well argued. Furthermore, it is not at all unusual to find up-to-date social commentary in other modern folklore—witness the many religious and sexual jokes and legends circulated by people who would not openly criticize a church or the traditional social mores. Folklore does not just purvey the old codes of morality and behavior; it can also absorb newer ideas. What needs to be done to analyze this is to collect what Alan Dundes calls "oral-literary criticism," the informants' own comments about their lore. How clearly would the girls who tell these stories perceive—or even accept—the messages extrapolated by scholars? And a related question: Have any stories with clear liberationist themes replaced older ones cautioning young women to stay home, be good, and—next best—be careful, and call a man if they need help?

After reading Brunvand's article, Courtney Schmidt wrote about her process of collecting an urban tale and its variants in her dorm.

THE ROOMMATE'S DEATH

I walked up and down the fifth floor of Harkin Residence Hall searching for a wonderful storyteller. As I soon found out, only one person was willing to step forward, and this was after a lot of coaching. Many people claimed "not to know any stories," and the people who did have stories proved to be very quiet once the recorder play button was hit. Finally, one brave soul out of the bunch put aside her shyness and spoke up to share the following story:

> This story is one of the first ones I heard here. I had heard it through my hall. It is about a girl who came in late one night from a date and found it odd that her door was locked. But being very tired, she decided not to turn on the light and not to wake up her roommate since it was extremely late. She got up the next morning to find a note on the mirror, in red lipstick, saying, "Aren't you glad you didn't turn on the light?" She looked over on the bed to find her roommate had been slaughtered.

Once my friend told this story, the rest of the group surrounding her wanted to tell their own—off the record. One girl told me that the message wasn't written in lipstick but in blood. Another girl told me that the victim had been raped before being slaughtered. Yet another shared that the girl had originally gone to a party that others had warned her about.

After the group told stories, I told them about urban folklore and explained how these stories are most often targeted to females and try to teach them how to act the correct way according to society's standards. I informed them that the basic theme of this legend revolved around the situation when, "as the adolescent moves out from home into the larger world, the world's danger may close in on him or her" (Brunvand 396). The girls and I agreed that the college freshman experience was indeed that of moving into a bigger world and that the story also had a huge warning to all those living in the hall. "If you don't lock your doors, the same thing could happen to you." The tale also contained a sexual theme, which stated that if you go out with a boy and come home late, you are probably up to no good. The roommate's death would be a direct punishment for not being discreet and not insisting that your date take you home right after the movie.

One of the messages of this story is for women to assume traditional roles—or else. I mean, what was the woman doing in college anyway? After I pointed out these ideas about the urban legend, the girls became very angry, and most of them admitted that they had never thought about it that way. Into the late night hours, they started taking old horror stories and analyzing them, even adding in the males as the "scairdy—cats" and laughing. I'm glad I could give them a little food for thought.

Like Courtney, our students went out, collected, and analyzed urban legends and shared their findings. Their urban legends, all cautionary tales, fell into three thematic categories: romance, food, and strangers. The first is a story about a high school romance, one you may have heard in a variant form in your own part of the country. This version takes place in North Carolina.

The Spillway

There is a story about this girl in high school. And she wasn't very wild. In fact, she had never been on a date. One night, she snuck out of her house to go on a date with a guy she had just met that day. She thought he was taking her to a movie, but her date convinced her that they needed to get to know each other better. So they drove down by the spillway, a bridge by a lake. Over the course of the evening, he persuaded her to have sex with him in the car. They both thought that since it was her first time, she could not get pregnant. But about after three months, the girl found out that she was pregnant. She didn't want to go through the humiliation of telling her family. She stole the boy's keys while he was in gym class, got in his car, and drove it down to the spillway. She ran the car off the bridge, killing herself. It is said that if a guy and a girl go down to the spillway and set their keys on the hood of their car, the girl will come by and start the car.

This urban legend serves to caution young women about having sex on the first date and includes folk beliefs about pregnancy. It feeds on young women's fears of family humiliation and community rejection. The gym class, the keys, and the car are details of our contemporary lives, but they are also symbols of power and freedom in our culture. The legend's main character uses these symbols to destroy herself. This tale has many elements of theme and structure that are traditional in lots of cultures, both modern and ancient. But if you were an outsider listening to this story, you would learn a lot about teenage culture in contemporary middle-class America: the place where kids park, the culture of the car, and a warning not to get into a similar situation.

Our next urban tale, which also includes a car, centers on the very American culture of the shopping mall. This legend elaborates on the traditional dictum "Never talk to strangers."

The Mall, the Car, and the Stranger

One day at the local mall, a young woman returned from shopping to her parked car. She thought that she had just had a normal day of shopping until she looked in and saw a little old woman sitting on the passenger's side. She walked up to the old woman and asked her what she was doing in the car. The old woman told her she was just tired. And then she asked the young woman if she could please give her a ride home. The young woman said no and asked the old lady to please get out of her car. The old woman persisted by saying how tired she was and how she only needed a ride home. Then the young woman decided to not argue anymore and to ask for help from the security officers at the mall. Soon the young woman and the security police returned to the car and found the old woman still sitting there. The security officer asked the old woman to get out of the car, but she would not budge. He had to take her by the arms and drag her out of the car. While they were doing this, the woman hit her head on the car door and her wig fell off. It turned out that the woman was not a woman at all but a man dressed as a woman. The police handcuffed him and praised the young woman for her action, saying that if she had taken the old woman's word for being tired and given her a ride home, she would probably never have made it.

This urban folktale centers around the fear of strangers, warning young women against an "outsider" who appears inside the young woman's car and tries to deceive her. It has traditional elements we might find in tales from many cultures: a stranger in disguise and a young woman who defends herself (with help from cultural authorities) against danger. But the legend uses details from suburban life: a mall with security police, an automobile as a private space that should never invite intruders. And it appears quite believable to any insider who lives and shops in contemporary America.

Like the mall story, urban legends are so loaded with familiar details that they seem quite believable. When we hear them, we are often fooled into thinking that they actually happened—recently, locally, among people who know people just like the people we know.

We suspect that you've heard urban legends about food, romance, strangers, and certainly many more themes, such as sudden wealth or poverty, mysterious disappearances of people, or superhuman feats. But we wonder if you've ever stopped to analyze which parts link back to traditional tales, which parts suggest cultural warnings or lessons, and which parts make them so believable to the insiders in our own culture.

BOX 16
COLLECTING URBAN FOLK TALES

If you were gathering legends in an unfamiliar culture, you'd notice elements of cultural tradition in those stories as well as details specific to that culture. As a fieldworker studying any culture or subculture, you'll want to collect important pieces of narrative folklore in order to interpret the teachings, anxieties, and fears of that group. Hearing these stories allows you to focus on the values that shape the subculture. If you have been working in your field site long enough, you might collect urban legends that will relate to your project or to the subculture you are investigating.

Record several urban legends or local ghost stories from willing storytellers as Courtney did. Choose one representative story to transcribe and share with a group of fellow fieldworkers. Be prepared to talk about some of the research issues you faced: finding a storyteller, taping and transcribing the story, and analyzing underlying themes, values, and beliefs.

Which of the stories are similar to others you have heard before? What parts seem to be the traditional core and which parts seem to be the creative variants? How do the details in the variant parts illustrate the values and belief systems in the culture or subculture? What fears, concerns, or anxieties does each story seem to address? What cultural lesson does it teach?

After you do some analysis, you might want to do some library research. Because of all these similarities and differences in folk narratives, folklorists keep carefully organized reference indexes. Most university libraries have *The Types of the Folk-tale* and the *Motif Index of Folk Literature,* which we mentioned earlier in this chapter. You may also want to read urban tales published by folklorists like Jan Brunvand. Hundreds of reference works are listed in both general catalogs and social science indexes in the categories of language, mythology, folklore, popular culture, anthropology, and ethnology. Library research will help you see the universal themes in folklore in all cultures and also help you track the details specific to the time and place of your own tale. You'll want to write up your research findings, along with the story itself, to include in your portfolio.

Response

Folklore researchers understand that these stories convey underlying fears and values within the culture. Debbie Smith collected a story about food. Although she was attending college in North Carolina, the story came from her elementary school days in Florida. Other students provided many variants from places where they had lived. When you read it, you may recognize this traditional urban legend from a variant you've heard. While outsiders to this culture of fifth graders might reject this legend as absurd, insider elementary children find it entirely plausible:

The Cafeteria Pizza

At lunch in my fifth grade, my class sat in the cafeteria wishing for any food other than what the cafeteria ladies made. We settled into the entertainment of vying for the story that could gross everyone else out. Over our shepherd's pie and gray peas and chocolate milk, tale after tale was offered depicting all things disgusting to our entranced audience.

And then a nerd, Andre, came through with the story to end all cafeteria stories. He told us about the mad cafeteria worker at another school who was tired of feeding all the nagging kids. He had been fired once but returned to seek his revenge. One night, he entered the school and sliced open all the boxes of processed pizza and carefully put in pieces of broken razor blades into each pizza. The next day, they had served about 50 slices before they found a piece of shiny sausage and went to ask the teacher about it. All the kids were taken to the hospital, but no one suffered from fatal cuts inside their throats. And they never found the maniacal cafeteria worker. We lost our appetites as we pondered this story and its consequences. The next day our school served pizza.

Our anxieties about food run deeper than we realize. In contemporary life, we often eat prepared, frozen, or institutional food. We don't always know the people who make it, we don't always make it ourselves, we don't even see it being made, so many of our urban legends center on food preparation. This tale is a variant of many modern urban legends about mysterious or sinister food preparation: an angry cafeteria worker takes revenge on fifth graders. But it also holds important cultural lessons: watch out for unidentified revenge seekers who lurk around in unexpected places, don't nag cafeteria workers, and be satisfied with boring but safe food. This urban legend is believable because the teller says "it happened at another school" and the worker quit and returned for revenge. We read news stories daily that share very similar details, so it is difficult to find the details that would make us doubt the story.

Reading the Story: A Fairy Tale for Our Time

When we first discover forms of verbal art like urban legends, we're often surprised to notice that they have such traditional and universal characteristics. Although we've told them and heard them for much of our lives, it's interesting to see how many cultural values they carry. As with the themes of urban legends, we grow up with the frames of other kinds of narratives, such as fairy tales, which begin early in our childhoods. The fairy tale is another form of verbal art that draws on oral traditions and reflects the values and belief systems of a culture. But unlike urban legends, which attempt to prove that they're true, everyone knows that a fairy tale is fiction and accepts that from the outset.

Fairy tales move through history and across cultures as verbal performance. Folklorists can document versions of Cinderella, Sleeping Beauty, Dracula, and Red Riding Hood, for instance, in hundreds of cultures. One of our students who grew up in Belize decided to write his grandfather's Mayan version of Hansel and Gretel, a well-known tale for centuries among his people, but one that had not been previously written down. Louis was surprised to learn that it had variants in other cultures. His Mayan version had three children instead of two: Delores, Sebastian, and

José. Instead of a forest leading to a little cottage, the three siblings cleared their way through a jungle, "slept the night in one big bunch under a fig tree," and came upon an ominous tropical hut. Instead of an old witch's hot oven, there was a talking dog inside with a pot of boiling water who threatened the children. But the basic traditional elements were unchanged: siblings must collaborate and look out for each other to survive when their parents are absent.

Fairy tales or magic tales (*märchen*) are not just stories for children; they are another way a culture preserves its traditions, values, and belief systems—that scholars call our *unconscious culture* or *unexamined mythology*. We don't often realize that the very nature of fairy tales means that there is no one original, authentic version. Those of us who listened to Grimm's fairy tales learned the 19th-century Western European versions written into books by the Grimm brothers and first published in Germany in 1812. But growing up in 20th-century North America, many of us also took in variants of those traditional fairy tales in Disney movies and more contemporary children's books and theater, TV productions, and audiotapes. Even though we are sometimes unaware of it, a great deal of classical literature originated in traditional folk tales. Because our mainstream American culture is so based on both print and electronic media, much of what we know to be our fairy tales come to us not as oral, shifting stories from a storyteller but in published form. We may have to look to our families and our ethnic or regional backgrounds to find more traditional oral forms of fairy tales.

Whether we've learned them from movies and books or from a relative, our fairy tales exist as unexamined mythology in our minds. Although most of us know better, a woman whistling the song from the Disney version of *Snow White*, "Someday My Prince Will Come," might have an unconscious belief that she will be saved from a jealous controlling person, get married, and live happily ever after. Simultaneously, her boyfriend might expect to charge his way toward a docile, forever smooth-skinned princess who can cook, clean, and transform his home each day while he's gone.

As with other forms of verbal performance, informed audiences of insiders know a fairy tale when they hear one. They know that it is a fiction and that there will be recognizable recurring features: a central human character or two, recognizable beginnings and endings ("Once upon a time," "And they lived happily ever after"), talking animals or distorted humans who express certain truths or have magical powers, and a series of trials or tests. Informed audiences know that the story will somehow illustrate an important piece of knowledge in the culture. As with other forms of folklore, the fairy tale has a traditional core (recognizable and recurrent features) and creative variants (details specific to the culture in which the tale takes place, and special details the storyteller adds to make it his or her own version).

We would like to close this chapter with a reading called "A Fairy Tale for Our Time," written by Jack Zipes, professor and storyteller. His book *Don't Bet on the Prince* is a collection of contemporary feminist fairy tales. As you read it, try to notice some of the recurring traditional features (animals who speak truths, a series of tests, two main characters of different ages) as well as the themes (urban, environmental, and feminist) that represent the values of contemporary American culture.

A Fairy Tale for Our Time

Jack Zipes

Steffie awoke with such a jolt that she fell out of bed. It was true, she thought. It must be. Her dreams never lied. The fairy tale had been kidnapped, and if she did not find it by nightfall, there would be silence, eternal silence, like the dreadful darkness that surrounded her room.

Haunted by her dream, Steffie got dressed as quickly as she could, and without realizing it she was soon outside the house and heading toward the country. When she reached the forest, she was overwhelmed by the devastating silence. It had already begun just as the sun was making its appearance felt. And yet, the sun was no help to her now. So she went straight to the massive oak trees and asked if they had seen the fairy tale. Without warning they all began to sob and told her that the magic had left their leaves. The entire forest was in danger. The dwarfs no longer worked in the caves, the pixies no longer swam in the ponds, the witches had thrown away their brooms, and the giants were scared of their own shadows. All of them had left the forest, but the trees could not tell her why.

So Steffie wandered deeper into the forest and gradually became aware that the birds had stopped chirping. Most of the animals looked ragged and sad, and the bushes seemed limp and paralysed. It was almost as if the entire forest had turned pale out of fright, and yet, Steffie did not see anything frightening. The only animal she encountered was a tiny rabbit who stood his ground when she approached him.

"So, you've come at last," the rabbit sighed and let his ears droop to the ground.

"Me?" Steffie responded.

"Well, get it over with," he said morosely.

"Get what over with?"

"Kill me!"

"What?" Steffie could not believe her ears.

"You've poisoned the fairy tale. You're destroying my home with sprays and guns," the rabbit asserted. "The least you could do would be to kill me right away!"

"Never," Steffie replied.

Then the rabbit stuck out his tongue at her and darted into some nearby bushes. Steffie hung her head and bumbled through a thicket. As she wandered into an open field wondering why the rabbit had picked on her, a huge cow with chocolate spots came trotting toward her.

"Hey you!" the burly cow bellowed.

"Me?" Steffie was surprised.

"What have you done with the fairy tale?"

"I haven't done a thing."

"You must have done something. We can hardly breathe here," the cow scowled. "First you bring these tools and instruments to torture us and steal our milk. Then you inject long needles into us to make us grow fat. You put chemicals into our food. You use all my friends in the farmyard for experiments. And you're telling me that you haven't killed the fairy tale, too!"

"That's not true," Steffie protested. "I'm looking for . . ."

"Get out of here, or else I'll call my friends," and she nodded to tremendous, sleek and powerful bulls and cows grazing at the other end of the field. "Moooove your self! Be quick!"

"But . . ."

"Mooooooooove!"

The cow started to nudge her, and Steffie began to run. She ran past the animals in

Reading the Story: A Fairy Tale for Our Time

199

the fields and heard taunts "Go baaaaaaaack home, baaaack! Cluck, cluck, cluck, cluck!" The howls and shrill sounds sent shivers up her spine. She felt like a criminal on the run, and she kept running until she reached the city.

Though the city was already at full speed, she had an eerie feeling that it, too, was in danger. As she walked through the streets, the people pushed and shoved her. And, whenever she tried to tell them what had happened to the fairy tale, nobody seemed to care. At one point she burst out crying, and a young woman dressed in an elegant business suit stopped by her side: "What's the matter, dear? Are you lost?"

"No, not really." Steffie dried her tears.

"Well, what's the matter?"

"It's the fairy tale. They've kidnapped it."

The young woman stared at Steffie as if she were crazy and moved on.

Just at that moment Steffie noticed a movie theater across the street with a big sign on the marquee: SLEEPING BEAUTY. Her eyes lit up, and she dodged the cars as she crossed the street.

"Watch out, you lunatic!" a driver yelled at her. But Steffie did not even hear him. She went up to the box office and asked the mousy-looking man who sold tickets whether she could go in and look for the fairy tale.

"Scram! I ain't got time to fool with kids like you!" the man threatened her with his fist.

"But, but . . ." Steffie stuttered and suddenly became aware of the pictures of nude sleeping beauties that lined the entrance to the theater.

The man made a motion as if he were going to run out after her, and Steffie scooted away. Now she walked aimlessly through the city with her bright eyes vacant and her shoulders slumped. After a while she became tired and sat down on a bench in the middle of a small park strewn with litter. Next to her was an old lady twirling a cane between her legs. She was dressed in a long, tattered calico gown, army boots, and a fancy, broadbrimmed hat with a navy blue veil.

"You're a sight!" the lady said to Steffie.

Steffie knew that she should not talk to the lady, but something inside her prompted her to smile.

"What are you looking at?" the lady pouted.

"Nothing, nothing," Steffie became afraid.

"Oh, don't become afraid." There was something tender now in the lady's face, a mournful but sympathetic look in her eyes.

"What's the matter?" Steffie asked.

"Oh, nothing, except that they're going to put me away tomorrow."

"Put you away? Why? Have you done something wrong?"

"No, not that I know of. I just don't have anyone. No money, no friends, and the boss people are kicking me out of my apartment, and some other boss people are going to cart me off."

"But where will they take you?"

"I don't know. Some home, maybe. I'm not sure," the lady suddenly began to sob.

"Please don't," Steffie tried to calm the old lady. "If I could, I'd take you home with me, but we don't have much money either, and I don't think that my mom and dad would like it. They've been in a terrible mood ever since my dad got fired."

"I know."

"You know?"

"I mean, I can imagine. I know what it's like to be without work," the lady bowed her head.

"Are you sure there's nothing I can do?" Steffie touched her arm.

"Maybe."

"I could help you find a hideout."

"No, no. I have to go. The boss people will find me. They always track you down."

"There must be something I can do," Steffie hoped.

"Well," the lady had a twinkle in her eye.

"Well, tell me." Steffie was getting impatient.

"No, You tell me. Tell me a story."

"But I can't," Steffie replied. "I don't know how."

"I'll bet you can," the lady looked square into Steffie's eyes.

"You don't understand," the girl resisted. "I've been searching for the fairy tale the entire day, and, if I can't find it pretty soon, then . . ."

"You said you wanted to help me, didn't you?" the old woman seemed upset.

So Steffie thought for a few seconds, and before she knew it, she began telling the lady a tale about a young woman in a calico dress who lived all alone in the city. "Nobody knew she had magic powers. But she did, you know. And one day she went into the forest, and she met a rabbit and a cow. They were dying. The trees, too. And all she had to do, you see, was touch them, and music exploded. It broke right through the dead silence, and they were well again. The young woman liked the forest so much that she decided to stay there for many years, and the animals and the trees loved her. Finally, when she became old, I mean, not all that old, she went back into the city. But, you see, nobody liked her magic powers. Nobody cared about her. So they didn't work anymore. She tried to get people to talk to each other and help each other. But they laughed at her. Nobody knew how wonderful she was, and . . ." Steffie fumbled for words. Then she said: "I'm not sure how the story ends." She blushed. "I mean, I'm sorry. I can't finish it."

There was a silence for a moment. Then the lady leaned over and gave her a kiss. "That's all right, Steffie. You're my fairy tale." The old lady smiled. "You're the fairy tale. I'm sure of it."

The lady stood up. She was a tall woman, and she glanced at Steffie with an impish grin. Then she turned from the girl, who remained seated on the bench, and she used her cane to propel herself down the path. In the twilight it seemed that a slight breeze twirled the calico gown and whisked the lady forwards. Steffie watched the large figure grow smaller, and at one point it seemed as if the lady had pushed herself into the air with her cane and was now riding on it like a broom. Steffie stood up, looked to make sure, and her heart told her that at that moment she had finally found the fairy tale.

Part of the contemporary twist or "spin" in this tale is the characters' acceptance of their own participation in it. Zipes leaves the ending open for the reader to complete. There is no "happily ever after" in this postmodernist mock ending.

The Research Portfolio: Synthesis

As you've worked your way through the exercises in this chapter, you've researched, read, and written a lot. Whether you chose to focus your exercises on your main fieldworking project or have done each exercise separately, you've probably piled up a lot of writing: transcripts, lists, short analyses, and written examples of verbal art.

One of the jobs of a research portfolio is to help you synthesize what you have collected and selected. It offers you an opportunity to reflect on what you've learned and on how your research writing fits into the larger picture of your research. It suggests how all this material will help you shape your future goals—both for the project and for yourself as a reader, writer, and researcher.

You've read one piece of fiction (Rebecca Rule's *Yankee Curse*), an excerpt from a classic published ethnography (Zora Neale Hurston's hoodoo doctor from *Mules and Men*), a folklorist's article about urban legends (Jan Brunvand's discussion of "The Roommate's Death"), and another folklorist's version of a fairy tale (Jack Zipes's "Fairy Tale for Our Time"). You've also read work that we, our colleagues, and our students have done: the interview with Danling Fu, Cheri Krcelic's and Rick Zollo's glossaries, Donna Qualley's waitress stories and reflection on her position, and other students' collections of sayings, proverbs, and urban legends.

And if you've tried the exercises, you have linked your own research project to extended writing about language in a cultural site. So far, you have

- Classified insider language by exploringthe word
- Clustered, categorized, and analyzed language used in occupational groups
- Gathered and interpreted a range of verbal art: proverbs, jokes, sayings, chants, and curses
- Collected, written, and shared urban folktales

At this point, for your portfolio, we suggest three ways to synthesize your studies of language and language use. You will want to write reflections and share them with your portfolio partner, and you will want to synthesize what all of these exercises, coupled with the readings, have taught you so far.

PERSONAL HISTORY

What is your own personal history with verbal art? In this chapter, we have offered several personal accounts of verbal art, but we have not invited you to think about your own. Here is an opportunity to synthesize with a personal reflection, applying what you've learned about verbal art by looking back at your own history. You may want to focus on one of these questions, or you may instead want to write a traditional story from your own cultural background to put in your portfolio.

- What proverbs or sayings governed your growing-up life?
- What special family language "events" happened in your home? At family celebrations? In the subculture of your workplace, your school, your church, or another subculture to which you belong?
- What kinds of stories were important in your background? Who were the important storytellers? How many different "informed audiences" have you been a member of? What has been your own role as a storyteller?

USE OF LANGUAGE

What have you learned about language and language use? The many forms of verbal art that you have studied and collected offer you an array of ways to look at language use and storytelling. Write a reflective analysis of yourself at this point as a language researcher.

- As you survey all the data, what themes do you see about your process as a researcher?
- Are there any themes you seem particularly interested in? Any themes you seem to always discard?
- How did your expectations match the data you actually assembled? What kinds of assumptions did you make before you began your research on language? What surprised you?
- What language behavior do you want to know more about? How would you go about obtaining more data?
- What kinds of personal filters did you notice you had that interfered with your interpretations?
- What have you learned about language and language use that will be important to you as a reader, a writer, and a researcher?

VERBAL ART

What do you now know about verbal art for your research project? If you related all these exercises to your field site, you have done important work toward your final project. As you reread all the data you've collected, which of the exercises will be most useful for describing the language practices of the subculture you are researching? Write a reflective response of yourself as a language researcher at this cultural site.

- What words, phrases or insider languages have given you insight into the culture you are studying?
- How do you serve as a "cultural translator" with your informants?
- What has surprised you most about the language use of the people at your site? What verbal behaviors would you like to know more about? How would you go about getting that data?
- What forms of verbal art (proverbs, jokes, curses, chants, stories, urban folk tales) have you looked for and found at your site?
- How have your informants reacted to your interest in their use of language? What were they eager to share? What made them nervous? What have you learned from them about researching language?
- What have you learned about yourself as a researcher of language? What are you good at? What kinds of skills do you need to practice?

Taping and Transcribing

Interviews provide the bones of any fieldwork project. You need your informants' actual words to support your findings. Without informants' voices, you have no perspective to share except your own. You bring to life the language of the people whose culture you study as you record them.

The process of taping and transcribing interviews has been advanced by sophisticated tape recorders and word processors. It's no coincidence that interviewing and collecting oral histories has become more popular in recent years with these accessible technologies; it's nice that cassette recorders are small, relatively inexpensive, and easily available. With a counting feature to keep track of slices of conversation and a pause button to slow down the transcription process, a simple cassette recorder becomes a valuable tool for the interviewer. Computer software, from the simplest word processors to the most specialized programs that create databases and recombine information, cut down the tedium of sorting, classifying, and organizing huge piles of written data.

But transcribing is tedious business nonetheless. Most researchers estimate 6 to 12 hours of transcribing for each hour of recording. You don't want to tape everything you hear, nor do you want to transcribe it all. That's why it's important to prepare ahead with research and guiding questions, but also with adequate equipment and knowledge about using it. We'd like to share some advice to make your taping and transcribing go smoothly.

1. *Obtain your equipment.* Borrow or purchase quality equipment. What's good for taping a concert or copying a friend's CD may not be the best equipment for recording an interview. You'll need a tape recorder that has a counting feature to track and locate sections of the interview and also a microphone that will be sensitive enough to pick up the human voice. Some tape recorders have built-in microphones, but often it is necessary to attach a separate directional mike to maximize the voice and minimize peripheral noise. Check to see if you can borrow interview equipment. Departments of anthropology, sociology, English, theater, or journalism usually lend equipment to students.

2. *Prepare your equipment.* Batteries can die when you least want them to, so you'll need to have an AC adapter as an additional power source. It is safer to use electrical outlets as your power source than to depend on batteries. Test your equipment before entering your field site by recording the date, your name, and your informant's name. Then, when you arrive at your interview, play it back. Most fieldworkers have stories about lost interviews due to bad tapes or malfunctioning equipment. Elizabeth, for example, only took one 60-minute tape to a two-hour interview session. After the first hour, her informant kept talking. Pretending she was still recording, she took notes furiously by hand. Check not only the length of each tape you purchase but also its quality. Medium-quality tape is quite adequate (higher-quality tape is made for recording music; low-quality tape can stretch or break). When you arrive on site, be sure to have extra batteries, extra tape, tape labels, a notepad and pencil, and perhaps a camera to gather contextual information. Remember to wear a wristwatch so that you can quietly keep track of interview time.

3. *Organize your interview time.* Ask the informant to suggest a convenient place and time for the interview. Arrive a few minutes early to set up and test your equipment. Try to minimize interruptions once you are at the field site. Arrange your tapes and note pads close by so that you won't bang or shuffle, distracting your informant or cluttering your tape with extraneous noise.

4. *Organize and listen to your audiotapes.* Nothing is more frustrating to the energetic researcher than a box full of unlabeled tapes. Use the stick-on labels

that accompany the tapes to identify the date, day, time, place, and person that you are interviewing. After recording, listen to the whole tape as soon as possible to get an idea of what may be valuable to transcribe. We sometimes do this in our spare time, on our car tape players and on our headsets. You may want to outline the topics covered and take notes to highlight the major themes or to think about what questions you'll want to ask in the next interview. Don't let the tapes gather dust until you have time to transcribe them fully. This initial listening process enhances your memory of the interview and the overall sense of purpose for your project.

5. *Log all your tapes.* Set the counter feature on the tape recorder to identify relevant chunks of data. List the topics and note the corresponding numbers on a piece of paper—for example, "015–138: CV: talks about her late mother's flower shop and her history of gardening" or "249–282: good quote on nature and spirituality." Summarizing your material and noting where it appears on the tape will allow for easy retrieval later. The more time you spend logging and describing what's on the tapes, the less time you'll need for actual transcription. Over time, you will develop a unique system of your own.

6. *Transcribe your tapes.* As soon as possible after the interview, transcribe your audiotapes. Use the pause button on the recorder to freeze the tape and the rewind buttons and play to reverse and review any material you need to hear again. If you are fortunate enough to have a foot switch (often used by professional transcribers), this allows you to start and stop the tape with your foot so that you can continue keyboarding as you listen. Transcribe word for word, using parentheses or brackets to indicate pauses, laughing, interruptions, sections you want to leave out, or words that seem unintelligible: "[CV talks about having a cold]" or "[unintelligible: maybe "hunch," "bunch," or "lunch"; check with CV]".

7. *Use your computer.* Word processors have features that enhance transcribing. You can make a separate file for each informant or separate interviews according to themes. The computer allows you to format a pattern of organization as you transcribe (date, person, topic) which you can sort again later when you need it. Be sure to back up important disks once you have a lot of data transcribed.

8. *Bring language to paper.* As a transcriber, you must bring your informant's speech to life as accurately and as appropriately as you can. When you transcribe oral language, you will find it difficult to capture intonations, speech rhythms, and regional accents on the page. Most researchers agree that a person's grammar should remain as spoken. If an informant says "I done," for example, it's not appropriate to alter it to "I did." If, when you share a transcript later with your informant and she chooses to change it, respect that change. All speakers "code-shift" between what linguists call "speech registers," which depend on topic, audience, and background such as regional or ethnic identity. For example, Bonnie's grandmother code-shifted with Yiddish expressions among her Mah-Jongg partners, but she'd use mainstream accented Philadelphia English in a department store. Many characteristics of oral language have no equivalents in print. It is too difficult for either transcriber or

reader to attempt to capture or understand oral dialect in written form. "Pahk the cah in Hahvahd Yahd" is a respelling of a Boston accent, meant to show how it sounds. But to a reader who's never heard it—even to an insider, a Bostonian who isn't conscious of her accent—the written version of her oral dialect looks artificial and complicates the reading process. Anthropologists and folklorists have long debated how to record oral language and currently discourage the use of spelling as a way to approximate oral language.

9. *Share your transcript.* Offer the transcripts to your informant to read for accuracy, but realize that you won't get many takers. Most informants would rather not plow through a whole transcript but would rather wait for your finished, edited version of the interview. In any case, the informant needs the opportunity to read what you've written. In some cases, the informant may make corrections or ask for deletions. But in most cases, the written interview becomes a kind of gift in exchange for the time spent interviewing.

FieldWriting: Language on the Page

In the fieldwriting section in Chapter 2, we reviewed how to cite your published and unpublished written data sources accurately for your reader. But we recognize that in doing fieldwork, the researcher has a special responsibility to use informants' words as carefully as any written source material. Fieldwriters choose the most appropriate way to represent oral language on the written page when they record informants' voices—on tape, in fieldnotes, and in transcripts and texts.

As fieldwriters, we need to create texts that embrace our informants' diverse voices and also include our own. Their voices speak of human difference, and it is that difference we need to preserve. When we research verbal art—gather words, assemble terms and sayings, conduct interviews and record stories—our data is language, the language of our informants. Rather than overwriting or erasing our informants' language, we want their voices to tell the fieldwork story along with ours.

When we wrote this chapter, we faced this very dilemma. We wanted to include informants we knew in our personal lives: our friends Danling Fu, whom we interviewed; Donna Qualley, whose waitress gossip study we quote; and Becky Rule, whose short story we heard her perform. We wanted to include our students' research from their informants: glossaries, lists of proverbs and sayings, and urban legends. And we wanted these voices to join those of the published writers, which came from our quirky collection of books—folkore, fiction, and nonfiction related to oral language. We combined these different sources in our chapter, oral and written, to illustrate the chapter's theme: how language represents culture.

To show this connection between oral language and culture, we made choices about how best to represent language on the page. When you write about your fieldwork, you'll choose among options, too. The fieldworkers whose projects we feature bring their informants' words to life using transcripts, ethnopoetics, and dialogue. They are able to do this only because they documented original conversations in their fieldnotes or in transcripts. Fieldworkers *cannot make up informants' words*, any more than scholars can plagiarize someone else's texts. It is critical to represent people's words with accuracy, for their integrity and for our own.

TRANSCRIPTS

Because most fieldworkers tape-record their informants' talk, one straightforward way to include these voices with our own is to quote from these transcripts. After interviewing, recording and transcribing their informants' words, researchers usually find their own transcripts fascinating to read. But we caution against quoting from transcripts at any great length because of the burden it places on a different reader, who can become easily bored because a long transcript, by itself, doesn't bring language to life.

Here is an excerpt from our original raw transcript of the interview we conducted with Danling Fu about the cultural significance of the word *silk*:

```
telephone interview                                      4/25/96
Bonnie & Elizabeth with Danling Fu                       005-150
B&E:  Were you unusual, or do all Chinese children keep pet silkworms?
D:    Our relationship with worms is like yours with cats and dogs. I
      grew up in Jian-Su province, a silk-producing place, and all
      children kept silkworms. Every family does it. The full name we
      use is "baby silkworms." We care for them, keep them clean,
      learn to hold them tenderly, and watch the whole life cycle
      process.
B&E:  How do you care for them?
D:    In early spring, we put eggs—thousands of little eggs, laid by
      the silk moth the year before—on little squares of paper in a
      shoebox. We put them in the sun for warmth. Sometimes we start
      them in school, like American children grow seeds in paper cups
      or chicken eggs in incubators. Eventually, a worm hatches—so
      tiny, so black, smaller than an ant. As the leaves come out, we
      feed them to the little worms. Day by day, we watch them grow
      bigger, as thick as a little finger, in different shades of
      white and black.
B&E:  Do children compete over how many silkworms they have?
D:    Yes, but only because we all want a few to live so we can care
      for them. They eat a lot of leaves, and we don't have enough of
      them. In cities, families protect their trees because children
      steal each other's leaves. Sometimes, I would buy extra leaves
      from farmers to feed my worms. Each year, if I had 10% survival
      rate, I would consider it a victory.
```

We excerpted this section of our longer interview with Danling from the beginning of this chapter, where we introduced the idea of the fieldworker as a cultural translator. We presented the entire interview to show how one important word can unlock a range of cultural information. We often read transcribed interviews with celebrities in popular magazines, and sometimes we see them in scholarly books as well: sociology, education, political science, anthropology, linguistics. Transcribed interviews can be tedious to read, so the fieldwriter needs to choose carefully only the excerpts that illustrate a specific point, as we've shown in other chapters: Karen and Liesl's dinner-making exercise and Rick Zollo's interview with Delia Moon, for example.

We prefer to interpret our transcripts with italicized interviewer commentary (as we did at the start of the chapter) so that the reader understands why we've chosen to ask the questions we have. And since our purpose is to teach interviewing skills, our commentaries emphasize ways of asking questions, as in our sample with Danling Fu and the ones you'll read in Chapter 5 with Paul Russ and Cindie Marshall. Other writers also include italicized commentaries, sometimes to give contextual information about the interview or historical or background information, such as where the interview is taking place or what the informant is wearing and doing.

When we transcribe an interview, we never know for sure where to place dashes or commas for pauses, periods for endings, or exclamation points for emphasis, or how to use quotation marks when our informants quote others. Since we're serving as translators from oral to written language, we must invent or borrow notations to indicate pauses, interruptions, endings, or overlapping conversations. Although there are some standard formats you might consult in books about oral history, linguistics, folklore, ethnography, or journalism, there is no one accepted method for transcribing interviews.

ETHNOPOETICS

Another way to present a transcript and to analyze it for its themes, rhythms, and language patterns is what folklorists and sociolinguists call *ethnopoetic notation*. Folklorist Dennis Tedlock used it to study and record Navajo speech. It has most recently been adapted by sociolinguist Deborah Tannen, author of the bestseller *You Just Don't Understand*, to analyze conversations in everyday living and in the workplace. Ethnopoetic notation is a procedure in which a language researcher turns oral speech into poetic form. Transforming oral speech into poetry allows a closer look, not only at an informant's language, but also at the informant's perspective. As you take the words, lay them out on a page, and identify repetitions, pauses, and themes, you capture the rhythms of your informant's everyday speech. Here is an excerpt from Danling's transcript, transformed into poetry on the page:

> In early spring we put eggs, thousands of little eggs
>> laid by the silk moth
>> the year before
>> on little squares of paper
>> in a shoebox.

> We put them in the sun for warmth; sometimes we start them in school
>> like American children
>> grow seeds
>>> in paper cups
>> or chicken eggs
>>> in incubators.

> Eventually, a worm hatches
>> so tiny
>> so black
>> smaller than an ant.

As the leaves come out, we feed them to the little worms.
    Day by day,
    we watch them grow bigger
    as thick as a little finger
    in different shades
        of white
        and black.

This layout of Danling's oral language in poetic form is similar to the oral context in which our conversation took place. The poetic notation allows you to see where she pauses and clusters images together: "so tiny / so black / smaller than an ant." In this poem, her figures of speech also stand out ("as thick as a little finger") and her cultural comparison is clear ("like American children / grow seeds / in paper cups / or chicken eggs / in incubators"). Ethnopoetic notation preserves the integrity of the oral conversation more closely than a written transcript. Although a word-for-word transcribed interview may seem more authentic, in fact, by writing it down we remove language from its oral context entirely. The process of ethnopoetic notation allows the researcher to recapture and study informants' language and thoughts more closely.

One contemporary poet who shares the fieldworker's concern over how to present language on the page is David Antin. In his "talk poetry," Antin tries to capture the way that conversations allow us to participate with others in real time. For Antin, ethnopoetics is an attempt to find an innovative and more realistic way to represent speech as an ongoing event.

In this short excerpt, Antin experiments with ways of making his poems look like ordinary conversation. First, Antin tape-records himself (and sometimes others), then he transcribes his words, omitting all capitalization and punctuation. Antin leaves empty spaces on the page to show pauses—breathing patterns that are seldom represented in taped transcriptions. To get the gist of his work, you may want to read the following section from his long poem *Tuning*, aloud, as it is the orality of poetry that he's after.

ive called this talk
tuning

        and you probably have no very good idea of what im going to
talk about   and it gave me a certain freedom from expectation
      as it gave to you   for it is part of my generosity and
    self indulgence   simultaneously   that what i will take for
myself i will allow to others..   which seems only fair
                      now i gave
a title to this piece long before coming here   and   if the
    title i gave was not intended to offer you a very precise image
      of what i was going to do and if you see me fiddling with
    this tape recorder   its mainly because i have no very precise
image of what im going to say   though i have a considerable
     notion of the terrain   into which i tend to move and
    the only way im going to find out whether it was worth doing

or not   is when i hear what ive got..........which has been
my way of entrapping myself   and the reason ive chosen to
entrap myself rather than to prepare in advance   a precise set
    of utterances   has been that i felt myself   ive written
        things before this   in the natural vacuum that is the
        artificial hermetic closet that literature has been in for some
        time   and the problem..........for me..........is in the closet
        confronting a typewriter and no person   so that for me
    literature defined as literature   has no urgency   it has no
    need of address   there are too many things   no there are
    not too many things there are only a few things you may want
        to talk about but there are too many ways you could talk
    about them   there are too many ways to proceed..........too many
        possibilities for making well crafted objects..........

DIALOGUE

Another way to present our informants' language on the page is by borrowing dialogue techniques from fiction, as Rick Zollo did in Chapter 1 with Delia Moon. And
in this chapter, you've read Donna Qualley's waitress gossip at Norton's Seafood
restaurant, which she presents in the form of a fictional conversation. Here, in this
conversation between waitresses Rae and Erin, you'll see the standard conventions
for writing conversation in dialogue: indenting each time the speaker shifts, framing
each sentence with quotation marks, and using strong verbs to indicate response
(notice that instead of *says*, Donna uses verbs like *interjects, mumbles, begins*, and
laugh). Donna doesn't need to identify Erin or Rae each time they speak because the
indentations and punctuation do it for her. As the researcher, Donna identifies herself in the conversation only twice, by using *I* outside the quotation.

"I had this young couple."

"How old?" Erin interjects.

"In their twenties I would guess. They order two fish and chips
and two glasses of water."

"Cheap. I'm surprised they didn't ask to split one meal," Erin
mumbles.

"When they are done I put the check on the table and tell them I
will be right back to collect it for them. I go into the kitchen and when I
come back, there is a ten-dollar bill, a dime, a nickel, and a penny on the
table."

"How much is the bill?" I ask.

"Ten fifteen."

"That makes me so mad . . ." Erin begins.

"But," Rae smiles, "the woman had left her coat on the chair.
They were in such a hurry to get out she forgot her coat! I grab the coat,
check, and money, and then I see her coming back for her coat . . ."

"I hope you kept it until they left a better tip," I laugh.

"I said to this woman, "Oh, did you come back for your change?"

"You really said that? How much was the bill again?" Erin asks.

"Ten fifteen, and they left me ten sixteen. Well, this woman turns all red and apologetic and says, "We didn't have any money—we thought this was a take-out place." Yeah, right. They knew what they were doing."

The waitress story from Greta Paules's book *Dishing It Out* illustrates another way to present an informant's dialogue. In this quotation, a waitress tells a whole stiffing story about herself and her friend Kaddie, and the researcher records it. Note that within this quoted transcript, the waitress quotes her friend, Kaddie, who participated in the stiffing story.

> This party of two guys come in and they order thirty to forty dollars' worth of food . . . and they stiff us. Every time. So Kaddie told them, "If you don't tip us, we're not going to wait on you." They said, "We'll tip you." So Kaddie waited on them, and they tipped her. The next night they came in, I waited on them and they didn't tip me. The third time they came in [the manager] put them in my station and I told [the manager] straight up, "I'm not waiting on them . . ." So when they came in the next night . . . [they] said, "Are you going to give us a table?" I said, "You going to tip me? I'm not going to wait on you" (31).

Sometimes, for variety and conciseness, a fieldwriter chooses to summarize rather than use a direct quote when she writes dialogue. Karen Downing combines summary and direct quotation to describe her phone encounter with Ginny James at Photo Phantasies:

> When I finally talk with Ginny during this second phone call, she leaves out the conversational niceties. Yes, my letter had arrived in the mail after all. "I'll have to clear this request with headquarters, which I can do tomorrow. I'm leaving for a Photo Phantasies meeting in Chicago. What kind of class is this for? Business? Sociology? I'll call you Wednesday night and leave a message about whether or not it's OK."

Bringing oral language to the page presents a challenge to the fieldwriter. We've shown you several ways we've done it in this chapter, including transcripts, ethnopoetic notation, and dialogue—directly quoted and summarized. When you work with the spoken words of an informant, your goal is to preserve the integrity of the informant's original verbal art and respect it. As with any art form, how you choose to display your informants' language for the reader must be a conscious and carefully considered choice.

FieldWords

Ethnopoetic notation: A procedure for analysis of transcripts in which a language researcher turns oral speech into poetic or fictive form.

Kinesics: The study of how individuals express themselves through body position and motion (facial expression, eye contact, posture, and gesture).

Linguist: A person who studies language and language behaviors.

Performance: In performance theory, an interaction between a performer and an audience who understands many of the cultural values and behaviors surrounding the act (joke, story, saying, curse).

Proxemics: The study of how individuals communicate nonverbally when in groups.

Variant: An alteration from the traditional core of a folk art, according to a performer's or artisan's specific history, cultural understanding, and personal creativity.

Verbal art: Language behaviors within a culture or subculture, ranging from informal everyday events (grunts, shouts, taunts, jokes, gossip, stories) to more highly ritualized forms (proverbs and taboos, songs and chants, urban legends, curses and spells, myths and tales, traditional stories and ceremonies).

FieldReading

Aarne, Antti. *The Types of the Folk-tale: A classification and Bibliography.* New York: Franklin, 1971.

Antin, David. *Tuning.* New York: New Directions, 1984.

Berger, Peter L., and Thomas Luckman. *The Social Construction of Reality.* New York: Anchor-Doubleday, 1967.

Brunvand, Jan Harald. *The Vanishing Hitchhiker: American Urban Legends and Their Meanings.* New York: Norton, 1981.

Chiseri-Strater, Elizabeth. *Academic Literacies: The Public and Private Discourse of University Students.* Portsmouth: Boynton/Cook, 1991.

Gleason, Norma, ed. *Proverbs from around the World.* New York: Citadel, 1992.

Hurston, Zora Neale. *Mules and Men.* New York: Harper, 1990.

Ives, Edward. *The Tape-Recorded Interview: A Manual for Fieldworkers in Folklore and Oral History.* Knoxville: U Tennessee P, 1980.

Jackson, Bruce. *Fieldwork.* Chicago: Illinois, 1987.

Kochman, Thomas. *Black and White Styles in Conflict.* Chicago: U Chicago P, 1981.

Moffatt, Michael. "The Discourse of the Dorm: Race, Friendship, and Culture among College Youth." *Symbolizing America.* Ed. Herve Varenne. Lincoln: U Nebraska P, 1986.

Momaday, M. Scott. *House Made of Dawn.* New York: Harper, 1966.

Paules, Greta Foff. *Dishing It Out: Power and Resistance among Waitresses in a New Jersey Restaurant.* Philadelphia: Temple U P, 1991.

Spradley, James P. *The Ethnographic Interview.* Fort Worth: Holt, 1979.

Spradley, James P. and Brenda Mann. *The Cocktail Waitress: Women's Work in a Male World.* New York: Wiley, 1975.

Tannen, Deborah. *You Just Don't Understand: Women and Men in Conversation.* New York: Morrow-Ballantine, 1990.

Thompson, Stith. *Motif: Index of Folk Literature.* Bloomington: Indiana U, 1965.

Turner, Patricia. *I Heard It Through the Grapevine: Rumor in African-American Culture.* Berkeley: U California 1993.

Zipes, Jack. *Don't Bet on the Prince: Contemporary Feminist Fairy Tales in North America and England.* New York: Routledge, 1987.

See also:

General Reference Works: "Language Dictionaries" for slang, allusions, jargon, and symbols, "Thematic Indexes," and "Folklore Guides."

Social and Behavioral Sciences: Mythology, folklore and popular culture dictionaries, specialized encyclopedias and handbooks.

Researching People:
The Collaborative Listener

Ethnography is interaction, collaboration. What it demands is not hypotheses, which may unnaturally close study down, obscuring the integrity of the other, but the ability to converse intimately.

Henry Glassie

Researching people means "stepping in" to the worldviews of others. When we talk with people in the field, or study the stuff of their lives—their stories, artifacts, and surroundings—we enter their perspectives by partly "stepping out" of our own. Insider and outsider stances are symbiotic; they support each other. You already know how to talk and listen to others from meeting new people. You've learned that you don't begin a conversation with a new person by talking only about yourself or failing to allow time or space for the other person to participate and collaborate in the conversation.

In an informal way, you are always gathering data about people's backgrounds and perspectives—their worldviews. "So where are you from?" "How do you like it here?" "How come someone from Texas wants to go to school in Minnesota?" "Did you know anyone when you first came here?" Not only do you ask questions about people's backgrounds, but you also notice their artifacts and adornments—the things with which they represent themselves: T-shirts, jewelry, particular kinds of shoes or hairstyles. The speculations and questions we form about others cause us to make hypotheses about the people we meet. We may just ask questions, or we may just listen. But unless we listen closely, we'll never understand others from their perspectives. We need to know what's it like for *that* person in *this* place. Our colleague Mark Shadle writes:

> At its best, this practice is called "cosmology"—the way each of us orders the world around us. Paradoxically, the only way we can find order for ourselves is to negotiate with others doing the same thing. This means that we must learn to respect in both nature and culture . . . "sensitive chaos."

In the quotation that begins this chapter, folklorist Henry Glassie stresses the interactive nature of field research, suggesting that we shed hypotheses that close down study. You may have formulated a hunch about someone only to find out through new data that your hypothesis is off-base. For example, you may dismiss the middle-aged woman who sits in your political science class and reminds you of your mother. But when you're assigned to a study group with her, you discover that as an army nurse who has traveled all over the world, she knows more about international politics than anyone else in the group. Glassie warns us not to "close down study and mask our informants' integrity" because this can prevent us from learning from them. The army nurse, as familiar as she may appear, turns into a great informant about international politics. The only way to learn with her is to be a listener. To learn from others, we must converse collaboratively. Fieldworkers and informants construct meaning together.

This chapter will help you strengthen the everyday skills of listening, questioning, and researching people who interest you. You'll gather, analyze, write, and reflect on family stories. You'll experience interactive ways to conduct interviews and oral histories. You'll look for and discover meaning in your informants' everyday cultural artifacts. And you'll read some examples of how other fieldworkers have researched and written about people's lives.

Gathering Family Stories

We often think of stories as pure entertainment, but as you saw in Chapter 4, there are many forms of storytelling—gossip, chants, curses, urban legends, and fairy tales, for example. Stories, like material artifacts, serve to tell us about our informants' worldviews and function as data in our fieldwork. Informants have entire repertoires of stories based on their childhoods, their interests, their occupations. When a fieldworker meets an informant, part of the listening process involves gathering the informant's stories. Our job as researchers is to elicit our informants' stories, record them, and carefully analyze what they mean. Researchers who study verbal art think about stories in these ways:

- Stories preserve a culture's values and beliefs.
- Stories help individuals endure, transform, or reject cultural values for themselves.
- Stories exist because of the interrelationship between tellers and audiences.

Waitresses' stories and gossip illustrate that one place where cultures pass on their values and beliefs is the job site. Waitresses build a kind of kinship—with insider language and stories that teach ways of behaving on the job. But the most influential kinship structure is, of course, the family. And stories begin in our families.

Families are not cultures, but they bridge the gap between individuals and their cultures. Because families are small enough units of people, we can, through interaction and collaboration, achieve intimate understandings. To understand someone's culture, we often need to understand the person's family, too. Through the individual we come to understand the culture, and through the culture we come to understand the individual. Family stories help us do that, and collecting them from our informants is part of the process of researching people.

Throughout your childhood, you heard and shared stories, but you may never have thought about them as verbal artifacts, to be analyzed for their core themes and variants. Family stories are narratives about family members, both living and deceased. They're the stories we grow up on—like the time your cousin Mattie was jilted the night before her wedding, or your uncle Tyrone, who remarried his high school sweetheart at 85 after his triple bypass, or your aunt Thelma, who took to her bed after raising 12 children, or the time Uncle Fritz won the state lottery and spent it all in a month. Because we first hear them when we're young, these stories influence and shape us.

In many cultures, family storytelling sessions are a deliberate way of passing along values. They are often expected events, almost ritualized performances. Judith Ortiz Cofer, in a memoir of her Puerto Rican childhood, writes about how the younger females in her extended family were encouraged to eavesdrop on the adult storytelling ritual:

> At three or four o'clock in the afternoon, the hour of the *café con leche*, the women of my family gathered in Mama's living room to speak of important things and retell family stories meant to be overheard by us young girls, their daughters. . . . It was on these rockers that my mother, her sisters, and my grandmother sat these afternoons of my childhood to tell their stories, teaching each other, and my cousin and me, what it was like to be a woman, more specifically, a Puerto Rican woman. They talked about life on the island, and life in Los Nueva Yores, their way of referring to the United States from New York City to California: the other place, not home, all the same. They told real-life stories, though, as I later learned, always embellishing them with a little or a lot of dramatic detail. And they told *cuentos*, the morality and cautionary tales told by the women in our family for generations; stories that became part of my subconscious as I grew up in two worlds . . . (64–65).

These stories from Cofer's childhood were not merely afternoon entertainment. Her family's stories recorded history and carried instructions about behaviors, rules, and beliefs. Like the legends, folk tales, and proverbs of specific cultures, family stories reflect the ways of acting and even of viewing the world sanctioned or approved by a family. Cofer's relatives conserve cultural traditions of their old country, Puerto Rico, and translate them into the "Los Nueva Yores" culture.

In addition to preserving cultural values, many writers suggest that the act of storytelling is also an act of individual survival. To endure in our families and the culture at large, we must explain our lives to ourselves. First we share our stories, and then we reflect on what they mean. Our own storytelling memories teach us about our personal histories. Why did I remember that story? What is important about that incident my father told me? What other stories does this one remind me of? Is my version the same as my cousin's? When you think of a family story, try to decide why it survived, which tellers have different versions, what parts of the story remain the same no matter who tells it, and how you've refashioned it for your own purposes.

We'd like to recall one of our own family stories for you. This is a story of family endurance in which five members reshape their own versions for their own purposes, playing out their personal histories in particular ways. A hostile teenager was sent to his room for complaining about the lumpy mashed potatoes during the family supper. He stormed away from the table, throwing his sneaker backward over his shoulder as he walked up the stairs. It landed in the massive bowl of mashed potatoes, splattering his five siblings and his parents and turning his defiance into comedy. On the surface, this is just a funny family anecdote, not a serious "family story." But its themes show why it survived and what it might teach each member.

After this incident, everyone in the family learned that "you never know when you throw something without looking exactly where it will land" and that even a person who is sent away from the family table holds the power to ruin a meal. In his absence, he can be the most present. The father's version of the story focuses on the shattered bowl. The older brother refashions it as a story about how the younger brother always found a way to get attention. The younger sister remembers wiping hot mashed potatoes off the crying baby's face. And the mother tells the story about making potato pancakes the next morning from the leftovers.

Within the family, the core of this story always includes the humor of the event, the mashed potatoes, and the central character of the angry teenager tossing his shoe backward as he walks up the stairs. Each family member's variant emphasizes an individual's values: power, property, jealousy, protection, economy. For the tellers, the story illustrates their own endurance within this family, emphasizing the values they hold most important. For example, the sister who protects the baby tells the story to her children about how she saved Aunt Alisha from being permanently scarred (by mashed potatoes?). And the hostile teenager tells this story to his own son as a warning against angry defiance. No one in this family may recognize the themes in each version, but a fieldworker would look for them and then try to confirm them with other data about the family's values. She would look at the theme of each member's version to see how it reflects their culture as a whole. In our interview with Danling Fu in Chapter 4, we uncovered cultural themes about the life cycle and the value of productivity when she recalled a Chinese song and a proverb about silkworms. Danling herself was unconscious of the values embedded in her verbal art. But in the process of the interview, as she told us about caring for pets in a crowded country and the importance of working hard, we confirmed the same themes that were in the song and the proverb.

When the values of the family and their culture converge, family stories can convey strong lessons, even warnings, to family members. Families are not cultures. They are extended kinship units, sanctioned by a culture's legal system to acknowledge rights or limitations for groups of related people. Like schools and churches, family units help nourish and conserve features of the larger culture. Individual family members can escape kinship boundaries more easily than they can escape the constraints of the culture as a whole.

In the following reading, a chapter from *The Woman Warrior*, by Maxine Hong Kingston, a mother tells a family story to her daughter in order to instill in her the cultural values of monogamy and sexual fidelity, values that have followed their Chinese family to San Francisco. Listening to her mother's story does not help the daughter escape her culture's values. But forming the story into a version for herself helps her endure and transcend the values that her mother handed down. As you read this, we hope you'll think about stories from your own family that convey teachings, warnings, or cultural messages.

No Name Woman
Maxine Hong Kingston

"You must not tell anyone," my mother said, "what I am about to tell you. In China your father had a sister who killed herself. She jumped into the family well. We say that your father has all brothers because it is as if she had never been born.

"In 1924 just a few days after our village celebrated seventeen hurry-up weddings—to make sure that every young man who went 'out on the road' would responsibly come home—your father and his brothers and your grandfather and his brothers and your aunt's new husband sailed for America, the Gold Mountain. It was your grandfather's last trip. Those lucky enough to get contracts waved goodbye from the decks. They fed and guarded the stowaways and helped them off in Cuba, New York, Bali, Hawaii. 'We'll meet in California next year,' they said. All of them sent money home.

"I remember looking at your aunt one day when she and I were dressing; I had not noticed before that she had such a protruding melon of a stomach. But I did not think, 'She's pregnant,' until she began to look like other pregnant women, her shirt pulling and the white tops of her black pants showing. She could not have been pregnant, you see, because her husband had been gone for years. No one said anything. We did not discuss it. In early summer she was ready to have the child, long after the time when it could have been possible.

"The village had also been counting. On the night the baby was to be born the villagers raided our house. Some were crying. Like a great saw, teeth strung with lights, files of people walked zigzag across our land, tearing the rice. Their lanterns doubled in the disturbed black water, which drained away through the broken bunds. As the villagers closed in, we could see that some of them, probably men and women we knew well, wore white masks. The people with long hair hung it over their faces. Women with short hair made it stand up on end. Some had tied white bands around their foreheads, arms, and legs.

"At first they threw mud and rocks at the house. Then they threw eggs and began slaughtering our stock. We could hear the animals scream their deaths—the roosters, the pigs, a last great roar from the ox. Familiar wild heads flared in our night windows; the villagers encircled us. Some of the faces stopped to peer at us, their eyes rushing like searchlights. The hands flattened against the panes, framed heads, and left red prints.

"The villagers broke in the front and the back doors at the same time, even though we had not locked the doors against them. Their knives dripped with the blood of our animals. They smeared blood on the doors and walls. One woman swung a chicken, whose throat she had slit, splattering blood in red arcs about her. We stood together in the middle of our house, in the family hall with the pictures and tables of the ancestors around us, and looked straight ahead.

"At that time the house had only two wings. When the men came back, we would build two more to enclose our courtyard and a third one to begin a second courtyard. The villagers pushed through both wings, even your grandparents' rooms, to find your aunt's, which was also mine until the men returned. From this room a new wing for one of the younger families would grow. They ripped up her clothes and shoes and broke her combs, grinding them underfoot. They tore her work from the loom. They scattered the cooking fire and rolled the new weaving in it. We could hear them in the kitchen breaking our bowls and banging the pots. They overturned the great waist-high earthenware jugs; duck eggs, pickled fruits, vegetables burst out and mixed in acrid torrents. The old woman from the next field swept a broom through the air and loosed the spirits-of-the-broom over our heads. 'Pig.' 'Ghost.' 'Pig,' they sobbed and scolded while they ruined our house.

"When they left, they took sugar and oranges to bless themselves. They cut pieces from the dead animals. Some of them took bowls that were not broken and clothes that were not torn. Afterward we swept up the rice and sewed it back up into sacks. But the smells from the spilled preserves lasted. Your aunt gave birth in the pigsty that night. The next morning when I went for the water, I found her and the baby plugging up the family well.

"Don't let your father know that I told you. He denies her. Now that you have started to menstruate, what happened to her could happen to you. Don't humiliate us. You wouldn't like to be forgotten as if you had never been born. The villagers are watchful."

Whenever she had to warn us about life, my mother told stories that ran like this one, a story to grow up on. She tested our strength to establish realities. Those in the emigrant generations who could not reassert brute survival died young and far from home. Those of us in the first American generations have had to figure out how the invisible world the emigrants built around our childhoods fits in solid America.

The emigrants confused the gods by diverting their curses, misleading them with crooked streets and false names. They must try to confuse their offspring as well, who, I suppose, threaten them in similar ways—always trying to get things straight, always trying to name the unspeakable. The Chinese I know hide their names; sojourners take new names when their lives change and guard their real names with silence.

Chinese-Americans, when you try to understand what things in you are Chinese, how do you separate what is peculiar to childhood, to poverty, insanities, one family, your mother who marked your growing with stories, from what is Chinese? What is Chinese tradition and what is the movies?

If I want to learn what clothes my aunt wore, whether flashy or ordinary, I would have to begin, "Remember Father's drowned-in-the-well sister?" I cannot ask that. My mother has told me once and for all the useful parts. She will add nothing unless powered by Necessity, a riverbank that guides her life. She plants vegetable gardens rather than lawns; she carries the odd-shaped tomatoes home from the fields and eats food left for the gods.

Whenever we did frivolous things, we used up energy; we flew high kites. We children came up off the ground over the melting cones our parents brought home from work and the American movie on New Year's Day—*Oh, You Beautiful Doll* with Betty Grable one year, and *She Wore a Yellow Ribbon* with John Wayne another year. After the one carnival ride each, we paid in guilt; our tired father counted his change on the dark walk home.

Adultery is extravagance. Could people who hatch their own chicks and eat the embryos and the heads for delicacies and boil the feet in vinegar for party food, leaving only the gravel, eating even the gizzard lining—could such people engender a prodigal aunt? To be a woman, to have a daughter in starvation time was a waste enough. My aunt could not have been the lone romantic who gave up everything for sex. Women in the old China did not choose. Some man had commanded her to lie with him and be his secret evil. I wonder whether he masked himself when he joined the raid on her family.

Perhaps she had encountered him in the fields or on the mountain where the daughters-in-law collected fuel. Or perhaps he first noticed her in the marketplace. He was not a stranger because the village housed no strangers. She had to have dealings with him other than sex. Perhaps he worked an adjoining field, or he sold her the cloth for the dress she sewed and wore. His demand must have surprised, then terrified her. She obeyed him; she always did as she was told.

When the family found a young man in the next village to be her husband, she had stood tractably beside the best rooster, his proxy, and promised before they met that she would be his forever. She was lucky that he was her age and she would be the first wife, an advantage secure now. The night she first saw him, he had sex with her. Then he left for America. She had almost forgotten what he looked like. When she tried to envision him, she only saw the black and white face in the group photograph the men had had taken before leaving.

The other man was not, after all, much different from her husband. They both gave orders: she followed. "If you tell your family, I'll beat you. I'll kill you. Be here again next week." No one talked sex, ever. And she might have separated the rapes from the rest of living if only she did not have to buy her oil from him or gather wood in the same forest. I want her fear to have lasted just as long as rape lasted so that the fear could have been contained. No drawn-out fear. But women at sex hazarded birth and hence lifetimes. The fear did not stop but permeated everywhere. She told the man, "I think I'm pregnant." He organized the raid against her.

On nights when my mother and father talked about their life back home, sometimes they mentioned an "outcast table" whose business they still seemed to be settling, their voices tight. In a commensal tradition, where food is precious, the powerful older people made wrong-doers eat alone. Instead of letting them start separate new lives like the Japanese, who could become samurais and geishas, the Chinese family, faces averted but eyes glowering sideways, hung on to the offenders and fed them leftovers. My aunt must have lived in the same house as my parents and eaten at an outcast table. My mother spoke about the raid as if she had seen it, when she and my aunt, a daughter-in-law to a different household, should not have been living together at all. Daughters-in-law lived with their husbands' parents, not their own; a synonym for marriage in Chinese is "taking a daughter-in-law." Her husband's parents could have sold her, mortgaged her, stoned her. But they had sent her back to her own mother and father, a mysterious act hinting at disgraces not told me. Perhaps they had thrown her out to deflect the avengers.

She was the only daughter; her four brothers went with her father, husband, and uncles "out on the road" and for some years became western men. When the goods were divided among the family, three of the brothers took land, and the youngest, my father, chose an education. After my grandparents gave their daughter away to her husband's family, they had dispensed all the adventure and all the property. They expected her alone to keep the traditional ways, which her brothers, now among the barbarians, could fumble without detection. The heavy, deep-rooted women were to maintain the past against the flood, safe for returning. But the rare urge west had fixed upon our family, and so my aunt crossed boundaries not delineated in space.

The work of preservation demands that the feelings playing about in one's guts not be turned into action. Just watch their passing like cherry blossoms. But perhaps my aunt, my forerunner, caught in a slow life, let dreams grow and fade and after some months or years went toward what persisted. Fear at the enormities of the forbidden kept her desires delicate, wire and bone. She looked at a man because she liked the way the hair was tucked behind his ears, or she liked the question-mark line of a long torso curving at the shoulder and straight at the hip. For warm eyes or a soft voice or a slow walk—that's all—a few hairs, a line, a brightness, a sound, a pace, she gave up family. She offered us up for a charm that vanished with tiredness, a pigtail that didn't toss when the wind died. Why, the wrong lighting could erase the dearest thing about him.

It could very well have been, however, that my aunt did not take subtle enjoyment of her friend, but, a wild woman, kept rollicking company. Imagining her free with sex doesn't fit, though. I don't know any women like that, or men either. Unless I see her life branching into mine, she gives me no ancestral help.

To sustain her being in love, she often worked at herself in the mirror, guessing at the colors and shapes that would interest him, changing them frequently in order to hit on the right combination. She wanted him to look back.

On a farm near the sea, a woman who tended her appearance reaped a reputation for eccentricity. All the married women blunt-cut their hair in flaps about their ears or pulled it back in tight buns. No nonsense. Neither style blew easily into heart-catching tangles. And at their weddings they displayed themselves in their long hair for the last time. "It brushed the backs of my knees," my mother tells me. "It was braided, and even so, it brushed the backs of my knees."

At the mirror my aunt combed individuality into her bob. A bun could have been contrived to escape into black streamers blowing in the wind or in quiet wisps about her face, but only the older women in our picture album wear buns. She brushed her hair back from her forehead, tucking the flaps behind her ears. She looped a piece of thread, knotted into a circle between her index fingers and thumbs, and ran the double strand across her forehead. When she closed her fingers as if she were making a pair of shadow geese bite, the string twisted together catching the little hairs. Then she pulled the thread away from her skin, ripping the hairs out neatly, her eyes watering from the needles of pain. Opening her fingers, she cleaned the thread, then rolled it along her hairline and the tops of her eyebrows. My mother did the same to me and my sisters and herself. I used to believe that the expression "caught by the short hairs" meant a captive held with a depilatory string. It especially hurt at the temples, but my mother said we were lucky we didn't have to have our feet bound when we were seven. Sisters used to sit on their beds and cry together, she said, as their mothers or their slave removed the bandages for a few minutes each night and let the blood gush back into their veins. I hope that the man my aunt loved appreciated a smooth brow, that he wasn't just a tits-and-ass man.

Once my aunt found a freckle on her chin, at a spot that the almanac said predestined her for unhappiness. She dug it out with a hot needle and washed the wound with peroxide.

More attention to her looks than these pullings of hairs and pickings at spots would have caused gossip among the villagers. They owned work clothes and good clothes, and they wore good clothes for feasting the new seasons. But since a woman combing her hair hexes beginnings, my aunt rarely found an occasion to look her best. Women looked like great sea snails—the corded wood, babies, and laundry they carried were the whorls on their backs. The Chinese did not admire a bent back; goddesses and warriors stood straight. Still there must have been a marvelous freeing of beauty when a worker laid down her burden and stretched and arched.

Such commonplace loveliness, however, was not enough for my aunt. She dreamed of a lover for the fifteen days of New Year's, the time for families to exchange visits, money, and food. She plied her secret comb. And sure enough she cursed the year, the family, the village, and herself.

Even as her hair lured her imminent lover, many other men looked at her. Uncles, cousins, nephews, brothers would have looked, too, had they been home between journeys. Perhaps they had already been restraining their curiosity, and they left, fearful that their glances, like a field of nesting birds, might be startled and caught. Poverty hurt, and that was their first reason for leaving. But another, final reason for leaving the crowded house was the never-said.

She may have been unusually beloved, the precious only daughter, spoiled and mirror gazing because of the affection the family lavished on her. When her husband left, they welcomed the chance to take her back from the in-laws; she could live like the little daughter for just a while longer. There are stories that my grandfather was different from other people, "crazy ever since the little Jap bayoneted him in the head." He used to put his naked penis on the dinner table, laughing. And one day he brought home a baby girl, wrapped up inside his brown western-style greatcoat. He had traded one of his sons, probably my father, the youngest, for her. My grandmother made him trade back. When he finally got a daughter of his own, he doted on her. They must have all loved her, except perhaps my father, the only brother who never went back to China, having once been traded for a girl.

Brothers and sisters, newly men and women, had to efface their sexual color and present plain miens. Disturbing hair and eyes, a smile like no other, threatened the ideal of five generations living under one roof. To focus blurs, people shouted face to face and yelled from room to room. The immigrants I know have loud voices, unmodulated to American tones even after years away from the village where they called their friendships out across the fields. I have not been able to stop my mother's screams in public libraries or over telephones. Walking erect (knees straight, toes pointed forward, not pigeon-toed, which is Chinese-feminine) and speaking in an inaudible voice, I have tried to turn myself American-feminine. Chinese communication was loud, public. Only sick people had to whisper. But at the dinner table, where the family members came nearest one another, no one could talk, not the outcasts nor any eaters. Every word that falls from the mouth is a coin lost. Silently they gave and accepted food with both hands. A preoccupied child who took his bowl with one hand got a sideways glare. A complete moment of total attention is due everyone alike. Children and lovers have no singularity here, but my aunt used a secret voice, a separate attentiveness.

She kept the man's name to herself throughout her labor and dying; she did not accuse him that he be punished with her. To save her inseminator's name she gave silent birth.

He may have been somebody in her own household, but intercourse with a man outside the family would have been no less abhorrent. All the village were kinsmen, and the titles shouted in loud country voices never let kinship be forgotten. Any man within visiting distance would have been neutralized as a lover—"brother," "younger brother," "older brother"—one hundred and fifteen relationship titles. Parents researched birth charts probably not so much to assure good fortune as to circumvent incest in a population that has but one hundred surnames. Everybody has eight million relatives. How useless then sexual mannerisms, how dangerous.

As if it came from an atavism deeper than fear, I used to add "brother" silently to boys' names. It hexed the boys, who would or would not ask me to dance and made them less scary and as familiar and deserving of benevolence as girls.

But, of course, I hexed myself also—no dates. I should have stood up, both arms waving, and shouted out across libraries, "Hey, you! Love me back." I had no idea, though, how to make attraction selective, how to control its direction and magnitude. If I made myself American-pretty so that the five or six Chinese boys in the class fell in love with me, everyone else—the Caucasian, Negro, and Japanese boys—would too. Sisterliness, dignified and honorable, made much more sense.

Attraction eludes control so stubbornly that whole societies designed to organize relationships among people cannot keep order, not even when they bind people to one another from childhood and raise them together. Among the very poor and the wealthy, brothers married their adopted sisters, like doves. Our family allowed some romance, paying adult brides' prices and providing dowries so that their sons and daughters could marry strangers. Marriage promises to turn strangers into friendly relatives—a nation of siblings.

In the village structure, spirits shimmered among the live creatures, balanced and held in equilibrium by time and land. But one human being flaring up into violence could open up a black hole, a maelstrom that pulled in the sky. The frightened villagers, who depended on one another to maintain the real, went to my aunt to show her a personal, physical representation of the break she had made in the "roundness." Misallying couples snapped off the future, which was to be embodied in true offspring. The villagers punished her for acting as if she could have a private life, secret and apart from them.

If my aunt had betrayed the family at a time of large grain yields and peace, when many boys were born, and wings were being built on many houses, perhaps she might have escaped such severe punishment. But the men—hungry, greedy, tired of planting in dry soil—had been forced to leave the village in order to send food-money home. There were ghost plagues, bandit plagues, wars with the Japanese, floods. My Chinese brother and sister had died of an unknown sickness. Adultery, perhaps only a mistake during good times, became a crime when the village needed food.

The round moon cakes and round doorways, the round tables of graduated size that fit one roundness inside another, round windows and rice bowls—these talismans had lost their power to warn this family of the law: a family must be whole, faithfully keeping the descent line by having sons to feed the old and the dead, who in turn look after the family. The villagers came to show my aunt and her lover-in-hiding a broken house. The villagers were speeding up the circling of events because she was too shortsighted to see that her infidelity had already harmed the village, that waves of consequences would return unpredictably, sometimes in disguise, as now, to hurt her. This roundness had to be made coin-sized so that she would see its circumference: punish her at the birth of her baby. Awaken her to the inexorable. People who refused fatalism because they could invent small resources insisted on culpability. Deny accidents and wrest fault from the stars.

After the villagers left, their lanterns now scattering in various directions toward home, the family broke their silence and cursed her. "Aiaa, we're going to die. Death is coming. Death is coming. Look what you've done. You've killed us. Ghost! Dead ghost! Ghost! You've never been born." She ran out into the fields, far enough from the house so that she could no longer hear their voices, and pressed herself against the earth, her own land no more. When she felt the birth coming, she thought that she had been hurt. Her body seized together. "They've hurt me too much," she thought. "This is gall, and it will kill me." With forehead and knees against the earth, her body convulsed and then relaxed. She turned on her back, lay on the ground. The black well of sky and stars went out and out and out forever; her body and her complexity seemed to disappear. She was one of the stars, a bright dot in blackness, without home, without a companion, in eternal cold and silence. An agoraphobia rose in her, speeding higher and higher, bigger and bigger; she would not be able to contain it; there would be no end to fear.

Flayed, unprotected against space, she felt pain return, focusing her body. This pain chilled her—a cold, steady kind of surface pain. Inside, spasmodically, the other pain, the pain of the child, heated her. For hours she lay on the ground, alternately body and space. Sometimes a vision of normal comfort obliterated reality: she saw the family in the evening gambling at the dinner table, the young people massaging their elders' backs.

She saw them congratulating one another, high joy on the mornings the rice shoots came up. When these pictures burst, the stars drew yet further apart. Black space opened.

She got to her feet to fight better and remembered that old-fashioned women gave birth in their pigsties to fool the jealous, pain-dealing gods, who do not snatch piglets. Before the next spasms could stop her, she ran to the pigsty, each step a rushing out into emptiness. She climbed over the fence and knelt in the dirt. It was good to have a fence enclosing her, a tribal person alone.

Laboring, this woman who had carried her child as a foreign growth that sickened her every day, expelled it at last. She reached down to touch the hot, wet, moving mass, surely smaller than anything human, and could feel that it was human after all—fingers, toes, nails, nose. She pulled it up on to her belly, and it lay curled there, butt in the air, feet precisely tucked one under the other. She opened her loose shirt and buttoned the child inside. After resting, it squirmed and thrashed and she pushed it up to her breast. It turned its head this way and that until it found her nipple. There, it made little snuffling noises. She clenched her teeth at its preciousness, lovely as a young calf, a piglet, a little dog.

She may have gone to the pigsty as a last act of responsibility: she would protect this child as she had protected its father. It would look after her soul, leaving supplies on her grave. But how would this tiny child without family find her grave when there would be no marker for her anywhere, neither in the earth nor the family hall? No one would give her a family hall name. She had taken the child with her into the wastes. At its birth the two of them had felt the same raw pain of separation, a wound that only the family pressing tight could close. A child with no descent line would not soften her life but only trail after her, ghost-like, begging her to give it purpose. At dawn the villagers on their way to the fields would stand around the fence and look.

Full of milk, the little ghost slept. When it awoke, she hardened her breasts against the milk that crying loosens. Toward morning she picked up the baby and walked to the well.

Carrying the baby to the well shows loving. Otherwise abandon it. Turn its face into the mud. Mothers who love their children take them along. It was probably a girl; there is some hope of forgiveness for boys.

"Don't tell anyone you had an aunt. Your father does not want to hear her name. She has never been born." I have believed that sex was unspeakable and words so strong and fathers so frail that "aunt" would do my father mysterious harm. I have thought that my family, having settled among immigrants who had also been their neighbors in the ancestral land, needed to clean their name, and a wrong word would incite the kinspeople even here. But there is more to this silence: they want me to participate in her punishment. And I have.

In the twenty years since I heard this story I have not asked for details nor said my aunt's name; I do not know it. People who can comfort the dead can also chase after them to hurt them further—a reverse ancestor worship. The real punishment was not the raid swiftly inflicted by the villagers, but the family's deliberately forgetting her. Her betrayal so maddened them, they saw to it that she would suffer forever, even after death. Always hungry, always needing, she would have to beg food from other ghosts, snatch and steal it from those whose living descendants give them gifts. She would have to fight the ghosts massed at crossroads for the buns a few thoughtful citizens leave to decoy her away from village and home so that the ancestral spirits could feast unharassed. At peace, they could act like gods, not ghosts, their descent lines providing them with paper suits and dresses, spirit money, paper houses, paper automobiles, chicken, meat, and rice into eternity— essences delivered up in smoke and flames, steam and incense rising from each rice bowl. In an attempt to make the Chinese care for people outside the family, Chairman Mao encourages us now to give our paper replicas to the spirits of outstanding soldiers and workers, no matter whose ancestors they may be. My aunt remains forever hungry. Goods are not distributed evenly among the dead.

My aunt haunts me—her ghost drawn to me because now, after fifty years of neglect, I alone devote pages of paper to her, though not origamied into houses and clothes. I do not think she always means me well. I am telling on her, and she was a spite suicide, drowning herself in the drinking water. The Chinese are always very frightened of the drowned one, whose weeping ghost, wet hair hanging and skin bloated, waits silently by the water to pull down a substitute.

Kingston's family tale about the Chinese community's violence and revenge gives the daughter a lesson "to grow up on," warning her against ruining the family name. The story teaches indirect messages such as "adultery is an extravagance" and "women are keepers of secret knowledge." You may have noticed other cultural messages in this story. You may reread it, looking just for those indirect messages carried from one generation to the next. In "No Name Woman," we can see that there is a stable core of details in the story of the aunt. But the Chinese-American daughter, listener and recipient, transforms and reinvents the story while her mother tells it, creating a variant. In her refashioning, she uses embellishments that were not part of the core.

Elizabeth's family tells a story about her mother's first love, David Perry, who is reputed to be the reason her mother came to marry her father. Alice, Elizabeth's mother, was engaged to David Perry, a respected high school English teacher. One day, when David left town on an errand, Alice went "motoring" with three friends, two of whom were males. They had an accident in the Model T, and Alice broke her arm. Hearing about the accident, David rushed to the hospital and ripped the engagement ring from the finger of Alice's broken arm, sure that she had been unfaithful to him. When he later discovered that this wasn't true, that Alice had just been on a friendly drive, he tried to reconcile, but to no avail. Three months later, on the rebound, Alice married Elizabeth's father. They remained married for over 50 years.

So what does this family story reveal? Because Alice broke the same arm twice again later in her life, perhaps the story—and the broken arms—recalled an early love for David Perry. In Alice's version to her daughters, this story conveyed the importance of ignoring gossip and rumors, retaining belief and faith in the one you love in spite of mitigating circumstances. Clearly, Alice was a steadfast woman, married for over half a century. As this story has been retold over the years by Alice's sisters, the fate of David Perry has changed in different versions. In Aunt June's version, he remained a bachelor all his life. And in Aunt Louise's, David had a teenage daughter named Allison who was never allowed to drive in boys' cars. Elizabeth tells this story to her two daughters with a lesson that echoes her contemporary feminist leanings. In her version, David Perry was her mother's only true love, and upon his loss, Alice could see no other choice but to marry someone else. This is the reason, she instructs her daughters, that every girl should have a profession and not rely on marriage.

Family stories are often transformed in oral retellings, but they clearly change when they are written down. In "No Name Woman," the aunt's ghost so haunts the narrator that she is driven to write, in part to make sense of what she has been told: "I alone devote pages to her." Although family stories belong to the oral narrative tradition, writing them down helps us analyze their meaning and potential relevance to our own lives. Think about a family story—not necessarily such a gloomy one. Stories about lost and found loves, courtship, and marriage are often shared as family tales.

BOX 17
WRITING A FAMILY STORY

Recall a family story you've heard many times. It may fall into one of these other categories: fortunes gained and lost, heroes, "black sheep," eccentric or oddball relatives, acts of retribution and revenge, or family feuds. After writing the story, analyze its meaning. When is this story most often told, and why? What kinds of warnings or messages does this story convey? For the family? For an outsider? What kind of lesson does the story teach? How does your story reflect your family's values? How has it changed or altered through various retellings? Which family members would have different versions?

Response

Cheri Krcelic wrote this family story about her parents' courtship.

The Blind Date
I've heard the story of how my parents met all through my life, but I never paid it much mind until now. My mom has used this story time and time again to teach me lessons about forming first impressions. I used to think it was just comical, but now I realize how it has affected my life.

My mother was only 18 years old when she met my father. She was a southern girl, born and raised in a small town in Mississippi. She was brought up by her parents on a farm. She often told stories of how her mother would cut off the heads of chickens in their kitchen and how it terrified her to watch the headless chickens run around the kitchen in a frenzy.

My father was from a small factory town in Pennsylvania. His parents divorced when he was young, and he was living with his mother and two younger brothers. When my father was in the tenth grade, he dropped out of school and got various jobs as a mechanic to support his family. My father eventually got his GED and then entered the navy and was by the age of 21 stationed at a naval base in Mississippi where my mother lived.

My mother had just graduated from high school and was working full time and still living at home with her parents. Her mother was a hypochondriac, and her father suffered from heart trouble. My mother had not begun to make any real plans for her future.

My mother was set up to go out on a blind date by a friend of hers. The guy she was to have gone out with bailed out at the last minute, and my dad was begged, and finally convinced, to be the last-minute replacement. My mom says that it was love at first sight the moment she laid eyes on him. Little did she know the adventure she was in for that night.

My mom and dad headed for the drive-in movies, accompanied by the couple who had brought them together. Once they reached their destination, the two guys brought out a case of beer. My mom was wearing a long blonde wig that night. She said that every time my dad tried to put his arm around her, the wig would go lopsided. She finally realized that my dad knew she didn't really have blonde hair, so she took it off and stuck it in the rear window of the car. This would help her later.

During the course of the evening, my mom and her best friend ventured from the car to the restrooms. On their way back, they couldn't remember where the car was parked. They began to walk up and down the rows of cars, looking for their dates. Finally, when my dad lit a cigarette, the blonde wig shined through the rear window, and my mom and her friend found their way back.

By the time the movie was over, my mom took it upon herself to drive them all home in order to meet her curfew. On the way out of the drive-in, my mom accidentally wrecked the car. The three others immediately sobered up, and my mom figured this was a good time to inform my dad that she didn't have a driver's license. After finding this out, my dad switched seats and took the blame for the accident.

One month after this disastrous blind date, my dad proposed to my mom. Three months later, they got married. They have been together ever since.

My mother used this story to teach me to be less judgmental and also to give me hope. If I ever came home upset because a date didn't go well, she'd tell me this story to remind me that sometimes the best things come out of bad events. She also wanted to convey that sometimes people alter their appearances in order to make a better impression, just as she had done when she wore the blonde wig and pretended that she could drive. This story has helped me give others a second chance instead of judging them by first impressions.

This story has shaped my own romantic life. I always thought that my mother exaggerated the part of the story about "love at first sight" and didn't think it was possible. When I met my fiancé, I knew the moment I saw him that no matter what, he was the one.

Family stories like Cheri Krcelic's preserve family beliefs through morality lessons with subliminal messages and subconscious instructions. Some family stories, like Kingston's, act as cautionary tales, or what Cofer calls *cuentos*, to pass on warnings about behavior to the next generation. Through storytelling, family tales can be transformed and reshaped to make them fit the teller's needs and life circumstances as the little girl does in Kingston's story, and as each family member does in the story about the mashed potatoes. As Elizabeth Stone suggests in her book *Black Sheep and Kissing Cousins*, family stories also allow individuals to break away from the family's values and form their own. Stone writes, "Still, to make one's family stories one's own in the truest sense is to achieve the greatest autonomy—the autonomy of one's point of view—while keeping hold of the best of one's connection to family" (224).

As they transform family stories, tellers can remain loyal to the family unit but released from it as well. Cheri, for instance, learns about first impressions and quick judgments from her parents' blind date story. In future versions, however, to her own children perhaps, Cheri might reshape the details. She could include the movie title, she might omit the part about the case of beer and the drinking, or she may change the amount of time between the blind date and the marriage. But Cheri also uses her family story to support her own love-at-first-sight narrative. She admits that although she had heard her mother's story, she didn't entirely believe in love at first sight until she met her own fiancé. So such stories can connect us with our families while allowing us our identities as we reshape them to fit our own lives and our own audiences.

When we hear a family story, as Cheri did, and retell it in our own words, it becomes our own story as much as the teller's. The embellishments Cheri would make with each retelling depend on her audience. Sharing it with her friends, her fiancé, her professor, or her own future children will demand different versions. However, if Cheri decides to write this story as told by either of her parents, she will need to record their versions—using their words rather than her own. When the hostile adolescent who threw his shoe into the mashed potatoes tells this story 20 years later to his son, he downplays the family humor and emphasizes the consequences of a teenager's defiance. Elizabeth found herself deliberately reshaping the David Perry story for her daughters to share with them her own contemporary beliefs about marriage.

One Family Story: The Core and Its Variants

Donna Niday decided to study one of her family's stories, "The Baby on the Roof." She expected to get different perspectives from the five Riggs sisters—her own mother and her four aunts who grew up on a farm in the rural Midwest of the 1920s. She wanted to record her family's history through the stories she had heard over the years. She began by interviewing her cousins to see what they remembered about the story, which would have been passed down to them by their mothers. Just as she suspected, each of Donna's cousins told the story with different details and points of emphasis. She confirmed the aunts' family reputations: "she was the daring one" or "she was always the chicken." Interviewing her cousins made it clear to Donna that she wanted to tape-record each aunt telling the tale of the baby on the roof.

Donna was realistic enough to know that there would be no "true" version of the tale, but the story would have a stable core, a basic frame, shared among the sisters. She also anticipated that there would be many variants, differences in details according to the tellers. She interviewed each elderly sister in her home, allowing time to look through family photo albums together and to visit before tape-recording their stories. As she listened and recorded, Donna gathered both the core story and its variants.

The oldest sister, Eleanor, who claimed responsibility for the secret family event, told the core story this way, emphasizing herself and the baby:

> I took Mary to the top of the house when Mom went out to work. You know, all four of us took the ladder—went down to the barn and got the big ladder. Mom just said to take care of Mary, and I did. I

took her everywhere I went. Mary was six months old. Well, she was born in January. This would be June, I suppose, when we were doing hay. I knew she'd lay wherever you put her. And so there was a flat place there on the roof. There wasn't any danger—I don't think there was ever any danger of her getting away at all. Yeah, we could see them mowing. If Mom had ever looked toward the house, she would have had a heart attack to see her kids up on the roof. Especially when we were supposed to be looking after the baby. Yeah, well see, I was ten when Mary was born, so I was ten then, a little past ten. I should have known better, but it shows that you can't trust ten-year-olds. I never got punished for that because Mom never did find out.

And so, with Eleanor's version, Donna had the core family story: four sisters spent the day on the roof with their 6-month-old baby sister while their mother and father mowed the fields. Each sister provided her own variation. One remembers that the parents were mowing hay; another insists they were cutting oats. Such details would also change the time of the story from June to late summer or early fall. The sisters debate other details. Donna's mother rejects the idea that they got a ladder from the barn, saying they climbed on a chair or rain barrel to reach the lower part of the farmhouse roof, which was accessible from their bedrooms. Another of the sisters tells the story as if she remained on the ground while the others climbed to the roof. When they challenge her version, this sister admits that she probably did follow the others. She confesses jealousy of the new baby—until then, she had been the baby of the family. "They weren't worried about me," she recalls. "They were only worried about Mary, the baby."

Baby Mary's version of the story deviates the most. She claims that she fell off the roof and that her sisters climbed down and put her "right back on." Because Mary's variant has no support from the other sisters, she retreats by saying, "Maybe I just dreamed that, but it seems like I fell off when I was up there—of course, I wasn't really old enough to remember."

After taping and transcribing all five versions of this story, Donna proposes that the "baby on the roof" story displays defiance of authority and rebellion against rules for these otherwise compliant farm girls. She also thinks that the story illustrates "pluck and adventure," as no harm was actually done. Donna admits that her mother and aunts would deny that these stories convey any meaning other than "pure entertainment" and confesses that any analysis of the meaning of these stories is her own. She recognizes that each sister embellished the story based on her family reputation, individual temperament, and storytelling ability. Donna's conclusions are consistent with what we know: that a story has a stable core of details but also many variants according to the tellers. Because Donna's stories were tape-recorded, she served as a kind of audience for the storytelling that took place between the aunts and their niece, and between Donna and her mother. Had these sisters told their story to another family member, like a grandchild, that audience would have affected the variants of the core story.

Donna repaid her aunts for their time with a copy of her research essay, "Secrets among Sisters: Stories of the Five Riggs Sisters," and she created a family album complete with photos of the old farmhouse from many angles, with several different views of the roof. Donna used her family photos as cultural artifacts. In a different project, she might also have used written artifacts such as family journals and diaries and letters among the sisters. Such material from a family's archives adds depth to a research project.

Donna followed several important steps in gathering her family stories, steps that any fieldworker considers:

- She conducted preliminary research by interviewing the people involved—in this case, her cousins. Had her cousins all told the same story, the project would not have illustrated the core and variants inherent in family stories.

- She interviewed her informants in their own home settings, making all participants comfortable as she taped and asked questions. To accomplish this, she traveled to four states and made some very long phone calls. She didn't rush her project; she allowed time for scheduling, visiting, interviewing, transcribing, sharing the transcripts, and writing her paper.

- She "triangulated" her data in two ways. First, by checking the five stories against one another, she could see how one story might verify another or disconfirm it. She shared her work with the sisters as she went along and afterward so that they might confirm, disconfirm, or add to each other's stories. The number of stories she gathered helped her build substantial evidence, which contributed to her analysis of the interview data. She analyzed her data by making a chart that detailed the core elements of the story and the variations in each one.

The "Baby on the Roof" farmhouse. (Photo: Donna Niday)

• She reciprocated to her informants. In this case, as they were her relatives, she presented her essay and the album as a gift in return for the time and energy they spent helping her learn how to listen to family stories. This kind of payback is crucial to the ethics of fieldworking.

BOX 18
STORIES AND VARIANTS

Try to collect one story and its variants. Donna's family story project took a long time to complete, but for this exercise, we suggest that you find a way to gather several variants of the same story in a shorter amount of time. If you are working in a field site, you might want to listen for an important story that has come out of a shared event, an important moment, or a special person whom everyone knows. For example, in a business, there are often stories about the boss and the boss's son or daughter that you might gather from several workers as well as the boss and his children. Retirement and holiday parties, Friday afternoon celebrations, and break time rituals are all events that yield stories. In families, dinners and holiday meals, vacations, and events like birthdays, weddings, and funerals often prompt storytelling. Malls, cafeterias, game rooms, dorm lounges, and sporting events invite storytelling as well.

You may want to record one storyteller relating the same story to three or four different audiences—a grandparent, for example, telling a family story to grandchildren, adult children, neighbors, and spouse, or a teacher's signature story as told to different students at different times. In these, you will find that the variants change according to the teller's perception of the audience's needs on particular occasions.

Another way to gather stories and variants is to focus on a moment in time, like John F. Kennedy's assassination in November 1963, the moon landing in August 1969, the *Challenger* disaster in January 1986, or the bombing of a federal building in Oklahoma in April 1995. As we wrote this paragraph, in fact, we found ourselves sharing our own stories about where we were during these moments. Elizabeth met her first husband, Michael Chiseri, at a bar in New York City, each waiting for a date that didn't arrive due to delays from Washington, DC, because of the Kennedy assassination. Bonnie was a high school senior, sitting in a writing class, who was assigned to write about her feelings at that moment. When Neil Armstrong landed on the moon, Bonnie watched it through an appliance shop window on a street in Greece, surrounded by emotional Athenians celebrating the United States' technological triumph. Elizabeth was living on her father's farm for the summer, thinking about going back to the land while watching this major advance forward.

Choose one way to collect several variants of one story. It is important to record the teller's version on tape or by careful word-for-word note taking. In each of these examples, whether you record several versions of one story or several stories about one event, you will need to look for the unchanging core elements as well as the variant details. After gathering stories on tape or on paper, analyze your data. Here are some things to look for. First, include the core details of the story: What facts are stable? What's the chronology of the story? What characters are key? What is the central conflict in the story? What is the theme? Does it contain a cultural message or lesson? Then ask, what are some of the variants as each teller offers her own version? List the features that change; then look at the list to speculate about why they change. What do the variants suggest about the tellers? You may find that some features do not fit the other versions, and those will provide clues about the tellers' positions and attitudes toward the story and toward the cultural themes that the story contains.

The Interview: Learning to Ask

With time and experience, each of us assembles a kind of personal archive, a collection of stories from our family, our workplace, and the people we've encountered. People's story repertoires are verbal artifacts; they become data for the fieldworker. As a fieldworker, you'll dig into these archives, uncover your informants' stories, and look for what they tell you about your informants' perspectives. Fieldworkers listen and record stories from the point of view of the informant—not their own. Letting people speak for themselves by telling about their lives seems an easy enough principle to follow. But in fact, there are some important strategies for both asking questions and listening to responses. Those strategies are part of interviewing—learning to ask and learning to listen.

Interviewing involves an ironic contradiction: You must be both structured and flexible at the same time. While it's critical to prepare for an interview with a list of planned questions to guide your talk, it is equally important to follow your informant's lead. Sometimes the best interviews come from a comment, a story, an artifact, or a phrase you couldn't have anticipated. The energy that drives a good interview—for both you and your informant—comes from expecting the unexpected.

It's happened to both of us as interviewers. As part of a two-year project, Elizabeth conducted in-depth interviews with a college student who was a dancer. Anna identified with the modern dancers at the university and also lived a lifestyle with interests in animal rights, organic foods, and ecological causes. Over time, Elizabeth wondered about a particular necklace that Anna always wore. She speculated that it served as a spiritual talisman or represented a political affiliation. When she asked Anna, she discovered the unexpected. The necklace actually held the key to Anna's apartment—a much less dramatic answer than Elizabeth anticipated. Anna claimed that she didn't trust herself to keep her key anywhere but around her neck, and that information provided a clue to her temperament that Elizabeth wouldn't have known if she hadn't asked and had persisted in her own speculations.

In a shorter project, Bonnie interviewed a school superintendent over a period of eight months. As Ken discussed his beliefs about education, Bonnie connected his ideas with the writings of progressivist philosopher John Dewey. At the time, she was reading educational philosophy herself and was greatly influenced by Dewey's ideas. To her, Ken seemed to be a contemporary incarnation of Dewey. Eventually, toward the end of their interviews, Bonnie asked Ken which of Dewey's works had been the most important to him. "Dewey?" he asked, "John Dewey? Never exactly got around to reading him."

No matter how hard we try to lay aside our assumptions when we interview others, we will always carry them with us. Rather than ignoring our hunches, we need to form questions around them, follow them through, and see where they will lead us. Asking Anna about her necklace, a personal artifact, led Elizabeth to new understandings about Anna's self-concept and habits that later became important in her analysis of Anna's literacy. Bonnie's admiration for Dewey had little to do directly with Ken's educational philosophy. Her follow-up questions centered on the scholars Ken had read, who did shape his theories. It is our job to reveal our informant's perspectives and experiences rather than our own. And so our questions must allow us to learn something new, something that our informant knows and we don't. We must learn how to ask.

Asking involves collaborative listening. When we interview, we are not extracting information like a dentist pulls a tooth, but we make meaning together like two dancers, one leading and one following. Interview questions range between closed and open. Closed questions are like those we fill out in popular magazines or application forms: How many years of schooling have you had? Do you rent your apartment? Do you own a car? Do you have any distinguishing birthmarks? Do you use bar or liquid soap? Do you drink sweetened or unsweetened tea, caffeinated or decaffeinated coffee? Some closed questions are essential for gathering background data: Where did you grow up? How many siblings did you have? What was your favorite subject in school? But these questions often yield single phrases as answers and can shut down further talk. Closed questions can start an awkward volley of single questions and abbreviated answers.

To avoid asking too many closed questions, you'll need to prepare ahead of time by doing informal research about your informants and the topics they represent. For example, if you are interviewing a woman in the air force, you may want to read something about the history of women in aviation. Reading a book about the WAFs (Women in the Air Force) will better prepare you for your interview. You might also consult an expert in the field or telephone government offices to request informational materials so that you avoid asking questions that you could answer for yourself, like "How many years have women been allowed to fly planes in the US Air Force?" When you are able to do background research, your knowledge of the topic and the informant's background will demonstrate your level of interest, put the informant at ease, and create a more comfortable interview situation.

Open questions, by contrast, help elicit your informant's perspective and allow for more conversational exchange. Because there is no single answer to open-ended questions, you will need to listen, respond, and follow the informant's lead. Because there is no single answer, you can allow yourself to engage in a lively, authentic response. In other words, simply being an interested "other" makes a good field interviewer. Here are some very general open questions—sometimes called *experimental* and *descriptive*—that try to get the informant to share experiences or to describe them from his or her own point of view:

- Tell me more about the time when . . .
- Describe the people who were most important to . . .
- Describe the first time you . . .

- Tell me about the person who taught you about . . .
- What stands out for you when you remember . . .
- Tell me the story behind that interesting item you have.
- Describe a typical day in your life.

When thinking of questions to ask an informant, make your informant your teacher. You want to learn about his or her expertise, knowledge, beliefs, and world-view. An interview can begin with a focus on almost any topic, as long as it involves the informant's point of view.

BOX 19
USING A CULTURAL ARTIFACT: AN INTERVIEW

This exercise mirrors the process of conducting interviews over time with an informant. It emphasizes working with the informant's perspective, making extensive and accurate observations, speculating and theorizing, confirming and disconfirming ideas, writing up notes, listening well, sharing ideas collaboratively, and reflecting on your data.

To introduce interviewing in our courses, we use an artifact exchange. This exercise allows people to investigate the meaning of an object from another person's point of view. It follows the model we used when we interviewed our friend Danling in Chapter 4 about silk and silkworms. This interview focuses on a concrete object, an artifact rather than language connotations.

Choose a partner from among your colleagues. You will act as both interviewer and informant. Select an interesting artifact that your partner is either wearing or carrying: a key chain, a piece of jewelry, an item of clothing. Both partners should be sure the artifact is one the owner feels comfortable talking about. If, for example, the interviewer says, "Tell me about that pin you are wearing," but the informant knows that her watch has more meaning or her bookbag holds a story, the interviewer should follow her lead. Once you've each chosen an artifact, try the following process. Begin by writing observational and personal notes before interviewing as a form of background research:

1. *Take observation notes.* Take quiet time to inspect, describe, and take notes on your informant's artifact. Pay attention to its form, and speculate about its function. Where do you think it comes from? What is it used for?

2. *Take personal notes.* What does it remind you of? What do you already know about things similar to it? How does it connect to your own experiences? What are your hunches about the artifact? In other words, what assumptions do you have about it? (For example, you may be taking notes on someone's ring and find yourself speculating about how much it costs and whether the owner of the artifact is wealthy). It is important here to identify your assumptions and not mask them.

3. *Interview the informant.* Ask questions and take notes on the story behind the artifact. What people are involved in it? Why is it important to them? How does the owner use it? Value it? What's the cultural background behind it? After recording your informant's responses, read your observational notes to each other to verify or clarify the information.

4. *Theorize.* Think of a metaphor that describes the object. How does the artifact reflect something you know about the informant? Could you find background material about the artifact? Where would you look? How does the artifact relate to history or culture? If, for example, your informant wears earrings made of spoons, you might research spoon making, spoon collecting, or the introduction of the spoon in polite society. Maybe this person had a famous cook in the family, played the spoons as a folk instrument, or used these as baby spoons in childhood.

5. *Write.* In several paragraphs about the observations, the interview, and your theories, create a written account of the artifact and its relationship to your informant. Give a draft to your informant for a response.

6. *Exchange.* Each informant writes a response to the interviewer's written account, detailing what was interesting and surprising. At this point, the informant can point out what the interviewer didn't notice, say, or ask that might be important to a further understanding of the artifact. You will want to exchange your responses again, explaining what you learned from the first exchange.

7. *Reflect.* Write about what you learned about yourself as an interviewer. What are your strengths? Your weaknesses? What assumptions or preconceptions did you find that you had that interfered with your interviewing skills? How might you change this?

Response

Here is an excerpt from the artifact exercise, written by EunJoo Kang about Ming-Chi Own's watch. Notice that in the final draft of her essay, EunJoo, the interviewer, includes many of her original notes as well as information added by Ming-Chi from both the oral interview and the written exchange.

> When I tried to locate an artifact on my classmate, Ming-Chi, I was first caught by her necklace. It was golden and very thin. I asked if it had any story behind it, but she said that it did not, she just wore it. So I changed my eyes to a different object. I saw that she was wearing a watch.
>
> Ming-Chi's watch is small and gold-plated and square. It has seven colors: gold, steel, silver, dark gray, light gray, brown, and black on the band. It has a snake leather band with an omega symbol on it. The band does not look new and does not seem cheap either because I could read the omega symbol, which is [used by] one of the most famous Swiss watch companies. The band has seven holes and two loops. The watch itself was made in Japan by Seiko. I recognized Seiko as another good and famous watch company.
>
> How I saw this watch depended on what I was likely to look at, what I was oriented to seeing. I should confess that once I dreamed to be a fine artist. And I find I have a tendency to look at objects by their colors, shapes, design, and usage all at the same time. This was borne out by my noting the seven colors in the watch. Ming-Chi seemed surprised at my finding so many colors in her watch. That told me something. Not everyone sees the same things. To Ming-Chi, the color had little meaning. Instead, her watch focused on keeping schedules and being on time.
>
> Ming-Chi shared that the watch was purchased by her father in Singapore. She got the watch as a graduation gift. She attended college in Australia, far from her family in Singapore. It was not common for families to

send their daughters to foreign countries to study, but Ming-Chi's father trusted her to be able to live by herself in Australia. Her father was happy with his grown daughter and bought her a watch that she could wear for a long time. And she did, as shown by the many scratches on it.

The most obvious thing to associate Ming-Chi's watch with is a concept of time. Even though she is from another culture, she has obviously adjusted to Western ideas of time. She has adjusted to our culture in which time is counted as "length," but time can be considered either monochronic, which comes from Western Europe, or polychronic. In monochronic time, for example, a host expects his guest would visit and leave by set times. In contrast, polychronic time is measured by quality and not length. Polychronic time should be measured by substance and satisfaction and not just by beginnings and endings. This is clearly a more Eastern way of observing time. I wonder whether or not Ming-Chi has experienced this way of being in time.

I am surprised at myself for finding this depth with an ordinary watch my classmate is wearing. This chance to look at a small artifact and describe it makes me understand what the ethnographic fieldworker does.

In interviews, sometimes researchers use cultural artifacts to enter into the informant's perspective. When we invite informants to tell stories about their artifacts, we learn not only about the artifacts themselves (Ming-Chi's watch) but also, indirectly, about other aspects of their world that they might not think to talk about. Artifacts, like stories, can mediate between individuals and their cultures.

In their short, informal conversation that began with a wristwatch, EunJoo uncovered the story of Ming-Chi's multicultural life: from Singapore to Australia to the United States. The watch gave them both, as Eastern students living in the West, an opportunity to theorize about different cultural attitudes toward time. Using Ming-Chi's watch as a focal point gave both the interviewer and the informant intense interaction and talk. Stories surfaced from Ming-Chi about herself as a student, a daughter, a foreigner in two cultures, and an amateur philosopher. Without the watch as mediator, it would have taken much longer to achieve such collaboration. That's why EunJoo was so surprised to find herself learning so much from looking at, speculating on, and thinking about her classmate's "ordinary watch."

Cultural artifacts provide data for a fieldworking project, much as stories do. Fieldworkers try to collect a wide range of artifacts from their individual informants and the culture at large to document their findings. If EunJoo were to write a full oral history of Ming-Chi, she might choose to use some of the following cultural artifacts: letters from Ming-Chi's father, a catalog and her school records from Australia, and her passport, family photos, or articles and books describing the complex mix of English and Chinese cultures in Singapore.

The Interview: Learning to Listen

Although most people think that the key to a good interview is asking a set of good questions, both we and our students have found that the real key to interviewing is being a good listener. Think about your favorite television or radio talk show personalities. What do they do to make their informants comfortable and keep conversation flowing? Think about someone you know who you've always considered a good listener. Why does that person make you feel that way?

Good listeners guide the direction of thoughts; they don't interrupt or move conversation back to themselves. Good listeners use their body language to let informants understand that their informants' words are important to them, not allowing their eyes to wander, not fiddling, not checking their watches. They encourage response with verbal acknowledgments and follow-up questions, with embellishments and examples. As Henry Glassie suggests in the quote that opens this chapter, interviewers need to keep the conversation open by keeping the "other" in the foreground.

But to be a good listener as a field interviewer, you must also have structured plans with focused questions. And you must be willing to change them as the conversation moves in different directions. With open questions, background research, and genuine interest in your informant, you'll find yourself holding a collaborative conversation from which you'll both learn. It is the process, not the preplanned information, that makes an interview successful.

Paul Russ conducted interviews with five AIDS survivors for an ethnographic film, *Healing without a Cure: Stories of People Living with AIDS*, sponsored by a local health agency. He developed a list of open and closed questions to prepare for and guide his interviewing process. Paul was a journalist teaching himself to do fieldwork and was very conscious of the difference between open and closed questions. He knew that closed questions would provide him with similar baseline data for all of his informants. For this reason, he formulated some questions that had one specific answer: "How many months have you lived with your diagnosis?" "When did you first request a 'buddy' from the health service?" "Does your family know about your diagnosis?" But the overall goal of his project was to capture how individuals coped with their diagnoses daily, drawing on their own unique resources. He wanted to avoid creating a stereotypical profile of a "day in the life of a person living with AIDS" since he knew that no one AIDS patient's way of coping could possibly illustrate another's.

The field interview draws on both collaboration and interaction. Being a good listener means becoming an active participant in the lives you're studying during the time you're in the field. It means posing questions from your informants' point of view, inviting them to answer from their perspective, from their own worldview. Paul constructed open questions to allow his informants to speak from their lived experiences. Here are a few of his open questions: "What did you already know about AIDS when you were diagnosed?" "How did others respond to you and your diagnosis?" "What has helped you most on a day-to-day basis to live with the virus?" "Have people treated you differently since you were diagnosed?"

In the following excerpt from his hundreds of pages of transcripts, Paul talks with Jessie, a man who had been living with his diagnosis for eight years. For Paul, this interview was a struggle because Jessie hadn't talked much with others about AIDS. And because Paul chose to study people whose lives were very fragile, he paid particular attention to the interactive process between himself and his informants. In the following transcript, Paul uses Jessie's dog Princess just as an interviewer might use an artifact.

P: What was your reaction when you were first diagnosed?

(This is one of the questions Paul posed to each of his five informants. Because he was making a training film for public health volunteers, he wanted to record people's initial reactions on discovering that they had a publicly controversial illness.)

J: My first reaction? How am I going to tell my family. And I put it in my mind that I would not tell anyone until it became noticeable. And I wondered who would take care of me. . . . I knew sometimes AIDS victims go blind. I panicked a little bit, and I started thinking of all the things I have to do to make my life livable. . . . I started thinking about the things I could do to make it go easier. And I started thinking of things I would miss.

P: Like Princess, your dog?

(Paul knew from previous talks that Jessie's dog was an important part of his daily life.)

J: I've had Princess for three years. I had another red dachshund, but she got away. I got Princess as a Christmas gift. . . . She comforts me. She knows when I'm not feeling right. She comes and rubs me. She goes places with me. If I'm in the garden, she's right there. She can't let me out of her sight. Sometimes I talk to her, late at night, we just lay there. She seems like she understands. . . . I don't think she can live without me. If something happens to me, she'll be so confused. I think she'll be so lonely, she'll go off somewhere and just die. . . . I want to give her to somebody. Maybe an older person, someone I believe will take care of her.

(In this part of the interview, the dog prompted Jessie to open his feelings to Paul. By following up on Jessie's comment about "things he'd miss," Paul deepened their interaction and intensified their talk. It was not the dog itself that was important in this exchange but what Princess represented from Jessie's perspective. Paul did not intend to make Jessie talk about his fear of dying, but it happened naturally as he talked about Princess. At this point, Paul found a way to ask another one of the prepared questions that he used with each of his informants. And Jessie's answer brought them back to Princess.)

P: What's your typical day like?

J: My typical day is feeding Princess, letting her out, doing my housework. I like to do my work before noon because I'm addicted to soap operas. . . . I like to work in the yard. I've got a garden. I have some herbs. And I like every now and then to pray. I go to the library. I do a great deal of reading.

(Paul continued to interview Jessie about his spirituality and his reading habits. He brought this interview around to another preplanned question that he asked of all his AIDS informants.)

P: What advice do you have for the newly diagnosed?

J: Don't panic. You do have a tendency to blow it out of proportion. And find a friend, a real friend, to help you filter out the negative. Ask your doctor questions. Let it out and forgive. Forgive yourself, you're only human. And forgive the person you think gave it to you. Then you will learn that the key to spirituality is to abandon yourself. . . . I don't want a sad funeral. I want music, more music than anything else. I don't want my family to go under because of this disease.

Paul's transcripts eventually became a training film for volunteers at the Triad Health Project and area schools that wanted to participate in AIDS support and education. In the film, Paul has the advantage of presenting his data, not just through verbal display, but visually as well. As Paul conducts his interviews, we hear his voice and see his informants—their surroundings and artifacts, their gestures and body language, and the tones of voices as they respond to Paul.

BOX 20
ESTABLISHING RAPPORT

You can tell from reading Paul's interview with Jessie that he worked hard to establish rapport with his informant. He achieves this connection with Jessie by turning his interviews into a collaborative and interactive process in which he makes himself sensitive to Jessie's feelings, position, and worldview. We'd like you to write a short paper about your subjective attitude toward an informant. Think about whether you've felt tentative or hesitant toward your informant, feelings that you may not want write about in your final paper but that you acknowlege and understand as part of your researcher self. Use the following list to guide you.

1. Describe your first meeting with your informant. What did you notice about yourself as you began the interview process?
2. Describe any gender, class, race, or age differences that may have affected the way you approached your informant.
3. Discuss ways you tried either to acknowledge or to erase these differences and the extent to which you were successful.
4. Discuss how your rapport changed over time in talking with and understanding your informant and her worldview.

Response

Paul Russ faced many race and class differences when he interviewed his informants about how they lived with AIDS. The most obvious was health, since his informants were facing death and he was not. Of the five informants Paul interviewed, as we write this book, three have not survived. Paul's response describes the many conflicting feelings he had when he interviewed Jessie:

I picked up Jessie to drive him to the Health Project office for the interview. At first, we didn't conduct the interviews at his house. I'm not sure if he was uncomfortable about me seeing the inside of his house, if he didn't want the neighbors seeing a tall white guy carrying a bunch of camera equipment into this house. Anyway, as Jessie rode in my car, I was incredibly aware of the two different worlds we came from. I had a bad case of white man's guilt. As he sat in my car, I apologized for the dog hair left from taking my two dogs to the vet. He said that it was fine, that he was used to it. Then he mentioned his dog, Princess. It was the first thing we had to talk about. Jessie admitted that he had little family support to cope with AIDS and that Princess was his family. I shared that my dog had had a difficult pregnancy and that I almost lost her. That's when he first opened up to me about his fear of living without Princess or Princess living without him. When it later came up in our interview, it was an obvious opportunity to encourage Jessie to speak personally.

It was essential to establish common ground with him because I felt I had nothing in common with Jessie. Perhaps this was because he did not come from where I came from and, perhaps, because he did not look like me. And while I've never considered myself prejudiced, I realize that we all have prejudices deeply buried inside no matter how intelligent or informed we are. In order to know him with some degree of intimacy, I had to be vulnerable and share myself. I had to address the baggage of race, class, education. I did this with all the informants in my project, and it scared me because being friends with someone who is facing mortality requires an emotional investment. I knew I had to establish a friendship.

While I was making a personal connection with Jessie, I also had professional distance. With everything that came out of Jessie's mouth, I was thinking about how it could be used in the final project. For me, interviewing is very active. It's not passive at all. You have to listen for meaning and listen for what's not being said. I had trouble getting Jessie to speak from the heart. His responses to early questions were pressed. I knew that if I were writing his story for a reader, I could project a much clearer sense of his identity than he gave me on camera. I knew that. But I wasn't writing his story. My mission was to record him telling his story in his own words. So I looked for opportunities to help him reveal himself to me. Princess was one of these opportunities.

Fieldworkers must turn interview transcripts into writing, making a kind of verbal film. As we mentioned in the FieldWriting section of Chapter 4, as interesting as interview transcripts are to the researcher, they are only partial representations of the actual interview process. Folklorist Elliott Oring observes, "Lives are not transcriptions of events. They are artful and enduring symbolic constitutions which demand our engagement and identification. They are to be perceived and understood as wholes" (258). To bring an informant's life to the page, you must use a transcript within your own text, sometimes describing the setting, the informant's physical appearances, particular mannerisms, and language patterns and intonations. The transcript by itself has little meaning until you bring it to life.

Cindie Marshall conducted a semester-long field project at Ralph's Sports Bar, frequented by men and women who describe themselves as bikers. Cindie had returned to school while she continued to worked at a law firm, and she completed this study in a second-semester freshman writing course. In "Ralph's Sports Bar," she combines her skills as a listener, an interviewer, and most of all a writer. In her study, her informants speak in their own voices, but Cindie contextualizes them, offering readers a look into the biker subculture as it exists at Ralph's. In her data analysis, she identifies three categories of biker patrons as they interact side by side at Ralph's: the "rednecks," the "regular bikers," and the "white-collar weekend professionals." Cindie uses her interviews with two key informants, Alice and Teardrop, to verify her data, along with her own extensive fieldnotes. As you read Cindie's research study, notice all the fieldworking skills she brings together.

Ralph's Sports Bar
Cindie Marshall

The Arrival

Ralph's Sports Bar isn't a sports bar at all really. When someone says "sports bar," I think of a bar that is neatly kept, full of white-collar professionals, a big-screen TV, billiard tables, and more than likely a dartboard or two. Oh, and let's not forget the line of high-dollar sports cars parked outside. Well, that does not come close to describing Ralph's Sports Bar.

As I pulled into the half-paved, half-graveled parking lot, the first thing I saw on the side of the small red-brick building was a large sign that said, "Urinate inside, not out here." I suppose had I been anywhere else I would have been shocked by the sign. However, I had come here to seek out bikers, and this small sign depicted just what I had expected of them. I am not quite sure how I came by such a negative image of bikers. Like anything else in life, I suppose I was conditioned to think this way. My white-collar family raised me to believe that there were different classes in the world and that my class was just better than theirs. The truth is that the sign struck another chord as well. The one thing I had always admired about them was the fact they didn't care what people like me thought of them. It is inspiring to think that there are actually people who simply "do their own thing."

After seeing that sign, I was hesitant to continue with my mission. But I had come here to seek out bikers and find out everything I could about them, and that was exactly what I had to do.

Unfamiliar Surroundings

I got out of my car and walked up toward the front of the building. On my approach, I could see three men and a woman sitting at an outdoor table, drinking beer and laughing. The table was brown plastic and was well worn. The four mismatched wooden chairs were unstable and varied in color. The concrete around them was littered with old cigarette butts, bottle caps, and other debris.

Beside the table was a small sidewalk area. This area served as a parking strip for Harley Davidson motorcycles. I had driven by the bar the weekend before and saw the bikes meticulously aligned, handlebar to handlebar, back tire to back tire. I noticed there were none there this evening and wondered if I would find any bikers at all.

As I turned from the table area toward the front entrance, I was greeted by a sign proclaiming my arrival at "Ralph's Sports Bar." The sign was so big, it took up half of the right-hand wall of the building. The entrance doors were glass that had been painted jet black and propped open with wooden straight-back chairs.

I entered the smoke-filled building to the sounds of Ozzie Osborne's "No More Tears" screaming from the jukebox. The smell of stale beer, cigarette ashes, and body odor was overwhelming.

"Ralph's" Sports Bar. (Photo: Minshall Strater)

Along the right-hand wall were four small pool tables with an even smaller one on a platform at the rear of the building. The pool tables were well worn, with cigarette burns, beer stains, and rips in the felt. Taking up the bulk of the right-hand wall was a huge 8 by 20 handpainted mural. It was a picture of the red dog from the Red Dog beer commercial. Through the mural ran a banner that said, "Mad Dog Ralphman." The space

"Ralph's" Sports Bar parking lot. (Photo: Minshall Strater)

remaining on the wall was filled with black velvet paintings of dogs playing pool. Most of these pictures were hung on the wall with tape or a punch pin and left unframed.

Immediately on the left was the L-shaped bar. On the wall to the left of the bar was a huge bulletin board covered by pictures of patrons both old and new. Most of the pictures captured smiling men and women while they toasted the camera with their beer. As you walked around the bar, it led to a small room. The room had a wooden table in the center and was surrounded by poker machines. I could only surmise that this room served as the arcade.

From the front door looking down the left wall of the building, there were two booths. The looked like they could have been in McDonald's at one point, with their yellow seats and tabletops. Behind the two booths was the jukebox. And beyond the jukebox were two more booths. As you passed the last booth, there was a wooden ramp leading to the bathrooms. (After entering the bathroom, I understood why one would opt to go outside.) The left wall was littered with pictures of Harley Davidson riders playing pool. It was a collection from the "Harley Davidson 25th Anniversary" prints. They were mounted in bent frames with shattered glass covering various snapshots of bikers at play. There were also a variety of neon signs scattered along the wall advertising Budweiser beer.

How Do You Read the Signs?

There were signs everywhere! I read them in hopes of finding out what behavior would be expected of me during my visit as well as what behavior I could expect from the patrons of this bar. The first thing that caught my eye was a sign that stated, "Break a cue, pay $25.00 or be barred." That wasn't the behavioral expectation I had hoped to find. And the bad news was, there were more. On the front door was a sign that stated, "We do not buy stolen merchandise." On the wall over the bar was a handwritten sign that said, "Ale law: no beer sold after 2 p.m." On each poker machine there was a handwritten sign that said, "By N.C. law no gambling allowed." What did all of these signs really mean? By talking to the owner's girlfriend, prior to my visit, I knew that stolen merchandise was sold and bought. I knew that if I played poker, I could cash in my points for money. I also knew that alcohol was served on many occasions as late as the patrons wanted to drink. What's more, I knew that drugs came and went out of this bar as frequently as the patrons. So these signs were really placed on the walls as a sign to the local police that the rules were in place and illegal activity was prohibited at Ralph's.

People Watching

There were thirteen people when I arrived; eight were men and five were women. I did not see the biker group that I had seen while driving by the previous weekend and was disappointed that they would not be the focus of my research. Since my target group was not there, I made my way to the back of the bar, where I thought I would be least conspicuous in my attempt to observe the culture of the bar.

The patrons were scattered around the bar in small groups. One group sat at the bar; they were all men who were mainly clad in black glasses (the doors were open and sun was coming in), blue jeans, T-shirts, and black leather boots of some sort. Each of them had chains attaching their wallets to their belts and had hair that was unkempt and hung at least to their shoulders.

The largest group in the bar surrounded the pool tables. This group was comprised of most of the remaining men and all of the women. They were clad in T-shirts, dirty blue jeans, and brown leather work boots. They were mainly involved in shooting pool and drinking beer, and some of them were dancing to the jukebox between shots.

At the back of the bar, closer to where I was located, were the remaining group of men. They were neatly dressed in blue jeans, button-down shirts, and tennis shoes. This group sat quietly talking while drinking their beers.

As I watched these three groups of people, I concluded that each section of the bar was the territory of distinct groups. The "bikers" were at the bar, the "rednecks" were at the pool tables, and the "white-collar professionals" made their way to the back booths. Each group was made up of individuals who were similarly dressed. They stayed in their own group and did not intermingle with the other groups unless it was a necessity. Anyone who wanted to get a beer had to speak to the bikers at the bar; otherwise you couldn't get to the bartender.

Everyone in the bar eyed me suspiciously during my visit. I appeared to be very different from the other women. I didn't dress like them, walk like them, or talk like them. Because of the illegal activity that goes on in the bar, I also guessed they were probably wondering if I was an undercover cop. After observing these groups for a couple of hours, I realized that given the way they marked their boundaries, they probably wouldn't be very inviting to a stranger asking a lot of questions about their "culture." Especially a female stranger who obviously didn't appear to belong there to begin with.

I decided that I would go to the table out front and perhaps there I could find someone to answer my questions. At the very least, I could get some fresh air and think about my approach.

Talking to Teardrop

When I arrived at the table, there was a woman sitting alone, drinking a beer. She had obviously had a lot to drink. But we talked for a minute, and she was really quite nice. I introduced myself, and she said her name was Teardrop. It was dark outside, so I couldn't see her very well. We talked about the weather for a few minutes, and that led her to tell me that she had moved here from Michigan three years ago and that she came to Ralph's every day.

I knew that this was my opportunity to talk to a patron. I wasn't sure which group she belonged in, but if she came to Ralph's every day, she must be in one of them. On a long shot, I asked her if she would like to shoot a game of pool. She agreed, and I was delighted. This was an opportunity to do two things—ask questions and be seen with a regular patron of the bar. I guessed that if others saw me talking to her, at the least her friends would be more relaxed about talking to me.

Once we were inside, I saw that Teardrop was wearing new Lee jeans, a nice pale yellow sweater, and a heart-shaped brooch. Her hair was brown but was showing signs of graying. She had it neatly pulled back, and her bangs were teased and carefully sprayed in place. It wasn't until she laughed that I noticed she was missing her front teeth, both top and bottom. She had a small tattoo around her wrist that served as a bracelet. It was dark green and was in the shape of a vine. Most of the tattoo was covered by the watch she was wearing.

As we played pool, I noticed something else. She had a very small black spot under her left eye, high on her cheek. At first I thought it was a mole or a birthmark. But after looking at it carefully, I noticed that it was a black tattoo in the shape of a teardrop. I asked her if it was a teardrop and she said yes; that was how she got her name.

When I asked her about her tattoo, she starting really talking to me. She told me that when she was 13, she had been kidnapped by a group of bikers. The biker that kidnapped her had eventually sold her to a fellow biker. This went on for years, being sold from biker to biker. Finally, three years ago, she got away from them and came to Greensboro. The teardrop was there because she couldn't cry anymore.

After hearing Teardrop's story, my admiration for the bikers' "do your own thing" attitude was lost. I had always been one who appreciated the freedom to express oneself, but this went far beyond freedom. What Teardrop had described was sheer abuse, and she wore that abuse both on her face, in the shape of a teardrop, and in her smile, which was darkened by missing teeth.

After talking with Teardrop, I left the bar to reflect on all that I had seen. I wanted to know why the groups in the bar kept themselves segregated. I also wanted to know why three groups in the bar would come together in a place just to be segregated. The only way I could get the answers to my questions was to talk to a person who had been in all three groups and had spent a lot of time at the bar. The likely candidate would be Alice.

Conversation with Alice

Alice was the receptionist at the law firm that I worked at. Her boyfriend, Ralph, owned the bar. She had worked there prior to coming to the law firm, and she could probably tell me all I wanted to know about these groups.

Alice agreed to my interview, and I prepared a list of the three groups, outlining what I thought their characteristics were. I felt that it was important to understand the groups before trying to understand their connection to this bar or to each other. Alice read my list, and we began our interview.

Characteristics of the "Rednecks"

We both agreed that one of the groups we would call "rednecks" for lack of a better term. My list conveyed the following characteristics for rednecks: they would be lazy; they would value freedom; they would not like or adhere to any rules imposed on them; they would have no self-pride, either in their work or appearance; they would demean women; they would have no materialistic values; they would have no work ethic; and they would have no moral code among themselves—it would be every man for himself.

After reviewing my list, Alice commented that actually, "they are hardworking and take pride in their jobs. Because they like to be able to say 'I do something well.' . . . Most of them are blue-collar workers—construction workers, electricians, people who do things with their hands. They're good at what they do to a certain extent. A lot of them change jobs frequently because of the drinking problem that they have, and I think the majority of them do have a drinking problem. . . . They are lazy in the sense that they don't aspire to be anything more than what they are."

We discussed how they treated their women, and Alice was quick to point out "that's the biggest thing that they do. . . . It makes them feel like they are bigger." We had talked prior to the interview about how uncomfortable I was at this bar. It seemed that all the men treated the women with little or no respect.

On the subject of the rednecks' commitment to their fellow rednecks, I felt that it would be every man for himself. I doubted that the rednecks had lasting bonds or would stand up for a buddy in trouble. Alice said that she had "seen where one night two guys would sit there and be buddy-buddy and would fight together side by side. Two weeks later, they would fight each other."

Overall, the only real corrections Alice made to my list of characteristics was that she strongly disagreed with my idea that rednecks were lazy. She said that they were not lazy and that they all worked. I asked her later outside the interview how they could all be working yet spending their entire day at Ralph's. She told me those individuals worked third shift and would simply go to work drunk.

Characteristics of the Bikers

I had made a similar list of characteristics for the bikers at Ralph's. I had decided that they, too, would value freedom and not like rules imposed on them, much like the rednecks. However, they would have a higher moral code among themselves. I guessed that they didn't care what other people thought of them and therefore would not be materialistic. They would likely believe in making their own way and have a higher work ethic than the rednecks. I would categorize them as more the "weekend warrior" type. I also concluded that unlike the rednecks, they were probably ritualistic in the way they meticulously parked their bikes. As for their treatment of women, after talking with Teardrop, my view on that was clear. To the bikers, women were property, and that was all.

Alice started her revision of my list by first telling me that "there are even two different classes of bikers. . . . There are some bikers that are construction workers, moochers, low lifes. They live from day to day in how they get their money, how they live. They come from a culture of brotherhood and "my buddy." They are more clannish in that, if a guy drives a bike, they will stand beside him no matter what. But also, there are a lot of bikers that come in there that are white-collar workers; they do this on the weekend and like to be someone different. They change their persona and how people perceive them. They put on their leather pants and leather jackets and ride these motorcycles all weekend long and go back to their jobs. There are four or five of them that nobody knows. . . . They are businessmen who own companies over in High Point . . . but you would never guess it by the way they look when they are sitting there on the weekends drinking."

When we talked about the stereotypical biker, I asked her if she felt they "treated women the same way the rednecks do." (I was fairly sure about the how the bikers treated women but unclear about the rednecks.) She said no. It was more a kind of ownership. She said, " 'My old lady' and 'my old man,' this is the way they talk. Rednecks are a little more respectful . . . 'this is my wife' or 'this is my girlfriend.' I think that the 'old lady' and 'old man' can change from week to week. I have seen [bikers] swap women around as if they were pieces of property." Surprisingly enough, she made her point about the way bikers treat women by telling me Teardrop's story.

We talked about the bikers and how they felt about freedom. Alice pointed out, "You will find that most of the bikers will be outside, they will not be inside the bar. . . . Bikers like the openness and the freedom—that's why they're bikers."

Conclusion

Alice is fascinating because she has been very deeply connected to all three of these groups. Therefore, she is a reliable source of information on all three groups. She works at Ralph's bar at night and at a law firm during the day. Unlike the white-collar biker, who takes on a persona to escape on the weekend, Alice truly does cross the line of the cultural boundaries. I believe that her stereotypes and ideas about each of these groups are based on her living in that culture. As she put it, "I've been there. I've been a drinker and down on my luck and slept in my car. I've been just where they are on many occasions. . . ."

My own stereotypes show in my list of characteristics that I mapped out for Alice to review. I am in the category of the white-collar professional. I have a high work ethic and would probably be tagged by the rednecks or the bikers as materialistic. But it really is more than that. I have pride in myself, and I value the opinions of others. I am uncertain where my stereotypes were born. In all fairness, I would have to say they came from the media, my parents, my friends, and my own attitudes about what is right and wrong.

As for Alice, it is clear that she, too, has stereotyped these groups. Even though she's been involved with each, when asked, "Which culture are you most comfortable with?" she replied, "The rednecks." During the interview, her tone of voice was forceful when she attempted to dispel the stereotype that I presented of rednecks' being lazy.

After talking with Alice and visiting the bar, my question still remained: Why would these distinctly different groups of people, each representing a unique culture, come to one small bar, each mapping their turf and intentionally staying separated? Alice felt that the common bond was Ralph. Ralph moved easily between the cultures and was actually a part of each group. She said that he did it much the same as she did, the difference being that Ralph held the role of "leader" or "policer" of each group. It was because of Ralph that the groups could all drink their beer in harmony while at the bar.

I feel that it goes much deeper than that. The one common bond that all of these groups share is love of freedom. I think that the culture of Ralph's Sports Bar is based on that love of freedom. All these people go to Ralph's to escape, to be free of the watchful eyes of a judgmental society. They like the comfort of not worrying what anyone else will think because they know no one will care or judge their actions.

The white-collar, part-time biker enjoys the freedom of wearing his leather and riding his Harley on the weekend without anyone knowing. The redneck enjoys the freedom to drink his beer and be totally wild if he wishes.

It all comes down to freedom. The group to which you belong simply indicates whether that freedom is experienced for a brief moment or for a lifetime; it states the extent to which the freedom is valued.

Commentary: With More Time . . .

I would love to have had more time to visit this bar and try to become part of this culture. I am certain that there are errors in my list of characteristics, and I know that these characteristics do not apply to every individual. It would have been interesting to make connections in the bar and test my ideas; to prove or disprove the stereotypes that I have about each group. With that research perhaps it would be more clear where the stereotypes actually come from. I have asked myself that question over and over again while writing this paper. At this point, I cannot clearly say where they come from. I think it is a combination of many sources.

I am still very intrigued with the biker culture. I wish I could have talked with more female bikers to get their ideas on the treatment-of-women issue. Teardrop really changed my attitude.

```
Three Distinct Cultures
My list of characteristics associated with each culture based on my
observations at the bar. (Alice's corrections and additions are in
italics.)
REDNECKS
Value freedom; do not like rules imposed on them
Lazy
No work ethic (Hardworking, but all they do is work and drink)
No self-pride; either in work or appearance
Demean women, think of them as possessions
Would rather drink than work or do anything else
```

No moral code among themselves; every man for himself

Minimal to nonexistent educational background

Don't care what other people think of them

Not materialistic or subject to cultural pressure such as fashion

BIKERS

Value freedom

Higher moral code than rednecks; stand up for each other; group is more important than the individual

Don't care what other people think of them

Believe in making their own way; higher work ethic than rednecks; "weekend warrior"

Not materialistic in terms of possessions but they are in terms of fashion; they all tend to want and have the same type of clothing

Ritualistic

PROFESSIONAL/WHITE-COLLAR

Materialistic

Care what others think of them; tend to worry a lot about the image they project

High work ethic; must work to obtain more material goods; more important than drinking; would give up weekend freedom to gain more material things

Attitude of being above the other two cultures

Interview with Alice

C: Let's go over the category list. You believe the rednecks value their freedom and are hardworking.

A: I think that they are hardworking and take pride in their jobs. Because they like to be able to say, "I do something well." But their whole goal in what I have viewed is that "I work to drink and I drink to work."

C: What kind of work do they do normally?

A: Most of them are blue-collar workers—construction workers, electricians, people who do things with their hands. They're good at what that do to a certain extent. A lot of them do change jobs frequently because of the drinking problem that they have, and I think the majority of them do have drinking problems.

C: We talked about their being lazy, and we concluded that they're lazy in the sense that they don't aspire to be anything more than what they are.

A: Yes. If their daddy taught them how to do construction or to build houses, they don't make goals other than that.

C: And no self-pride in terms of their appearance?

A: Yes.

C: And we talked about how they demean women.

A: Yes, very much so. That's the biggest thing that they do. It makes them feel stronger and feel like better people. It makes them feel like they are bigger.

C: We talked about every man for himself, and you were saying that there were no lasting bonds between the members of this particular culture within the bar.

A: This is true. Because I have seen where one night two guys would sit there and be buddy-buddy and would fight together side by side. Two weeks later, they would fight each other. If the situation changes. The alcohol changes people's personalities, and it varies day to day who is buddy-buddy.

C: The other culture that I saw when I was there is—you have your rednecks and you have your bikers. What is the difference between the bikers and the rednecks?

A: I think that there are even two different classes of bikers.

C: In this bar?

A: In this bar. In the sense that there are some bikers that are construction workers, moochers, low life. They live from day to day in how they get their money, how they live. They come from a culture of brotherhood and "my buddy." They are more clannish in that if a guy drives a bike, they will stand beside him no matter what. But also there are a lot of bikers that come in there that are white-collar workers—they do this on the weekend and like to be someone different. They change their persona and how people perceive them. They put on their leather pants and leather jackets and ride these motorcycles all weekend long and go back to their jobs. There are four or five of them that nobody knows. They are very honest and they tell you what they do, that they are businessmen who own companies over in High Point and one thing and another. But you would never guess it by the way they look when they are sitting there on the weekends drinking.

(*Need to ask her how these guys are treated by the full-time bikers. Do they tell the full-time bikers about their other identity*?)

C: So those particular guys really fit both in among the bikers and the white-collar professionals.

A: Yes.

C: So they are just choosing what culture they want to be in on weekends basically. They could go into the biker thing or the professional white-collar worker thing if they wanted to, just whichever way they wanted to go.

A: Yeah.

C: OK. Back to your basic stereotyped biker, which is what we were talking about at first. What do you think the differences are that they treat women the same way the rednecks do? It is my understanding that the bikers in general have a different kind of moral code. Do you find that's true within this environment?

A: I think the bikers have much less respect for women.

C: Is it more of an ownership kind of thing? That is what I've heard.

A: Ownership? Yes. "My ol' lady," "my ol' man," that is the way they talk. Rednecks are a little more respectful, I guess if you can call it respect, in the sense that they'll say "this is my wife" or "this is my girlfriend." I think that the "ol' lady" and "ol' man" can change from week to week. I have seen them swap women around as if they were pieces of property.

C: Do the women go along and just do what they want them to do?

A: The women go along with it because this is . . . I've heard stories where women were caught up in the gangs when they were thirteen or fourteen years old and were passed along from biker to biker and city to city and everything. There is one girl named Teardrop. She started this when she was thirteen years old. She was a biker from out in the Midwest. She now lives here; she waits tables sometimes. She has a little teardrop under her eye. She was sold or bargained off from biker to biker and she is like in her late forties now and she has no life.

C: Tell me something. I met her, and it is my understanding that she finally got off the biker thing and came here from Michigan. If she came here and she's trying to escape the biker lifestyle and the biker culture, why would she end up at Ralph's, right in the middle of these two cultures?

A: Because it is all she's ever known.

C: Do you think the familiarity makes it comfortable for her?

A: The familiarity does make it comfortable for her. She's aware, she knows the code of ethics, she knows where she stands with these type of people. But there is also that chance that she might meet somebody that might be a little bit more respectful than the way she has been treated in the past. There is always that chance.

C: When I met her, the one thing that I noticed about her was that she didn't dress like a lot of the bikers or rednecks dressed. It's almost like with her dress she's trying to escape it, but she's putting herself back in the same place.

A: This is true.

C: Could it be that she is switching from the biker culture to the redneck culture now?

A: Oh, yeah. I think that she is looking for a way out. She's looking for someone to love her and take care of her now that she's getting older. She has nothing to offer. She has no education, she has no family. Nothing.

C: How would you describe . . . . If I walked into this bar, could I tell who the bikers are and who the rednecks are just by their appearance or what they're wearing?

A: Yes. All bikers wear leather of some sort. Either a leather jacket, leather vest, or leather hat. Most of the time it is leather pants or leather vest. The majority of them wear leather vests that would mark their colors of their group, who they ride with.

C: What's the deal with the little rounded helmets? Is there any significance to that?

A: Yes. I do know. It's more of a fad for that group of people. The law says you have to have a helmet on. This is one way of skirting it, because it is a very light helmet. It's more like a hat.

C: I never knew that. How would the rednecks dress?

A: Blue jeans, plaid shirts, T-shirts.

C: I saw a lot of work boots. Is that normal?

A: Yes.

C: Even on a Friday night when they are dressed up to go out?

A: Yes.

C: When you are in this bar, and you've spent a lot of time in there, do these people tend to segregate? Do they pretty much stay with their own?

A: Yes.

C: So there are three distinct groups of people, and you can sort of walk in and know immediately that this is this group, this is this group.

A: You will find that most of the bikers will be outside; they will not be inside the bar. They come and get their beer, they may talk to a woman, they may talk to someone they know, but most of the time they will go back outside to drink their beer, day or night. Bikers like the openness and the freedom, that's why they're bikers.

C: How would you describe the overall culture of the bar? I know that's kind of broad.

A: I would call it a blue-collar worker, family-type bar in the sense of everybody pretty much knows everybody else. They've been in on a day-to-day basis, and they each know other. They know who is a moocher, who works, who pays their bills, who will try to get you for a beer, and who won't get you for a beer.

C: What attracts them, do you think? What makes these three very distinct groups of people come to one place?

A: Do you want my honest answer?

C: Yes.

A: Ralph.

C: That's what the people in the office came up with too when we were talking about this earlier.

A: He is so entertaining, he is so intelligent that it's scary. It's scary in the fact that I think he could have been a Jim Jones. He has a control over people, and he knows that he has this control. He can convince people that they are the best, that they are important, and that they are considered important in this group of people when he speaks to them.

C: So it's self-gratification for these people to come there.

A: He is very, very good at it.

C: So Ralph would really be the common ground. I was trying to find some common ground, other than the beer, which is obvious, and the pool, which is obvious—all these groups tend to like to do that. So if you had to put Teardrop in a category now, would you put her in the biker category or the redneck category?

A: Redneck category.

C: When the bikers come, she tends to go to the redneck guys?

A: She tends to [unintelligible] away from them.

C: What is your point of view? In describing this culture, where do you fit in? What's really interesting is that you as an informant actually cross the line into each of these cultures and actually become part of each culture, which is really unusual. For example, when the white-collar professionals become bikers on the weekends, they're not really crossing the cultural boundary, they are just putting up the facade that they are crossing the boundary. However, you have actually crossed into each culture. The one thing that I've noted is that you would go to the bar and work and actually be part of that culture and would leave that and come to a law office where there is different language, different norms, expectations, etc. When you are talking about the bar, where are you in that? Are you looking at it from the perspective of being one of them, or is from the perspective of being on the outside looking in?

A: I treat everybody, everybody in that bar that walks in the door the same way I would want to be treated, with respect and—"hello, how are you?"—a friendly tone. No matter who they are, where they come from, what they've done, what they haven't done. I pretty much know most of the background on just about everybody because everybody loves to gossip. Every one of them has my respect and admiration because they have all been through, somehow, somewhere, some type of trouble that has made them tougher and made their character. So I think that they respect me that I don't think that I'm any better than they are and I have never thought that. But they think that I am because I work in a law office and I work a lot of hours and I come in and hang out with them, but I don't drink with them. I think they have a lot of respect for that. I am their buddy as well as somebody they can relate to. I have been there, I've been a drinker and down on my luck and slept in my car. I've been just where they are on many occasions. They won't listen to anybody's advice, and I don't give them any advice. I listen to what they say and don't offer advice because everybody's going to do what they want to do no matter what.

C: How do you function in both cultures? I noticed that when I walked in the bar, there are signs that say, "We don't buy stolen merchandise" and the gambling sign, "Break a cue, pay $25.00." How do you learn the rules of these cultures? Is it spoken?

A: I guess because they are there on a day-to-day basis, once something happens, they know that there's a penalty for it.

C: So you're saying they see it? They aren't necessarily told that unless they buddy up with somebody.

A: No. Right.

C: Do the patrons buddy up and tell each other what the rules are, what Ralph will accept and not accept?

A: No. Because that could differ from day to day. It all depends on who exactly it is. If it's somebody that has pissed off Ralph as bad as he's pissed off the guy that broke the cue stick over the guy's head, well, "Don't worry about it—it's no big deal, but you do need to replace my cue stick. But don't worry about it— whenever you can." But if he broke it because he missed a ball— "By God, you're going to pay for the stick—learn to control your temper."

C: That's the way you learned it too, then? When you went into that bar, you were just there a lot and just sort of watched and observed and that's how you learned how to interact with these people and what to say and not to say?

A: Yes.

C: Which culture are you most comfortable with?

A: The rednecks. There are a few guys that come in there in the daytime that want to escape from reality because they have so many pressures. I wanted to mention that to you, because there are a couple of guys that I know that own furniture companies and are millionaires but they ride all the way over to Ralph's and sit down for a couple of hours and drink beer to get away from the pressure because there is no pressure there except "How do I pay for my next beer?"

C: I'm different from you in that I feel most comfortable in the white-collar culture. I feel very intimidated by both the redneck and biker cultures, and I think a lot of that has to do with how they treat women. I think if I were a man, it might be different.

A: But see I've been down there where I've been demeaned, beaten, and hit and told I wasn't worth the time of day. What makes me comfortable in it is because now I'm not intimidated by it. I can stand there and say, "You can't talk to me that way." I can enjoy the freedom of it without the repercussions of it.

C: Where does Ralph fit in all of this? Ralph is like a chameleon. It's hard to figure out where Ralph belongs. I don't know if he really belongs in all three categories.

A: Ralph doesn't belong in any category.

C: I think everybody belongs in one category more predominantly than another.

A: No. I don't think you've ever sat down and talked to Ralph like I've talked to Ralph.

C: Well, no, probably not.

A: He is a superintelligent human being. It's amazing. His memory and his thought process on society and financial situations. He reads the exchanges, the financial part of the paper. He can say this company is getting ready to come down, you can see it in the stock. He is a white-collar person in that sense. But he can't tell that to any of these rednecks—half of them don't even read or write. But as I said before, he is a Jim Jones, and he convinces these people that they are worth something and that is what makes him so special to them. Everybody, no matter who they are, where they come from, what they do, how much they make or don't make, he makes them feel as comfortable as possible and that he's their best buddy in the whole wide world. But when he walks out that door, he couldn't give a shit about them.

C: But that's what I'm saying. I've been to your house, I see the way he dresses, I see the way you dress, which I think is all inherent in these cultures. That's what you are comfortable with, and that reflects who you are. If I had to look at Ralph and pulled him out of the bar—like Teardrop. If I pulled her out of the bar and put her somewhere else, it wouldn't matter. I would still categorize her the way I would categorize her if she were sitting there in the bar. With Ralph, however, if you pull him out of that bar, you're not going to categorize him with these two groups—at least I wouldn't—not by looking at him or talking to him. If you had to put a percentage on it, I think he is more the white-collar, educated professional.

```
A:   He has a college education. But that doesn't make any difference.
     Ralph is for Ralph and Ralph only. It doesn't matter. His only
     concern is that he is happy at this moment, at this time, and
     that he is doing what he enjoys and what he wants. He could do
     anything he wants in this world—there is no doubt in my mind that
     he could be sitting up on the Supreme Court if he wanted to. What
     I'm saying is, you can't put a category on him because he can be
     whatever he wants to be whenever he wants to be.

C:   So you feel he truly is a chameleon and is just as comfortable in
     one group as the other.

A:   Anywhere. Because he is going to be the leader of any one he's
     in. . . . He learned a very hard lesson from the time he was born
     till this day: "Nobody is going to make me happy, nobody is going
     to make it for me except me. So I have to remember that and
     remember that this guy may be my buddy right this minute but
     tomorrow he may be my enemy—so I need to make sure that I take
     care of me. It's not in the sense of the 'me generation,' it's
     not all for me, it's that nobody can do it but me." Ralph would
     give you the shirt off his back because he knows that he has
     enough shirts at home, that he has another one.

C:   So as long as he's covered, he's happy.

A:   Yes.
```

One of the strengths of Cindie's study is that she acquires different perspectives about Ralph's Sports Bar, which mirror the three categories of patrons she is attempting to understand. One is the perspective of the "white-collar weekend professional." Cindie positions herself honestly at the outset as part of this group, admitting her own stereotypes as she reflects: "I am not quite sure how I came by such a negative image of bikers. Like anything else in life, I suppose I was conditioned to think this way. My white-collar family raised me to believe that there were different classes in the world and that my class was just better than theirs [the bikers]." The second perspective is what Cindie calls the "regular bikers," and her informant Teardrop has belonged to that "regular biker" culture much of her life. Although no longer a biker's girlfriend, Teardrop speaks from insider experience. The third perspective comes from Alice, Cindie's colleague at the law firm and Ralph's girlfriend, who defends the "redneck" position. Since "redneck" is such a negative term, Cindie would have to work hard to find out what Alice implied when she used it. In the South, *redneck* traditionally refers to a manual laborer, someone whose neck is burned from picking crops under the hot sun.

Cindie was fortunate to find Teardrop, who was in many ways an ideal informant. Teardrop frequents Ralph's every day, so she is an insider to the culture. But Teardrop had "stepped out" of the biker culture long enough to be able to reflect on it. As a female, she held a unique view of this predominantly male group. Teardrop was also an ideal informant because Cindie interacted with her informally, gathering data as they shot pool together. During their pool game, Teardrop offered the story about the meaning of her tear-shaped tattoo. Cindie didn't tape-record the story but remembered it and wrote it into her fieldnotes. While shooting pool, she didn't worry about forgetting Teardrop's story because it was indelible; the tattoo was there "because she couldn't cry anymore." Cindie learned this story from

Teardrop as they interacted, each gaining trust for the other. Had Cindie pulled out her tape recorder and tried to interview Teardrop by asking, "So tell me how you got your name?" she probably wouldn't have heard Teardrop's story. It was the process of interaction and rapport that allowed Cindie to acquire such good insider data.

Cindie's interview with Alice was entirely different because it was structured and planned. Cindie prepared a list of questions based on her own fieldnote observations of the three categories of patrons at the bar. Because Alice was already a friend from the law firm where Cindie worked, she didn't need to establish rapport. As Ralph's girlfriend, Alice was a different kind of insider at the bar who identified with both the rednecks and the white-collar professionals. In this way, Alice had a position of double access.

Alice confirmed and extended Cindie's understanding of the "white-collar biker" with her own observations and insider status. Alice knew that this group was neither "regular" nor "redneck," that these people transformed themselves for the weekends. "They change their persona and how people perceive them. They put on their leather pants and leather jackets and ride these motorcycles all weekend long and go back to their jobs." While Cindie used Alice both to verify and to disconfirm her own observations, Alice rejected some of Cindie's stereotypes of rednecks: "During the interview, her tone of voice was forceful," Cindie wrote, when Alice "attempted to dispel the stereotype of rednecks' being lazy." Alice also confirmed Cindie's observations about two groups of patrons at Ralph's Sports Bar.

Both Teardrop's and Alice's perspectives give weight and evidence to Cindie's own field observations, allowing her to confirm and disconfirm her data. When researchers use multiple data sources (interviews, fieldnotes, artifacts, and library or archival documents), they *triangulate* their findings. In this semester-long study, Cindie collected and analyzed varied sources (interviews, fieldnotes, and artifacts), but if she were to layer her data further in another revision, she would need to interview different patrons, selecting among informants in her three categories. Cindie's perspective was that of a woman who interviewed other women about a predominantly male subculture. To learn more about the male biking culture, she'd have to conduct research with a few of the male bikers and also probably Ralph, the owner.

Cindie's final written account illustrates the systematic process of fieldworking. Short fieldwork accounts like this one may display different points of emphasis, depending on the topic, the data, and the researcher's interests. Some may foreground the culture; others may foreground the people. Whereas Rick Zollo's "Friday Night at Iowa 80" included many informant interviews, his final account focuses on the culture of trucking using his informants mainly to support his account of the culture. Karen Downing's study of Photo Phantasies achieves a balance between looking at the glamour culture and looking at the people who inhabit it: herself, the customers, the management, and the staff. And unlike the researcher Reema's boy in *Mama Day*, who pokes his tape recorder into everyone's face, Cindie Marshall learned how to ask, how to listen, and how to collaborate with her informants at Ralph's Sports Bar.

Because Cindie's final account is so smoothly written and her research skills are so well integrated, it might not be apparent that she has included so much of the fieldworking process. A summary of her many fieldworking strategies demonstrates that Cindie was able to do all of the following:

- *Prepare for the field*

  She gained access through her colleague Alice, an insider at Ralph's.

  She read other research studies and material about fieldworking.

  She drafted a research proposal that explained her interest in the biker subculture.

  She wrote about her assumptions and uncovered her prejudices about bikers and rednecks.

- *Use the researcher's tools*

  She established rapport by hanging out at Ralph's and by locating Teardrop, an insider informant.

  She observed, taking detailed fieldnotes about the physical environment.

  She participated in the culture by shooting pool with Teardrop, talking and interacting at the same time.

  She gathered cultural artifacts, taking photos and noting the signs outside and inside and what these implied.

  She interviewed two informants, Alice formally and Teardrop informally, taking fieldnotes on their physical characteristics as well as their stories.

  She transcribed Alice's interview, selecting potential sections to use in her final project.

- *Interpret the fieldwork*

  She read her data, proposal, fieldnotes, interview notes, and transcripts, looking for themes and patterns.

  She categorized her data into findings according to the three groups she observed.

  She made meaning collaboratively with her informants:

    With Alice, she verified her categories and disconfirmed her own cultural stereotypes in her interview.

    With Teardrop, she reflected on her data, particularly after her interview, and expanded her findings with insights about the treatment of women within the biking culture.

  She reflected on how her data described a subculture.

- *Present the findings*

  She acknowledged and wrote about her position as an outsider.

  She used descriptive details in her writing, selecting particular written artifacts (various signs) that convey the meaning of the culture: "please urinate inside," "we do not buy any stolen merchandise."

  She turned her informants into characters by melding her fieldnotes and her transcripts.

  She integrated her informants' voices with her narrative by using direct quotations from her transcripts.

  She designed sections with subheadings to guide her reader through the project: "The Arrival," "Unfamiliar Surroundings," "How Do You Read the Signs?" "People Watching," "Talking to Teardrop," "Conversation with Alice," "Characteristics of the Rednecks," "Characteristics of the Bikers," and her commentary called "With More Time. . . ."

She drew conclusions without shutting down further exploration of the topic as she reflects on what other sorts of data she would need to continue her research in her final commentary called "With More Time. . . ."

BOX 21
ANALYZING YOUR INTERVIEWING SKILLS

Reviewing and analyzing an excerpt from your transcripts can help you refine your interviewing skills and see ways to improve them. Pausing to look closely at your interviewing and transcribing techniques may smooth the way for the rest of your project. Select and transcribe a short section from a key interview, no more than a page, to share. Play the corresponding portion of the audiotape as your colleagues read the transcript and listen. Have your colleagues jot down notes and suggestions about your interview so that you can discuss their observations together afterward.

- Has the interviewer established rapport with the informant?
- Who talks the most, the informant or the interviewer? Does that seem to work?
- What was the best question the interviewer asked? Why?
- What question might have extended to another question? Why?
- How did the interviewer encourage your informant to be specific?
- Were any of the questions closed?

Try using the line-by-line analysis in a small section, like the ones we've presented in the interviews with Danling Fu in Chapter 4, Paul Russ's interview with Jessie, and the following example from Cindie Marshall.

Response

Here we'll analyze one of Cindie's transcripts, a portion of her interview with Alice. In this excerpt, both interviewer and informant struggle with what they mean by the word *redneck* and its associated cultural stereotypes. Fieldworkers need to be sensitive to words that have different meanings for insiders in a culture. From her outsider perspective, Cindie knew that the word *redneck* is a loaded term and that it's used differently in different areas of the country. She was eager for Alice to help her clarify what it meant to different groups at Ralph's.

C: You believe the rednecks value their freedom and are hardworking?

(*Cindie wants confirmation from Alice about one group of people she has observed frequenting Ralph's Sports Bar. She tries to get Alice to untangle her own perspective about this category of patrons in the bar.*)

A: I think that they are hardworking and take pride in their jobs. Because they like to be able to say, "I do something well." But their whole goal from what I have viewed is that

"I work to drink and I drink to work."

C: What kind of work do they normally do?

(Cindie follows Alice's lead, asking for more information, trying to find out more about what they each mean when they use the term redneck. *When the researcher recognizes that one word has different meanings among different informants, she ought to try to understand it.)*

A: Most of them are blue-collar workers—construction workers, electricians, people who do things with their hands. They're good at what they do to a certain extent. A lot of them do change jobs frequently because of the drinking problem that they have, and I think the majority of them do have drinking problems.

C: We talked about their being lazy, and we concluded that they're lazy in the same sense that they don't aspire to be anything more than what they are.

(Rather than trying to get more information from Alice about biker patrons who "do things with their hands," Cindie introduces her own stereotype—that bikers are lazy, an idea that she and Alice had discussed before. Cindie's question represents her indecision about whether her stereotypes of bikers were true or if they came from movies.)

A: Yes. If their daddy taught them how to do construction or to build houses, they don't make goals other than that.

(Alice tries to move the conversation away from yet another stereotype—that bikers are lazy—by offering her own observation—that bikers seem to have limited career goals. Both interviewer and informant struggle to understand each other's stereotypes.)

C: And no self-pride in terms of their appearance?

(This is a leading question, and in the end a closed question. Alice has no choice but to answer yes or no. Later in the interview, Cindie asks a descriptive question that prompts Alice to talk about what bikers actually do like to wear.)

A: Yes.

C: And we talked about how they demean women.

(Cindie raises yet another topic based on earlier conversations with Alice and also based on stereotypes of bikers that, in her later interview with Teardrop, proves to be true.)

A: Yes, very much so. That's the biggest thing that they do. It makes them feel stronger and feel like better people. It makes them feel like they are bigger.

Gathering Oral Histories

An oral history is a life's story shared collaboratively with a fieldworker, emphasizing the individual's life against the cultural significance of that life. Cindie Marshall uses her interviews to support her research on the biker subculture. But if she were to do an oral history, she would have interviewed Teardrop in depth to record her whole life's story. Teardrop's role as a biker's companion would be a major part of her oral history, but the emphasis would be on Teardrop. Donna Niday's family story project did not focus on any single sister's whole life. But if Donna were to undertake an oral history, the "baby on the roof" story would become only a minor part of the study of one sister's life as a midwestern farm girl. Paul Russ recorded enough information from five people living with AIDS to write oral histories about each one, but instead his goal was to produce a documentary film.

In an oral history, the fieldworker gathers real-life stories about the past experiences of a particular person, family, region, occupation, craft, skill, or topic. The fieldworker records spoken recollections and personal reflections from living people about their past lives, creating a history. One of the most successful contemporary oral history projects in this country comes from the fieldwork of high school students in rural Georgia. In the 1970s, teenagers in Rabun Gap, Georgia, began to document the stories, folk arts, and crafts of elderly people in their Appalachian community. They wrote about making moonshine, building log cabins, faith healing, dressing hogs, and farming practices in their mountain culture and published their fieldwork in the many *Foxfire* anthologies.

Anthropological fieldworkers who record an entire life's history as well as speculate on the relationship between that life and the culture it represents are called *ethnohistorians*, and their studies span many years. Over 10 years' time, Henry Glassie visited, interviewed, and wrote about one 4-square-mile Irish community in *Passing the Time in Ballymenone*. Shirley Brice Heath, who researched literacy in the Piedmonts of the southeastern United States in her study *Ways with Words*, spent 14 years gathering data from parents, teachers, and children there. Ruth Behar wrote a life history of Esperanza, a Mexican street peddler, in her book *Translated Woman*. Behar traveled back and forth between the United States and Mexico for over five years collecting data and writing about Esperanza.

But not all oral histories need to be full-length ethnographic studies. During the Great Depression in the United States of the 1930s, when writers were among the many unemployed, the government sponsored the Federal Writer's Project, which put writers to work as interviewers. Among them were Claude McKay, Richard Wright, Saul Bellow, Loren Eiseley, and Ralph Ellison. This project's goal was to record the life histories of ordinary American people whose stories had never been told; carpenters, cigar makers, dairy people, seamstresses, peddlers, railroad men, textile workers, salesladies, and chicken farmers were among their informants.

One collection of these life histories, *These Are Our Lives* (1939), assembled for the Federal Writer's Project, includes the life story of Lee Lincoln, an African-American who learns to read and write as an adult. The fieldworker, Jennette Edwards, inserts her own observations and description into the interview while quoting Lee's words directly as she collected them. As you read this piece, remember it was written in 1939, when black Americans were called Negroes, when jobs were difficult to get, and $65 a month was a decent living. You may want to think about other cultural assumptions, attitudes, and beliefs that have changed in the past six decades as you read this piece.

 I Can Read and I Can Write

Jennette Edwards

The Negro houses on Jackson Avenue are strung out like ragged clothes on a wash line. Unpainted. Run down. Lee Lincoln's house—centering the East side of the Seventh block—stands lopsided from added rooms. One room takes care of Lee. Home-made book cases, racks, stands, tables, piled to the limit with books, crowd the room.

"I can read and I can write and I can figure," Lee said. "Every day I am thankful that I had a chance to learn. A man can't get anywheres much these days without schooling."

Lee wore the blue overall uniform of freight packers on the L. & N. railroad. His powerfully built frame tallied with his occupation. Lee pointed out his books with pride. He talked slowly, carefully.

"I'm fifty-three years old, still studying. Still buying books. I have almost five hundred books here on all kinds of subjects. Lots of them I have read from cover to cover."

He took a pair of silver rimmed spectacles from his inside coat pocket and fitted the hooks to his ears.

"My parents didn't have time to fool with schooling for themselves or any of us children. They were sharecroppers. By the time we would get five or six years old, the cotton field got us. I can remember playing about Pappy and Mammy and the older children when they were making the crop and at picking time, wishing I was old enough to help. Before long I was right there slaving too."

Lee pulled a dark oak rocker to a clear space in the center of the matting rug for his visitor. He settled in a straight chair.

"We didn't make much money. Not ever enough to get along easy. But from year to year we'd manage to get by some way. Corn pone, sorghum and sowbelly was the most we had to eat. I didn't mind. I like 'em to this good day. Going to the meeting on Sunday or to some neighborhood shindig at night was the way we had our fun."

Lee took off his glasses and polished the lenses with a clean white cotton handkerchief.

"Mammy died when I was sixteen. Then I pulled out for myself. I worked around for different planters for a couple of years. Then I got a job on the L. & N. Railroad at Memphis trucking outbound freight. It was the best job I had ever had and I was set on not getting fired."

He sighted the glasses for clearness.

"That was the job that learned me a man's got to have schooling to get anywheres. Signboards were posted on the freight cars with the name of the town where the car was to go. You had to know how to read to know what to load up. When the boss would say, 'This truck-load goes to the Nashville car,' I'd ask one of the truckers on the quiet— 'Which one's the Nashville car?' One day the Boss heard me. He called me over, picked up a freight bill. 'Read what that says, Lee,' he said pointing to the words, 'The Louisville & Nashville Railroad.' I was scared stiff. I knew it wasn't any use to give a guess. Mammy and Pappy had learned me that a lie always got you in a fiddle. 'I just don't know, Boss,' I said right out. 'I can't read a line.' "

Lee shifted his weight in the chair. A smile of satisfaction spread over his honest face.

"Next day at noon-time the Boss brought a first reader book and a tablet and a pencil. He commenced to teach me to read and spell. I was mighty tickled when I could tell him what some of the words were. At noon-times while I was eating my lunch and every night I studied. Before long I could read most of the signs that said where the freight went. I learned how to write my name. I learned to copy and read back everything in the primer. My, I was one proud Negro! Boss was tickled, too. I never will forget him. Never. He was the best man I ever knew. I've got a little picture of him. I never have framed it. I got a lady artist to fix it on a card for me and I keep it for a bookmarker."

Lee left his chair and went to the iron bed in the far corner of the room. He pulled back the clean quilt—tucked at the head over the pillows—and found the book with last night's reading place marked. He left the book face down on the quilt and brought back the boss' picture.

"There he is. Fine-looking, don't you think? I never will forget him, because he was so good to me and learned me to read and write. I worked at that freight trucking job until the railroad transferred me to Nashville. That was a big promotion. I was made a regular officer. I had a badge with 'L. & N. Railway Police' on it. I worked all up and down the line on excursion trains and in the Nashville yards. I was about thirty years old then. I knew I never would have gotten that promotion if I hadn't picked up what little education I had. I kept right on. I went to night school two or three terms. For more than two years while I was an officer I got a white man to come to my room two nights a week and teach me. I paid him fifty cents a night and there wasn't a night that I didn't learn more than a dollar's worth. He was real educated and had a lot of patience with me. Pretty soon I could read newspapers good as white people and books too. There were a lot of words I didn't know the sense of, so I got me a dictionary. I paid twenty-two dollars for it."

Lee went to the center table and straightened the scattered newspapers and books. He dusted off the large dictionary for display.

"My teacher told me this was a good one. It is, too. Wish I knew just half the words in it. He was all set on me getting good books. One hour of my lesson he would teach me words and reading and the other hour arithmetic. He would work up all sorts of simple problems he thought I'd have need of in work. He never did just stick to the book. I never will forget the night he told me how to take the carded weight of a carload of coal, figure how many tons and bushels was in the car. Then how much it would bring at so much a ton. Now that was fun. Just as much fun as reading those freight car names. I got so at lunch hour I'd pick out a car of coal in the yard every day, maybe more than one, figure up tons and bushels. He showed me how to figure lumber, too. I planned and figured ever' bit of the lumber for my coal house last fall. Figured it all by myself. I was right proud when my figuring came out just exactly like the lumber man's."

Lee got things on the center table settled to his liking. He rubbed his large hands clean on his pants legs and came back to his chair.

"I know I can read and figure better than I can write. I got to worrying about people not knowing what I meant if I put it down, so I got me a typewriter. They can read my letters now. I am secretary of my union and that typewriter is a big help there. Minutes look nice. Most anything makes a good show when you get it fixed up like print. I use it to make out my rent receipts. This house here I don't use but one room—this one. I pay the whole house rent and sublet all but this room. I've got two families here now. They're good renters, pay on time. The difference in what I pay rent and what I get from them helps me a lot since I lost my good job."

Lee slowly buttoned up the brass buttons of his overall jacket.

"About three years ago I got cut off from the railroad police 'cause I was the only Negro officer left on the system. They put me back to trucking freight, though I mostly packs freight in the cars to go out. I watch for thieving on the platform. I don't get paid for that, just paid for packing freight. They told me I'd have to take this job or nothing as they had to cut expenses. I took it. There were a lot of white men officers that didn't have thirty-two years experience behind 'em like I did. Not easy to pick up a job when you getting along in years—I had to take it. Everything that had been coming in for so long went out sooner than I got it. My wife, now, was one to help a man save. She could have helped. She was a good woman. I spent more'n two thousand dollars on doctor's bills for her. Maybe they eased her some. I don't know. Anyway doctors didn't save her."

Lee rammed his hands deep in his pants pockets.

"Since she died I never have come across a woman I felt like I could trust. We didn't have any children. I never was much on raking up relatives, so I'm going it by myself. I do my own cooking, most of the cleaning too. One of the women that rents does my washing. I had a little saved together from my officer's salary after I got the main of the doctors' bill paid. I had it in a bank. It busted along with the rest of them. The bank got all I had but wages—and those about a fourth of what I got as an officer."

Lee took off his glasses. He unbuttoned the top buttons of his coat and stored them in the inside pocket.

"If I can just keep my job I'll be satisfied. I'd rather work for what I get. There's lots better folks than me out of work now.

"I ain't going to have a preacher telling me I lost my officer's job for some wrong living. I didn't. I don't hold much with churches and less with the preachers. I loaned my preacher twenty-five dollars more'n two years back. I haven't heard a word about it since. If a man lives best he can he'll get along. I'm getting along. You can't do a big lot of things on sixty-five dollars a month but you can live and help a few out besides. A preacher's after my money a sight more than he is my soul."

Lee left his chair and went back to the dictionary. He was silent while he hunted a word.

"I thought so. Not any such word. That Methodist preacher tried to trip me on it last time he came here snooping. I seldom go to church. I do like a good moving picture when I'm not too tired to set. I go to union meeting once a week. I'm secretary."

He closed the dictionary noisily.

"I'd rather get a good case of beer and settle right here with time enough to read on any book I pick up than anything I know of in the world. I remember when I used to have to drink and play poker and shoot craps to make me feel big. I don't now. I don't crave going around a lot like I used to."

This interview is a good example of several techniques for writing up oral histories. The writer begins Lee's story with a simile describing the houses on his street, "strung out like ragged clothes on a wash line." Although the interview begins with Edwards's observations, the story belongs to Lee. The writer strikes an important balance between Lee's voice and her descriptions of his clothing and his mannerisms ("he took off his glasses and polished the lenses with a clean white cotton handkerchief"). Edwards includes details about body language as Lee tells his story ("he dusted the dictionary for display," "he shifted his weight in his chair," "he rubbed his large hands clean on his pants legs and came back to his chair"). The writer retains Lee's language patterns ("That was the job that learned me a man's got to have schooling to get anywheres"), doesn't alter his grammar ("This house here I don't use but one room—this one"), and keeps his colloquial expressions as they were ("A preacher's after my money a sight more than he is my soul.").

Although at first the reader may not understand why the fieldworker chooses the particular details she does, none is extraneous. The details themselves bring Lee's story to life with an emphasis on the artifacts of reading and literacy: glasses, the dictionary, his mentor's picture, and then finally Edwards ends with her own observations as Lee "closes the dictionary noisily." In this oral history, the fieldwriter keeps herself in the background, allowing Lee to remain in the foreground telling his own story.

BOX 22
STARTING AN ORAL HISTORY

Many oral histories today are gathered from ordinary people who have lived through extraordinary times and experiences, as Lee Lincoln did. Contemporary informants can share their life histories and experiences from, for example, the Cultural Revolution in China; the Vietnam, Korean, and Gulf wars; the women's movement; the civil rights movement in the United States; the Holocaust in Europe; the dissembling of the Berlin Wall; or the end of apartheid in South Africa. Other oral histories can record the everyday life of an occupation that no longer exists, like Jack Santino's study of Pullman porters, "Miles of Smiles"; Theodore Rosengarten's life history of Nat Shaw, a black sharecropper; or A. B. Spellman's study of jazz musicians, *Black Music: Four Lives*. Studs Terkel's journalistic oral histories are probably among the best known. His collections of occupational stories, *Working*, and of Depression stories, *In Hard Times*, offer examples of short histories from real people whose voices are seldom heard or recorded.

Possible projects for an oral history are limited only by your imagination and access to the people you wish to interview. Many people begin an oral history by interviewing their relatives, friends, or teachers about living through a particular era or a time of personal struggle that resulted in dramatic life changes. Perhaps you know someone who's lived through a major catastrophe such as an earthquake, a hurricane, a tornado, or a flood or someone who's been caught personally in a social or political entanglement like war, bankruptcy, or discrimination. Such people make good subjects for oral history.

Many local and compelling oral history projects can emerge in unexpected places and on unexpected topics. Think about someone you know who has a particular skill, such as cooking ethnic food, whittling wooden figures, weaving, or embroidering, or an unusual hobby such as clogging, playing the bagpipes, or raising llamas. Or perhaps someone's lifelong passion can yield interesting oral histories—like doll or coin collecting, fly fishing, boar or duck hunting, or a naturalist interest like wildflowers, mushroom hunting, or bird watching. Good subjects for oral histories also hide in places where people spend their time alone, for example, in garages tinkering with engines or in antique shops restoring items others have discarded.

If you're interested in pursuing an oral history project, spend some time interviewing someone who fascinates you. Like any other interviewing project, all of the information you record in your fieldnotes may not be what you'll use in a final write-up, but you'll need to record it nonetheless. As Jennette Edwards used Lee Lincoln's surroundings to support his talk, your choices of details in an oral history will help you feature your subject without distracting the reader from the life story as it is told in informant's own words. An elaborate oral history takes a great deal of time, like many of the other research projects we describe in this book. We hope that what you'll learn by reading and writing oral history is that it's important to foreground the informant and her words and to background the topic, yourself, and her surroundings.

Response

Many wonder but few dare to ask how some people become homeless. Our colleague Steve VanderStaay's book *Street Lives* is a collection of oral histories of homeless Americans. Steve's project was a large one, and as a professional writer, teacher, and researcher, he could devote many years to competing it. For six years, Steve interviewed people across the country, visiting soup kitchens and homeless shelters, city parks and alleys, tape recorder in hand, gathering their stories. He found that many of the homeless wanted to share their stories and welcomed Steve as a listener. In his introduction, Steve claims that many of the narratives he presents "contradict current and accepted notions of homelessness. . . . I learned that our present crisis of homelessness, while fueled by societal trends and forces, is most essentially a personal one: a crisis in the life of someone with hopes, dreams, and a name. Someone we can know" (x).

In the following oral history, a homeless mother, Tanya, shares her gradual life struggle. We meet her in Philadelphia four years after she had been a college student and soon after she had lost her children to the welfare system. In this example of oral history, Steve as the interviewer remains in the background, foregrounding Tanya's story in her own voice. Unlike Edwards's history of Lee Lincoln, Steve separates—in italics—his words from those of his informant.

TANYA

Steve VanderStaay

Philadelphia, Pennsylvania

Tanya is a quiet, gentle woman with soft features and a languid, pensive expression that rarely changes. She speaks slowly, breaking up her narrative with long, motionless pauses. Tanya spends large portions of her day thinking and staring, and remains puzzled and confused about all that has happened to her.

Another portion of Tanya's testimony appears in the chapter "The Homeless Mentally Ill." She is an African American and perhaps 30 years old.

This is not really the first time I've been homeless, but this is the first time I've been homeless since I've had a child. Lots of times they tell me, "You should sell your body. Go over there in that hotel, get fifty dollars overnight." I don't do it, but when people get down and out, see, their mind is like . . . well it's open. Anything somebody got to offer, if you're homeless you're gonna hop on it most of the time.

Jobs is it, I guess, 'cause, the prices these days . . . a one-bedroom apartment is at least $320, and you have to pay your own utilities, such as your gas and electric. And a lot of people out here that are working are not even getting enough to keep up with those bills. You try anyway, you know. You put a little bit on this and a little bit on that, but that's how people end up being homeless. All of a sudden they'll cut the electric off. You'll say, "Oh well, I'm not gonna let that bother me." They cut the gas off: "I won't let that bother me, I'm gettin' in enough income to pay my rent so I'm just gonna pay that."

Then the landlord gonna come out: "I don't want you livin' here, I'm gonna find somebody that's gonna take care of the place." Which they can. And you're out there again, trying to find a place to live.

And then you lose your kids. 'Cause you ain't got a place, or they don't think the way you live is fittin'. Most of the girls here in this shelter, their children have been taken away from them that way. And it leaves them home-less. It leaves you homeless if you have been a mother for so many years and you don't have a work history. Just like the situation I had. When they took my children away from me, that's when it all started.

I was like . . . left alone. I spent the first nights in University City, under an awning. It's part of the University of Pennsylvania, across the street from a big bank. It's a big area; most of the time I was there. Or I would wrap up in a blanket and just, you know, go right off to sleep on a vent. I was hop-ing someone would see me and tell me how to get back on my feet, but it didn't happen.

Then I found a little shelter where you could go during the day. It was for women. Nights you would have to find some place to go. Just by going to the shelter I'd meet people who had an apartment and they would say, "Well, you can stay the night" or "You can stay a couple of days, but I can't let you stay forever." And it just kept going and going and going.

There were a couple of McDonald's and Burger King's and Roy Rogers that would stay open all night and they noticed me. You know, "Oh I seen that girl around a lot this year." And they'd say, "Hey, do you want some-thing to eat?" And I'd say yes and they'd say, "Well here, you can't eat it in here, and don't hang around, don't let people notice that you're, you know, that you're . . . outdoors."

I stayed in subways too. Most of the people stay around 30th Street Station. Or sleep on the street. I mean these days you can just lie down on the sidewalk. As long as you don't look like you fell off somethin' or you're sick nobody'll say anything to ya.

The Informant's Perspective: "An Anthropologist on Mars"

Most field interviews in their final form look smooth and polished, as if nothing had ever gone wrong throughout the process of working with an informant. They make it seem that there have been no fumbling, false starts, missed appointments, or mud-dled communication and that the equipment always worked. Because fieldworking takes a long time, once interviewers and informants establish rapport, the early messiness and hesitations of the relationship fade into the background. Paul Russ admits to his initial discomfort with Jessie, for example, but even his transcripts show a rather smooth interviewing process. When there are troubles with interviewing, most researchers decide not to write about them. But they talk about them a lot. Our favorite interviewer's story comes from the *Foxfire* collection. In this excerpt, a high school student named Paul Gillespie, working alongside his teacher Eliot "Wig" Wigginton, interviews an elderly informant named Aunt Arie at her house in the Appalachian Mountains. Aunt Arie had been interviewed many times; she had been the subject of a *Life* magazine article and much oral history research. But Paul was a novice interviewer, as you will see in this excerpt about students' interviewing experiences. Aunt Arie is 90 years old, and the year is 1963.

CHAPTER FIVE   Researching People: The Collaborative Listener

[W]e walked in on her on Thanksgiving morning. She had her back to the door, and we startled her. There she was trying to carve the eyeballs out of a hog's head. I was almost sick to my stomach, so Wig helped operate on this hog's head while I turned my head and held the microphone of the tape recorder in the general vicinity of the action.

They struggled for at least fifteen minutes, maybe more, and then I witnessed one of the most amazing events of my life. Aunt Arie took an eyeball, went to the back door, and flung it out. When she threw it, the eyeball went up on the tin roof of an adjoining outbuilding, rolled off, snagged on the clothesline, and hung there bobbing like a yo-yo. I had Wig's Pentax, so I took a picture of it, and it appeared in a subsequent issue of the magazine. It was very funny, remarkable (56).

We close this chapter with one fieldworker whose smooth and polished story-telling intrigues us but whose primary work is in medicine. Oliver Sacks describes himself as a "neuroanthropologist in the field," but he is neither an oral historian nor an anthropologist. He's a doctor who specializes in disorders of the nervous system and uses some fieldworking strategies to understand the perspectives of his patients. Rather than examining them in a hospital setting, Sacks visits his patients in their own contexts to explore their lives "as they live in the real world." In fact, in the preface to his bestselling collection of interviews, *An Anthropologist on Mars: Seven Paradoxical Tales*, he describes his fieldwork as "house calls at the far borders of human experience" (xx).

In one interview, he visits Temple Grandin, a woman with autism who, as a professor of animal science at Colorado State University, studies animal behavior. In this interview, Sacks describes autism's neurological issues as "a triad of impairments: of social interaction, of verbal and non-verbal communication, and of play and imaginative activities" (246). A common stereotype is that autistic people have no concept of feelings for others or even for themselves. Autistic children are often bypassed and misunderstood, both in and out of school, and some autistic people spend their lives institutionalized. Sacks wanted to find out about autism from an insider's perspective. He knew that Grandin was unusual because she had successfully integrated herself into society, had written a book about autism, and was professionally recognized in her field. After researching autism from a medical point of view, he realized that he needed a person to give it voice, to create a portrait of the autistic person. Grandin told him that in her daily life, she feels like an outsider, like a researcher from another planet who is constantly studying the culture in which she lives in order to understand it. She provided Sacks with a critical understanding of her autistic world view with the comment, "Much of the time I feel like an anthropologist on Mars."

He arranged to interview Grandin in her office and in her home. Sacks recounts his first meeting with Grandin at the university, detailing her physical features, clothing, body language, and the deviations of her gait and handshake. Sacks shows us, rather than tells us, through selected detail, creating a portrait of Temple Grandin:

I made my way to the university campus and located the Animal Sciences Building, where Temple was waiting to greet me. She is a tall, strongly built woman in her mid-forties; she was wearing jeans, a knit shirt, western boots, her habitual dress. Her clothing, her appearance, her manner, were plain, frank, and forthright; I had the distinct impression of a sturdy, no-nonsense cattlewoman, with an indifference to social conventions, appearance, or ornament, an absence of frills, an absolute directness of manner and mind. When she raised her arm in greeting, the arm went too high, seemed to get caught for a moment in a sort of spasm or fixed posture—a hint, an echo, of the stereotypies she once had. Then she gave me a strong handshake and led the way down to her office. [Her gait seemed to me slightly clumsy or uncouth, as is often the case with autistic adults. Temple attributes this to a simple ataxia associated with impaired development of the vestibular system and part of the cerebellum. Later I did a brief neurological exam, focusing on her cerebellar function and balance; I did indeed find a little ataxia, but insufficient, I thought, to explain her odd gait.] (256).

In a later section of his article, Sacks visits Grandin at her house. Notice that each of the details he offers is like a puzzle piece, fitting one item at a time into this description. Sacks depicts her range of interests at her home by describing her collection of identification badges and caps from hundreds of conferences, contrasting those, for example, from the American Psychiatric Association and the American Meat Institute. When he looks in her bedroom and finds the "squeeze machine," he doesn't only rely on her description or on her 20-minute demonstration of the machine. Sacks actually enters Grandin's invention, lies in it, and experiences the sensations she designed it to provide.

 An Anthropologist on Mars
Oliver Sacks

Early the next morning, a Saturday, Temple picked me up in her four-wheel-drive, a rugged vehicle she drives all over the West to visit farms, ranches, corrals, and meat plants. As we headed for her house, I quizzed her about the work she had done for her Ph.D.; her thesis was on the effects of enriched and impoverished environments on the development of pigs' brains. She told me about the great differences that developed between the two groups—how sociable and delightful the "enriched" pigs became, how hyperexcitable and aggressive (and almost "autistic") the "impoverished" ones were by contrast. (She wondered whether impoverishment of experience was not a contributing factor in human autism.) "I got to love my enriched pigs," she said. "I was very attached. I was so attached I couldn't kill them." The animals had to be sacrificed at the end of the experiment so their brains could be examined. She described how the pigs, at the end, trusting her, let her lead them on their last walk, and how she had calmed them, by stroking them and talking to them, while they were killed. She was very distressed at their deaths—"I wept and wept."

She had just finished the story when we arrived at her home—a small two-story town house, some distance from the campus. Downstairs was comfortable, with the usual amenities—a sofa, armchairs, a television, pictures on the wall—but I had the sense that it was rarely used. There was an immense sepia print of her grandfather's farm in Grandin, North Dakota, in 1880; her other grandfather, she told me, had invented the automatic pilot for planes. These two were the progenitors, she feels, of her agricultural and engineering talents. Upstairs was her study, with her typewriter (but no word processor), absolutely bursting with manuscripts and books—books everywhere, spilling out of the study into every room in the house. (My own little house was once described as "a machine for working," and I had a somewhat similar impression of Temple's.) On one wall was a large cowhide with a huge collection of identity badges and caps, from the hundreds of conferences she has lectured at. I was amused to see, side by side, an I.D. from the American Meat Institute and one from the American Psychiatric Association. Temple has published more than a hundred papers, divided between those on animal behavior and facilities management and those on autism. The intimate blending of the two was epitomized by the medley of badges side by side.

Finally, without diffidence or embarrassment (emotions unknown to her), Temple showed me her bedroom, an austere room with whitewashed walls and a single bed and, next to the bed, a very large, strange-looking object. "What is that?" I asked.

"That's my squeeze machine," Temple replied. "Some people call it my hug machine."

The device had two heavy, slanting wooden sides, perhaps four by three feet each, pleasantly upholstered with a thick, soft padding. They were joined by hinges to a long, narrow bottom board to create a V-shaped, body-sized trough. There was a complex control box at one end, with heavy-duty tubes leading off to another device, in a closet. Temple showed me this as well. "It's an industrial compressor," she said, "the kind they use for filling tires."

"And what does this do?"

"It exerts a firm but comfortable pressure on the body, from the shoulders to the knees," Temple said. "Either a steady pressure or a variable one or a pulsating one, as you wish," she added. "You crawl into it—I'll show you—and turn the compressor on, and you have all the controls in your hand, here, right in front of you."

When I asked her why one should seek to submit oneself to such pressure, she told me. When she was a little girl, she said, she had longed to be hugged but had at the same time been terrified of all contact. When she was hugged, especially by a favorite (but vast) aunt, she felt overwhelmed, overcome by sensation; she had a sense of peacefulness and pleasure, but also of terror and engulfment. She started to have daydreams—she was just five at the time—of a magic machine that could squeeze her powerfully but gently, in a huglike way, and in a way entirely commanded and controlled by her. Years later, as an adolescent, she had seen a picture of a squeeze chute designed to hold or restrain calves and realized that that was it: a little modification to make it suitable for human use, and it could be her magic machine. She had considered other devices—inflatable suits, which could exert an even pressure all over the body—but the squeeze chute, in its simplicity, was quite irresistible.

Being of a practical turn of mind, she soon made her fantasy come true. The early models were crude, with some snags and glitches, but she eventually evolved a totally comfortable, predictable system, capable of administering a "hug" with whatever parameters she desired. Her squeeze machine had worked exactly as she hoped, yielding the very sense of calmness and pleasure she had dreamed of since childhood. She could not have gone through the stormy days of college without her squeeze machine, she said. She could not turn to human beings for solace and comfort, but she could always turn to it. The machine, which she neither exhibited nor concealed but kept openly in her room at college, excited derision and suspicion and was seen by psychiatrists as a "regression" or "fixation"—something that needed to be psychoanalyzed and resolved. With her characteristic stubbornness, tenacity, single-mindedness, and bravery—along with a complete absence of inhibition or hesitation—Temple ignored all these comments and reactions and determined to find a scientific "validation" of her feelings.

Both before and after writing her doctoral thesis, she made a systematic investigation of the effects of deep pressure in autistic people, college students, and animals, and recently a paper of hers on this was published in the *Journal of Child and Adolescent Psychopharmacology*. Today, her squeeze machine, variously modified, is receiving extensive clinical trials. She has also become the world's foremost designer of squeeze chutes for cattle and has published, in the meat-industry and veterinary literature, many articles on the theory and practice of humane restraint and gentle holding.

While telling me this, Temple knelt down, then eased herself, facedown and at full length, into the "V," turned on the compressor (it took a minute for the master cylinder to fill), and twisted the controls. The sides converged, clasping her firmly, and then, as she made a small adjustment, relaxed their grip slightly. It was the most bizarre thing I had ever seen, and yet, for all its oddness, it was moving and simple. Certainly there was no doubt of its effect. Temple's voice, often loud and hard, became softer and gentler as she lay in her machine. "I concentrate on how gently I can do it," she said, and then spoke of the necessity of "totally giving in to it . . . I'm getting real relaxed now," she added quietly. "I guess others get this through relation with other people."

It is not just pleasure or relaxation that Temple gets from the machine but, she maintains, a feeling for others. As she lies in her machine, she says, her thoughts often turn to her mother, her favorite aunt, her teachers. She feels their love for her, and hers for them. She feels that the machine opens a door into an otherwise closed emotional world and allows her, almost teaches her, to feel empathy for others.

After twenty minutes or so, she emerged, visibly calmer, emotionally less rigid (she says that a cat can easily sense the difference in her at these times), and asked me if I would care to try the machine.

Indeed, I was curious and scrambled into it, feeling a little foolish and self-conscious—but less so than I might have been, because Temple herself was so wholly lacking in self-consciousness. She turned the compressor on again and filled the master cylinder, and I experimented gingerly with the controls. It was indeed a sweet, calming feeling—one that reminded me of my deep-diving days long ago, when I felt the pressure of the water on my diving suit as a whole-body embrace.

The Research Portfolio: Documentation

Whether you've chosen to learn to research people by continuing your major field-work project or by trying separate short studies, we hope you've seen that the researcher-informant relationship is a symbiotic one. It is full of interaction, collaboration, and mutual teaching and learning. In this chapter, people are a dominant source of data in the field—through family stories, remembered histories, responses to questions, the personal artifacts they consider important, and your own observation of them. You've exercised the skills of gathering and analyzing family stories and oral histories, and you've conducted some interviews and transcript analysis.

We wanted the readings to illustrate that people, when we research them with their cooperation, teach us much about their cultures. With the professional readings, you met Judith Ortiz Cofer's Puerto Rican New Yorker relatives, Maxine Hong

Kingston's No Name Woman, Jennette Edwards's Lee Lincoln in 1939, Steve VanderStaay's Tanya, the homeless mother, and Oliver Sacks's Temple Grandin, the autistic scientist who feels like an anthropologist on Mars. Our own and our students' work offered more readings: Cheri Krcelic's and Elizabeth's family stories of their parents' courtship, Donna Niday's five Riggs girls' "baby on the roof" stories, Paul Russ's Jessie, who was living with AIDs, EunJoo Kang's investigation of Ming-Chi Own's wristwatch, and Cindie Marshall's journey into the culture of Ralph's biker bar.

The research portfolio is an important place to record, keep track of, and make sense of the skills you've learned, the routines and organization you've used, and your responses to readings that illustrate how other fieldworkers have written about their work. Listing and categorizing your research processes illustrates your progress as a fieldworker. We like to call this charting process "reflective documentation." Just as we reviewed Cindie Marshall's research process in the completed version of "Ralph's Sports Bar," you might review and document your fieldworking skills at this point in your project. This chapter's portfolio suggestions focus on documentation of your research skills and not on the actual stories, oral histories, and interviews you've collected, the products of your research process.

For your portfolio, try listing, mapping, outlining, or charting the skills you've learned and the variety and amounts of material you've gathered. You may want to document each of your projects from this chapter separately: family stories, oral histories, and interviews. Or if you are working on a large project, use the questions to document what is relevant in your project. Here is an outline, framed around the same categories as our summary of Cindie's work. You might choose a few questions under each category, try to work with them all, or document your work in a different way.

I. Prepare for the field
   A. What did you read to prepare for your fieldwork? Where did you find it?
   B. What did you learn from reading the fieldwork of others?
   C. How did you select your informants? How did you prepare before meeting them?
   D. How did you gain access to your informants and your field sites? Were there any problems? What might you do next time?
   E. What assumptions did you have going into the field? How did you record them? What did you expect to see, and what did you actually find?

II. Use the researcher's tools
   A. How did you record your fieldnotes? Did you separate observation notes from personal notes? Did you invent your own method for organizing your fieldnotes?
   B. What equipment did you use? What would you want if you could do this work again?
   C. How did you transcribe your tape recordings?
   D. What interviewing skills did you develop? What skills would you like to work on?

E. What different types of data did you gather? Print sources? Cultural artifacts? Stories and interviews?

III. Interpret the fieldwork

A. Which initial impressions turned out to be part of your final piece? Which ideas did you discard?

B. What strategies did you develop to categorize your data? Did you use patterns that were linear? Thematic? Chronological? Abstract to concrete? Concrete to abstract?

C. What strategies did you develop to analyze your data? What didn't fit?

D. What is your favorite piece of data—or data source—and why?

IV. Present the findings

A. What decisions did you make about writing up your fieldwork?

B. How much of your voice is in the final project? How much of your informants' voices?

C. What details did you select to illustrate key points so as to bring your informant to life?

D. Did you use subheadings to guide your reader in your final paper or some other way to organize your material?

You might decide to use these questions to help you write an essay or commentary about your process as a researcher.

FieldWriting: From Details to Verbal Portraiture

To bring an informant to the page from a pile of data, fieldwriters must pay close attention to informants' personal characteristics, surroundings, and the overall themes they want to highlight. Creating verbal portraits means studying your fieldnotes, selecting your most relevant details, and drafting sentences that portray the informant against a cultural backdrop. In this chapter, the fieldwriters who gave us portraits—Jennette Edwards, Steve VanderStaay, Paul Russ, Oliver Sacks—wrote them on the basis of carefully gathered observations from their fieldnotes and other sources and their own interpretations confirmed by their data.

DETAILS OF CHARACTER

Choosing the details to describe an interview with an informant is hard work. Fieldwriters must gather and record far more information than they will ever use because during data collection, they won't yet know the themes they'll eventually want to highlight. Written portraits of an informant require noting the same kinds of details that fiction writers use: physical features, material artifacts, body language, oral language patterns, and personal history. But those details are borne in fieldnotes, interviews, artifacts, and documents. Cindie's fieldnotes about Teardrop provided the details she needed to create her verbal portrait. Some of them follow.

- *Physical features*: vine-shaped tattoo around wrist; brown hair with gray, neatly pulled back, teased and sprayed bangs; top and bottom front teeth missing; small black spot under left eye, high on cheek
- *Material artifacts*: new Lee jeans, pale yellow sweater, heart-shaped brooch, wristwatch
- *Body language*: sitting alone drinking beer, shooting pool
- *Personal history*: goes to Ralph's every day, moved from Michigan three years ago, kidnapped by bikers at 13 and sold from biker to biker for years

From her list of these specific character details, Cindie created a tightly written portrait of Teardrop, and she tried not to interject her own judgments. She presents the descriptions of the most startling details—Teardrop's missing teeth and her tattoos—without judgmental qualifiers. Those details affect the reader because she presents them without value statements. In spite of these attempts, she was probably unaware, as we all are, that she did interpret a few details with qualifiers. Here are three examples of adverbs and adjectives that reflect Cindie's assumptions: a "nice" pale yellow sweater, "carefully sprayed" and "neatly pulled back" hair. To write verbal portraiture, fieldwriters must know their fieldnotes so well that they'll select the ones that most reveal a character—like Teardrop's tattoo, which Cindie at first mistook for a mole or a birthmark. Here is an excerpt from Cindie's description of Teardrop; the character details that help her create her portrait are in italics:

> When I arrived at the table, there was a woman *sitting alone*, drinking a beer. . . . I introduced myself, and she said her *name was Teardrop*. It was dark outside, so I couldn't see her very well. We talked about the weather for a few minutes, and that led her to tell me that she had *moved here from Michigan* three years ago and that *she came to Ralph's every day*. . . .
>
> Once we were inside, I saw that Teardrop was wearing *new Lee jeans*, a *nice pale yellow sweater*, and a *heart-shaped brooch*. Her *hair was brown* but was showing *signs of graying*. She had it *neatly pulled back*, and her *bangs were teased* and *carefully sprayed* in place. It wasn't until she laughed that I noticed she was *missing her front teeth, both top and bottom*. She had a *small tattoo* around her wrist that served as a bracelet. It was *dark green* and was in the *shape of a vine*. Most of the tattoo was covered by the *watch* she was wearing.
>
> As we *played pool*, I noticed something else. She had a very *small black spot* under her left eye, high on her cheek. At first I thought it was a birthmark. But after looking at it carefully, I noticed that it was a *black tattoo in the shape of a teardrop*. I asked her if it was a teardrop and she said yes; that was *how she got her name*.

DETAILS OF SETTING

When fieldwriters paint verbal portraits, they also create a backdrop for their informants. In Chapter 3, we discussed how writers present landscapes or what we called "verbal snapshots." In addition to her portrait of Teardrop, Cindie creates a cultural backdrop for the other patrons at Ralph's Sports Bar using her fieldnote observations. As we showed in Chapter 3 with Myerhoff's details of the Senior Center, Glassie's details of the Irish landscape, and Karen's description of the Photo Phantasies store, setting details must be organized from notes about time, place, weather, color, and other sensory impressions at the field site.

To bring her reader into Ralph's, Cindie moves from exterior to interior. She selects details of texture and space to represent Ralph's Sports Bar outside, focusing first on the half-paved half-graveled parking lot with Harleys "meticulously aligned, handlebar to handlebar, back tire to back tire." She zooms in on a large exterior sign that announces "Urinate inside, not out here."

As she moves inside, she describes tastes and smells in an atmosphere of smoke, stale beer, cigarette ashes, and body odor. And Cindie also listens to the sounds of Ozzie Osborne's "No More Tears" screaming from the jukebox, a detail with special significance that supports the "teardrop" theme. She chooses among much visual data to represent the biker subculture: four pool tables, McDonald's plastic booths, neon Budweiser signs, and black velvet paintings of dogs playing pool. But her major interior visual focus is on the printed signs in the bar that give her clues to insiders' shared values: "Break a cue, pay $25.00 or be barred" is not a gentle sign. "We do not buy stolen merchandise" may imply that they do. The handwritten sign on each poker machine smacks of irony: "No gambling allowed." And Cindie's selection of details to present an image of Ralph's, a so-called sports bar, defies her earlier assumptions about such bars, "full of white-collar professionals, a big-screen TV, and a line of high-dollar sports cars parked outside."

DETAILS OF THEME

As you write your informants into your text, you might draw on an important metaphor or theme buried in your notes about the place or the person. Like the houses on Lee's street "strung out like ragged clothes on a wash line," which offers a contrast to the literate man who lives inside, or Temple Grandin's squeeze machine, which she invents to comfort her animals and also herself, fieldwriters must choose details to support the themes they want to highlight. One artifact might uncover an important theme, as EunJoo's focus on Ming-Chi's watch began a discussion of cultural differences about time or the dog hairs in Paul Russ's car that got Jessie talking about his fears about his dog Princess. Lee Lincoln's story about learning to read was enhanced by the writer Edwards' decision to describe his glasses, the dictionary he paid for, and his book collection. And Steve VanderStaay's portrait of Tanya highlighted her descriptions of temporary housing: shelters, temporary apartments, sidewalks, and outdoor sleeping spaces.

In fieldworking, themes don't emerge directly from lists in fieldnotes, words in transcripts, or library books and collected artifacts, but such sources suggest them. Themes *do come* from active interpretation of your data, as you study it, triangulate it, organize it, reflect on it, and write about it. Themes are bigger than the actual details you record, but those details, as they cluster into categories of data and images from your observations, generate larger interpretations.

For example, in her study of Ralph's Sports Bar, Cindie's themes work off of the contrasts she observed within the subculture in the biker bar. She arrives at Ralph's with a mental image of what a sports bar was like, and immediately that image contrasts with the reality of this biker sports bar. She is greeted by the sign "Urinate inside, not out here" and realizes that the sports here are limited to playing pool and biking. As she spends more time and takes more notes, Cindie sees other contrasting themes within this subculture.

Another set of contrasting themes is that of bikers as a community of independent people who "do their own thing," but Cindie sees that within this subculture, they come together only to be separated: "I also wanted to know why three groups in a bar would come together in a place just to be segregated." Cindie interprets still another contrast when she notices that the biking subculture includes many women. Her fieldnotes report 13 people at the bar, 8 men and 5 women. But this inclusion is deceptive when her informant Teardrop describes her life as a biker woman: "What Teardrop had described was sheer abuse, and she wore that abuse both on her face, in the shape of a teardrop, and in her smile, which was darkened by missing teeth."

Fieldwriting is a skill that requires close observation, careful documentation, and the rendering of data into what anthropologist Clifford Geertz calls "thick descriptions" of informants within their cultural spaces. To be an accurate and sensitive fieldwriter, you'll need to manipulate your multiple data sources, call on your informants' voices, examine your reflective writing, and craft a text so that it will give your reader a sense of participating in the fieldwork you've experienced.

FieldWords

Archives: Public records belonging to a community; also, the place where such records are stored.

Dialect: A regional variation in language, such as English spoken in Tidewater Virginia, Downeast Maine, or South Texas.

Ethnohistorian: A trained ethnographer who conducts oral and life histories.

Family stories: Narratives shared in extended families about other family members that convey messages about acceptable behaviors, rules of conduct, or shared values.

Oral history: Real-life stories recorded about the past, gathered from living people about their experiences, crafts, skills, or occupations.

Rapport: A feeling of connection and trust established between people.

Reciprocity: Giving back, a mutual exchange of favors and rights. In fieldwork, it is important to give something to the informant in exchange for time spent.

Triangulation: The process of verifying data using multiple sources of information. In spite of the prefix indicating "three," triangulation does not mean simply obtaining three pieces of evidence or three perspectives. Researchers use the term to discuss ways in which data is validated, cross-checked, or disconfirmed.

FieldReading

Behar, Ruth. *Translated Woman: Crossing the Border with Esperanza's Story.* Boston: Beacon, 1993.

Cofer, Judith Ortiz. "A Partial Remembrance of a Puerto Rican Childhood." *Silent Dancing*. Houston: Arte Publico Press, 1990.

Geertz, Clifford. "Thick Description: Toward an Interpretive Theory of Culture." *The Interpretation of Cultures*. New York: Basic, 1973.

Gillespie, Paul in *Foxfire: 25 Years*. Wigginton, Eliot et al., Eds. New York: Doubleday, 1991.

Glassie, Henry. *Passing the Time in Ballymenone: Culture and History of an Ulster Community*. Philadelphia: U Pennsylvania P, 1982.

Heath, Shirley Brice. *Ways with Words: Language, Life, and Work in Communities and Classrooms*. Cambridge: Cambridge UP, 1983.

Humphries, R. R., Ed. *These Are Our Lives*. Durham: U North Carolina, 1939.

Kingston, Maxine Hong. *The Woman Warrior: Memoirs of a Girlhood among Ghosts*. New York: Vintage, 1977.

Rosengarten, Theodore. *All God's Dangers and the Life of Nat Shaw*. New York: Harper, 1966.

Russ, Paul. *Healing without a Cure: Stories of People Living with AIDS*. Film. 1994.

Sacks, Oliver. *An Anthropologist on Mars: Seven Paradoxical Tales*. New York: Knopf, 1995.

Santino, Jack. "Miles of Smiles, Years of Struggle: The Negotiation of Black Occupational Identity through Personal Experience Narrative." *Journal of American Folklore* 96 (1983): 393–410.

Shostak, Marjorie. *The Life and Works of a !Kung Woman*. New York: Vintage, 1981.

Spellman, A. B. *Black Music: Four Lives*. New York: Shocken, 1970.

Stone, Elizabeth. *Black Sheep and Kissing Cousins: How Our Family Stories Shape Us*. New York: Times Books, 1988.

Terkel, Studs. *In Hard Times: An Oral History of the Great Depression*. New York: Pantheon, 1970.

Terkel, Studs. *Working: People Talk about What They Do All Day and How They Feel about What They Do*. New York: Pantheon, 1974.

VanderStaay, Steve. *Street Lives: An Oral History of Homeless Americans*. Philadelphia: New Society, 1992.

FieldWriting: From Talk to Text

The fieldworker must choose, shape, prune, discard this and collect finer detail on that, much as a novelist works who finds some minor character is threatening to swallow the major theme, or that the hero is fast talking himself out of his depth. But unlike the novelist . . . the fieldworker is wholly and helplessly dependent on what happens. . . . One must be continually prepared for anything, everything—and perhaps most devastating—for nothing.

Margaret Mead

This book is about conducting fieldwork, but we hope you've noticed that it's also very much about fieldwriting—transforming words and images from talk to text. The writing process of a fieldworker, as anthropologist Margaret Mead describes in the quotation, is something like that of a novelist. The fieldworker must "choose, shape, prune, discard and collect" material—or data. Mead, whose fieldwork reached both scholarly and popular audiences, knew how to write for both. Her research on Samoan family life informed not only her professional colleagues but also the readers of *Redbook, Parents, The Nation*, and other magazines—as well as the viewers of early TV talk shows. She learned how to translate the reality of her distant field experiences to her home culture in the United States in an inviting and accessible way. This is what you'll want to do, too, as you re-create the conversations and experiences of your fieldwork into writing for an audience.

The business of writing up fieldwork has always been a controversial part of anthropological research. Like Mead, fieldworkers have often compared their task to other kinds of writing—drama, poetry, nonfiction, and fiction. In Chapter 1, for instance, we introduced Hortense Powdermaker's comparison between fieldwriting and fiction:

> The novelist and the playwright, as well as the anthropologist, write out of their immersion and participation in a particular situation from which they have been able to detach themselves. But they write of the particular. . . . [T]he particular illuminates the human condition (296).

And today, perhaps more than ever before, anthropologists pay close attention to how language shapes and influences their work. The fieldworker, Mead reminds us, invents neither informants nor descriptions of their cultural spaces. Rather, as Mead observed decades ago, you as a fieldworker are "helplessly dependent" on the reality of what takes place in the field—both as you see it and as your informants see it. Representing reality depends on how a fieldworker uses language to describe "what's going on."

In conversations with our informants, we make a contract to try to understand them and represent their ideas in writing as they've been presented to us. And as in any negotiation, the ability to understand and interpret the point of view and situation of an "other" depends on both participants. It also depends on how deeply our informants allow us to understand their worldviews and on how well we participate and listen. The special ethics of fieldwriting demand that we respect our informants' worldviews and voices. At the same time, we must respect and represent ourselves as narrators, as fieldworkers telling a story about an "other." This critical issue—representation of self and other—marks the difference between fiction and fieldwriting.

So fieldwork is not just about *what* you write but also about *how* you write it. This final chapter will link fieldworkers' writing with the theories and practices of composition studies. Much of college work, for students and instructors, requires the fieldworker's lenses—for reading and for writing. Every day, we step into languages and step out of our own, and hundreds of others'. Many of us spend much time with other people's words. We read, respond, confer, and analyze layers of talk and text that our peers and our mentors produce. Then we analyze those layers of talk and text and write about them again.

We'd like to share some examples from our lives as composition instructors who've also done a lot of fieldwriting. Elizabeth studied the invented reading strategies of kindergarten children in research called "Reading to Mr. Bear" (a children's book club bought this article and marketed it with a stuffed red bear). She's worked with university faculty in engineering, life sciences, forestry, nursing, and occupational therapy to help them create writing assignments and curricula for their students. And she followed middle schoolers through their daily routines to understand what it meant to "do school" from their perspective.

Bonnie studied college freshmen as they wrote science papers and considered how they drafted and revised using metaphors: a two-way road to understand the spinal column, for example, a platoon of soldiers to describe tonsils, and many more. She assisted high-tech employees and executives as they crafted both business reports and science fiction stories and guided older women as they recalled and wrote memories of childhood writing and reading. Bonnie analyzed the classroom behavior of disabled children, her own included, whose school language worksheets prevented them from sharing their thoughts in words. And she researched the "literary canon" with senior English majors as they wrote about their college reading. Between us, we've had thousands of writing conferences with students and watched the process of drafts growing and becoming polished papers. It's a satisying job to work constantly with language, with both the talk and text of others.

Throughout *FieldWorking*, we've leaned on our own backgrounds as composition teachers to emphasize the fieldwork process. But in this chapter, we'll switch the focus and emphasize the composing part of fieldwork. From our own field studies and our years of teaching writing, we've learned that writing and research are intimately related. What's in the background and what's in the foreground—the writing or the research—constantly shifts as we work. Part of the discipline of fieldwork is inherent in the process of creating a text; as our New Hampshire colleague Thomas Newkirk says, "The scholarship is in the *rendering*." And so the fieldworker writes.

As we devote this chapter explicitly to the writing part of fieldworking, we'll draw on some of the composition scholars whose ideas have most influenced ours. We want to share with you a few of the people in our own intellectual kinship of composition studies, the discipline that shapes the direction of most freshman English programs. It's important, we believe, for fieldworkers to identify the people whose ideas inform their own thoughts and practices and make up the subculture that guides their writing. We discover much about ourselves—and the ways we look at our data—when we are able to acknowledge such kinships, even those that exist only on the page.

No matter how you've used this book so far, you've accumulated a stack of fieldwriting: fieldnotes or journal entries, short observations and descriptions, transcribed interviews, responses to readings, and reflections on your research process. You're probably ready now to transform your stack of data into a polished ethnographic essay that you'll shape for a reader. But from our own experience we know that even when you're prepared to begin writing, there are myriad and insidious ways to avoid it—from the beginning of the fieldworking process to the end. One of Bonnie's colleagues spent most of a year vacuuming when she should have been writing. Others iron, hang out, cook, swim, jog, sharpen pencils, spend hours on the Internet—anything but write. While we wrote this book, in fact, we ate candy, made coffee, talked to our families on the phone, and took long walks on the days we couldn't put our thoughts to words. It took over three years to write this book. Writing is not easy for any writer.

Even professional writers procrastinate. Our colleague Don Murray has spent time gathering quotes from writers about their writing processes and habits and describing his own writing processes to students and teachers. In his book *Shoptalk: Learning to Write with Writers*, Murray writes: "The single quality that distinguishes the unpublished writer from the published is not talent but work habits. . . . Many times I think everything is wrong, it will be impossible to write, and yet when I whip myself to my writing, the writing goes well" (43). Here are a few of our favorites about the stubborn stage when the talk must begin to turn to text and notes into a coherent paper:

Woody Allen: "If you work only three to five hours a day, you become quite productive. It's the steadiness that counts" (46).

Isaac Asimov: "Rituals? Ridiculous! My only ritual is to sit close enough to the typewriter so that my fingers touch the keys" (47).

Annie Dillard: "Writing . . . is like rearing children—willpower has very little to do with it. If you have a little baby crying in the middle of the night, and if you depend only on willpower to get you out of bed to feed the baby, that baby will starve. You do it out of love" (50).

Madeline L'Engle: "Inspiration usually comes during work, rather than before it" (57).

John McPhee: "After college, I sat all day in a captain's chair up on 84th Street trying to write plays for live television. Each morning I would thread my bathrobe sash thought the spokes of the chair and tie myself in" (58).

Planning and Unplanning: From Hanging Out to Informal Writing

At the outset of your fieldwork, you may have questioned the importance of writing. Why not just hang out, observe, and listen to others? Why take notes at all? Why can't a good fieldworker just be a participant-observer? A person who can scope out a place, schmooze with others, and make witty or astute observations about whatever new group of people she happens to meet? Why not just develop your observational powers by sitting around, watching people and places?

Why? Because the difference between doing fieldwork and just "hanging out" is the *writing*. Without writing, all of the sharp, incisive details about people, places, and cultures are lost to us. The overheard conversation, the aftereffect of an image, or the undertone of an encounter dissipate without writing about it. Without writing, it's just hanging out. The fieldworker turns hanging out into a scholarly art form.

One of our own projects began with just hanging out, sitting in Elizabeth's stuffy gray Caravan. It was a casual conversation after celebrating a colleague's graduation, late on a humid summer night. Bonnie was collecting data about teachers in a summer writing program in which Elizabeth was teaching. Worried about her research, Bonnie whined, "I'm not seeing anything interesting. I just don't know what to focus on, and I'm taking notes on everything. It feels like nothing. I'm not getting any sleep, and it's taking up all my time."

Elizabeth reassured her. "You're taking fieldnotes, right? All data is something. Tell me what you're seeing." Giving Bonnie no chance to answer, Elizabeth changed the subject. "Hey, how are those deaf teachers doing in Terry's class? Did the interpreters show up today?" Our colleague Terry Moher was teaching a class of high school teachers, three of whom were deaf and taught at an urban high school for the deaf.

"Oh, yeah, they're there. And it's really neat to watch the interpreters—their movements are so expressive. Sort of like dancers. Wish I understood what they're doing. Terry was rattled at first—too many extra people in the class—me as researcher and two interpreters at all times. She's got twenty-seven high school teachers in that group now, and she's really enjoying them. But I'm not studying the deaf teachers anyway. Or their interpreters. It just wasn't in my plan."

Ignoring Bonnie's plan, Elizabeth suggested, "So if you want to understand them, why don't you interview them? Why don't you pay more attention to what's happening with the deaf teachers? Do they have a chance to talk about their deaf students? These teachers probably have something important to teach us about literacy."

Bonnie listened, still wanting to follow her "plan." But she was eager to talk through her anxiety with her friend. Elizabeth continued, "You know, I've always stayed away from deaf people. I've been 'hard of hearing' all my life and I'm afraid as I get older, I'll become even more deaf than I already am. Wearing a hearing aid hasn't made me any more sympathetic. But I've really become interested after watching the interpreters at the poetry reading yesterday. How is sign language a language? What kind of translation processes do the interpreters go through?"

Elizabeth was really talking to herself, but it made Bonnie think about those three teachers who had not been in her original plans for interviewing. Aloud she replied, "Well, maybe I should take some more notes on them. We're staying in the same dorm, and last night they bought a dozen donuts and we ate them in the lounge. They all read lips, just like you do sometimes." This brief talk was the beginning of a theme that emerged in Bonnie's research and eventually became part of her full-length study of the writing program that summer. The conversation about the deaf continued throughout the summer in both planned and unplanned ways. Talking to Elizabeth helped Bonnie clarify what she was learning about the culture of the deaf.

All researchers need collaborative partners, people with whom to share their research plans and talk through the next stage of their projects. All fieldworkers need to invite an interested "other" to help question and talk through their thinking. At different places in this book, especially in the boxes and the Research Portfolio sections, we've indicated different ways to use talk to clarify, expand, and reflect on fieldwork projects:

- Portfolio partners: to talk over fieldnotes, transcripts, other data
- Small groups: to share drafts in progress, portfolios as they illustrate your processes
- Artifact exchanges: to understand the cultural objects gathered from the research site
- Paired reading responses: to exchange ideas about readings and background research
- Collaborative exercises: to learn with another fieldworker about the research process

Conversation, even casual talk, has power. Talk generates both further thinking and further text. At the beginning of her project, Bonnie's collaborative conversation with Elizabeth took her off course into surprising but important new directions. When we discuss our plans with an "other," we can hear the "self" aloud—which is a different process than thinking alone. Often informal conversation encourages us to stretch, shift, or refashion our plans. Even if we make no changes at all, talk clarifies as we shape our thoughts into words for another person.

And writing holds the same generative power as talk. We agree with writer E. M. Forster's comment, "How do I know what I think until I see what I say?" (Murray *Shoptalk*, 101) Language, unarticulated but felt, turns into words and ideas as it moves from mind to page. Pencils, pens, paper, and word processors are tools for making meaning out of the chaos of our thoughts. In the field of composition studies, much attention has been given to the writing activities that precede formal drafting: freewriting, journal writing, double-entry notebooks, mapping, brainstorming.

At different points in this book, we've suggested that you write to find out where you are in the fieldworking process and where your project is going. Portfolio reflections, for example, ask that you stop and review what you've collected and write about what the whole collection means—periodically, while you continue to shape your research and your writing. Most fieldworkers find that this kind of writing loosens them up and makes them more aware of their research choices. Freewriting is a kind of uninhibited doodling with words, and it is helpful for blocked writers who sometimes have trouble getting started. Peter Elbow, a scholar of composition, writes extensively and powerfully about the potential of freewriting as a way of "priming the pump." We present his chapter about freewriting here.

 Freewriting

Peter Elbow

Freewriting is the easiest way to get words on paper and the best all-around practice in writing that I know. To do a freewriting exercise, simply force yourself to write without stopping for ten minutes. Sometimes you will produce good writing, but that's not the goal. Sometimes you will produce garbage, but that's not the goal either. You may stay on one topic, you may flip repeatedly from one to another: it doesn't matter. Sometimes you will produce a good record of your stream of consciousness, but often you can't keep up. Speed is not the goal, though sometimes the process revs you up. If you can't think of anything to write, write about how that feels or repeat over and over "I have nothing to write" or "Nonsense" or "No." If you get stuck in the middle of a sentence or thought, just repeat the last word or phrase till something comes along. The only point is to keep writing.

Or rather, that's the first point. For there are lots of goals of freewriting, but they are best served if, while you are doing it, you accept this single, simple, mechanical goal of simply not stopping. When you produce an exciting piece of writing, it doesn't mean you did it better than the time before when you wrote one sentence over and over for ten minutes. Both times you freewrote perfectly. The goal of freewriting is in the process, not the product.

Here is an example of freewriting—this one done in a group led by an experienced writer but not a writing teacher:

> The second class of no teacher and I'm finding it hard to see how anything will come of it without someone who *knows* something being here. I really mean who knows *some*thing about writing. I know a little about writing, even that speed writing cramps the muscles just inside the thenar curve and I know the grip on my pen is too tight. I know what sounds right when I write right or when someone else writes right. But, is that right just because I hear it right or someone else's right writing listens right. If no one who knows what is right is here to right what we write rightly to our own ears, how will we know who's right really?
>
> The sound of "-ite" and "-ight" and "r's" rolling around is pleasant or sibilant I believe is the right word to describe writing by rule rightly for right writers to hear or rule on. Does sibilant have to have "s's" hissing or are "r's" running rapidly reasonably rationale for sibilance without "s's".

My cramp is gaining on me even though I remember my father writing my mother all "f's" in a letter from Frankfurt in the days when "f's" had other meaning than what my youngest son at eight called the "King of Swears."

"Dear Effie," he wrote from Frankfurt. "Four foolish fellows followed me from fearful . . ." I can't go on with it. To follow my original thought, "It doesn't sound right." And with the cramp now slowing me down and running off the paper, I'm hoping our non-leader tells us to stop. She did.

Russell Hoxsie, M.D.

The Benefits of Freewriting

Freewriting makes writing easier by helping you with the root psychological or existential difficulty in writing: finding words in your head and putting them down on a blank piece of paper. So much writing time and energy is spent *not* writing: wondering, worrying, crossing out, having second, third, and fourth thoughts. And it's easy to get stopped even in the middle of a piece. (This is why Hemingway made a rule for himself never to end one sheet and start a new one except in the middle of a sentence.) Frequent freewriting exercises help you learn simply to *get on with it* and not be held back by worries about whether these words are good words or the right words.

Thus, freewriting is the best way to learn—in practice, not just in theory—to separate the producing process from the revising process. Freewriting exercises are push-ups in withholding judgment as you produce so that afterwards you can judge better.

Freewriting for ten minutes is a good way to warm up when you sit down to write something. You won't waste so much time getting started when you turn to your real writing task and you won't have to struggle so hard to find words. Writing almost always goes better when you are already started: now you'll be able to start off already started.

Freewriting helps you learn to write when you don't feel like writing. It is practice in setting deadlines for yourself, taking charge of yourself, and learning gradually how to get that special energy that sometimes comes when you work fast under pressure.

Freewriting teaches you to write without thinking about writing. We can usually speak without thinking about speech—without thinking about how to form words in the mouth and pronounce them and the rules of syntax we unconsciously obey—and as a result we can give undivided attention to what we say. Not so writing. Or at least most people are considerably distracted from their meaning by considerations of spelling, grammar, rules, errors. Most people experience an awkward and sometimes paralyzing *translating* process in writing: "Let's see, how shall I say this." Freewriting helps you learn to *just say* it. Regular freewriting helps make the writing process *transparent*.

Freewriting is a useful outlet. We have lots in our heads that makes it hard to think straight and write clearly: we are mad at someone, sad about something, depressed about everything. Perhaps even inconveniently happy. "How can I think about this report when I'm so in love?" Freewriting is a quick outlet for these feelings so they don't get so much in your way when you are trying to write about something else. Sometimes your mind is marvelously clear after ten minutes of telling someone on paper everything you need to tell him. (In fact, if your feelings often keep you from functioning well in other areas of your life frequent freewriting can help: not only by providing a good arena for those feelings, but also by helping you understand them better and see them in perspective by seeing them on paper.)

Freewriting helps you to think of topics to write about. Just keep writing, follow threads where they lead and you will get to ideas, experiences, feelings, or people that are just asking to be written about.

Finally, and perhaps most important, freewriting improves your writing. It doesn't always produce powerful writing itself, but it leads to powerful writing. The process by which it does so is a mysterious underground one. When people talk about the Zen of this or that I think they are referring to the peculiar increase in power and insight that comes from focusing your energy while at the same time putting aside your conscious controlling self. Freewriting gives practice in this special mode of focusing-but-not-trying; it helps you stand out of the way and let words be chosen by the sequence of the words themselves or the thought, not by the conscious self. In this way freewriting gradually puts a deeper resonance or voice into your writing.

But freewriting also brings a surface coherence to your writing and it does so immediately. You cannot write *really* incoherently if you write quickly. You may violate the rules of correctness, you may make mistakes in reasoning, you may write foolishness, you may change directions before you have said anything significant. That is, you may produce something like "Me and her we went down and saw the folks but wait that reminds me of the thing I was thinking about yester oh dam what am I really trying to say." But you won't produce syntactic chaos: language that is so jumbled that when you read it over you are frightened there is something the matter with you.

However, you wouldn't be frightened if you looked more closely at how you actually produced that verbal soup. If you had movies of yourself you would see yourself starting four or five times and throwing each start away and thereby getting more and more jumbled in your mind; finally starting; stopping part way through the sentence to wonder if you are on the wrong track and thereby losing your syntactic thread. You would see yourself start writing again on a slightly different piece of syntax from the one you started with, then notice something really wrong and fix it and lose the thread again; so when you finally conclude your sentence, you are actually writing the conclusion of a different sentence from the ones you had been writing. Thus, the resulting sentence—whether incorrect or just impossibly awkward—is really fragments of three different syntactic impulses or sentences-in-the-head tied together with baling wire. When you write quickly, however, as in freewriting, your syntactic units hang together. Even if you change your mind in mid-sentence, as above, you produce a clear break. You don't try to plaster over two or three syntactic units as one, as you so often do in painstaking writing. Freewriting produces syntactic coherence and verbal energy which gradually transfer to your more careful writing.

What to Do with Freewriting

If you can view freewriting as an exercise to help you to grow in the long run rather than give you good writing in the short run, then you can use some of the good pieces that freewriting sometimes produces. But if you slip into freewriting for the sake of producing good pieces of writing, then you put a kind of short-run utilitarian pressure on the process and hinder yourself from getting all the other benefits.

I suspect there is some added benefit if you read freewriting over after you have written it (better yet out loud) and if you let someone else read it. I think it may help you integrate better into your conscious controlling mind the energies that are available to your innards. But don't get criticism or comment of any sort.

If reading over your freewriting or giving it to someone else gets in the way of future freewriting, as it may well do, then it's better just to throw it away or stash it somewhere unread. Reading it over may make you too self-conscious or make you feel "YEEEcchh, what garbage this is," or "Oh, dear, there must be something the matter with me to be so obsessed." This may start you censoring yourself as you engage in more freewriting. Don't read over your freewriting unless you can do so in a spirit of benign self-welcoming. I used to be fascinated with my freewritings and save them and read them periodically. Now I just throw them away.

A Hunch about Resistance

I remember agonizing over a particular section of something I hoped I would be able to publish. It seemed forever that I struggled and still couldn't get my thought right. I was knotted and incoherent. Finally I broke through into fluency. What a relief. For two days I hadn't been able to say what I wanted; then I could say it. But when I read the whole thing over a day or two later I noticed that the passage was particularly dead. It was limp, it was like a firehose after someone turns off the water.

This illustrates a kind of a myth I have come to believe without quite knowing how to integrate it into the rest of my beliefs about writing. To write is to overcome a certain resistance: you are trying to wrestle a steer to the ground, to wrestle a snake into a bottle, to overcome a demon that sits in your head. To succeed in writing or making sense is to overpower that steer, that snake, that demon.

But if, in your struggles to write, you actually break its back, you are in trouble. Yes, now you have power over it, you can say what you need to say, but in transforming that resistant force into a limp noodle, somehow you turn your words into limp noodles, too. Somehow the force that is fighting you is also the force that gives life to your words. You must overpower that steer or snake or demon. But not kill it.

This myth explains why some people who write fluently and perhaps even clearly—they say just what they mean in adequate, errorless words—are really hopelessly boring to read. There is no resistance in their words; you cannot feel any force-being-overcome, any orneriness. No surprises. The language is too abjectly obedient. When writing is really good, on the other hand, the words themselves lend some of their own energy to the writer. The writer is controlling words which he can't turn his back on without danger of being scratched or bitten.

This explains why it is sometimes easier for a blocked and incoherent writer to break into powerful language than for someone who is fluent and verbal and can always write just what he wants. Picture the two of them: one has uneven, scrunched handwriting with pointy angles, the other has round, soft, even handwriting. When I make these two people freewrite, the incoherent scrunched one is often catapulted immediately into vivid, forceful language. The soft handwriting, on the other hand, just continues to yield what it has always yielded: language that is clear and perfectly obedient to the intentions of the writer, but lifeless. It will take this obedient writer much longer to get power. It will take the scrunched writer longer to get control.

The reason the scrunched writer is so incoherent and hates writing is that he is ruled by the steer, the snake, the demon. He is unable to take charge as he writes and make all those tiny decisions you must make second by second as you write. When I force him to do a freewriting exercise—or he forces himself to do one—he finally gets words on the page but of course he is still not completely in charge. He is not instantly transformed into someone who can make all the micro-decisions needed for writing. He gets words down on the page, but a lot of the decisions are still being made by the words themselves. Thus he has frequent bursts of power in his writing but little control.

The rounded fluent writer on the other hand is so good at making the quick decisions involved in writing—at steering, at being in charge—that even though he writes fast without stopping, his writing still lacks the vitality that comes from exploiting the resistant force.

The goal of freewriting, then, is not absolutely limpid fluency. If you are a blocked writer, freewriting will help you overcome resistance and move you gradually in the direction of more fluency and control (though your path will probably involve lots of writing where you feel totally out of control). But if you are a very controlled writer who can write anything you want, but without power—if you have killed the demon—freewriting will gradually bring it back to life. Forcing yourself to write regularly without stopping for ten minutes will put more *resistance* back into your language. The clay will fight you a bit in your hands as you try to work it into a bowl, but that bowl will end up more alive and powerful.

Elbow reminds us that informal writing helps to produce more writing; it gives us "all-around practice" in writing. The goal for informal writing is to loosen up the process, not to create a perfect product. In fact, as Elbow mentions, "so much time is spent not writing" that such informal writing can just help us "get on with it." Our colleagues have favorite expressions, like "lower your standards," "outrun your censor," and "let's just get down some language." Freewriting, brainstorming, and mapping are all similiar to conversation in that they have no predetermined plan. Words call up other words, and consequently words call up ideas. When the ideas are on paper, when we have cooked the "verbal soup," as Elbow calls it, then we can find the "life force" in the writing. We can begin to search for tensions, look for important details or controlling metaphors, or add new data to the mix.

As we were writing the first few pages of this chapter, Bonnie asked Elizabeth if she'd ever freewritten about her lifelong difficulty hearing. "No journal entries? No little personal pieces? Come on, I don't believe it. You never wrote about being almost deaf?" Bonnie was amazed. Elizabeth's quiet and persistent interest in deafness had allowed Bonnie to explore a whole topic, discover much about deaf English teaching, and write the piece of fieldwork we share with you later in this chapter. And yet Elizabeth had never written about it. Not even in a journal.

"No," Elizabeth answered.

"Well, how about writing it now? Try a little freewrite. A memoir thing. See what you already know." Bonnie suggested. "If you never do anything else with it, it would be an addition to our chapter on fieldwriting." Elizabeth agreed, spending 20 minutes writing alone about her deafness. Here is what she wrote:

> Third grade, teacher had a soft voice. Couldn't hear her but didn't want to admit it. Asked to be moved to front row because of my eyes. Seemed safer to say that I couldn't see. Whenever the lights went out at camp, I couldn't see to read lips. All that late-night activity. Jokes about our counselor, plans for sneaking around after taps. They just grabbed me out of my bed and I followed. Stillness at nighttime for me was frightening. That's why all those movies about the deaf take place at night when the protagonist is alone. Most deaf say they prefer deafness to blindness. But Helen Keller wrote that deafness was a greater handicap. Choices are

never choices—would you rather have $200,000 over two years or ten years? Prefer a Pearson 28 sailboat or a new Saab? A kind of Publisher's Clearing House of Disasters asks, Would you rather have eyes or ears? Your kidneys or your heart? Paste a sticker in the "Earlybird Entry Box" and send it in before midnight. High school drama teacher with bleached blonde hair who eventually married the principal insisted that I get a hearing aid. My first aid was attached to my eyeglasses, cumbersome device, made me feel awkward, weird. All the sounds I had not heard before. Birds interested me especially. But whispering was what I had missed out on most. So much of teenage life is experienced in undertones and asides, in hushes and shhh's! Yet I sleep better than most people I know because when I take my hearing aid out, all I have are my dreams. I tune annoying music out when I no longer want to listen—there are a few advantages. I know that I have been shaped by my deafness. I listen more intently than some. I watch people's facial expressions closely.

In her sample of freewriting, Elizabeth doesn't care about chronology of events or cohesion of images. She mixes memories of third grade, high school and camp, sounds of whispering with birds and darkness, adult thoughts and childlike observations. References to deafness for her call up humorous thoughts of lotteries—life's unexpected fortunes and misfortunes. Her writing here is free of conventional constraints.

Many people use personal journals as a kind of freewriting space. For some, their purpose is fluidity; for others, regularity. For her project, Bonnie kept a researcher's journal as she studied the summer writing program for teachers. Because the program lasted only three weeks, she disciplined herself to keep detailed fieldnotes, and nightly she reflected on them in her researcher's journal, which she kept as a separate file on her computer. Here are some excerpts from her researcher's journal that very summer night as she was beginning to change her plan:

MEMO 7/21/90
1:25 a.m.

Party for Sherrie at Cindy's. Eight days to rewrite her dissertation and then move to Mississippi. Yuck. It's hot and sticky and we danced a lot. Eliz danced near the music so she could hear it. Sherrie taught me the cowboy two-step. I feel guilty because I took off two hours from collecting data. Anyway, at midnight, I talked with Eliz in her car, in the driveway. She was so encouraging—said, "Bonnie, you can't fail at this. There's no way to fail. You have great stuff. It's all in how you organize it." Always get more than you need. Talked about the importance of having a metaphor for controlling the whole thing—or a part of it. Then we talked about marginalized populations, how they need to adapt—and how they fit when a system (or program like this) allows them to. God, do I know that from parenting Amy and Steve. It's emotional and disturbing, but exciting. Lee, Ruth, and Linda are so articulate about it. Last nite they brought donuts and we sat in the lounge and talked about deaf teachers teaching English to deaf kids. I love watching the inter-preters, seeing L, R, and L make strong statements to their class of "hear-ing" others. Bet they've got a lot to say, and "reading" how they see this experience might tell me a lot about others' experiences too. But I didn't plan to do it. I have enough to do. Maybe I need another year to do more research. These deaf women are really teaching me a lot. A good ethnography comes, Eliz says, by looking at contrasts—setting one thing against another. Deafness and hearing? "Traditional language" and "interpreted language?" Reading and writing? Silence and speech?

Rats! I just don't know enough about it.

But Bonnie knew more than she realized. And she added to her knowledge with more research. Later in this chapter, we'll show you how she pieced together what turned out to be a six-page section of her book. Bonnie's journal writing allowed her to trace back her thinking and offered important details—talk and observations—that she used later in her finished text. Whatever you prefer to call a daily personal account—journal, log, daybook, diary, commonplace book—it is a space in which you can record and track your thinking and your experience as it develops. Our col-league Cinthia Gannett studied the history of journals and their functions for jour-nal keepers, men and women alike. In her book *Gender and the Journal*, she mentions the metaphors writing teachers use to describe journals: "a seedbed where ideas can be planted; it is a mine where precious concepts or images lie in wait for excavation; it is a practice ground where one works out—prewrites or drafts—as a preliminary to formal writing. . . . [T]he journal offers an invitation to serve as the recordbook of the mind's life—the hard disk for the soft human memory" (25–26).

Freewriting and journal writing are each kinds of informal writing, but a more structured kind of informal writing is the double-entry notebook. We introduced it in Chapter 2 as a way of taking fieldnotes: first the researcher records observations on one half of a page, usually the left, and then reflects on her notes on the other half of the page. Throughout this book, we've offered many examples of researchers using this note-taking technique: double-entry notes on Samuel Scudder's fish, Donna Niday's molding bread, Harvey Du Marce's description of his childhood home, and Karen Downing's observation of the Photo Phantasies store. As you've seen, the power of this note-taking strategy lies in the mind's engagement and its commentary on itself. Composition theorist Ann Berthoff introduced the idea of the double-entry notebook in her book *The Making of Meaning* (1981) and later expanded the idea, calling it a dialectical notebook. She allows us to see how writers can "audit" their own thoughts as they create them, searching for patterns, bringing order to what may have seemed random observations.

Critical awareness is consciousness of *consciousness* (a name for the active mind.) Minding the mind, being conscious of consciousness, is not the same sort of thing as thinking about your elbows when you're about to pitch a baseball: nor is it *self-consciousness*. Consciousness, in meaning-making activity, always involves us in interpreting our interpretations.

We believe that process, that consciousness, is critical to writing about research. It is a reflexive encounter among the researcher, the research, and the researched, a document of the original plans and the changed plans. Bonnie, in her project, had written a detailed outline for her whole project and was resistant, as many people are, to the idea of altering the plan. But through talk, listening to herself and to Elizabeth, and journal writing, she undid her plan and discovered an important way to rebuild her research project. Just as conversation often meanders and loops through topics and around themes and ideas, so does informal writing invite such flexibility. Writers (and researchers) return again and again to conversation and to informal writing in order to clarify their existing plans and to develop new ones. This process—planning, unplanning, and planning again according to our new thoughts—is the way in which we develop the theories that drive our fieldwriting. By writing, we discover theories or hunches about what's going on in the field.

Our colleague Don Graves is fond of saying, "You can't get out of bed in the morning without a theory." We don't realize how much we use theories, he reminds us. We just aren't conscious of them. He writes:

> I think doing research is like chaperoning an eighth grade dance. You can't wait to see which ungainly guy is going to dance with which ungainly girl. You have all those ideas and theories bouncing around like so many ungainly adolescents. So, you experiment by pairing them up. That's where the writing comes in. You put two ideas on the page, right next to each other, and see if they dance. It's a bit herky-jerky at first but then they get a bit smoother as you work and rework them it's exciting. When students do research they aren't going to know anything until they write. They say, "I can't write yet, I don't have anything." Of course, it's the theories that save time. You know a little better who to send out together on the dance floor. A kind of wild image. Poetry and research dance well together. Theories and metaphors dance well together. Einstein got his theory of relativity from a metaphor (Graves, March 1996).

We cannot keep track of such ideas unless we record everything. And often, in the recording, we find a metaphor that explains a theory or an idea that reminds us of another piece of data. Strategies for informal writing enable fieldwriters to create plans for the research project and also to change them. Planning and unplanning are equally important.

Writing about the "Other": Drafting Twin Tales

Piles of informal and formal writing accumulate throughout the fieldworking process: observational fieldnotes, interview transcripts, and analyses of cultural artifacts are all pieces of fieldwriting. The mounds of data a fieldworker confronts may seem overwhelming, like a bad dream that began with a good experience. But the good news about this rich stack of material is that you've already written some of your final formal piece. You may decide, for example, in a first sweep through your data, that you'll be able to use a memorable quote from a transcript, a key image from your field description, or a reflective piece about your own position in your final draft. It's reassuring, then, to go through your notes with a colored highlighter or a pad of Post-its and mark the data you may use. This initial sweep should also help you locate gaps and missing spots that call for further information. Evaluating your raw material, of course, is not just a mechanical process. Selecting the best snippets of language and describing and reflecting on your data require time and thought. And while you look through your materials for the pieces to use, you'll begin to note possible themes and ideas for your essay.

Like other kinds of research writing, the first draft serves to pull together many data sources into potential sections. Some people lay their data on the floor and move pages around. Others use color-coded or hanging file folders to review and organize their data. Of course, you can cluster and shift data into separate files on a computer using key words as guides. Whichever method you use, it needs to be flexible so that you can order and reorder your disparate data as the themes emerge. This is an intellectually challenging process. Fieldworkers most often accumulate too much data, far more than they can use. Like movie directors, who use only 10% of the footage they shoot, and professional writers, who publish only a quarter of what they write, fieldworkers must learn to let go of the data that doesn't work, fit, or enrich the study. Selecting the appropriate data is the most complicated part of creating a first draft.

In Karen Downing's study, she interviewed six customers about their experiences with Photo Phantasies. As the theme of customer satisfaction emerged in her data, Karen cut and pasted sections of her interviews together in a folder she labeled "Customer Satisfaction." When Rick Zollo began to notice the cowboy metaphor, he used an orange highlighter to mark all the references that might make their way into the theme: *outlaws, fugitives, loners* from his background readings; *hats* and *boots* in his field data. For fieldwriters, early first-draft writing means retrieving and organizing data around potential themes and nascent ideas.

When you get your data into some kind of working order, there are three key questions you'll need to ask of it to guide you in the drafting process:

1. What's going on here?
2. Where's the culture?
3. What's the story?

"What's going on here?" asks descriptive questions of your data—about informants' rituals and routines, about how people and places interact. "Where is the culture?" refers to language practices, place observations, background research, and artifacts you've gathered in the field to understand the group and its history. But the final question, "What's the story?" is the main concern of this chapter and one you must ask continually as you turn your data into an essay. In trying to answer "What's the story?" you must consider not only your informants' explanations (their theories) but also your own.

Every field study has two stories to tell. One is about the culture itself, what it means through the perspective of informants. The other story is the one about you as the researcher and how you did the research. The story about your research process is what compositionist Ken Macrorie calls the "I-search paper." While the story about the culture you're investigating is the critical one, the subplot of how you negotiated your entry, conducted your interviews, and collected other data should also be part of your study. Just as documentaries about the making of a movie offer an inside look at how a finished film came about, your story of your fieldwork will offer your readers the same. There is no formula for the balance between these twin narratives; they form and inform a dialogue between self and other. We can see from the fieldwork we've included in this book that both tales are present to greater or lesser degrees.

The opening section of Karen's study, "Smiling Women," narrates the story of her buying running shoes and irises to set the scene for her study of the mall photography enterprise. As readers, we learn about her mixed feelings about the beauty industry and her own spending habits. Karen's story of herself as the researcher recedes, and the story of Photo Phantasies takes over. In "An Anthropologist on Mars," Oliver Sacks uses a different device to call attention to himself as a researcher throughout his interwoven narratives. While his focus is always on Temple Grandin, Sacks tells us how he makes his discoveries about Grandin's difference and her adaptability. Sacks is ever-present throughout his tale.

Whatever way you choose to balance the twin tales, it is the power of narrative that will carry your essay to your reader. For an illustration of this, we return to Don Murray, writer and writing teacher who has influenced our teaching and scholarship. He writes about the power of narrative in "Where Do You Find Your Stories?" In this essay, Murray reflects on storytelling in his own life and, he suggests, the lives of us all.

 ## Where Do You Find Your Stories?
Donald M. Murray

The question always surprises me. I imagine everyone swims in an ocean of narrative. How else can anyone experience—and understand—the world except through stories? The stories I tell my readers are but a millionth of those I tell myself. Each day overflows with narrative and every night I dream.

When does a fish know it is a fish? I was a writer before I had language. We all are.

Literacy precedes reading, precedes language; literacy is, first of all, the silent-to-others narratives you tell yourself in your head to make order of your world. The story that Mother will return from the other room is made up, tested by reality, and retold before its teller has developed the spoken language to share this wondrous story of abandonment and return.

We all carry stories into this world. My stories were passed down in the blood from flint users who came to the land that would be known as Scotland, inherited from the makers of fire, the ax carriers, herders, sowers, beaker people and cairn builders and on through to Pict, Scot, Celt; their stories all in me at birth, stories of loyalty and betrayal, love and hate, gain and loss, defense and attack, survival and belief. When I first heard the bagpipe tell a story I was not hearing it for the first time.

I was a writer long before I could read, before I could write, before I could speak. I do not make up stories by writing them; the stories are there, grown on their own inevitable telling. I write a few of them down so they can escape and make room for the new stories that are telling themselves.

I was a writer when my finger traced the brown roads in the faded Oriental rug on the living room floor of the house I can hardly remember, and even now I can explore the boxed red squares in which there were secret places I later called forts.

Visiting my year-old-grandson, I see him, with one tiny finger, trace the roads on his Oriental rug, different than mine and the same. His stories come from Russia, Germany, Scotland and he knows, now, before we can understand the stories he tells, the terrible, glorious history of the Jews.

Playing on the Oriental rug of my own childhood, I read the mysterious signals sent by strange fingered hand shadows I would later discover matched maple leaf and oak outside the window. When those shadows left, I told myself about the people who lived in the cities Jack Frost etched on the window pane. On bright days I told myself the stories sent by reflected light, bright spots, circular and oblong, that bounced along ceiling and wall.

I was born to a house with a family that lived in the wall. I cannot remember the last name of the tiny family—small as lead soldiers—that lived in the walls, but one boy was named Donald. He had brothers and sisters and was not an only child. Our rooms were small, but the world within the wall was large; it held oceans, mountains, valleys, cities, ships, Indian tribes, Crusader castles.

Only once did I run away from home, making it only to the next block, returning to the family in the wall, knowing I could escape any room in that house of grown-ups—grandmother, mother, uncle, father—tall people who were given to silences and looking away.

Once, I grew careless and talked to the wall family out loud but the giant people with whom I lived only laughed. They were never worried about the family in the wall, never knew they were my favorite family. They did not know how much time I spent within the wall, how little with them; that when they praised me for being a good little boy—"seen but not heard"—they didn't realize that I was not only silent but also gone.

At first stories were my escape, later they would be my vocation. For now, it was enough to pass into the wall, watch what was happening to what they thought was the real Donald. There was violence in our house, discreet Baptist violence kept from the neighbors—our curtains were always drawn to the proper height—and even, it seemed, from ourselves. Everyone ignored an unfortunate sudden rage, a crying out that was quickly choked back down, the slammed door, the night walk alone.

The rod was not spared. My pants were yanked to my ankles and the slick brown leather shaving strap, pronounced strawp, snaked down or the hair brush, its backside dipped in water to make it sting, beat against me, again and again and again. We were all born in sin. We could only work towards unachievable virtue, doing good works that were never good enough, trying to be what we were not, in the hope of salvation: in the hereafter, when the roll was called up yonder, we would be there, rising on a smug column of righteousness while most of those around us would fall screaming into the sea of flames.

That was a story, the story of salvation, the story of damnation. The Bible was filled with stories; the evangelist strode the platform telling stories. Religion was true narrative—Jonah and the whale, the loaves and the fishes, Jesus and the money changers in the temple, the crucifixion and the resurrection.

I also learned family history through stories: how we came to the lands beyond the sea, from island and moor, croft and textile mill; how the Black Watch fought in the war against Napoleon and how the ancestor for whom I was named took a ball in the knee and his brother stepped into his place; how each family made a first voyage across the ocean, then returned, then made a second voyage back.

Grandmother brought with her the Black Watch shawl, trunks of clothes and dishes and books—my grandfather had been a bookseller, his father a poet—as well as stories from Scotland, every story with its own terror, its own moral. Father brought home deacon stories from church—we had roast minister for Sunday dinner—and his buying trips to New York City; Mother told the stories of neighbors, friends, and her brother's wives.

We talked indirectly, through stories, discovering why people were hired or let go, were unhappy or happy, married or single, with family or childless, ill and sick to death or both hale and hearty.

My real family created and defined themselves by their stories and I created myself by living stories with the family in the wall. I can remember the joy of myselfness I must still admit to, the pleasure of solitude, the comforting escape into loneliness, the passage into the wall. I was not abandoned or punished but grateful to be left alone in rooms or hallways or on that Oriental rug, doors shut against me. There were no silences but make believe. The rug was a magic carpet, I had a Newfoundland dog, my rocking horse was real.

I lived a guerrilla life, a life of surveillance and betrayal; hiding under tables, covered by the tent of hanging tablecloth; watching from behind a sofa or sitting on a closet floor, the door cracked open; listening from under the draping forsythia bush where grown-up stories fell out the summer window, or hearing, hidden by the lattice of the under porch, their rock-rock-rocking chairs and discovered one night I could understand what was not said; lying in the upstairs hall at the heating grate I could follow the stories not for children's ears that rose like invisible smoke from downstairs. I was spy to my life and grew to like my secretiveness, what I knew they did not know I knew and could only share with the family in the wall.

When I came to reading—and I cannot remember when I could not read—it was all familiar. Others were telling stories, the stories I had told myself. I knew all about narrative; I lived a life of stories. My world was make believe: they told the stories I had written in my imagination from what was not said, the narratives that spring up in silences, the worlds to which I escaped, within the walls. I slid into books as easily as I passed into the wall. I walked through the pages and lived within their narratives—and out of their stories, I made more stories of my own.

I was Daniel in the lion's den; I was my grandmother when she was attacked by the bull while taking a shortcut to school in Scotland. I did not hear stories, I entered stories. I was the Little Engine That Could, Billy Goat Gruff, Pinocchio, Long John Silver, Little John ever loyal to Robin Hood.

School was an uncomfortable place for a boy who lived in stories. In class and playground, I remained for years in my story life, staring out windows, standing at the edge of the playground, walking to school alone, watching the street games from the sickly child's window, happy, content to participate in imagination.

I was shy, an only child, late and, I imagine, unexpected; a Scots Protestant in a world of Irish Catholics; a bookish, bespectacled kid in a neighborhood of rowdies. I ran to hide from strangers, walked the long way home to avoid the loud boys, brash and confident, bare knuckled. "Wanta knuckle sandwich, four-eyes?"

I read in the library and head down—a dangerous habit in my neighborhood—read walking home from the library. I read on the worn Oriental rug, kneeling in front of the wicker chair that became a book rest, curled up in the chair, at the kitchen table, on the back steps, up in the apple tree, on the pot, in bed at night with a flashlight, all day when

I was taken to Cape Cod by Uncle Will and left alone in the car. I was blessed with a sickly childhood, spent almost all of one year out of school with a tutor; experienced in visions in delirium and was granted long days and weeks convalescence when I could read and daydream—half dozing—and nightdream—half waking. My life was narrative, secret narrative, and I remember the fear of growing up, of leaving that secret life, feeling that if I went out in the world, I would leave behind all my stories and the family in the wall.

Sadly, with enormous fear, I left the family in the wall, left the world invisible to others and dove, head first, into reality. I survived the sad way we all learn to survive, by becoming what we are not. I accomplished this, I suspect, by stories, telling myself the narratives the world expected and then entering their stories. I did not know this. I thought I had put make believe behind. I learned costumes, manners, and appearance. More masks fitted than I could have imagined: the class play mask, the church youth leader mask, the delivery boy mask, the newspaper reporter mask, the right tackle mask, the combat paratrooper mask.

But I had not left the imagined world. I found these masks were as effective as the table cloth that hid me as I listened to grown-up talk. Wearing a mask I was never seen. I could live my secret life with the families—now there were many—that lived in the wall. My masks were many and none revealed the voices in my head, the cave drawings on the inside of my skull, the stories in which I was both writer and character.

I learned to deny Jesus and not turn the other cheek, to use knuckle and knee, eventually to speak to rooms full of the devout at church, to go to work, to deliver and even sell, to play football, to bump into people who terrified me, and to shoot back when Germans shot at me. I became whoever I had to be to graduate, to advance, to administer, to make my way in the world which was, of course, never my way but theirs.

I learned to dissemble, to smile, to laugh, to agree, to communicate what I was expected to communicate, to cultivate a shell of personality that allowed me to pass as one of the boys. I was hearty, outgoing, a public person who was once even charged with being a "people person" in the 1960s, pleasingly plump, good natured, hale, open.

I survived because of my inheritance from my family in the wall. They had taught me the great worlds within us. They had encouraged my secretiveness, my habit of observation, and, I suppose, my talent for betrayal, comparing what my family and other grown-ups said with what they did. No one saw the fantasies I created going to school and back, in classroom and church, all as much my life as were the stories I read, heard on the radio, or later saw on movie or television screen.

In high school I began to fear this habit of withdrawal. There was great fear in the land—and in my home. I heard my mother confess her worry to her cronies: I was a "bookworm," I was becoming an "introvert." They knew an introvert would not get ahead, would live a lonely life. I worried just the opposite. My interior life was far more interesting than the life of saddle shoes and beer jackets that was going on around me, certainly more interesting than the life of women's hosiery sales and prayer meetings my father led.

I did sense that there would be a price to pay for my escape into myself and there was: I have never had a vacation from observing others and, worst of all, myself, keeping score on all sins of commission—and omission, my own as well as those of others. The eye that turns on others, turns on the self. I thought that perhaps this habit, this compulsive self-observation, self-examination would end when I grew up and found myself. But myself was the person I was, here, now, and there, now.

When I became a journalist, I found a new word to describe my interview style: empathy. When I talked to victim or criminal, detective or DA, I passed through the wall, found their lives there and entered into them. I could be doctor and patient, alcoholic and social worker, Chairman of the Joint Chiefs of Staff and enlisted man; labor leader and labor exploiter; environmentalist and polluter; politician and statesman; male and female; performer and audience. As a ghost writer I became Vice President Nixon's secretary, Rose Mary Woods; the U. S. Secretary of Labor, the CEO of a national corporation. No problem. They were all in the wall, waiting.

I worried, of course, about such writerly arrogance, my confident stealing of the lives of others. I feared what I made up could never be, what I wrote could never exist in "real" life. But like most writers, I learned that what some readers think could never happen, has happened to the writer—those are often the most autobiographical parts. And when I think I have gone too far, life provides post-draft documentation. My novel opens with a scene that I doubted; then I visited a town where it almost happened. Sometimes I wonder if the family in the wall doesn't even influence the life within the room, causing real people to perform the acts created by imaginary ones.

I have learned to accept the world I first shared with my family in the wall, a life counterpoint to what others call reality. Walking alone through the winter woods of the Ardennes in 1944, my rifle carried before me at the ready, assigned to find the British army turning south to cut off the German advance, I was the boy in Wollaston who had played snowball war or a city teenager at a New Hampshire camp grown comfortable in the woods. This morning, an old man walking to my 6:30 AM breakfast at the Bagelry, my hands still cradle my rifle, my ears hearing the owl, force my eyes to search for Germans. Later, at my desk, I write a story of war, making once again a narrative, drawing on the narratives I have lived, imagined, read, watched, dreamt, heard.

I live by narrative: the life of love and betrayal, fear and courage, said and unsaid, done and undone. Imagination extorts its price. I almost drowned three times but I had died by drowning hundreds of times before I learned to swim. I was captured and tortured, wounded, killed a thousand times in a war from which I returned without a physical scratch. As right tackle I scored one accidental touchdown on the field, ten thousand on my way to school, in class, at night in bed. In life you can only lose your virginity once, but I lost it a million times.

Sometimes I think the ability to live a life of stories is a curse: the sound at night is an animal more terrifying than any I have ever seen, every lump a tumor, the smell of smoke a conflagration, the wife or daughter late a victim of accident.

But I have no choice and each story is, I suppose, a preparation. When I was suddenly paralyzed and took my first ambulance ride, I surprised the attendant by saying it was just as I had described it in a novel years before. The life of make believe allows no escape, I am compelled to tell myself the story of my daughter's dying as it is happening—and the story of the father of a dying daughter. That real story was far worse than I imagined going down the corridor to her bedroom, night after night. The world tilts with vertigo: there is guilt in living in the wall and in the hospital waiting room—and therapy.

During my almost fatal heart attack, as six nurses and technicians bustle above I told myself the quiet story of at last meeting my daughter once more: Lee stands in her blue jumper waiting at the end of the brightly lit tunnel. I do not pass through the tunnel this time but she was there and there are tears in my eyes writing this and, guiltily, enough detachment to write it.

I have wondered at my strange life of narrative I grew to understand, living with the family in the wall, and think I stand apart from those around me, but when I write of what is most private, most personal, most unusual and unexpected in my life, readers write to tell me that I have articulated their stories. I discover my readers have been neighbors, waiting in the walls of my office to have their stories told.

But our stories are not our own. They were passed down and I will pass them down. None of them belongs to me; not the stories I have experienced here, in this world; not those I have experienced in the wall with my make-believe family; not the narratives that have been woven from what was lived here and there, overheard, read, observed, dreamed, made up, drawn up from that memory of the times so long before now, times when we first discovered the shelter of a cave, the warmth of fire, and the satisfaction of narrative.

Murray's essay stresses ideas about narrative shared by thinkers in other fields who believe that we experience our lives through stories. He observes that narrative is the primary device we use for making meaning in our lives. Life circumstances and personal necessity dictated that Murray create a second family for himself in his imagination—his "family in the wall." This fictional family could *be all* and *do all* that his stern and frozen family could not. Although he actually lived in an apartment in Boston as an only child of aging parents, with his invented family Don creates brothers and sisters, a Newfoundland dog, and even a horse. As he grew older, his reading about the lives of others added still another dimension to his imaginative life; he "slid into books," he writes, as easily as he "passed into the wall." His creative powers helped the adult Don Murray play out the various roles, along with the appropriate masks, costumes, and manners to assume these parts. Finally, when he became a journalist, Murray called on his imaginative abilities to interview others. Once again, he "passed through the wall, found their lives and entered them."

Fieldwriters must learn to "pass through the wall" in order to capture and record the stories of others' lives. An important but difficult job of fieldwork is to allow informants to tell a tale about their lives—and find a way to show the fieldworker doing it. Oliver Sacks, like Murray, "passed through the wall" by breaking down barriers between Temple Grandin and himself by entering her squeeze machine, entering her worldview, and understanding what it felt like to be autistic, like "an anthropologist on Mars." Fieldwriters need to be open and receptive to their informants' tales and honest about their own roles in those tales. Cindie Marshall's story of Teardrop emerged because they played pool together. The informant's tale is always there for the telling. And so is the researcher's. Without these tales, the study of any culture would be devoid of human interest.

In fact, key informants' narratives are so important that they often lend shape to an entire study by uncovering a subculture's belief systems and values. The story of the trucker, the glamour photo manager, or the "motorcyle woman" connects to deeper themes and ideas a subculture shares—even to their shared stories. In a way, fieldwriters often make new stories out of old ones. Karen's informants' stories, for instance, connect directly to cultural myths that promise to make the ugly duckling into a swan or Cinderella into a princess. Without a traditional belief in the transformative energy of beauty, women would not be convinced to dress up in special clothes and makeup to have their pictures taken. Finding a connecting traditional myth will help guide you through the telling of an informant's story. But of course, the myth cannot smother what you discover in the field. As Mead tells us, fieldworkers are dependent on what happens.

Culture on the Page: The Rhetoric and Aesthetics of Representation

Narrative choice means taking a stand on the page: How do you decide to combine your data? How will you portray yourself, the others, their culture and yours, and the twin tales you're telling? Here are three lists we've developed for considering some of the writing strategies available to fieldworkers, strategies that will bring life to your work—and bring your work to life.

Selected Strategies for Cultural Representation		
Experiential	Rhetorical	Aesthetic
Fieldnotes	Positionality	Metaphor and simile
Double-entry notebooks	Voice of the researcher	Sensory image
Researcher's journals	Voice of the "other"	Concrete image
Interview transcripts	Point of view	Ethnopoetic notation
Photos and artifacts	Analytical section heads	Spatial gaze
Background sources	Analytical titles	

EXPERIENTIAL STRATEGIES

This list of strategies refers to your layers of data: fieldnotes, double-entry notes, notes from your background reading, and other fieldwork records like tapes and transcripts, photos, and artifacts. We like to call this mass of field material **experiential**, firsthand accounts of your experience—at specific times and in specific places. As we've described in all the other chapters of this book, your job is to convince readers that *you were there*—that you saw the places, heard the people, and tried what they were doing.

RHETORICAL STRATEGIES

Another way to represent yourself and your informants originates with the rhetorical choices you make as a writer: choices of voice, purpose, and audience. Our Western rhetorical tradition owes much to Aristotle's advice about effective communication. Aristotle described the position and voice of the communicator as "ethos." He referred to the communicator's sensitivity to audience as "pathos." And he called the body of information, the communicator's actual data, "logos." Composition scholars refer to similar basic principles when they teach effective written communication: voice, purpose, and audience.

As you craft a final text working with informants' words, background information, field experiences, and observations, you ask questions that help shape a rhetorical stance. These questions can help you determine your purpose, your voice, and the needs of your audience:

1. Whose views of this culture am I representing? Mine, my informants', or background information? What is the balance among these sources?

2. How do I organize data? How can I include my informants' perspective or worldview? Through my own? Or through some theme from my data?

3. How am I representing my informants? What data do I use to re-create an informant on the page? Have I given my reader enough details to portray my informant?

4. What sense of place am I offering? What details of setting do I use to organize and locate what I saw? What data do I use to re-create this place? Will my readers feel as if they've been there as I have?

5. What values and assumptions do I bring to my interpretations? Where did they come from? Will my reader know enough about me to understand them?

6. Would I offer my reader the same information if I presented it a different way? Could I shift point of view and tell a similar story?

Your answers to these questions can help guide the writing process. Creative options give us much rhetorical power as writers. Our chart offers a sample of rhetorical choices, many of which we've already discussed in this book. Not every strategy is useful for every study. Each setting, each culture, each person suggests different rhetorical decisions about the chronology or the shape of the narrative. What fieldworkers actually experience governs the shape of the written text.

AESTHETIC STRATEGIES

Finally, we must employ knowledge of the writer's craft as we choose aesthetic ways to represent what we've studied. Like good fiction or poetry, a well-written ethnography needs artful design to allow the reader in. Throughout this book, we've pointed out writers' conscious uses of aesthetic features. For example, Harvey Du Marce uses sensory description of his childhood home in Chapter 3: the buzz of crickets and the sound of his mother's soft voice, the contrast between the bright hot light outside her house and the cool shade inside the living room, the smell of the fry bread and steaming corn soup. In Chapter 4, Danling Fu uses metaphor and simile when she describes silkworms as pets: "Our relationship with worms is like yours with cats and dogs." Her description of the worms themselves draws on imagery and simile: "thick as a little finger," "smaller than an ant," "tastes like a peanut." She makes a comparison between the silkworm and Chinese workers when she says, "Such a little body, so much hard work." She employs the metaphor of the silkworm to describe the whole life cycle process: "We see how silk comes into our lives, not only how we wear it, but how we live with it." And when we see how easily Danling's prose becomes poetry, we understand the effect her figurative language has in bringing her culture to the page.

Culture on the Page: Drafting a Text

Now we'd like to show how all these strategies come together for a writer using layer upon layer of data to draft a text. Our example comes from Bonnie's research on the deaf teachers in the summer writing program, which we discussed earlier in this chapter. It turned into a seven-page "intertext" (a smallish chapter between larger ones) in her book *Composing a Culture*. The selection is titled "Getting the

Words Second Hand: Deaf People Can Do Everything—Except Hear." In it, she uses many of the formal experiential, rhetorical, and aesthetic writing strategies we've just introduced. As you read through this excerpt from her book, notice how Bonnie has employed these to craft her text.

Getting the Words Second Hand
Deaf People Can Do Everything—Except Hear
Bonnie S. Sunstein

"Everything you hear directly is what we hear second hand." As we sit in the lobby of Sackett Hall, Lee explains to a few of us how it is to be deaf in a hearing world. She and her colleagues, Ruth and Linda, live down the hall and I see them daily in Terry Moher's class with Therese and Dorothy. As temporary neighbors, we've shared food, drink, dorm woes, and writing. They are here with two other colleagues this summer from an English department at a high school for the deaf. As a hearing teacher who has spent a long professional lifetime in public schools, I learn much that I never knew about the languages, culture and politics of deafness.

The university has hired several free-lance sign interpreters for each day of the writing program. They are not always the same people. Every week there is a new crew of interpreters, probably because it is summer and many of them teach or go to school. Few of the rest of us know how to sign, but we can see there are differences in the interpreters' interpretations. Lee explains to me that there is American Sign Language (ASL), considered a language, and Signed English, a coding system. Each interpreter appears different as we watch, but, like translators, their job is to interpret spoken text as closely as possible. To an outsider, the interpreters are performers. As hearing observers, we enjoy watching the texts of our spoken words dance in their hands and on their faces. It adds a poetic dimension to the summer and some dramatic physical action to all our talk about writing. The language of Sign is an artful mix of letters, facial expressions, and gestures.

But the complexities are more than poetic for those who must rely on the interpreters' work for language. As in all languages, we discover, translation is not exact. It is a special verbal literacy that requires quick and careful thinking on the part of the hearing interpreter as well as the deaf recipient. I ask Lee if it's difficult to get oriented to so many different interpreters, and mention that I've noticed major differences in them. "Of course," she signs while her mouth forms the words, her oral English a bit blurry. "You are very observant." In this encounter, we talk about language and writing with a twist I hadn't considered.

On the lawn in front of the dorm, we lie in the bright sun together, pick at the grass, and talk about how crucial it is for all students to maintain the connection between reading and writing, especially those who are "at risk" with physical disabilities like deafness that block mainstream language acquisition. Lee and I watch each other's mouths carefully and we secure our notebooks under our legs. We do not need an interpreter. Occasionally, we need to write out a word that one of us doesn't understand.

Deaf Students Are Bilingual Interpreters

Lee shows me a record she keeps of her students' "malapropisms." Until now, I have not thought of her students as interpreters. To me, their approximations in using English written language are both amusing and poignant. They remind me of all teenagers as they pursue making their own sense of the adult world. But Lee's students' written words illustrate the extra job a deaf adolescent has as she interprets Sign into writing:

"Oh, thank gosh."

"A shovel slaps the snow."

"Going camping, I wear my pack-back."

"There was a terrible plane crush."

"It is time to clam down."

"When I went to my girlfriend's house, I rang the door bellring," and then we had an "argumen."

I put the words in "alphabetable order."

There is a "broadwalk at Ocean City."

I found a "secret passway."

"After the argument, my mouth was wild open."

"I had to go to the hospital to get an x-tray."

"The police arrived in a helicopper"

"The weather is short of warm"

"The dance was wowderful, fan-static."

"I ran the lawnmotor"

"I saw a hummerbird."

In each of these little misuses, there is inherent logic and figurative language. The words illustrate creative understanding of meaning, as well as contextual interpretation. "Wild-open" mouths and beachside "broadwalks," weather that is "short of warm," and crushed planes and police in helicoppers conjure up lucid poetic imagery. We must understand that deaf students are bilingual, and, Lee believes, given an environment rich with reading and writing, they thrive.

We Read with Our Eyes, of Course

Lee is deeply aware of the unnecessary disenfranchisement her students suffer. She and her colleagues tell many stories to support this position. Because her school is a demonstration school in a large city, her students are often "on display" to administrators, politicians, foreign diplomats, and other interested people. The visitors are not always enlightened. She incorporates one of those stories into her own writing about disability and power. In her paper, Lee writes:

> . . . This spring, one of my classes was visited by a South American dignitary from a country where educating deaf people is not the norm. My students had just finished reading *Sounds of Silence*, a young adult novel by Marilyn Levy that includes a mainstreamed deaf teen as a major character. The dignitary watched with visible awe as the class worked individually and in teams writing an additional chapter to the novel, drafting invitations for the character to come to our school and experience the Deaf culture the students themselves enjoyed.

Our visitor could suppress her confusion no longer. "You mean these deaf students have all READ this book? But how?"

Julie, a junior, confidently stated what was to her the obvious. "With our eyes, of course." And Julie was perfectly correct. . . .

Lee's story illustrates a moment that is at once embarrassing and triumphant. As I see it, this is a story of all marginalized populations in school: the foreign language speaker, the ghetto dialect speaker, the person who is "educable mentally retarded" or physically handicapped. Like Julie and her classmates, our marginalized students deserve *more* fully connected language opportunities in school, *not fewer*. A rich mix of reading, writing, speaking, and listening in the company of other English language users is critical for their literacy. This means reading and writing literature, not executing grammar worksheets. (Sunstein in Stires, ed., 1991)

Deafness as Deficit: A Self-Fulfilling Prophecy

Lee and I discuss the "deficit model" thinking that we see in curricula for students who carry the label "disabled." As long as schools see human difference as deficit, difference will always be sorted out. On the other hand, schools *could* view difference as opportunity, we agree. The mere act of living in the mainstream demands that "disabled" students develop extra abilities: interpreting and signing, jumping comfortably between two national or ethnic cultures, or understanding the biology of a physical or mental handicap. Students with difference have extra information to contribute.

"If our deaf students cannot read and write literature on a level with their hearing peers," Lee writes, "it may very well be that they've never been exposed to real literature at all. . . . Too long, we have been making deficit assumptions and spoon feeding (sometimes force-feeding) our students with a conceptual mash unable to create or sustain intellectual or linguistic growth. By thinking deaf students incapable of reading and writing real literature, we've created a self-fulfilling prophecy. . . . Reading and writing are power, and empowered students are hooked for life on their own learning."

It is not any lack of intelligence that prevents a student from fuller literacy; it is often the self-fulfilling prophecy of the "disability testing and remediation" she must endure. If these students are given little pieces of language to exercise their broken parts, they will never have a chance to use English whole, or to see how others use it. As these teachers experience reading and writing for themselves here this summer, they rethink their own teaching practices and reflect on their teacher-training histories. Lee's colleague Ruth writes:

> Teacher training programs set the pace for the field of education of the deaf. When I began teaching deaf children over twenty years ago, I took classes towards a certificate that showed I understood deafness and how it made deaf children different . . . in Language Development I learned ASL was to be ignored . . . in Speech and Speechreading the hearing professor was embarrassed about having deaf students in his class . . . in Audiology we learned about how language development is affected by degree of hearing loss . . . in Psychology of Deafness, we learned certain personal traits deaf children have, and that the teachers were martyrs . . . there was rarely a course in American Sign Language, the language that most deaf people used . . . but there were newly developed systems of signs to help children learn English. . . .

Ruth explains that many educators of deaf students still have a clinical, pathological point of view. As a deaf person herself, she writes "We prefer to be seen as a culture, with a rich heritage passed on by children of deaf parents. . . . It will be a long time before my rage is completely gone. Like Toni Morrison said of white people, 'historically, we were seldom invited to participate in the discourse even when we were its topic.' " (Morrison in Zinsser, 91)

Language Forbidden

Although Lee grew up struggling as a deaf child in a hearing home, her colleagues Ruth and Linda are among the 5 percent of the deaf population who come from deaf families. The deaf child born into a deaf family has a distinct advantage in literacy, Linda tells me, a home environment rich in language. Their "home language" is American Sign, and English is a learned second language. Linda's parents and grandfather signed stories to her when she was a child, creating a context for learning much the same as in any privileged home. But for deaf children like Lee born into hearing homes, there is minimal communication.

Linda observes that Don Murray's term "inner voice" was a new idea to her (1990). She tests herself. "I noticed that *I do* have a 'deaf voice' based on the dreams I dream. The characters in my dreams have conversations in ASL. With the interpreters, the ones who signed in ASL, I received the messages very comfortably and directly whereas those who signed in Signed English, I had to translate into ASL—especially the phrases, idiomatic expressions, sounds, and puns, and then into English." Linda writes:

> For most of us whose first language is ASL, writing is a laborious chore. We have to translate our native language into English and then put it down on paper. In order to write well, we must read a lot, so we can switch our language into English comfortably when we write.

One of Linda's pieces during the three weeks is a poem called "The Forbidden Language." It details her "seven solid years of battle" during the nineteen-fifties, in a residential school in which ASL was prohibited. At night in the dorms, one student would stand in the doorway, watching for the housemother: "A circle of kids would watch another kid, the storyteller, signing, secretly" and then they would scatter when the housemother came. Although they were punished severely, they "dared to continue the risks." The scars on her sister's thigh clued Linda's parents to the hairbrush beatings they received for signing stories together. A formal, legally filed grievance and a subsequent victory placed Linda and her sister in a different school where signing was respected. Had her parents not been deaf, Linda and her sister and their classmates might have stayed there for more years, deprived of their native language.

A Bond of Stars: The Plastic Spots of Difference

On one night during the first week, Lee, Ruth, and Linda sit in a circle on Lee's bed in their pajamas, eating candy, drinking Diet Coke, joking, and reading one another's writing. Linda is wearing her favorite tee shirt. It is black with white letters across the chest: "Deaf People Can Do Everything—Except Hear." Lee's computer is printing out her latest piece of writing, her cloth-bound journal sits inside her folded legs, and the floor is messy with wads of discarded drafts. They are signing wildly to each other when I walk by.

Ruth invites me to take a walk down the hall with her. She has just discovered a planetarium in her room. She points upward and then turns off the light. The ceiling is covered with plastic stars, affixed in configurations that reproduce a few constellations. They don't twinkle; they glow plastic yellow-green over our heads. We can't talk in the dark, but we jab each other and laugh together at the hidden legacy from a recent college student.

When she turns the light on, the stars disappear. It is a fitting metaphor for the shared literacies we are all experiencing this summer. When the lights go on, the eerie spots of plastic difference disappear. But they become a bond between us, the knowledge that each of us has a secret in the dark worth exploring together. Whether we get the words "straight" or "second hand," it is in talking, reading, and writing about those differences that we can celebrate our human abilities to communicate.

Bonnie's dilemma as a researcher was that she had collected mounds of different kinds of data about the deaf subculture. She had no idea how she would present these three separate and very different stories from her deaf informants, Lee, Ruth, and Linda. Her data included

- Journal entries from conversations with Elizabeth, Terry Moher (the instructor), and the interpreters who were in the three informants' class
- Observations and fieldnotes about the interpreters in the classroom and public readings
- Observations and fieldnotes about the three informants in the dorm and in the classroom
- Taped interviews with each informant, including histories about deafness in their own schooling and family lives and accounts of their teaching
- Written artifacts from each informant: letters, poetry, narratives, and essays
- Photos of the three informants in their dorm rooms, in their classroom, and at summer program activities, such as picnics
- Background source material on the difference between American Sign Language and Signed English, as well as the politics of deafness
- Background source material on marginalized students in schools

As she surveyed her mass of data, Bonnie thought of many options for presenting this story to her reader. Maybe she could offer three separate case studies, one about each informant. Or she could write a chronological account of her significant encounters with every informant throughout the three weeks of the summer writing program. She could perhaps choose to show how they entered into the life of the dorm, the tenor of the classroom, and the program's shared events. She had enough data to organize her text in any of these ways, but at this point in her project, she wanted to think about her audience, other teachers of writing.

To begin writing, she asked herself, "What do I want my readers to learn about these teachers and this subculture?" Her decision, interestingly enough, came from two insider clues: one was Linda's T-shirt, which announced "Deaf People Can Do

Everything—Except Hear," which turned into the subtitle for the intertext. The other was a quote from Lee in a transcript, "Everything you hear directly is what we hear second hand," which became her lead sentence. Bonnie's decision about how to begin to offer her data to her reader came from what she had learned about the subculture itself—in the informants' own language.

Culture on the Page: Strategies

EXPERIENTIAL STRATEGIES

To tell her own researcher's story with the deaf teachers (her part of the twin tales), Bonnie chose data from her fieldnotes that would show the reader how she worked with the deaf teachers, meeting them in their dorms, classes, and outside. She didn't bother with the conversation in Elizabeth's Caravan. It had been an important catalyst for Bonnie, but it was not relevant for the purposes of the three informants' stories. To help the reader believe in the research, it's important that fieldworkers disclose the kinds of relationships they form with their informants. Bonnie does this in the scene on the lawn in which she and Lee communicate without an interpreter. And Bonnie's fieldworking methods come in again in the final scene, where, turning out the lights and looking at the plastic ceiling constellations in Ruth's room, she illustrates how she's been invited into the lives of those she's researched. Depicting the actual fieldworking "in process" develops the narrative voice that allows a reader to participate in the story a researcher has to tell.

RHETORICAL STRATEGIES

Bonnie organized her writing around five main themes or ideas about the deaf that she used as subheadings. Both the intertext's complete title, "Getting the Words Second Hand: Deaf People Can Do Everything—Except Hear," and the five section headings serve to guide her reader through the text without interrupting the narrative flow:

Deaf Students Are Bilingual Interpreters
We Read with Our Eyes, of Course
Deafness as Deficit: A Self-Fulfilling Prophecy
Language Forbidden
A Bond of Stars: The Plastic Spots of Difference

Subheadings serve a rhetorical purpose for a fieldwriter: they stand as a kind of outline for the whole. And for readers, these headings quietly signal the important themes that the text will develop.

Bonnie made other rhetorical choices for her intertext. Because the topic of her book is a summer writing program for teachers, she chose to include these teachers' stories, as they wrote and told them. She was careful to bring as much of the teachers' writing into the text as possible, to achieve a balance between her voice and that of the teachers she studied.

She employs still another rhetorical strategy in this piece of writing: background source material about American Sign Language and Signed English. Bonnie hadn't previously known much about sign languages, but after working with these teachers and reading books and articles about the deaf, she wove basic informative material into her text. In the same way, she included information about the inclusion and exclusion of marginalized populations in school to give force—rhetorical power—to her unstated argument that the deaf are unfairly treated both in and out of schools.

AESTHETIC STRATEGIES

Writers cannot tell feelings to their readers; they must show the feelings instead. Well-chosen imagery and careful use of poetic devices are not extraneous details. Rather, they can sensitize a reader toward a point of view, an argument, or an idea. For the purposes of fieldwriting, researchers draw on the same aesthetic strategies that all writers use to elicit strong emotional responses from their readers.

The major but subtle metaphor Bonnie evokes in this short piece is that of dance—an idea that came from her earliest talk in Elizabeth's van. She invokes this metaphor to show how she begins to see sign language as more than just physcial motion, as "an artful mix of letters, facial expressions, and gestures." And just as dance does not translate directly into words, neither is sign language an exact translation. She learns, with the help of Lee, Ruth, Linda, and the interpreters, that there are gains and losses in the translation process.

Another metaphor Bonnie employs is the plastic stars in Ruth's room. These symbolize how Bonnie began her relationship with these teachers, separated from them by "eerie spots of plastic difference." In fact, the difference between the deaf and the hearing are important and ever present, but when both share the secret of the stars by turning off the lights, elbowing and chuckling as friends and fellow teachers—at a student's contribution to a dorm room—the differences disappear. Her metaphor, though somewhat schmaltzy, really did represent Bonnie's emotional response to working with deaf teachers.

Culture on the Page: Revising, Editing, and Polishing

To us, the word *draft* suggests wind blowing through a piece of writing, with holes left to fill as you craft your writing into something your reader will understand. All writers have their own drafting styles. Just as fieldworkers establish various habits for organizing information during data collection, so do writers develop successful drafting habits. First drafts need to be exploratory, and sometimes we must force them out of a strange paradox. We write to release ourselves from that stuck-tight, closed-up feeling that we can't write because we don't know the answers or the meaning of what we want to say. But to understand the theories behind what we think and feel, we must write. We learn more about what we know as we draft. Writing a first draft is not the same as freewriting. Freewriting uncorks your writing process and helps you become fluid, fast, and fluent. Drafting frees all the ideas and research about a topic that you've been holding in your mind. With subsequent drafts, you can fill in the holes—for yourself and for your reader. But the trick in getting that first draft down is to "just do it."

Anne Lamott is a professional writer whose book *Bird by Bird: Some Instructions on Writing and Life* considers not only writing but also the writer's habits of mind. Her title comes from a family story. When her brother, at age 10, became overwhelmed while writing a report on birds, her writer father's comforting advice was, "Bird-by-bird, Buddy. Just take it bird by bird." In the following selection, Lamott writes about the power and the usefulness of first drafts, of getting ideas on paper just for the purpose of later expanding, clarifying, and organizing them. For many writers, just as for Lamott's brother, there's reassurance in allowing yourself to write a messy first draft, knowing that each subsequent draft will refine what's already there.

 Shitty First Drafts

Anne Lamott

Now, practically even better news than that of short assignments is the idea of shitty first drafts. All good writers write them. This is how they end up with good second drafts and terrific third drafts. People tend to look at successful writers, writers who are getting their books published and maybe even doing well financially, and think that they sit down at their desks every morning feeling like a million dollars, feeling great about who they are and how much talent they have and what a great story they have to tell; that they take in a few deep breaths, push back their sleeves, roll their necks a few times to get all the cricks out, and dive in, typing fully formed passages as fast as a court reporter. But this is just the fantasy of the uninitiated. I know some very great writers, writers you love who write beautifully and have made a great deal of money, and not *one* of them sits down routinely feeling wildly enthusiastic and confident. Not one of them writes elegant first drafts. All right, one of them does, but we do not like her very much. We do not think that she has a rich inner life or that God likes her or can even stand her. (Although when I mentioned this to my priest friend Tom, he said you can safely assume you've created God in your own image when it turns out that God hates all the same people you do.)

Very few writers really know what they are doing until they've done it. Nor do they go about their business feeling dewy and thrilled. They do not type a few stiff warm-up sentences and then find themselves bounding along like huskies across the snow. One writer I know tells me that he sits down every morning and says to himself nicely, "It's not like you don't have a choice, because you do—you can either type or kill yourself." We all often feel like we are pulling teeth, even those writers whose prose ends up being the most natural and fluid. The right words and sentences just do not come pouring out like ticker tape most of the time. Now, Muriel Spark is said to have felt that she was taking dictation from God every morning—sitting there, one supposes, plugged into a Dictaphone, typing away, humming. But this is a very hostile and aggressive position. One might hope for bad things to rain down on a person like this.

For me and most of the other writers I know, writing is not rapturous. In fact, the only way I can get anything written at all is to write really, really shitty first drafts.

The first draft is the child's draft, where you let it all pour out and then let it romp all over the place, knowing that no one is going to see it and that you can shape it later. You just let this childlike part of you channel whatever voices and visions come through and onto the page. If one of the characters wants to say, "Well, so what, Mr. Poopy Pants?," you let her. No one is going to see it. If the kid wants to get into really sentimental, weepy, emotional territory, you let him. Just get it all down on paper, because there may be something great in those six crazy pages that you would never have gotten to by more rational, grown-up means. There may be something in the very last line of the very last paragraph on page six that you just love, that is so beautiful or wild that you now know what you're supposed to be writing about, more or less, or in what direction you might go—but there was no way to get to this without first getting through the first five and a half pages.

I used to write food reviews for *California* magazine before it folded. (My writing food reviews had nothing to do with the magazine folding, although every single review did cause a couple of canceled subscriptions. Some readers took umbrage at my comparing mounds of vegetable puree with various ex-presidents' brains.) These reviews always took two days to write. First I'd go to a restaurant several times with a few opinionated, articulate friends in tow. I'd sit there writing down everything anyone said that was at all interesting or funny. Then on the following Monday I'd sit down at my desk with my notes, and try to write the review. Even after I'd been doing this for years, panic would set in. I'd try to write a lead, but instead I'd write a couple of dreadful sentences, xx them out, try again, xx everything out, and then feel despair and worry settle on my chest like an x-ray apron. It's over, I'd think, calmly. I'm not going to be able to get the magic to work this time. I'm ruined. I'm through. I'm toast. Maybe, I'd think, I can get my old job back as a clerk-typist. But probably not. I'd get up and study my teeth in the mirror for a while. Then I'd stop, remember to breathe, make a few phone calls, hit the kitchen and chow down. Eventually I'd go back and sit down at my desk, and sigh for the next ten minutes. Finally I would pick up my one-inch picture frame, stare into it as if for the answer, and every time the answer would come: all I had to do was to write a really shitty first draft of, say, the opening paragraph. And no one was going to see it.

So I'd start writing without reining myself in. It was almost just typing, just making my fingers move. And the writing would be *terrible*. I'd write a lead paragraph that was a whole page, even though the entire review could only be three pages long, and then I'd start writing up descriptions of the food, one dish at a time, bird by bird, and the critics would be sitting on my shoulders, commenting like cartoon characters. They'd be pretending to snore, or rolling their eyes at my overwrought descriptions, no matter how hard I tried to tone those descriptions down, no matter how conscious I was of what a friend said to me gently in my early days of restaurant reviewing. "Annie," she said, "it is just a piece of *chicken*. It is just a bit of *cake*."

But because by then I had been writing for so long, I would eventually let myself trust the process—sort of, more or less. I'd write a first draft that was maybe twice as long as it should be, with a self-indulgent and boring beginning, stupefying descriptions of the meal, lots of quotes from my black-humored friends that made them sound more like the Manson girls than food lovers, and no ending to speak of. The whole thing would be so long and incoherent and hideous that for the rest of the day I'd obsess about getting creamed by a car before I could write a decent second draft. I'd worry that people would read what I'd written and believe that the accident had really been a suicide, that I had panicked because my talent was waning and my mind was shot.

The next day, though, I'd sit down, go through it all with a colored pen, take out everything I possibly could, find a new lead somewhere on the second page, figure out a kicky place to end it, and then write a second draft. It always turned out fine, sometimes even funny and weird and helpful. I'd go over it one more time and mail it in.

Then, a month later, when it was time for another review, the whole process would start again, complete with the fears that people would find my first draft before I could rewrite it.

Almost all good writing begins with terrible first efforts. You need to start some-where. Start by getting something—anything—down on paper. A friend of mine says that the first draft is the down draft—you just get it down. The second draft is the up draft—you fix it up. You try to say what you have to say more accurately. And the third draft is the dental draft, where you check every tooth, to see if it's loose or cramped or decayed, or even, God help us, healthy.

What I've learned to do when I sit down to work on a shitty first draft is to quiet the voices in my head. First there's the vinegar-lipped Reader Lady, who says primly, "Well, *that's* not very interesting, is it?" And there's the emaciated German male who writes these Orwellian memos detailing your thought crimes. And there are your parents, ago-nizing over your lack of loyalty and discretion; and there's William Burroughs, dozing off or shooting up because he finds you as bold and articulate as a houseplant; and so on. And there are also the dogs: let's not forget the dogs, the dogs in their pen who will surely hurtle and snarl their way out if you ever *stop* writing, because writing is, for some of us, the latch that keeps the door of the pen closed, keeps those crazy ravenous dogs contained.

Quieting these voices is at least half the battle I fight daily. But this is better than it used to be. It used to be 87 percent. Left to its own devices, my mind spends much of its time having conversations with people who aren't there. I walk along defending myself to people, or exchanging repartee with them, or rationalizing my behavior, or seducing them with gossip, or pretending I'm on their TV talk show or whatever. I speed or run an aging yellow light or don't come to a full stop, and one nanosecond later am explaining to imaginary cops exactly why I had to do what I did, or insisting that I did not in fact do it.

I happened to mention this to a hypnotist I saw many years ago, and he looked at me very nicely. At first I thought he was feeling around on the floor for the silent alarm button, but then he gave me the following exercise, which I still use to this day.

Close your eyes and get quiet for a minute, until the chatter starts up. Then isolate one of the voices and imagine the person speaking as a mouse. Pick it up by the tail and drop it into a mason jar. Then isolate another voice, pick it up by the tail, drop it in the jar. And so on. Drop in any high-maintenance parental units, drop in any contractors, lawyers, colleagues, children, anyone who is whining in your head. Then put the lid on, and watch all these mouse people clawing at the glass, jabbering away, trying to make you feel like shit because you won't do what they want—won't give them more money, won't be more successful, won't see them more often. Then imagine that there is a vol-ume-control button on the bottle. Turn it all the way up for a minute, and listen to the stream of angry, neglected, guilt-mongering voices. Then turn it all the way down and watch the frantic mice lunge at the glass, trying to get to you. Leave it down, and get back to your shitty first draft.

A writer friend of mine suggests opening the jar and shooting them all in the head. But I think he's a little angry, and I'm sure nothing like this would ever occur to you.

We like Lamott's description of the drafting process, first the "down draft" and then the subsequent "up drafts" as the writer moves slowly "up," shaping her text for a reader. Eventually, of course, comes what Lamott calls the "dental draft," in which the writer must polish and edit carefully to meet the expectations and con-ventions appropriate to her intended audience. This "dental draft" is the last stage of manuscript preparation, an important distinction. The process of working a "dental draft" is quite separate from the process of revision. Your English department probably has a "dental" policy, one that describes the conventions a piece of writing must follow in its final form. There are many good handbooks available, too, for that final polishing stage.

Revising is *not* editing. Both editing and revising can take place during the drafting process, but revision always involves making substantial changes, not just fine-tuning a sentence or two. As you draft and redraft, adding and subtracting pieces of data and discovering new connections, you should not bother to make your writing look perfect. Save the editing for later. To revise means to rewrite with an eye toward emerging ideas, themes, and voice. The term *revision* implies the reseeing and reimagining of the original material.

In writing this book, we've worked together to write the "down draft" and then revised afterward. In this final chapter, our major problem was that we had left many informational holes in our down draft, holes that we needed to fill and expand. To illustrate how our ideas grew from draft to draft, we'll show you an early version of the first paragraph in this chapter and how it changed through different "up drafts" and through the process of response from a few readers.

The first paragraph of this chapter, we think, discusses one of the most difficult ideas in our entire book, an idea that also concerns many other researchers: how to represent culture on the page. The concept of representing other people and places from your fieldwork in your writing is complex and fraught with ethical dilemmas. How do we take the words of others and put them into our language while remaining faithful to theirs? As we've mentioned so many times in *FieldWorking*, whether a researcher can successfully bring the lives of different cultures onto a page depends very much on how well that fieldworker writes.

The difficulty of these wedded processes—research and writing—is what we tried to present at the outset of this chapter. Here's our first draft of the first paragraph of this chapter, followed by comments from our reader, Julie Cheville. This is the "down draft" as we first wrote it—six sentences that first appear on the first page:

DRAFT 1

Today, perhaps even more so than ever before, anthropologists pay close attention to how language shapes and informs their work. As Mead suggests, the fieldworker invents neither informants nor their cultural spaces but is "helplessly dependent" on the reality of what takes place in the field. Representing reality depends on how a fieldworker uses language. This is the special ethic of fieldworking. It demands that you *be true* to your informants' worldview and their language—which you must translate into your own words. The critical issue of informant representation makes the difference between fiction and fieldwriting.

In this draft, the idea of representation enters the chapter with little warning. We realize that the word could confuse a fieldwriter who might not associate *representation* with the process of writing. When Julie, who had read every draft of each chapter for us, got to the phrase "representing reality," she put a big question mark beside it and wrote "too vague" and, next to "representing reality," she wrote "Big gap for me. See notes." She also wrote us comments that showed her dissatisfaction with how we presented the idea: "For me, there is a wide gap between the Mead sentence and the one which introduces the idea of 'representing reality.' I suggest that you start a new paragraph after Mead and develop a number of points here. I am also confused by the issue of 'being true.' What exactly does that mean? Since for you both the issue of how to write is the 'special ethic' of fieldwriting, I want those dimensions spelled out for me more fully."

And so we redrafted, with Julie's comments in mind. We tried to explain what we meant by "representing reality" and to "be true." We agreed that these were vague and confusing ideas as we had written about them. We didn't want our reader to get bogged down in theories of writing and representation, but we needed to explore these points with care. In our next draft, the idea appears later, and we've expanded the paragraph from 6 to 13 sentences:

DRAFT 2

Today, perhaps more than ever before, anthropologists pay close attention to how language shapes and influences their work. As Mead reminds us, the fieldworker invents neither informants nor their cultural spaces. Rather, you as a fieldworker are "helplessly dependent" on the reality of what takes place in the field—both as you sees it and as your informants see it. Representing reality depends on how a fieldworker uses language. In any talk (or text), we make a silent contract between speaker and listener—the participants in the conversation. We try to understand the ideas as they filter from speakers (or writers) through language toward listeners (or readers). Whenever we use language—talk or text— we share conventions with the people who participate—speakers, writers, listeners, and readers. In any conversation—or any piece of writing—our understanding of situations and conventions depends on how much others allow and help us understand. This is the special ethic of fieldwriting. Fieldwriting demands that you respect your informants' worldviews and language—and then represent them, translating into your own words. At the same time, you must respect and represent yourself as narrator. This critical issue—representation—makes the difference between fiction and fieldwriting. As Mead observed decades ago, "Unlike the novelist . . . the fieldworker is wholly and helplessly dependent on what happens."

But it still wasn't right. The beginning of the chapter needed more context for the whole debate about whether or not the researcher represents or constructs informants and their worlds. In our third draft, we split the paragraphs, added an earlier note to remind the reader about Hortense Powdermaker, and wrote a little more about Margaret Mead. Most important, though, we retalked the theory—over the phone and in e-mail messages. We consulted a few more articles and books and had conversations with other colleagues as well. In this draft, the idea shows up as the fourth and fifth paragraphs in our text.

DRAFT 3

Today, perhaps more than ever before, anthropologists pay close attention to how language shapes and influences their work. As Mead reminds us, you as a fieldworker invent neither your informants nor their cultural spaces. Rather, you are "helplessly dependent" on the reality of what takes place in the field—both as you see it and as your informants see it. Representing reality depends on how you use language.

In conversations (talk) with our informants, we make a contract with them to try to understand and represent their ideas in writing (our text) as they've presented those ideas to us. And as in any conversation, the ability to understand and interpret the point of view and situation of an "other" depends on both participants. It also depends on how informants allow us to understand their worldviews and on how well we participate and listen. The special ethics of fieldwriting demand that you respect your informants' worldviews and their language. At the same time, you must respect and represent yourself as narrator, as the fieldworker telling the story. This critical issue—representation of self and other—makes the difference between fiction and fieldwriting. As Mead observed decades ago, "Unlike the novelist . . . the fieldworker is wholly and helplessly dependent on what happens."

And if you check the final version that appears at the beginning of this chapter, you'll see that after drafting, we edited, clarifying and changing some of our phrasing. At the editing stage, we worked through what Bonnie calls "word dust." Just as some people love to vacuum, Bonnie loves to tinker with words, dusting and clarifying ideas once they are in place within a draft (*talk* and *text* in parentheses, for example, and mixed-up pronouns like *we* and *you*). Finally, when the book went into production, our editor and our copy editor helped with the "dental" flossing, polishing, and proofreading process.

So revision in the case of this chapter's first paragraph was about clarification. In other instances, revision can be about deletion, reorganization, or changes to tone and style. But revision is *always* about changes, about opportunity. Revision demands that a writer step outside of the original frame of the work and adopt an open and willing attitude toward making changes. Since most people view change as scary, it's not unusual that many beginning writers resist revising. Making changes also requires allowing enough time for the writer to accomplish those changes. Every draft demands a different kind of revision. When a first draft is also a final draft, there is no chance to think about or take advantage of the opportunities that revision would offer.

We want to end with a voice whose work has guided us throughout this chapter, Don Murray. Murray is the first composition scholar to acknowledge both the risk taking and the rewards involved in the drafting process. His attention to revision has helped writers and writing teachers for the past three decades. Here's a short piece he calls "Some Notes on Revision," which he first presented to a writing class.

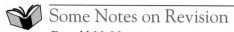

Some Notes on Revision

Donald M. Murray

February 15, 1995

- Revision is not failure but opportunity. It is an essential part of the process of thinking that produces a series of drafts that clarify and communicate significant meaning to a reader. Writing is not thought reported but the act of thinking itself.

> The artist Philip Baxter: "I don't paint what I see, I see what I paint."
> Murray: "I don't write what I know, I know what I write."
> John Kenneth Galbraith: "There are days when the result is so bad that no fewer than five revisions are required. However, when I'm greatly inspired, only four revisions are needed before, as I've often said, I put in that note of spontaneity which even my meanest critics concede."
> Neil Simon: "Rewriting is when playwriting really gets to be fun. In baseball you only get three swings and you're out. In rewriting, you get almost as many swings as you want and you know, sooner or later, you'll hit the ball."
> Bernard Malamud: "I love the flowers of afterthought."

- Revision begins before the first draft when writers talk to themselves, make notes, begin to draft in their head and on the screen.

> Wallace Stevens: "The tongue is an eye."

- Find the edge. Revision is first of all a search for the central tension, the knot, the conflict, the intersection, the questions, the news, the contradiction, the surprise that will involve the reader in the draft.
- Do not look first for error. Look for what works, develop the strengths. Ironically, the strengths of the draft are often found in the failures, in the places where the writing is new, awkward, not yet clear because the writer has not written it before.
- Start as near the end as possible. No background information before the draft really begins. Weave in background material when the reader needs it. Often we write our way toward the subject. It is scaffolding similar to the staging we construct to put up a building. It should be taken down before the text is shown to a reader.
- Revision is fun because of the surprise. The draft teaches us and we are surprised by what we didn't know we knew.

> Saul Bellow: "I'm happy when the revisions are big. I'm not speaking of stylistic revisions, but of revisions in my own understanding."

- There is a logical sequence to revision:

  Message: What do I have to say?

  Order: How can I say it?

  Develop: What does the reader need to know?

  Voice: What is the voice of the draft?

- Write for yourself, *then* your reader.
- Write and edit out loud. Listen to your voice and tune it to the meaning, purpose, and audience of the draft.

- Enter the work. Work within the evolving draft, taking instruction from the evolving work. Enjoy the gift of concentration.

  > Bernard Malamud: "If it is winter in the book, spring surprises me when I look up."

- Cut what can be cut. Everything must advance the evolving meaning.

  > Kurt Vonnegut, Jr.: "Don't put anything in a story that does not reveal character or advance the action."

- Develop. Answer the reader's questions in the order they will be asked with specific, accurate information.

  > John Kenneth Galbraith: "I would want to tell my students of a point strongly pressed, if my memory serves, by Shaw. He once said that as he grew older, he became less and less interested in theory, more and more interested in information. The temptation in writing is just reversed. Nothing is so hard to come by as a new and interesting fact. Nothing so easy on the feet as a generalization."

- When do you stop revising? On deadline or when there are no more surprises as you read and edit the draft.

- The effect on the writer of revision—re-seeing, re-feeling, re-thinking—is powerful.

  > E. L. Doctorow: "Everytime you compose a book your composition of yourself is at risk. You put yourself further away from whatever is comfortable to you or you feel at home with. Writing is a lifetime act of self-displacement."

  > Don De Lillo: "I think after a while a writer can begin to know himself through his language. He sees someone or something reflected back at him from these constructions. Over the years it's possible for a writer to shape himself as a human being through the language he uses. I think written language, fiction, goes that deep. He not only sees himself but begins to make himself or remake himself."

There is no formula for revision. How to revise depends on the demands of each draft you've written. So Murray's notes are just that, musings about the process from his perspective and that of other writers. He's been collecting writers' quotes for decades and likes to include perspectives from creators in other artistic media—artists and musicians, for example—and he collects quotes that compare writing to other processes, such as playing baseball. The quotes Murray offers and his commentary in this short piece represent revision as play and surprise. His advice about revising includes indentifying tensions, conflicts, and contradictions in a draft. He tells writers to develop material and to cut it. He suggests reading your work aloud and talking to others about your writing.

Murray never sees revision as failure or punishment. One of Elizabeth's students, a reluctant reviser, described his negative attitude toward rewriting this way: "If you bang a nail in once, why would you want to take it out and bang it back in again?" Murray is eager to remove that nail and examine it before he pounds it back in. Revision, he's taught us, is a way to gain energy and insight about your topic.

And it's also a way to gain insights about yourself and your writing, since as we revise, we reflect on the meaning of our work—and the way we figured it out. Under the most generous of circumstances, revision can become a way of remaking the self in the process of remaking a text.

A Final Comment

As you wend your way through your fieldwork, you will shuttle often between research and writing, and each process will enable the other. Research always involves, of course, searching for and finding answers to questions. Fieldwork is no different in that respect. As philosopher Roland Barthes writes, "Research is the name we give to the activity of writing. . . . [W]hatever it searches for, it must not forget its nature as language . . ." (198). Attention to language is critical when we write about the lives of others and bring their cultures to the page. As you work with the words of your informants and with your own, as you haul them from your notes and layer them into text for your reader, you will engage in the rigors and joys of writing and researching. We think it's a stimulating process.

Now it's time for us to step out of this chapter—and our book—so that you can step back into your own fieldwriting project. We hope that our advice and experience have been interesting to you and that we've introduced you to students, colleagues, teachers, and writers whose fieldwork and writing will inform and invigorate your own. For us, writing *FieldWorking* has been a rich journey, one we've discussed with you throughout this text as we break through and speak to you about ourselves and our fieldwork. For you, depending on the topic and the courses you're taking, you may want to journey back through the book as you continue your fieldworking and fieldwriting.

FieldReading

Berthoff, Ann E. *The Making of Meaning: Metaphors, Models, and Maxims for Writing Teachers*. Portsmouth: Boynton/Cook, 1981.

Didion, Joan. "On Keeping a Notebook." *Slouching toward Bethlehem*. New York: Farrar, 1968.

Dillard, Annie. *The Writing Life*. New York: Harper and Row, 1989.

Elbow, Peter. *Writing with Power: Techniques for Mastering the Writing Process*. New York: Oxford UP, 1981.

Elbow, Peter. *Writing without Teachers*. New York: Oxford, 1973.

Friedman, Bonnie. *Writing Past Dark: Envy, Fear, Distraction, and Other Dilemmas in the Writer's Life*. New York: Harper, 1993.

Fletcher, Ralph. *What a Writer Needs*. Portsmouth: Heinemann, 1993.

Gannett, Cinthia. *Gender and the Journal: Diaries and Academic Discourse*. Albany: State U of New York P, 1992.

Goldberg, Natalie. *Writing Down the Bones: Freeing the Writer Within*. Boston: Shambhala, 1986.

Graves, Donald. *A Researcher Learns to Write*. Portsmouth: Heinemann, 1983.

Heard, Georgia. *Writing Toward Home*. Portsmouth: Heinemann, 1996.

Howard, Jane. *Margaret Mead: A Life*. New York: Ballantine, 1984.

Huddle, David. *The Writing Habit: Essays*. Salt Lake City: Peregrine, 1991.

Lamott, Anne. *Bird by Bird: Some Instructions on Writing and Life*. New York: Pantheon, 1994.

Lowenstein, Sharyn. "A Brief History of Journal Keeping." *The Journal Book*. Ed. Toby Fulwiler. Portsmouth: Boynton/Cook, 1987.

Macrorie, Ken. *Searching Writing*. Rochelle Park: Hayden, 1980.

Macrorie, Ken. *The I-Search Paper: Revised Edition of Searching Writing*. Portsmouth: Boynton/Cook, 1988.

Marshall, Paule. "From the Poets in the Kitchen." *The New York Times Book Review* 9 Jan. 9, 1983: 3+.

Mead, Margaret. *Letters from the Field, 1925–1975*. New York: Harper, 1977.

Moore, Lorrie. "How to Become a Writer." *Self-Help: Stories*. New York: Knopf, 1985.

Murray, Donald. *Crafting A Life in Essay, Story, Poem*. Portsmouth: Boynton/Cook, 1996.

Murray, Donald. *Shoptalk: Learning to Write with Writers*. Portsmouth: Boynton/Cook, 1990.

Payne, Lucille Vaughan. *The Lively Art of Writing*. New York: New American Library, 1975.

Romano, Tom. *Writing with Passion*. Portsmouth: Boynton/Cook, 1995.

Sunstein, Bonnie S. *Composing a Culture: Inside a Summer Writing Program with High School Teachers*. Portsmouth: Boynton/Cook, 1994.

Thomas, Lewis. "Notes on Punctuation." *The Medusa and the Snail*. New York: Viking, 1979.

Welty, Eudora. *One Writer's Beginnings*. Cambridge, MA: Warner, 1983.

Woodruff, Jay. *A Piece of Work: Five Writers Discuss Their Revisions*. U Iowa P, 1993.

Zinsser, William. *On Writing Well*. 3rd ed. New York: Harper, 1988.

Works Cited

Aarne, Antti A. *The Types of the Folktale*. Trans. Stith Thompson. Helsinki: Soumalainen: Tiedeakatemia, 1961.

Ackerman, Diane. *A Natural History of the Senses*. New York: Vintage, 1991.

Antin, David. *Tuning*. New York: New Directions, 1984.

Baldwin, James. "Stranger in the Village" *Notes of a Native Son*. Boston: Beacon, 1955.

Barthes, Roland. "Writers, Intellectuals, Teachers." *Image-Music-Text*. Trans. Stephen Heath. New York: Hill and Wang, 1977.

Behar, Ruth. *Translated Woman: Crossing the Border with Esperanza's Story*. Boston: Beacon, 1993.

Benedict, Ruth. *Patterns of Culture*. 2nd ed. New York: New American Library, 1953.

Berger, John. *Ways of Seeing*. New York: Penguin, 1972.

Berthoff, Ann. *Forming, Thinking, Writing*. 2nd ed. Portsmouth: Boynton/Cook, 1988.

Birdwhistell, Ray. *Introduction to Kinesics*. Louisville: U Kentucky, 1952.

"Black Astronaut Carries Navajo Flag." *Cedar Rapids Gazette* 10 Feb. 1995: A7.

Brown, Byron. "Church Opens Doors to Vietnamese." *Nashua Telegraph* 10 Aug. 1994: A3.

Brunvand, Jan. *The Vanishing Hitchhiker: American Urban Legends and their Meanings*. New York: Norton, 1981.

Chiseri-Strater, Elizabeth. *Academic Literacies: The Public and Private Discourse of University Students*. Portsmouth: Boynton/Cook, 1991.

Cofer, Judith Ortiz. "A Partial Remembrance of a Puerto Rican Childhood." *Silent Dancing*. Houston: Arte Publico, 1980.

Didion, Joan. "On Keeping a Notebook." *Slouching toward Bethlehem*. Farrar, 1968.

Edwards, Jennette, Ed. *These Are Our Lives*. New York: Norton, 1939.

Elbow, Peter. *Writing with Power: Techniques for Mastering the Writing Process*. New York: Oxford UP, 1981.

Gannett, Cinthia. *Gender and the Journal: Diaries and Academic Discourse*. Albany: State U New York P, 1992.

Geertz, Clifford. *The Interpretation of Cultures*. New York: Basic Books, 1973.

———. *Local Knowledge: Further Essays in Interpretive Anthropology*. New York: Basic Books, 1983.

Glassie, Henry. *Passing the Time in Ballymenone: Culture and History of an Ulster Community*. Philadelphia: U Pennsylvania P, 1982.

Goodenough, Ward. *Culture, Language, and Society*. Menlo Park, CA: Benjamin/Cummings, 1981.

Graves, Donald. E-mail to the authors. Mar. 1996.

Hall, Edward. *The Silent-Language*. Garden City, NY: Doubleday, 1959.

———, *Healing without a Cure: Stories of People Living with AIDS*. Dir. Paul Russ. TRIAD Health Project, 1994.

Heath, Shirley Brice. *Ways With Words: Language, Life, and Work in Communities and Classrooms*. New York: Cambridge UP, 1983.

Hurston, Zora Neale. *Mules and Men*. 1935. 3rd Ed. New York: Harper Perennial, 1990.

Jackson, Jean. "I Am a Fieldnote: Fieldnotes as a Symbol of Professional Identity." Ed. Roger Sanjek. *Fieldnotes: The Making of Anthropology*. Ithaca, NY: Cornell U, 1990.

Kincaid, Jamaica. "On Seeing England for the First Time." *Harper's* Aug. 1991: 13–16.

Kingston, Maxine Hong. *The Woman Warrior: Memoirs of a Girlhood among Ghosts*. New York: Vintage, 1977.

Lado, Robert. "How to Compare Two Cultures." *Encountering Cultures: Reading and Writing in a Changing World*. Englewood Cliffs, NJ: Blair, 1992.

Lamott, Anne. *Bird by Bird*. New York: Pantheon, 1994.

Lopez, Barry. "Losing Our Sense of Place." *Teacher Magazine*. Feb. 1990: 38–44.

Macrorie, Ken. *The I-Search Paper: Revised Edition of Searching Writing*. Portsmouth: Boynton/Cook, 1988.

Mead, Margaret. *Letters from the Field: 1925–1975*. New York: Harper, 1977.

Miner, Horace. "Body Ritual among the Nacirema." *American Anthropologist* 58 (1956): 503–507.

Moffatt, Michael. *Coming of Age in New Jersey: College and American Culture*. New Brunswick, NJ: Rutgers UP, 1989.

Momaday, M. Scott. *The Way to Rainy Mountain*. Albuquerque: U New Mexico P, 1969.

Murray, Donald M. "Notes on Revision." Letter to the authors. 15 Feb. 1995.

———. *Shoptalk: Learning to Write with Writers*. Portsmouth: Boynton/Cook, 1990.

———. "Where Do You Find Your Stories?" Ed. Alice Brand and Richard Graves. *Presence of Mind: Writing and the Domain Beyond the Cognitive*. Portsmouth: Boynton/Cook, 1994.

Myerhoff, Barbara. *Number Our Days*. New York: Touchstone, 1978.

Naylor, Gloria. *Mama Day*. New York: Vintage, 1988.

Oring, Elliott. "Generating Lives: The Construction of an Autobiography." *Journal of Folklore Research* 24 (1987): 241–262.

Paules, Greta Foff. *Dishing It Out: Power and Resistance among Waitresses in a New Jersey Restaurant*. Philadelphia: Temple UP, 1991.

Peacock, James L. *The Anthropological Lens: Harsh Light, Soft Focus*. Cambridge: Cambridge UP, 1986.

Powdermaker, Hortense. *Stranger and Friend: The Way of an Anthropologist*. New York: Norton, 1966.

Rosaldo, Renato. *Culture and Truth: The Remaking of Social Analysis*. Boston: Beacon, 1989.

Rosenblatt, Louise. *Literature as Exploration*. New York: Noble and Noble, 1976.

Rule, Rebecca. "Yankee Curse." Hanover, NH: UPNE.

Sacks, Oliver. *An Anthropologist on Mars: Seven Paradoxical Tales*. New York: Knopf, 1995.

Sanjek, Roger. *Fieldnotes: The Makings of Anthropology*. Ithaca: Cornell UP, 1990.

Santino, Jack. "Miles of Smiles, Years of Struggle: The Negotiation of Black Occupational Identity through Personal Experience Narrative." *Journal of American Folklore* 96 (1983): 393–410.

Scudder, Samuel. "In the Library with Agassiz." *Every Saturday* 4 April 1874.

Shadle, Mark. Letter to the authors. Sep. 1995.

Spellman, A. B. *Black Music: Four Lives*. New York: Shocken, 1976.

Stires, Susan, Ed. *With Promise: Redefining Reading and Writing for Special Students*. Portsmouth: Heinemann, 1989.

Stoller, Paul. *The Taste of Ethnographic Things: The Senses in Anthropology*. Philadelphia: U Pennsylvania P, 1989.

Stone, Elizabeth. *Black Sheep and Kissing Cousins: How Our Family Stories Shape Us*. New York: Times, 1988.

Sunstein, Bonnie S. *Composing a Culture: Inside a Summer Writing Program with High School Teachers*. Portsmouth: Boynton/Cook, 1994.

Tannen, Deborah. *You Just Don't Understand: Women and Men in Conversation*. New York: Morrow/Ballantine, 1990.

Tedlock, Dennis. *The Spoken Word and the Work of Interpretation*. Philadelphia: U Pennsylvania, 1983.

Terkel, Studs. *Hard Times: An Oral History of the Great Depression*. New York: Pantheon, 1970.

———. *Working: People Talk about What They Do All Day and How They Feel about What They Do*. New York: Pantheon, 1974.

Thompson, Stith. *Motif-Index of Folk Literature*. Bloomington: Indiana U, 1955.

Toth, Jennifer. *The Mole People: Life in the Tunnels of New York City*. Chicago: Chicago Review P, 1993.

VanderStaay, Steve. *Street Lives: An Oral History of Homeless Americans*. Philadelphia: New Society, 1992.

Walker, Alice. "Everyday Use." *In Love and Trouble: Stories of Black Women*. Harcourt, 1967.

Wigginton, Eliot and students, eds. *Foxfire: 25 Years*. New York: Doubleday, 1991.

Williams, Raymond. *The Sociology of Culture*. New York: Schocken, 1982.

Wolf, Margery. *A Thrice-Told Tale: Feminism, Postmodernism, and Ethnographic Responsibility*. Stanford: Stanford UP, 1992.

Zinsser, William. *Inventing the Truth: The Art and Craft of Memoir*. 2nd ed. New York: Houghton, 1995.

Zipes, Jack. *Don't Bet on the Prince: Contemporary Feminist Fairy Tales in North America and England*. New York: Routledge, 1987.

Credits

p. xiii: Sal Biondello. "Self and Other." *Anthropology and Humanism Quarterly*, 4:1, February 1989. Reprinted by permission of the American Anthropological Association.

pp. 9–12:   Horace Miner. "Body Ritual Among the Nacirema." *American Anthropologist*, 58:3, June 1956, pp. 503–507. Reprinted by permission of the American Anthropological Association. Not for further reproduction.

pp. 17–18:   "Black Astronaut Carries Navajo Flag." Reprinted with permission by *The Des Moines Register*, 1996.

p. 18:   Photograph from AP/Wide World Photos.

pp. 49–54:   Gloria Naylor. *Mama Day*. Copyright © 1988 by Gloria Naylor. Reprinted by permission of Ticknor & Fields/Houghton Mifflin Company. All rights reserved.

pp. 75–76:   Roger Sanjek. *Fieldnotes: The Makings of Anthropology*, p. 135. Ithaca: Cornell University Press, 1990. Reprinted by permission.

pp. 76–77:   Margery Wolf. *A Thrice-Told Tale: Feminism, Postmodernism, and Ethnographic Responsibility*. © 1992 by the Board of Trustees of the Leland Stanford Junior University. Reprinted by permission of Stanford University Press.

pp. 82–87:   Alice Walker. "Everyday Use" from *In Love and Trouble: Stories of Black Women*. Copyright © 1973 by Alice Walker. Reprinted by permission of Harcourt Brace & Company.

pp. 99–105:   Barry Lopez. "The American Geographies." *Orion* magazine, reprinted as "Losing Our Sense of Place" in *Teacher*, February 1990, pp. 38–44. Copyright © 1990 by Barry Holstun Lopez. Reprinted by permission of Sterling Lord Literistic, Inc.

pp. 108–109:   Henry Glassie. *Passing the Time in Ballymenone: Culture and History of an Ulster Community*, pp. 95–96. Bloomington: Indiana University Press, 1982. Reprinted by permission of Indiana University Press.

p. 113:   Henry Glassie. Map from *Passing the Time*. Bloomington: Indiana University Press, 1982. Reprinted by permission.

pp. 124, 125–126, 132, 164:   Barbara Myerhoff. *Number Our Days*. Copyright © 1978 by Barbara Myerhoff. Used by permission of Dutton Signet, a division of Penguin Books USA Inc.

pp. 133–136:   Jamaica Kincaid. "On Seeing England for the First Time." *Harper's*, August 1991, pp. 13–16. Copyright 1991 by Jamaica Kincaid. Reprinted by permission of Wylie, Aitken & Stone.

p. 143:   Jenny Joseph. "Warning" from *Selected Poems*. London: Bloodaxe Books Ltd. Copyright © Jenny Joseph 1992. Reprinted by permission of the author.

Index